AFTER THE RUINS

RESTORING THE COUNTRYSIDE OF
NORTHERN FRANCE
AFTER THE GREAT WAR

AFTER THE RUINS

RESTORING THE COUNTRYSIDE OF NORTHERN FRANCE AFTER THE GREAT WAR

Hugh Clout

UNIVERSITY
of
EXETER
PRESS

First published in 1996 by
University of Exeter Press
Reed Hall, Streatham Drive
Exeter, Devon EX4 4QR
UK

British Library Cataloguing in Publication Data
A catalogue record of this book is available
from the British Library

ISBN 0 85989 491 6

Typeset in 11 on 13 pt Sabon
by Exe Valley Dataset, Exeter

Printed and bound in Great Britain
by Short Run Press Ltd, Exeter

Contents

Figures

Tables

Plates

Preface

Between August 1914 and November 1918 the northernmost districts of France experienced death and destruction on a scale unparalleled in human history. Farms and factories, villages and market towns were reduced to ruins, and fields that had yielded some of the finest crops in the land became the 'fields of death' (Slowe & Woods 1988). Three-quarters of a century later the horrors of what contemporaries called the 'Great War' attract our attention through the photographs, paintings and writings of the time. Popular accounts continue to present memories of events, while more scholarly works interpret the conflicts, analyse the roles of leading personalities, and recount the hardships experienced by the armed forces and by ordinary civilians caught up in the war (Gilbert 1994). By contrast with this enormous outpouring of information, the months and years of what the French called *reconstitution* have been allowed to pass by relatively unnoticed.

As a geographer with research interests in the French countryside in the past as well as in the present, I had examined a fraction of the archival record of agricultural change during the nineteenth century and appreciated that the most productive *départements* were to be devastated so savagely during the Great War (Clout 1980, 1983). As an academic visitor travelling slowly along the country roads of those areas I became aware that many northern landscapes still display evidence, albeit now rather muted, of the patient reconstitution of what had been lost as well as examples of modest innovation with respect to property boundaries, villages and farmsteads. I began to wonder how this restoration had come about. Was it conceived according to some grand design, formulated by the state, and undertaken by its employees? Was it left to individual property holders to tackle as best they could? Or was it undertaken in some other way? These were some of the leading questions that prompted my subsequent enquiries.

It was understandable that historians of the Great War should end their account at the Armistice and exclude peacetime recovery from their field of study, but I was surprised to find that geographers and historians had paid rather little attention to material reconstruction, and especially so in the specific context of France in the 1920s (Edmonds 1947; Bowden 1982; Diefendorf 1990; Geipel 1982). However, comparative research on cities destroyed by earthquakes proposed a four-fold sequence of recovery, which is not irrelevant to what happened in the northern *départements* after the Great War. In this model, initial emergency work is succeeded by a brief restoration phase, then a longer period of replacement reconstruction, and a final commemorative period (Haas, Kates & Bowden 1977: xxvii). In addition, the 1920s seem to have attracted rather little research by French scholars, with Alfred Sauvy expressing his astonishment at how the interwar period in France had been neglected by economic historians (Sauvy 1965 I: 7). The classic geographical monographs on Picardy by Albert Demangeon (1905) and on Flanders by Raoul Blanchard (1906), and the less well known study on Champagne by Emile Chantriot (1906), had been completed a few years before the war broke out, but subsequent geographical monographs made very little mention of the crucial task of rural recovery. The paragraphs by Pierre Brunet on rural life in Soissonnais form the most notable exception, and have been quoted in textbooks (Brunet 1960: 396–98; Fohlen 1972: 31). Precious few books or articles by geographers focused specifically on the recovery of France's devastated countrysides (Bloch 1925; Musset 1922; Alexandre 1928a; Hartke 1932). By contrast, Edmond Michel's (1932) masterly economic study of the principles and practices of monetary compensation offers an account of the broad financial context within which material reconstruction took place, and books by George B. Ford (1919a) and William MacDonald (1922) provide very helpful contemporary accounts. Some urban and industrial aspects of post-war restoration were certainly subjected to academic analysis, with the city of Reims attracting particular interest, and much attention being devoted to neighbouring areas in Belgium (Rigaud & Bédarida 1988; Smets 1985, 1987). But the recovery of the French countryside during the 1920s passed almost without scholarly comment (Barral 1968: 199). Even Eugen Weber dismisses the topic in half a page in *The Hollow Years* (1995: 16). In a more popular vein, numerous 'before and after' photographs by early photo-journalists, such as A.J. Insall, captured scenes of wartime devastation and their subsequent restored state two decades later, but virtually no photographic record has been found of the *processes* of land restoration or village reconstruction (for example, Swinton 1936). However, the Musée Albert Kahn at Boulogne-Billancourt contains a collection of colour photographs by Frédéric Gadmer of freshly rebuilt farmsteads, which formed part of the photographic Archives de la Planète assembled by the banker Kahn and the geographer Jean Brunhes (Favier 1991: 44).

The major exhibition entitled 'Reconstructions et modernisation, la France après les ruines 1918, 1945' that was arranged by the Archives de France in 1991 emphasized the recovery of towns and industrial enterprises, especially after 1945, but very little attention was paid to the revival of the countryside in the 1920s (Favier 1991). Perhaps not surprisingly, the ambitious Historial de la Grande Guerre, housed in a modern building within the framework of the *château* at Péronne, is focused firmly on the events and experiences of the war, and devotes only a small fraction of its spacious display galleries to the vital task of reconstruction (Sherman 1995: 53). Likewise, a well-signposted circuit directs motorized visitors out from the Historial to a selection of battle sites and to military cemeteries, as well as indicating in the present landscape where the front line stood at critical moments during the war. But virtually no mention is made of the farmsteads, houses, churches, schools and *mairies* that were rebuilt during the 1920s and form the major components in the present settlement pattern. I suspect that most visitors following the circuit pass them by in complete ignorance, seeing only the monuments and the graves.

My initial reaction to this apparent lack of study was one of encouragement since here, I felt, was a theme that was calling out for attention. But, I did note that Richard Kuisel had warned that: 'We may never know the full story of this episode [of economic recovery] because the essential ministerial records seem to be missing' (Kuisel 1981: 293). Given that responsibility for the *régions libérées* had been shifted among four ministries between 1917 and 1933, and had been entrusted to no fewer than forty-five ministers or secretaries of state, such a warning was hardly unexpected (Héricault 1934: 163). However, I hoped that my proposed enquiry into the restoration of the countryside might produce more solid conclusions. To this end I sought the advice of rural geographers, historians and academic librarians in both Britain and France and my thanks are extended to them for their general encouragement. In fact, little detailed advice on likely sources proved to be forthcoming and I stumbled along a number of time-consuming false trails. In short, I was thrown back to my own devices.

My quest for information dealing with emergency restoration in the immediate aftermath of war and *reconstitution* during the calmer years of the 1920s took me to the Archives Nationales in Paris, to Archives Départementales in a dozen northern cities, and to the archival collections of the Ministère de l'Agriculture and the Ministère des Finances. In addition to this variety of manuscript sources, I made considerable use of published reports and journals held in the Bibliothèque Nationale (Paris), the most useful Bibliothèque de Documentation Internationale Contemporaine (Nanterre), the British Library, the Imperial War Museum, the resource centre of the Confédération Générale du Travail (Montreuil), a number of other libraries on both sides of the Channel (including, of course, the Historial de la Grande Guerre), the Institut Géographique National (Saint-Mandé), and the Institut National de la Statistique et des Etudes Economiques (Paris).

Successive visits to these archives and libraries confirmed my earlier suspicions. Despite suggestions to the contrary, there are no grand reports dealing with the process of rural reconstruction across the complete sweep of the northern *départements*. The few sets of contemporary statistics that do survive are shot through with inconsistencies and tantalizing ambiguities. As Marin explained, contemporary estimates of loss and recovery suffered from 'difficulties of nature, method, classification and calculation' (cited in Michel 1932: vii). Dessaint made the point more crisply, remarking that much of the official statistical documentation conveyed 'a false air of mathematical rigour' (Dessaint 1922: 749). Instead, reliance has had to be placed on fragmentary evidence, ranging from 'official' reports submitted by northern prefects to their respective *conseils-généraux*, which tended to stress what had been achieved, to articles by journalists in the agricultural, architectural, regional and national press, which often conveyed critical views on how slowly *reconstitution* was being accomplished and reported the hardships endured by many of those who returned to their devastated farms and villages.

Some archivists greeted my enquiries about documentation with shocked surprise, arguing that no records of any kind relating to rural reconstruction survived for their *départements*. In each case a brief perusal of the proceedings of the *conseils-généraux* immediately after the war served to prove them wrong. Other archivists ushered me to floor-to-ceiling stacks of documents relating to compensation claimed by tens of thousands of households in their *département*, and then explained that this amazingly detailed financial and legal documentation had been neither catalogued nor summarized into any kind of manageable form. For example, even after massive disposal of material, the documentation recording damage, compensation claims and subsequent payments occupies 1,500 m of shelf space in the Archives Départementales du Pas-de-Calais at Arras. To sample such detailed records of claims and settlements for even a single *département* would require the energies of a research team working over many years. Such a task was clearly far beyond my own capabilities, especially since I wished to explore trends of rural recovery across northern France as a whole. In any case some of this financial material related to families with members who are still alive and, I was advised, was therefore not only confidential but was effectively doubly so, since I was not a French citizen. I must confess that this information came to me as a considerable relief. *Faute de mieux* I was thrown back to scrutinizing official and unofficial commentaries which had been presented in a multitude of ways and with a variety of objectives in view. Since I had become used to working with substantial bodies of apparently coherent statistical matter, this enforced reliance on qualitative and quantitative fragments proved an extremely uncomfortable adjustment process which consumed many months (Clout 1980). The pages which follow attempt to bring some order to the story of the complex activities and achievements of rural *reconstitution* in ten northern *départements*. In this account, considerable reliance will be placed on the words used by contemporary observers. The details of recovery within specific *départements* may be found in a number of complementary articles (Clout 1992, 1993a & b, 1994a & b).

When the black crepe draped over the female statue representing Strasbourg in the Place de la Concorde was removed at eleven o'clock on Armistice Day, attention was drawn to the reincorporation into France of three *départements* that had been lost as a result of the Franco-Prussian War (Smith & Hill 1920: 1). However, rural reconstruction in Alsace and northern Lorraine was to be carried out in rather different ways from the rest of northern France, and contemporary reviews rarely included information on the recovery of those areas (Picard 1937). For these reasons, Bas-Rhin, Haut-Rhin and Moselle must remain beyond the scope of the present study (Clout 1994c).

Throughout northern France, recovery did not wait until the Armistice had been signed but began even as the events of war continued to rage. Emergency restoration of land and patching up of buildings were tackled hastily by voluntary organizations and a suite of state agencies (Illaire 1991: 105–11). But the intricate process of financial compensation involved a discrete contract between each individual who had suffered loss (*sinistré*) and the French state, which, as will be shown, never intended to undertake material reconstruction according to a grand design or with the help of its own labour force. The initiative had to come from each property owner or, more usually, from groups of *sinistrés* who sacrificed part of their fierce individualism so that they might establish cooperatives to rebuild villages and farmsteads and, more rarely, to reorganize their landholdings into more rational mosaics.

In order to organize my account I have chosen to distinguish hastily undertaken emergency work from reconstruction proper, and then to separate the restoration of land from the rebuilding of settlements. Of course, this enforced distinction tends to oversimplify highly complicated processes and overlapping organizations, whose inefficiencies frustrated *sinistrés* and administrators alike. The end result casts light on the material recovery of the ten northern *départements* which had made—and were to continue to make—a major contribution to the economic life of the nation. However, I have to note that Richard Kuisel's warning about the absence of documentation on industrial and economic recovery is equally valid for the rural environment. As a consequence, it seems to me that many aspects of the story can be recounted only in part, and many questions simply remain unanswerable. The chapters that follow can only offer a reasoned introduction to a frustratingly elusive topic.

A few more comments must be made. As a child born to middle-aged parents, I have been intrigued to explore the countrysides over which two eighteen-year-old men fought and in which they were wounded, and which an older man mapped out as he helped install railway lines behind the British lines. In subsequent months, the two teenagers recovered in adjacent beds in a military sanatorium in the Home Counties, where they were visited by a young secretary from London who had been engaged to be married to another man during the course of the war. Circumstances turned out differently. The young woman was to be my mother, and the two teenagers my father and my uncle; the platelayer was my mother's father. They had no personal experience of rural reconstruction in the *régions libérées* but the photographs taken by one of my aunts, on her annual pilgrimage during the 1920s to the grave of her first husband, depicted settlements being restored and landscapes being shaped to commemorate the supreme sacrifice that had been made by so many. Each member of my parents' generation in my family had died before I started on this research and, apart from the photographs and a few tiny mementoes, nothing remains about northern France in the 1920s in our family archive. The best I could do was to keep my parents, aunts and uncles in my thoughts as I scrutinized documents, traversed ordinary landscapes, and visited the Great War cemeteries across the Channel.

After the Ruins does not attempt to explore the intricacies of French domestic politics and Franco-German relations during the 1920s, or the amazingly complicated political and financial circumstances surrounding the issues of reparations, reconstruction loans and compensation (Michel 1932). Nor does it review the tragic impact of 1914–18 on the national economy which was discussed systematically in a series of major research reports funded by the Carnegie Foundation and published in the late 1920s and early 1930s. It is, most emphatically, *not* another book about the Great War; rather it is a story of hope and achievement amid the hardships of peace.

I am pleased to acknowledge that several of my research visits were assisted by small grants from the British Academy, the Central Research Fund of the University of London and by the Dean's Fund, Faculty of Arts, University College London. The artwork was prepared efficiently by Tim Aspden and other members of the Cartographic Unit, Department of Geography, UCL, to whom I express my thanks. As always, my students formed the first sounding board for the substance of my research and I am grateful to them for their questions and interest. My colleague Hugh Prince gave wise advice on many matters and read the whole manuscript. I extend my sincere thanks to him. Malcolm Ward accompanied me to battlefields, memorials, war graves, cafés, bars and restaurants from the Channel to the Rhine, and shared the good days of discovery and put up with the bad, despairing ones associated with compiling statistics that refused to make sense and writing up accounts that had to remain partial and incomplete. Although neither a geographer nor a historian, his support and insights have been invaluable. I wish to express my gratitude to the editors of *Agricultural History Review, Erdkunde, Geografiska Annaler*, and *Rural History* for their kindness in allowing me to include revised versions of illustrative material which appeared in my articles in their journals. The miracles and pitfalls of Amstrad and IBM should not be allowed to pass without mention in these secretary-less times. And, finally, I must thank Paul Schooling for restoring my sanity twice, once after hard disk failure on my personal machine, and again when my office computer was ripped apart by thieves in search of marketable components.

1
The War-Torn Zone

Defining the War-Torn Zone

Three-quarters of a century have passed since the signing of the Armistice halted the Great War. There are very few left who remember 'the nightmare landscape of the battlefields' (Bury 1972: 23). For subsequent generations the war has been relegated to history, to be explored through the occasional exhibition, novel, film or television programme, or more rarely on a journey across northern France. As one speeds along the railway or the motorway from a Channel port toward Paris or some holiday destination, it is easy to miss the indicators of that long and tragic war. But the moment one takes to the side roads through the former battle zones and begins to read the landscape, it is obvious that testimony is all around. As Pierre Flatrès has insisted, the battle zone 'remains a fact in the geography of northern France many decades after the conclusion of the war' (Flatrès 1980: 96). At one extreme are the military cemeteries and great memorials, which are such unusual insertions in an otherwise ordinary scene (Becker A 1988, 1991; Borg 1991; Reynes 1929). Less striking but arguably none the less significant are the roadside houses, farmsteads, schools, whole villages and urban neighbourhoods which are clearly all of a period if not all of a piece. Their design and building materials evoke a single reconstruction phase, as do many rather gaunt hotels that were built to accommodate the 'pilgrims' from many nations who came during the 1920s and 1930s to honour the war dead. To a more practised eye, the surprising juxtaposition of styles and fabrics in the walls and roofs of churches, town halls, railway stations and ordinary homes evokes essential restoration work to much older structures.

The events of fifty-two months of war have been recorded in numerous ways, from the great official histories to the evocative memoirs of combattants, written soon afterwards or with the wisdom of hindsight (Fussell 1975). By contrast, the story of the restoration of great swathes of devastated farmland to a state of productivity and the rebuilding of damaged and destroyed rural settlements remains largely untold. History textbooks dealing with the 1920s afford the challenge and achievement of recovery no more than a passing mention, citing a few figures (usually on industrial production) and implying that the damage was repaired quickly and was completed by the mid 1920s (for example Aldcroft 1978: 51). The story of reconstruction in northern France was, of course, far more complicated than a rehearsal of economic statistics might have us believe. Adopting a broad view of time and space, A.J.P. Taylor argued that 'the material destruction was . . . temporary' and 'on a map of Europe the areas of destruction appear as tiny black dots' (Taylor 1966: 279). Setting things in sharper focus, Denis Brogan captured the enormity of the challenge when he described reconstruction in France as 'the greatest economic achievement of post-war Europe' (Brogan 1940: 599). Unlike the emergency work undertaken by special services organized by the state, material reconstruction was not implemented in a standardized way by government agencies; instead, much was left to the ingenuity of those who had suffered loss (*sinistrés)* and to the differing capability of prefects and other administrators in the northern *départements*. Just as the character and intensity of devastation varied from place to place, so did the organization and chronology of reconstruction.

What exactly was the war-torn zone? The question may seem banal, since the evidence of destruction was there for all to see in an area extending from the international boundary that had removed Alsace and northern Lorraine from French control at the conclusion of the Franco-Prussian War, as far west as Amiens and as far south as Meaux and Vitry-le-François. It embraced a suite of *pays* from the Vosges mountains, through the plateaux and valleys of Lorraine and Champagne to the plain of Picardy, the hills of Artois and the damp, low-lying farmlands of Flanders (Figure 1.1). The war-torn zone included some of the very best agricultural land and most important manufacturing districts in

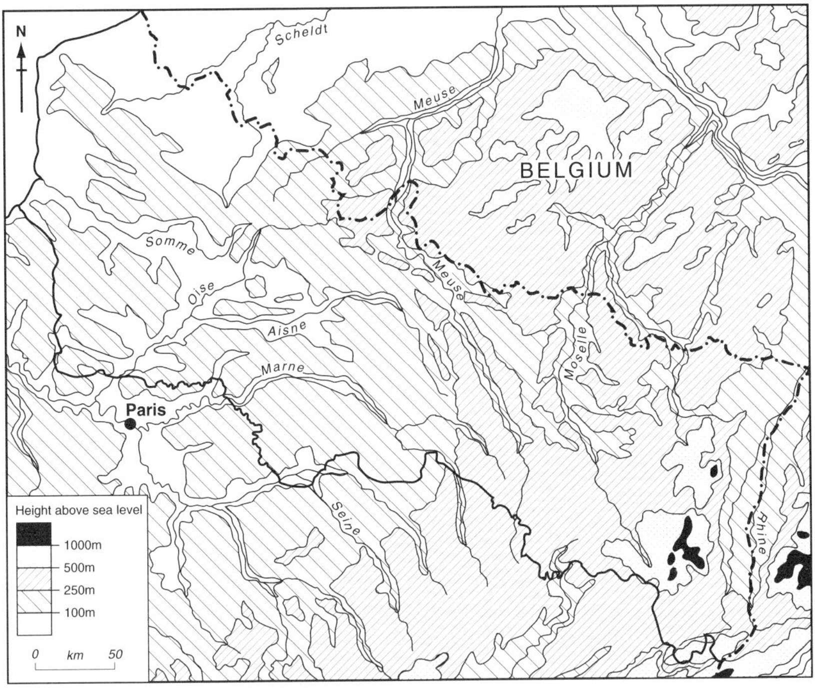

Figure 1.1 The relief of northern France

the whole country, whose occupation and devastation dealt a savage blow to the French economy (Fohlen 1972: 31). Its great significance may be summarized by the fact that it covered only one-fourteenth part of national territory but had contributed one-fifth of the nation's tax revenues on the eve of the war (Reibel 1924a: 565). Writing about it six months after the Armistice, Senator Paul Doumer described 'a desert, a zone of death, assassination and devastation . . . There are corpses of horses, corpses of trees covering the corpses of men' (Doumer 1919: 33). In his treatise on *Le Déclin de l'Europe*, written at about the same time and published in 1920, the eminent geographer Albert Demangeon also evoked 'a zone of death, 500 km long and 10–25 km broad, following the battle front in which good land has been transformed into a desert, a wild steppe, where the very fields have erupted . . . farm buildings need to be restored, agricultural equipment renewed and the fertility of the soil made anew wherever the "cyclone" has passed' (Demangeon 1920:

33–34). Adopting another natural metaphor, journalist Léandre Vaillat likened the devastation to 'a lava flow, submerging living beings, villages, towns, houses, forests, crops, running without a break between Nieuport and Bâle' (Vaillat 1919: 780). While to Henri Thierry the tortured landscapes of the battle zone resembled 'the sea, whose waves are formed by the rise and fall of shellholes' (Thierry 1919: 217).

During more than four years of war the location of the battle front shifted many times but also remained quite stable for long periods (Augé-Laribé 1925: 93). For example, the total area invaded by the Germans in 1914 exceeded 38,850 km^2 but their retreat of March 1917 returned roughly one-tenth of that ground, and courageous but perhaps foolhardy farmers in the western *département* of Somme risked bombardment as they started re-working their land in the shadow of the battle zone (Augé-Laribé 1923: 95). By contrast, the German advance of March and May 1918 covered an additional 5,950 km^2. The multiple excavations of the trench system were carved across the northern countryside, being relatively stable for much of the war but on occasions shifting just a few hundred metres or a few kilometres, always at appalling cost to human life (Trenard 1972: 486–87). Together they formed a 'terrible gash' across the devastated *départements* which would have to be restored before agricultural life could start again (Becker J-J 1991: 21). The northernmost 60 km of the trench-lined western front lay beyond the Belgian border, the next 140 km extending southward to the river Ancre were in British hands, while the remainder of the front was held by the French (Fussell 1975: 36).

In the chaos of wartime, accurate statistics were not collected and even those relating to basic territorial divisions which had been drawn up by a variety of administrative organizations in peacetime proved not to be completely compatible. Thus the Service Géographique de l'Armée, the Service du Cadastre and the respective prefects produced differing totals for as fundamental an element as the combined surface of ten *départements* in northern France (Michel 1923: 26; 1932: 91). Of course, the war-torn zone needed to be expressed in terms of the complete mosaic of hierarchically arranged administrative units, composed of *communes*, *cantons*, and *arrondissements* as well as *départements* (Figure 1.2). This was not just a matter of pedantic

Figure 1.2 Administrative units of northern France

concern but was of great practical importance, since the vital issue of entitlement to compensation would depend on exactly how the devastated zone had been delineated and would give rise to detailed and repeated complaint in the years ahead (AN F2 2102 Lettre du Préfet 17.09.21).

In 1919 official attempts to define the *régions libérées* produced a total of 3,800,000 ha in ten *départements* extending from Vosges to Nord. A second attempt recognized that 4,095,662 ha had been subject to invasion or bombardment in those *départements*, plus a further 159,427 ha in adjacent areas to the south, but these figures did not include information on Alsace or northern Lorraine (Michel 1932: 91). To clarify matters a decree was issued on 12 August 1919 by the Ministre des Régions Libérées with the purpose of defining territorial limits within which the fundamental law of 17 April 1919 relating to war damages should be applied (MacDonald 1922: 1; Peytral

1927; Picard 1922: 1010) (see Chapter 8). Thus, the *régions libérées* were specified in the following terms.

(i) All territory invaded and occupied by the enemy for a sufficient time for it to experience pillage and destruction, from the first advance of the Germans in 1914 to their last offensive in 1918.
(ii) Areas close to the front which had to be evacuated by the civilian population under the pressure of war, and where enemy bombardment, defensive measures, and conditions due to military operations led to the destruction of property or personal goods or other losses.
(iii) Adjacent areas which, without experiencing invasion or evacuation, suffered in a general way from the operations of war.

In accordance with these criteria, the *régions libérées* comprised all French territory east or north of a line which started at the Belgian border, ran along the Channel coast to the south-west corner of Somme *département* and then extended across north-eastern France eventually to reach the Swiss border (Figure 1.3). In more detail, the line followed the western limits of Nord and Pas-de-Calais, the western and southern boundaries of Somme and Oise and of the *arrondissements* of Meaux, Coulommiers and Provins (each in Seine-et-Marne), the southern boundary of Marne, of three *communes* in Aube (Semoine, Mailly-le-Camp and Poivres) and of Meuse, and the southern and western limits of Meurthe-et-Moselle, of the *arrondissements* of Epinal and Remiremont (in Vosges) and finally of the territory of Belfort (Peytral 1927: 82).

The 'liberated regions' defined in this way covered the whole of nine *départements*, notable parts of Seine-et-Marne and Vosges, and a tiny fraction of Aube (Dautresme 1919: 4). The total amounted to 6,453,000 ha, roughly half as large again as the earlier definitions which had related more specifically to invasion and bombardment. The disruption brought to normal life obviously figured in the minds of the legislators as they devised this broader definition. As William MacDonald explained, 'the larger part of the Nord, Pas-de-Calais, Somme and Oise, for example, was in general completely disorganized by the war,

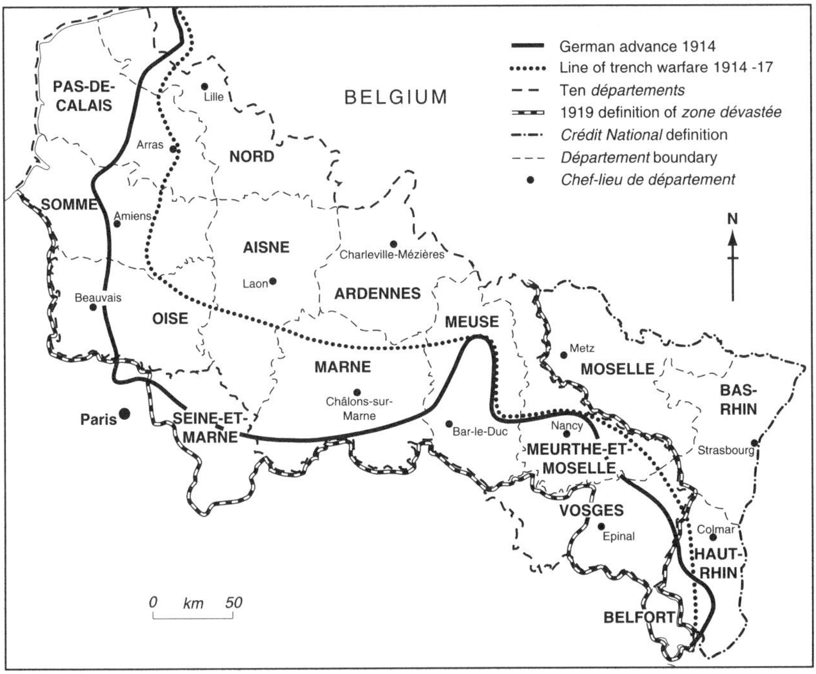

Figure 1.3 Definitions of the war-torn zone

notwithstanding the fact that scores of *communes* never saw a German soldier, except as a prisoner, and did not suffer from German guns' (MacDonald 1922: 3). Despite the unquestionably broad specification of the liberated regions, the government was to be called upon also to consider compensation claims for damage from half a dozen *départements* further south. In due course, the recovered *départements* of Bas-Rhin, Haut-Rhin and Moselle and the territory of Belfort would be included in the liberated regions for purposes of compensation, thereby adding 1,452,180 ha to the territory that had been recognized on 12 August 1919. However, their restoration will not be examined in the present discussion.

This broad definition retained legal validity with respect to compensation but the more narrowly defined 'devastated regions' (3,337,000 ha) were recognized on 1 June 1921, embracing the whole of Aisne and Ardennes and parts of eight other *départements* (Michel 1932: 7). German documents mentioned by Michel suggest that 3,750,000 ha had been occupied by their troops at one time or another during the war (Ibid.). The surface of the devastated regions was greater than that of Belgium or the Netherlands, or the combined territory of Massachussetts and Connecticut (Dervaux 1917; MacDonald 1922: 4). By virtue of minor adjustments in three *départements* the total area was reduced subsequently to 3,306,350 ha (excluding Alsace-Lorraine) (Bédarida 1991: 263). This fundamental definition was used in the statistical publications of the Ministère des Régions Libérées (1923) and the Ministère des Travaux Publics (1929) and will be employed in the present discussion. However, in the absence of more detailed information it will be necessary in some instances to refer to the ten *départements* in their entirety, even though only 4,329 of the 6,832 *communes* in those *départements* were embraced by the ministerial definition of *régions libérées* (Ministère des Régions Liberées 1923).

Before the War

On the eve of war the territory that was to be recognized as the 'war zone' had housed 4,790,062 people (1911) and the ten northern *départements* in their totality had contained 6,523,000 (Table 1.1). Rich agriculture, flourishing manufacturing and crucially important coal-mining activities supported over three million people in the two western *départements* of Nord (1,961,780) and Pas-de-Calais (1,068,155) (Braudel & Labrousse 1980: IV2). At the other extreme, the largely rural *département* of Meuse on the western marchlands of Lorraine contained a mere 277,955 inhabitants. The cities of Lille (217,800) and neighbouring Roubaix (122,700) headed the urban hierarchy of northern France, with Nancy (119,950), Reims (115,170) and Amiens (93,200) not far behind. A dozen other towns housed more than 20,000 inhabitants apiece in 1911 but almost all *communes* in the war zone were nucleated settlements with populations that could be counted by the hundred or at most a couple of thousand apiece (Bédarida 1991: 263).

The ten northern *départements* had supported on average 108.5 persons/km^2, with very high densities encountered only in the strongly urbanized *arrondissements* of Lille (979), Valenciennes (416), Béthune (431) and Nancy (189). Constellations of long-established rural industries inflated densities in villages around

Table 1.1 Population of whole *départements*, 1891 and 1911

	1891	1911	1911/1891 (%)	Density/km² 1911
Aisne	545,493	530,226	97.2	71.4
Ardennes	324,923	318,896	98.1	60.7
Marne	434,692	436,310	100.4	53.2
Meurthe-et-Moselle	444,150	564,730	127.1	107.0
Meuse	292,253	277,955	95.1	44.5
Nord	1,736,341	1,961,780	112.9	339.7
Oise	401,835	411,028	102.5	69.8
Pas-de-Calais	874,364	1,068,155	122.2	158.3
Somme	546,495	520,161	95.2	82.8
Vosges	410,196	433,914	105.8	73.5
Total	6,010,742	6,523,155	108.5	96.6

Source: Ministère de l'Intérieur, 1892, 1912

the market towns of Picardy (Demangeon 1905). Family-run workshops for making hosiery were found on many farms on the plateau of Santerre but, by virtue of their dispersed location, they were 'virtually invisible' to the casual visitor except in a few places where clusters of small factories were to be found (Ardouin-Dumazet 1916: 305). Despite the existence of this non-agricultural employment, rural depopulation had been occurring in Picardy for several decades before the war (Pinchemel 1957). Further to the north and east, the mining of coal and iron enhanced population densities in Pas-de-Calais, Nord and Meurthe-et-Moselle. In predominantly rural *arrondissements* in Picardy and eastern Lorraine average densities were still above 50 persons/km^2 but they fell to half that figure in the farmlands of Champagne and across the wooded countrysides of western Lorraine, with the *arrondissements* of Sainte-Menehould and Vitry-le-François supporting only 23 and 27/km^2 respectively.

During many decades the attractions of better-paid jobs in urban factories and mines had triggered important flows of labour away from the rural areas of northern France, as from other parts of the country, and had a profound impact on the redistribution of population during the quarter century before the war (Zimmermann 1922: 39) (Table 1.1). Between 1891 and 1911 the ten northern *départements* increased their collective population by 8.5 per cent, with phenomenally rapid growth in urban and industrial *arrondissements* (e.g. Briey +87 per cent but also Nancy +26 per cent) contrasting with pronounced decline not only in the rural east (parts of Ardennes, Marne, Meuse and Vosges) but also in Somme in the heart of Picardy.

Figure 1.4, derived from a comparison of *canton* returns for the Dénombrements de la Population for 1896 and 1911, plots the picture in more detail. Six zones of population growth embraced the Channel ports and resorts, the interior of Nord and Pas-de-Calais with its factories and coal mines, the industrializing Meuse valley north of Charleville, the iron-mining area of northern Lorraine, the environs of Nancy, and eastern sections of Vosges. In addition, a number of free-standing urban centres (Amiens, Reims, Saint-Quentin) and southern sections of Oise were becoming markedly more populous. However, there were

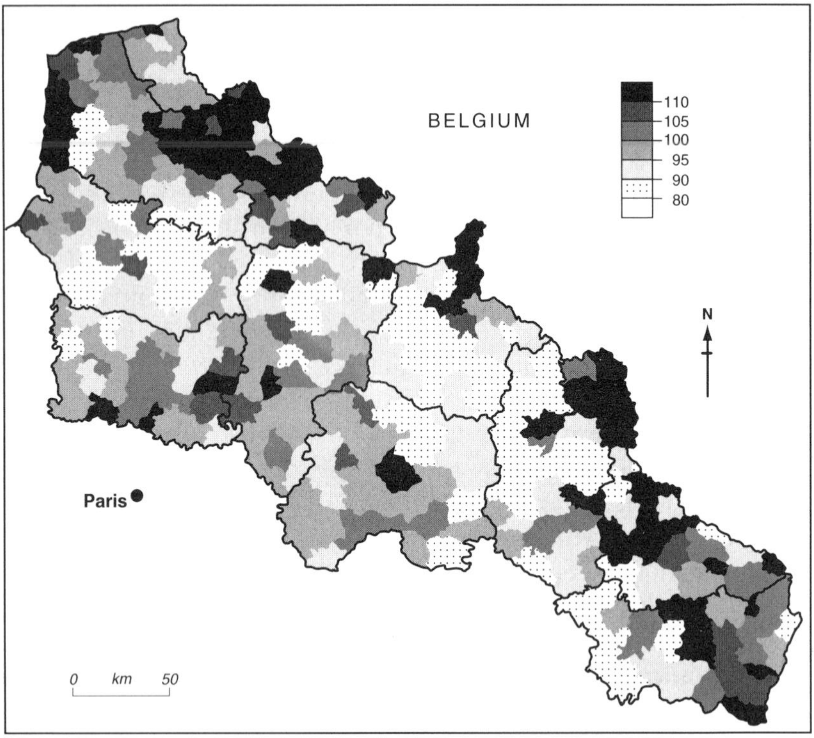

Figure 1.4 Population change, 1896–1911 (1896=100%)

exceptions to the general rule, since the population in almost 300 of the 369 *cantons* in the ten northern *départements* was declining, with losses in excess of 10–20 per cent during the fifteen-year period characterizing southern areas of Ardennes, northern Marne, and northern and central parts of Meuse, as well as western sections of Vosges and much of Somme (Emery 1922: 7). A series of *département* reports published in 1909 provided detailed confirmation of the fact that rural decline was widespread across four-fifths of northern France well before the events of war were to wreak their devastation (Ministère de l'Agriculture 1909). In addition, many rural dwellers were taking off-farm work, and making use of local train services to travel to and from factory employment each day. Agricultural labour was being 'drained away' in each part of the northern *départements* and in districts of Ardennes and Meurthe-et-Moselle, where industrial work was especially plentiful, running the family holding was becoming increasingly the responsibility of women (Ibid.: 27). Permanent paid agricultural labour had become very rare across northern France except on some of the largest farms, and hence harvesting of sugar beet and other intensive crops relied on bands of seasonal workers recruited from Belgian Flanders and Luxembourg. A second response to the declining number of workers on northern farms during the decades before the war was for some large and well-funded estates to invest in mechanization. Finally, some farmers put an increasing share of farmland down to less intensive forms of production, namely down to grass.

Despite the presence of large cities and very important factories and coal mines, over 96 per cent of what was to be recognized as the war zone was given over to farming and forestry, although housing, roads, railways and factories covered more than 5 per cent of Nord, Marne and Meurthe-et-Moselle (Table 1.2). Two-thirds of the total area had been under the plough, with arable occupying over four-fifths of the land surface on the rolling plateaux of Picardy (for example, 84 per cent in both Somme and Pas-de-Calais). Only one-eighth of the war zone was under grass, but the surface had been increasing in recent decades. The enclosed pastures of Thiérache raised the importance of grassland in Nord, and other extensive areas of grazing land were found in the northern portions of Ardennes and Meuse. Not surprisingly,

Table 1.2 Land use by whole *départements* on the eve of the war (ha)

	Arable	Permanent grass	Wood-land	Lakes & marshes	Built-up	Total
Aisne	446,602	70,306	72,453	12,528	18,678	620,567
Ardennes	254,626	103,000	139,982	500	25,408	523,516
Marne	178,910	11,007	69,726	6,583	16,358	282,584
Meurthe-et-Moselle	242,136	52,403	112,527	5,109	17,825	430,000
Meuse	179, 000	41,000	20,000	1,000	20,510	261,510
Nord	200,000	90,000	34,000	500	82,794	407,294
Oise	99,565	7,767	36,922	2,568	6,618	153,440
Pas-de-Calais	128,054	6,982	3,046	5,350	9,360	152,792
Somme	307,000	17,000	19,000	12,000	12,000	367,000
Vosges	60,730	6,865	70,317	161	224	138,297
Total	2,096,623	406,330	577,973	46,299	209,775	3,337,000

Source: Michel, 1932: 90 (attributed to official statistics of the Ministère des Régions Libérées)

woodland was sparse on the fertile agricultural plains of Picardy but very considerable stretches were devoted to timber in Ardennes, Meurthe-et-Moselle and more especially Vosges, where trees covered half of the land surface (Figure 1.5).

A fundamental gradation in the intensity of rural activity which declined from west to east was reflected not only by land use and settlement but also with regard to land values and rents. Taxation documents confirm that on the eve of war arable land in Nord commanded remarkably high average rents (135 F/ha), substantially ahead of what was being paid in Pas-de-Calais (90), Somme (65) and Oise (63) and in a completely different league from average land rents in the eastern *départements* of Meurthe-et-Moselle (28), Marne (25), Vosges (23) and Meuse (22) (Michel 1932: 190) (Table 1.3). Grazing land displayed a comparable gradation, with rentals being rather higher than for arable throughout the northern *départements*. For example, a hectare of ploughland could be sold for more than 4,000 F in Nord and might command 3,000 F in Artois (Pas-de-Calais), Santerre or Vermandois (Somme), and more than 2,000 F in Aisne. By contrast, 500 F was more like the purchasing price in the eastern half of the future war zone, falling to as low as 200 or 300 F in the poorest parts of *la Champagne crayeuse* in Marne.

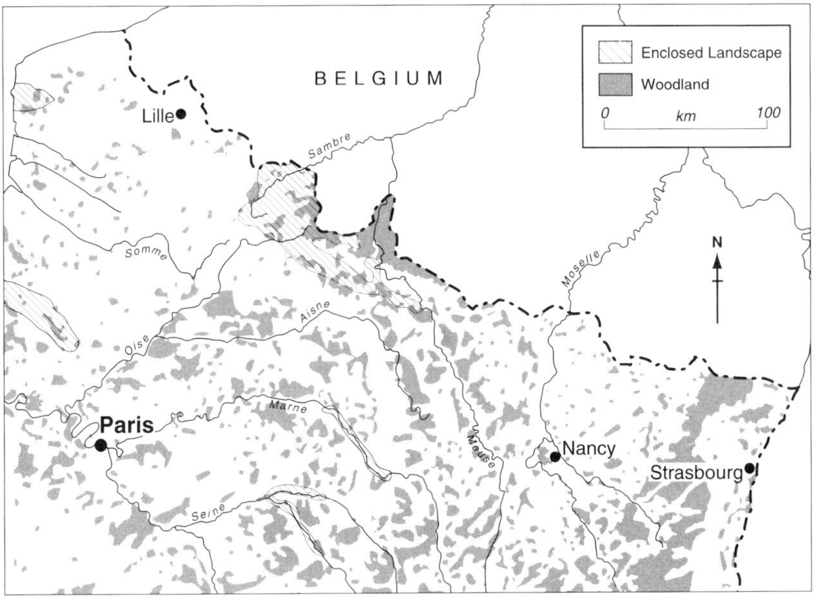

Figure 1.5 Woodland cover of northern France

Table 1.3 Land values on the eve of the war (average rental francs/ha)

	Arable	Meadows & pastures	Woodland	Vines
Aisne	54	76	27	59
Ardennes	35	48	17	46
Marne	25	44	18	263
Meurthe-et-Moselle	28	59	29	35
Meuse	22	68	22	29
Nord	135	142	56	0
Oise	63	74	24	66
Pas-de-Calais	90	114	29	0
Somme	65	92	23	0
Vosges	23	55	44	13

Source: Michel 1932: 190 (attributed to enquiries of the Service des Contributions Directes)

Unfortunately, there is no way of knowing the number or size of farms in the war zone just before the outbreak of hostilities, since the most recent *enquête agricole* had been undertaken as far back as 1892, but at that time 669,351 farms had been recorded in the ten northern *départements* (Ministère de l'Agriculture 1897). Tiny holdings of less than 1 ha apiece had made up 45 per cent of all northern farms, and the proportion rose to half in Meurthe-et-Moselle, Nord and Oise (Table 1.4). A great many of these smallholdings belonged to households which were committed at least in part to industrial work (Ford 1919b: 221). Only 2.6 per cent of units in the ten *départements* were greater than 40 ha, with 4.5 per cent of the total being exceeded in the large farm territory of Aisne and Marne. Regrettably, but understandably, no official survey of the structure of farm holdings was undertaken during the years that surrounded the Great War and the next major agricultural enquiry was not to be held until 1929. Estimates made by the agronomist Professor Ringelmann in May 1918 for seven *départements* or parts thereof gave a very comparable size distribution to that for 1892, with 46.4 per cent of northern farms being under 1 ha apiece and 2.6 per cent exceeding 40 ha (Ringelmann 1918: 130).

On the eve of war the ten *départements* contained only 12 per cent of the total land of France but included 15 per cent of the nation's arable surface and 22 per cent of its improved grasslands (*herbages*), which were particularly widespread in Ardennes and Nord (Ministère de l'Agriculture 1911–14) (Table 1.2). In the French context, agricultural productivity was high, however it

Table 1.4 Farm structures 1892, by whole *départements*

	Total	<1 ha (%)	1–10 ha (%)	10–40 ha (%)	>40 ha (%)
Aisne	66,145	46.7	38.3	10.4	4.5
Ardennes	48,412	44.8	38.8	13.0	3.3
Marne	62,766	41.3	38.1	15.7	4.7
Meurthe-et-Moselle	63,077	49.4	40.4	7.6	2.5
Meuse	59,016	39.6	45.0	13.4	1.9
Nord	86,463	49.3	39.3	10.1	1.3
Oise	52,762	49.8	33.8	12.4	3.9
Pas-de-Calais	86,265	45.2	41.6	10.9	2.3
Somme	69,674	38.9	43.3	15.3	2.4
Vosges	74,771	44.3	47.1	7.9	0.7
Total	669,351	45.0	40.8	11.5	2.6

Source: Ministère de l'Agriculture 1897

was measured (Barral 1968: 181). For example, these ten *départements* embraced 15 per cent of France's wheat-growing surface but yielded no less than 27 per cent of total output (calculated as the average for 1910–13), giving a regional average yield of 22.37 qx/ha, which was almost double the national mean (12.81). Average yields by *département* ranged from a very impressive 30.35 qx/ha in Nord down to 13.32 qx/ha in Meuse. Despite this pronounced gradation in productivity between west and east, wheat yields for each of the ten *départements* were above the national average on the eve of the war. In terms of volume of output, the five western *départements* (Aisne, Nord, Oise, Pas-de-Calais and Somme) together produced one-fifth of the nation's home supply of wheat. Sugar beet entered sophistic-

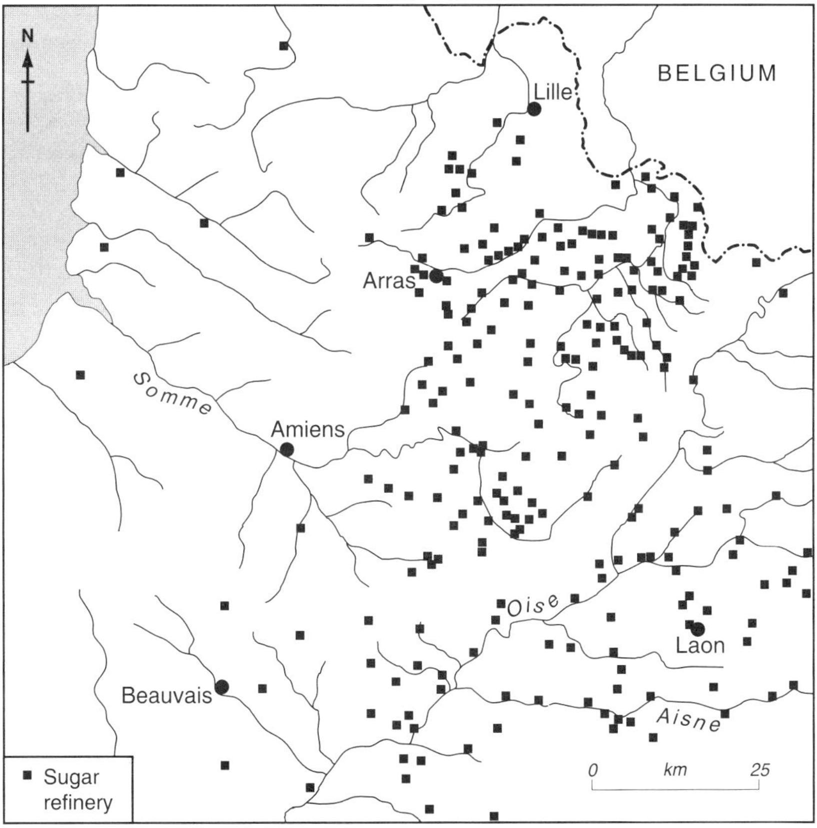

Figure 1.6 Sugar refineries *c.* 1905

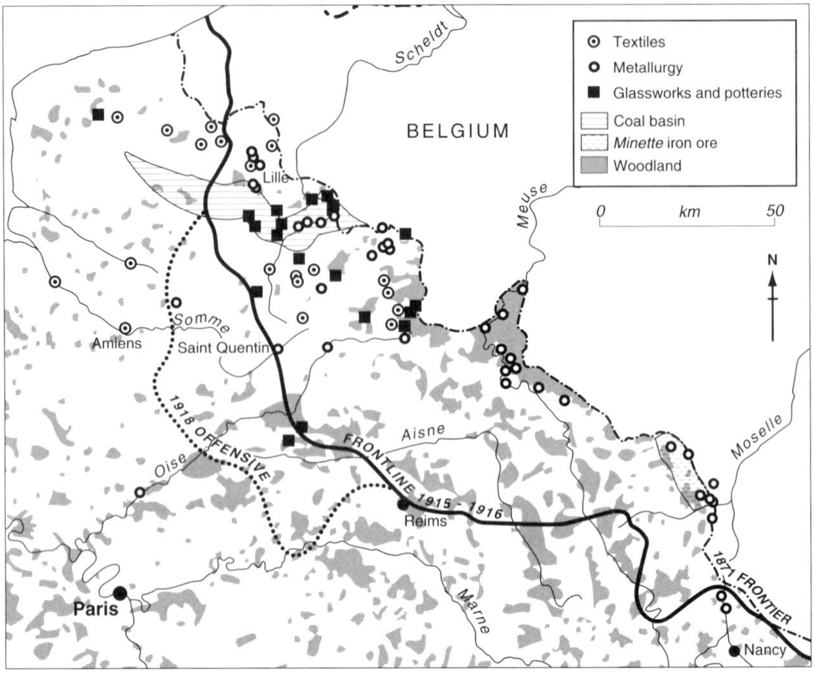

Figure 1.7 Industrial features of northern France, *c.*1913

ated rotations in seven of the northern *départements* which together produced 83 per cent of all French beet (Figure 1.6). The five *départements* mentioned above yielded no less than 79 per cent of the nation's output of sugar, with Aisne alone producing 21 per cent (Augé-Laribé 1923: 49). With respect to livestock, the ten northern *départements* accounted for one-tenth of the nation's cattle, sheep and pigs, and one-fifth of its horses. Nord and Pas-de-Calais came in first and second positions in the ranking of French *départements* according to the value of agricultural production in 1913 (AN F12 8030 Le Rôle de l'Office de Reconstitution Agricole, 1917). Further south, carefully organized rotations and heavy applications of fertilizer enabled the *limon* soils of the Santerre district of Somme to generate high yields of wheat, sugar beet and fodder, and to support large numbers of livestock (Hitier 1917b: 580).

As well as accounting for so much agricultural strength, the areas that were to make up the war zone had an even more vital role since they contributed one-third of French industrial output at the eve of the war, and for specific products the proportion was much higher (Picard 1922: 1010). Three-quarters of French coal production had come from the invaded basin of Nord and Pas-de-Calais, and the basins of Briey and Longwy (Meurthe-et-Moselle) had supplied nine-tenths of French iron ore (Boulin 1927) (Figure 1.7). Two-thirds of the nation's cast iron and steel had been produced in parts of French Lorraine that would suffer invasion (Collinet & Stahl 1928: 99). Sixty per cent of French cotton spindles had been in areas to be invaded subsequently by German troops, and for wool (85 per cent) and linen (90 per cent) the proportions had been even higher (Ford 1919b: 218). Over half the nation's textile looms had been housed in the future devastated regions, together with by far the greater share of its breweries and sugar refineries (Fontaine 1925: 218; Gide & Oualid 1931: 170). At the Armistice northern France was to present a desolate picture not only of devastated farmland and ruined farmsteads, but also of flooded mines, of empty shells of factories from which machinery had been removed to Germany, and of straightforward destruction, with thousands of manufacturing plant reduced to heaps of ruins (Bowman 1921: 77). The details of this formidable industrial loss and of the subsequent restoration of mines and factories, and of the towns and cities that accommodated the majority of them, were critical to the revival not only of northern France but of the nation as a whole, but they lie beyond the scope of the present rural study (Kuisel 1981).

2
The Intensity of Devastation

Recording and Classifying the Damage

The damage caused to the land of France by the events of the Great War was quite different in both extent and intensity from the results of previous hostilities. For example, in 1870 invading German armies had encountered no serious obstacle apart from the fortress of Metz, and had managed to move rapidly across the plains and valleys of the eastern Paris Basin to put Paris under siege. Fighting had been of short duration, the population had not been evacuated, and damage to land and other forms of property had been localized (MacDonald 1922: 4). It is certainly not my intention at this point to rehearse the major engagements of the Great War, suffice it to say that the devastation resulting from it was of quite a different order of size to anything experienced before, and, of course, the challenge of restoration was of unprecedented magnitude (Ibid.: 23). On the basis of personal observation during and just after the war, the American town planner, George B. Ford remarked 'so stupendous is the destruction in the devastated regions of France that no-one can begin to realize what it means. It is only by travelling day after day in an automobile through village after village and town after town, often where nothing is standing erect more than a few feet above the ground, that one can begin to have any conception of its enormousness' (Ford 1919a: 218). From the perspective of our own time, the historian Jean-Jacques Becker insists that 'nothing in the French memory equals the formidable sacrifices made during the first world war' with respect to material goods and to human life (Becker J-J 1991: 17).

In the peaceful, but in many respects chaotic, months that followed the signing of the Armistice a vital start was made on recording the extent and intensity of damage to land and property, and on compiling statistics on the number of dwellings and other buildings that had been utterly destroyed or might be liable to repair. Heavy artillery of both sides in the conflict had, of course, wrought the most horrific destruction not only where battle lines had remained relatively static for months or even years on end or where engagements had been particularly fierce, but also where there had been rapid movements. For example, a campaign of frighteningly systematic destruction was implemented as the Germans were driven back through Somme, Oise and Aisne in the spring of 1917 (Ford 1919a: 27–30; Morain 1918: 65). In the early stages of their retreat the Germans caused relatively little damage in these *départements*. Many buildings were burned but often their exterior and sometimes interior walls remained standing so they could be repaired quite speedily by replacing roofs and installing doors and windows (Ford 1919a: 219). But in the latter part of the retreat there was sufficient time to burn or blow up many settlements across a wide stretch of countryside to the east of Bapaume, Péronne, Ham and Noyon, so that, as Ford remarked, 'in some cases one can ride through a village without knowing it' (Ibid.). During the great German advance of the following spring such towns as Albert, Montdidier, Noyon, Château-Thierry and their surrounding villages were destroyed, and many more distant places, including Paris, experienced long-range shelling or aerial bombardment. Even more destruction of villages, farms, towns, factories and mines accompanied the final German retreat during the summer and autumn of 1918, when quantities of livestock, farm implements and other moveable goods also were carried off (Ducasse, Meyer & Perreux 1962: 435).

The impact on the landscape as well as on the economy and society of northern France was, of course, appalling. After four years of warfare, the battle zone of Pas-de-Calais formed 'a panorama that had never been seen before' (Tribondeau 1937: 121). Weeds flourished among shellholes, trenches, barbed wire and concrete bunkers, carpeting the countryside with quite a different vegetation from the cereals and lush fodder crops that it had supported for so long. Across some stretches every tree had been felled by gunfire or had been cut down intentionally. No bird song was heard; no birds remained. Whole villages had been destroyed in the fighting or had been mined as the Germans withdrew (Figure 2.1). It seemed, as numerous commentators would suggest, to form a 'lunar landscape' (Ibid.). Districts away from the battle zone were less affected but they too suffered from

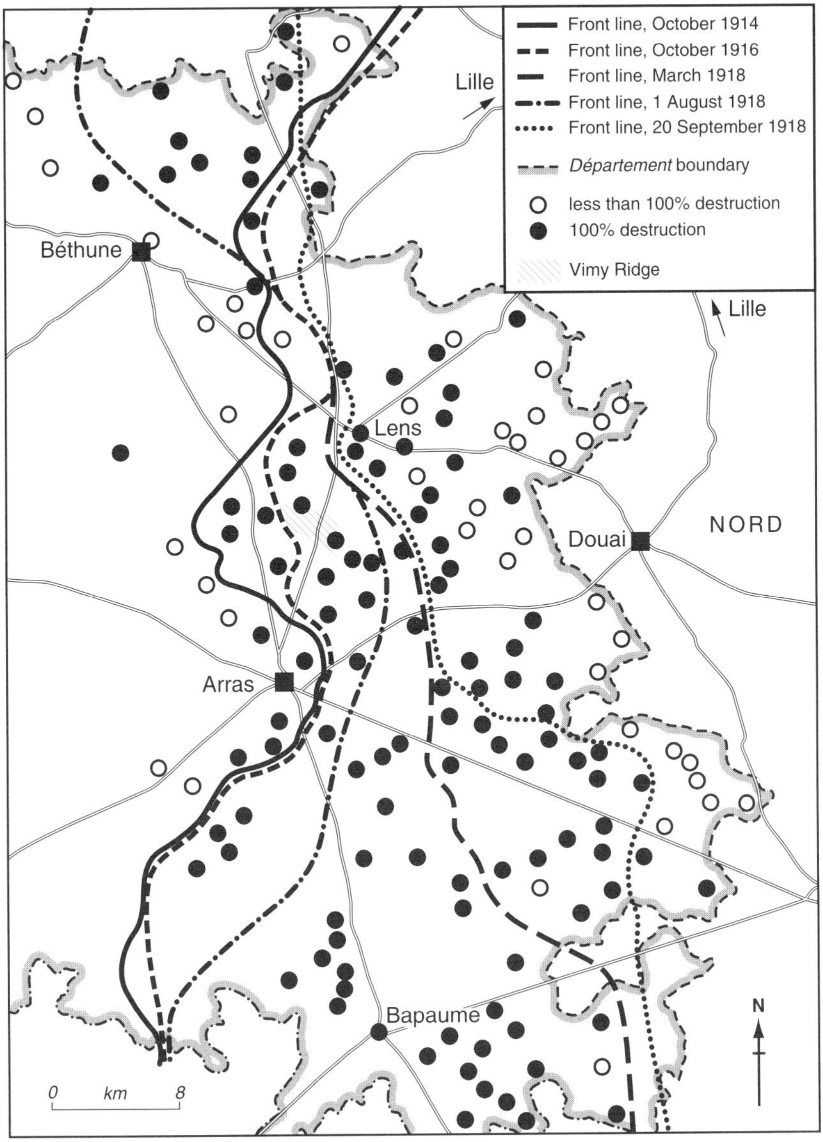

Figure 2.1 The battle zone of Pas-de-Calais; only the devastated settlements visited by Mlle Guyot have been marked (ADPC 1J200 Enquête en Artois)

damage caused by the enforced presence of troops and by the effects of scorched earth policies.

Recording and classifying such information proved to be a difficult and necessarily haphazard business. Early in the war mayors had been instructed to produce regular and detailed reports on the degree of destruction across their territory. But, as time elapsed and civilian administrations were evacuated from increasingly wide areas, that source became both sporadic and unreliable. A number of French ministries and military authorities attempted to remedy the deficiency and undertook their own enquiries at various dates. For example, a report was drawn up by the Ministère de l'Intérieur in May 1916 covering 754 *communes* in ten *départements* in which 46,263 buildings were noted as having been damaged; however this enquiry excluded 450 *communes* that were too near the front line to be surveyed (Ford 1919a: 220). A further statement was made in July 1917 embracing 1,223 *communes* where 50,756 buildings had been destroyed and a fractionally larger number had been damaged. No fewer than 414 factories were reported to have been destroyed by that time (Ibid.).

Three intensities of destruction were often recognized, as in 1917 in the *département* of Somme (Figure 2.2). Nothing remained in the battle zone proper. The agricultural writer Henri Hitier remarked, 'where there had been villages one sees nothing but shellholes and trenches, not a square metre of top-soil is in place, everything has been disturbed and the sub-soil has been turned up to the surface' (Hitier 1917b: 237). Shells needed to be removed from an intermediate zone of devastation, while outer areas might be brought back into cultivation if farmers could be provided with shelter, foodstuffs and some financial support to tide them through. Thus, one year before the Armistice, the plateau of Santerre in south-eastern Somme had taken on the appearance of an 'immense prairie', with some fields of rye and wheat having been sown by the Germans and a few old patches of luzerne still being recognizable (Ibid.: 238). As in other sections of the *régions dévastées* which remained to the east or north of the front line, German authorities, or local farmers working to their orders, had sown wheat for three years in succession in eastern Somme with total disregard for rotations or fertilizers (Hitier 1917a: 586). As a result, yields plummeted and

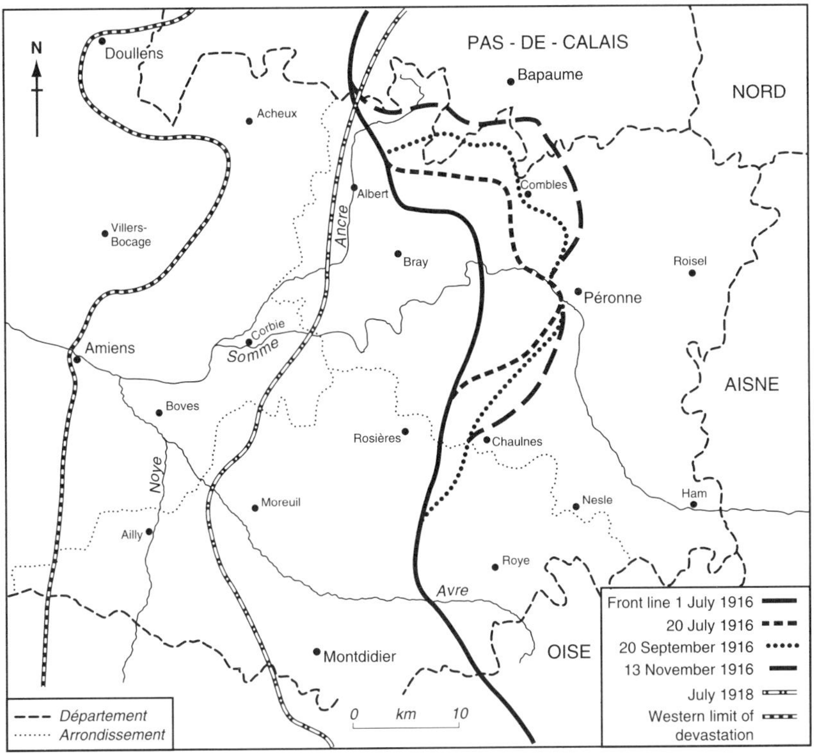

Figure 2.2 The battle zone of Somme

the soil became infested with weeds. Before the German offensive of spring 1918 new enquiries into the local impact of devastation were launched in some parts of the war zone. For example, in Aisne staff of the Génie Rural, the director of agricultural services, and representatives of local farmers' associations had started an investigation into rural conditions early in the year (Saint 1920: 90). Unfortunately, their painstakingly collected results were rendered redundant as soon as the Germans re-advanced.

Shortly before the Armistice was signed, a government circular (31 October 1918) required the engineers of the Génie Rural to classify in a standardized way all the land in each *commune* of the war zone, according to whether they considered: it could be returned to cultivation or other forms of normal use after simple clearance of debris; it would require considerable restoration work; or it was so devastated that the likely costs of restoration would outstrip its intrinsic value. Three months later, instructions were issued for special maps to be drawn up, using blue, yellow and red tints to identify each of these three appraisals which were then marked on 1:20,000 *plans directeurs* held by the Service du Cadastre of each *département* (Amat 1987: 229; Becker J-J 1991: 21). Green was reserved to indicate the location of woodland (Saint 1920: 90). More detailed maps at the scale of 1:10,000 were to be prepared for the so-called red zone where destruction was most intense. All this information was duly collated by the Ministère des Régions Libérées (Table 2.1).

It was believed that the bulk of recovery work in the blue zone might be entrusted to private initiative, although the state's emergency organizations would be required to identify and remove shells and undertake other urgent tasks (Picard 1922: 1010). In those parts of the blue zone where farmhouses and other shelters had been destroyed, squads of prisoners of war and other emergency workers would have to be brought in each day (Lebrun 1918: 492). The blue zone typically embraced land that was a substantial distance from areas where the battle front had been stabilized for a considerable length of time. It was characterized by southern and western parts of the war zone which had been overrun rapidly during the German advance of summer 1914, and also by extensive districts which had been behind the German front line throughout the war (Figure 2.3(a)). The main agricultural problems encountered in the blue zone included land abandonment or very poor methods of cultivation having been used. For example, land in Ardennes had been subjected to four years of 'enforced abandonment' under German occupation, so that at the Armistice 'uncultivated fields stretched as far as the eye could see' and were interrupted only by a few patches of cabbages and turnips which had been a source of food for the few wretched *envahis* who had not been deported (Hubert 1923: 189, 197). To Lucien Hubert it seemed as if 'life itself had withdrawn from these accursed areas; none of the thousand familiar sounds of the countryside broke the silence' (Ibid.: 197). He argued that 'At the Armistice . . . everything had to be restored. Most land was left as uncultivated waste, crops had been removed, livestock were virtually inexistant, buildings were damaged or destroyed' (Ibid.: 214).

Table 2.1 Types of devastation to land (ha)

	Needing simple clearance	Demanding considerable work	Cost of work exceeds value of land	Total
Aisne	342,755	262,622	15,190	620,567
Ardennes	365,654	157,862	0	523,516
Marne	89,967	169,317	23,300	282,584
Meurthe-et-Moselle	233,206	176,794	20,000	430,000
Meuse	204,000	40,510	17,000	261,510
Nord	72,500	331,794	3,000	407,294
Oise	50,440	101,200	1,800	153,440
Pas-de-Calais	34,000	92,352	26,440	152,792
Somme	206,000	152,000	9,000	367,000
Vosges	120,565	16,822	910	138,297
Total	1,719,087	1,501,273	116,640	3,337,000

Source: Michel 1932: 90 (attributed to official statistics from the Ministère des Régions Libérées).

More serious destruction and disruption was found in the intermediate, or yellow, zone which was demarcated roughly by a line traced some 15 km from the furthest points reached by the enemy between the start of trench warfare (September 1914) and the Armistice (Michel 1932: 89). In this zone, shells would have to be identified, removed and disposed of; trenches and shellholes needed to be filled; and barbed wire and all the other abandoned paraphernalia of war had to be removed. Agricultural recovery would doubtless take several years and would require considerable input of labour from the state's emergency services or other sources in such districts, which were particularly extensive in the western and central parts of the war zone.

Places in which fighting had been most intense or prolonged formed the red zone, where surface damage was extreme and the possibility of agricultural restoration was far from certain in the minds of the staff of the Génie Rural. Across Champagne and to the north of Verdun this zone of profound devastation was 10–15 km broad, and it was even wider in parts of Picardy. For example, no trace remained of four villages along the road between Albert and Bapaume where the landscape had been turned into chaos by 'millions upon millions of shells' raining on

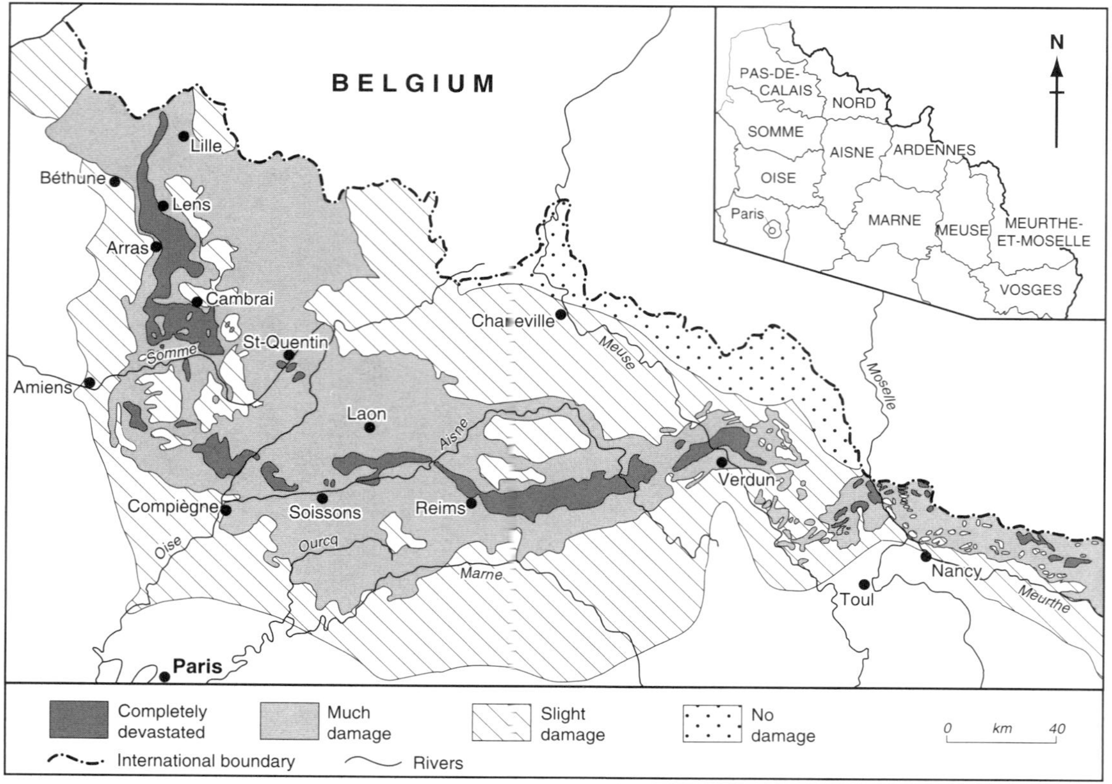

Figure 2.3(a) Degrees of destruction across northern France

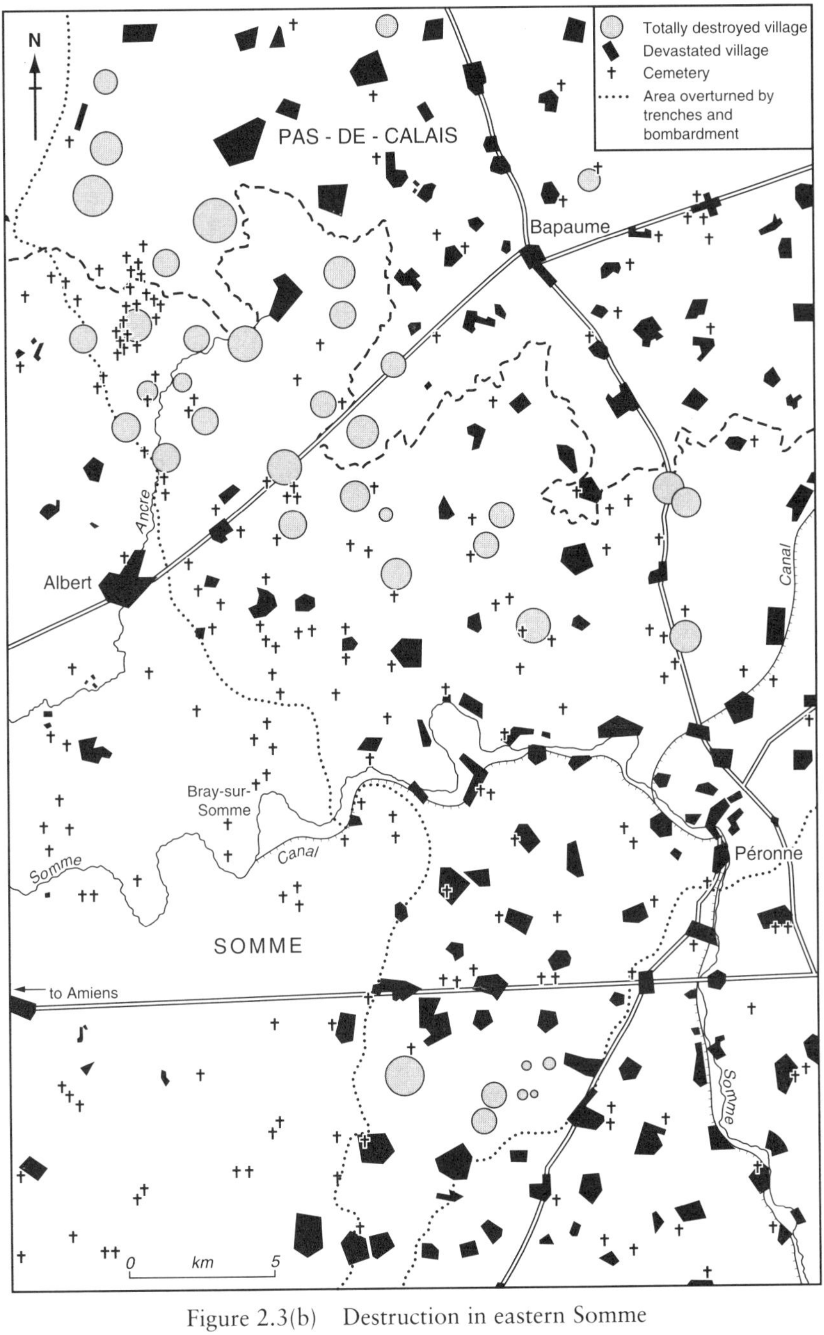

Figure 2.3(b) Destruction in eastern Somme

to a labyrinth of trenches (Figure 2.3(b)) (Bechmann 1917: 672). As a result 'not only had buildings been destroyed but also the ground itself' (Ibid). As well as the volume of shelling that had occurred, there was the deadly estimate that one-fifth of the projectiles had not exploded, with grenades being even more dangerous than large, more visible shells to those moving about on foot (Ibid.: 673). The utter devastation of these localities impressed itself on many councillors for central and southern provinces who were brought there on official visits in October 1917. As a result of the devastation, the politician André Tardieu insisted that it was possible to drive for many kilometres across the northern *départements* without coming across a single house, for example between Soissons and Saint-Quentin, between Armentières and Péronne, and between Soissons and Laon (Tardieu 1921: 384). In areas where the topsoil was not particularly thick, trenches, shellholes and craters brought the underlying rock to the surface (Flatrès 1980: 95). Land restoration in the red zone, if it were to prove feasible, would have to be an extremely painstaking, time-consuming and costly affair.

Some commentators were much more pessimistic and argued that the technical difficulties and likely financial implications of reconstitution were so great that the red zone would never be returned to agricultural use (see Chapter 10). Even the experienced agricultural writer Henri Hitier, who normally placed great faith in the prospect of agricultural revival, remarked bluntly that he could not 'see how one might hope to restore cultivation in such places' (Hitier 1917a: 582). It was widely advocated that, as far as possible, the red zone should be made safe and then afforested to form a national memorial, or alternatively be provided with a *voie sacrée* that would be lined with monuments and cemeteries (Vaillat 1919: 781). This kind of opinion disregarded the ferocious attachment of the farming population to its devastated land which, some would maintain, formed a sentiment that had been strengthened by enforced absence during the years of war (Picard 1922: 1023). As the historian Denis Brogan was to argue, the pessimists simply 'overlooked the irrational courage and tenacity of the French peasant' which insisted that the red zone be reduced in size and that extensive stretches be released for farming with the minimum of delay (Brogan 1940: 599). Faced with such claims, the extent of the red zone was to be challenged repeatedly and would undergo considerable revision in the decade following the Armistice (see Chapter 10).

Early statistics from the Ministère de l'Agriculture identified 178,511 ha of extreme devastation located in nine *départements* (none in Ardennes), with no less than 53,000 ha being found in Somme alone (Michel 1932: 89). However, a distinction was drawn between 55,898 ha that were judged to be beyond any chance of restoration, and 122,613 ha where agricultural recovery was believed to be technically possible but probably only at a cost far outstripping the intrinsic value of the land. Individual prefects recorded their own estimates which incorporated local perceptions and, not surprisingly, differed from those of the Ministry. For example, immediately after the Armistice, and in response to the strong wish of farmers to start working the

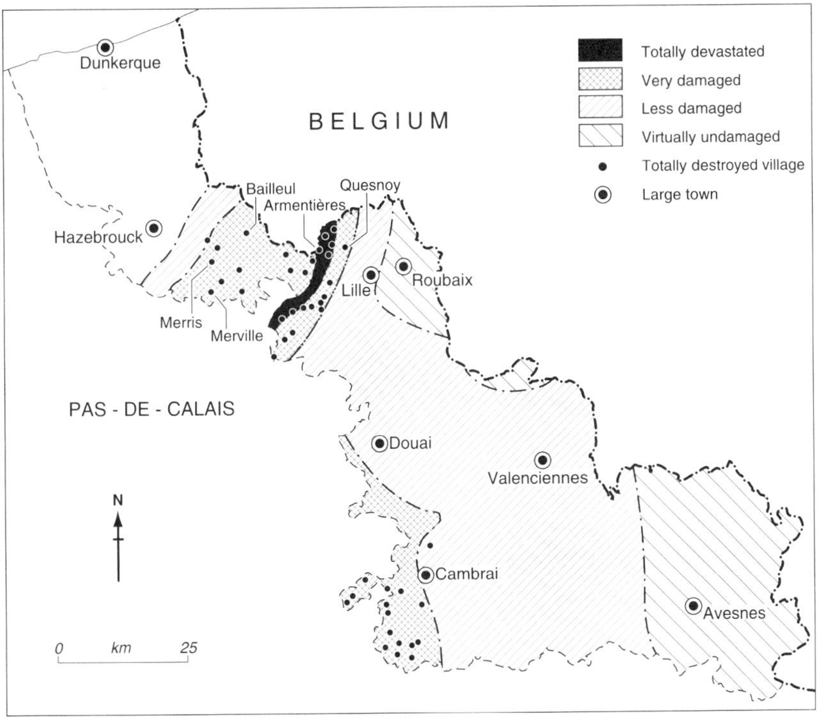

Figure 2.4 Destruction in Nord

land, Prefect Morain recognized a red zone of only 28,000 ha in Somme (Morain 1920: 19).

According to the so-called official statistics assembled by the Ministère des Régions Libérées and released by it in 1923, the red zone covered 116,794 ha in parts of nine *départements*, with particularly large stretches being recognized in Pas-de-Calais (26,440 ha), Marne (23,300 ha), Meurthe-et-Moselle (20,000 ha) and Meuse (17,000 ha) (Table 2.1). By contrast, in Nord only 3,000 ha were classified as red zone which covered land adjacent to the front line established in 1914 and along the subsequent Hindenburg Line to the west of Cambrai (Figure 2.4) (Vezin & Vandamme 1937: 334). This official definition of extreme devastation covered some 3.5 per cent of the complete war zone but occupied as much as 17.3 per cent of it in Pas-de-Calais and 8.2 per cent in Marne.

Damage to Woodlands and Vineyards

Extensive areas of trees had been destroyed or degraded, with Picard estimating that three-quarters of woodland throughout the ten *départements* had suffered in one way or another as a result of military events and over-exploitation during the war (Picard 1922: 1011). The report sponsored by the Carnegie Foundation noted that timber had been destroyed across 200,000 ha and premature or 'abusive' felling had been undertaken over a further 150,000 ha (Chevalier 1927: 122). The most savage devastation was found in former battle zones such as the woodlands between Epernay and the Chemin-des-Dames, where as late as summer 1920 *The Statist* could report that 'nothing remains of the once flourishing forests save a few blasted tree trunks whose blackened and naked branches symbolize the desolation that meets the eye for miles on all sides' (Epernay, *TS*, 03.06.21: 1054). Behind the allied front line, woods had been exploited by troops to meet their many regular needs, for example for heating, building, or supporting trenches, regardless of the damage caused (Ratineau & Gaillot 1928: 127; Amat 1987: 218). Northern woodlands behind the German lines had also been exploited heavily by military, civilian and prisoner-of-war labour to obtain timber for many purposes (Raux 1921: 9). For example, in Ardennes the Germans installed sawmills for processing timber which was used for bolstering trenches and fuelling military locomotives as well as for supplying troops with firewood and charcoal (Poquet 1986: 27). In the southern part of the *département*, military camps and vehicle parks were hidden in woodlands for the duration of the war, which were further mutilated as the line of fire moved rapidly northwards during the violent combat of autumn 1918 (Adam 1928: 112).

Starting in 1915, intensive exploitation also had occurred in the oak woods of Nord, where the best timber was selected for dispatch to Germany (Ardouin-Dumazet 1915: 572; Rabouille 1922: 395). Normal and narrow-gauge (0.60 m) railway lines served the sawmills and labour was supplied by Russian and Italian prisoners who, according to Rabouille, were subjected to 'iron discipline' (Rabouille 1922: 396). Vast areas of woodland had been cleared from the *département* by the end of the war, with stumps left protruding 40–60 cm from the ground and sawmills having been set alight by the retreating Germans. The Forêt de Mormal (5,400 ha) had been felled completely and a total of 15,386 ha, or almost three-quarters of the 21,026 ha of state and communal woodland recorded in Nord in 1914, had been over-exploited by the enemy or destroyed by shelling (Morain 1923: 97). In a bizarre way the German commander at Valenciennes made use of elephants to pull up tree roots and to load logs on to wagons, with one particular working elephant called Jenny from Hagenbeck's circus in Hamburg acquiring fame by being portrayed in German news magazines (Rabouille 1922: 396, 1928: 434; Boulin 1927: 37–38).

Allied and enemy troops alike had been stationed in camouflaged forest clearances for the duration of the war (Forget 1927). Deprived of their normal supplies of coal, the remaining civilians also ravaged the woods (Jolyet 1916: 404). Bastide estimated that almost all the woodlands in Ardennes *département* and in the Argonne district had been devastated, and he suggested optimistically that it would take at least a generation for the damage to be made good (Bastide 1923: 592). A survey of woodlands throughout the northern *départements* undertaken in 1919 recorded about 100,000 ha where the soil needed to be restored, an equal amount in need of replanting or reseeding, and roughly 150,000 ha which had suffered because of ruthless cutting (MacDonald 1922: 168). It was estimated that it would take half a century for these areas to return to a condition in which they would be able to produce decent timber. Recently, the biogeographer Paul Arnould has written of the 'forest trauma' of northern France, explaining that in 1930 and even later some 'particularly affected parts of the forests still remained disrupted; the ground littered with fallen trees, set among barbed wire entanglements in the craters of shellholes' (Arnould 1992). Even now the traces of damage inflicted during the Great War can still be seen on the trunks of older trees in some northern woodlands (Bach 1975; Gouttin 1979). Other forms of vegetation also suffered as a result of over four years of war (Amat 1987: 217, 1988a: 192). For example, osier beds had not been maintained and osiers became thick and branch-like rather than slender and pliable and hence were useless for basket making (Hubert 1923: 229). They would have to be cleared and the areas used in other ways, for example for growing poplar trees (Renaudin 1936: 236).

The vineyards of northern France formed a rather special case of destruction during the war. Small areas under vines were devastated in Meurthe-et-Moselle but the story of northern viticulture was essentially that of Champagne. On the eve of the war the *département* of Marne had contained 11,750 ha of vines, of which half were diseased because of phylloxera but continued to produce grapes (Moreau-Bérillon 1924: 292). The Germans occupied the vineyards around Reims for just a few days in September 1914; indeed initially they respected the vines and it was argued that they wished to appropriate 'this jewel in the viticultural crown of France' (De Polignac 1920: 16). But as circumstances changed, shelling from the heights of Moronvillers, Berru and Nogent-l'Abbaye, aerial bombardment and drifting gas devastated the surface of the Montagne de Reims over the next four years (Comité d'Action des Régions Dévastées 1925: 160). Trenches were cut, gun emplacements were installed across sections of vineyard, and vine-growing villages were destroyed during 1918. In addition, mobilization had deprived the vineyards of necessary labour; women, children and old men were unable to tend the vines and work the soil in the habitual way. Normal fertilizers were unobtainable so that insects and plant diseases flourished unchecked; phylloxera made more progress in a mere four years than in the preceding three decades. Special permits had to be obtained by all who wished to work in the vineyards where, of course, they were easy targets for enemy fire. For this reason the military authorities evacuated most of the vine-growing *communes* during 1918. *The Statist* reported that 'the vines lost in the Champagne district directly from war causes, such as bombardment, trampling by troops, digging of trenches, and gun attacks, amount to only one-third of the losses caused by disease and unavoidable neglect' (The Champagne industry, *TS*, 03.06.20: 1051). By the Armistice, the vineyards of Marne had declined to 10,600 ha, including 4,284 ha where vines had been uprooted or abandoned and 3,009 ha which had succumbed to phylloxera but were still in production (Moreau-Bérillon 1924: 293). In six *communes* vineyards had virtually disappeared and the vine-covered slopes of Verzenay, which had been much visited and admired by tourists before the war, were reduced to an immense stretch of scrub, with only 75 ha of the former 500 ha of vines remaining in cultivation.

The simple presence of military forces took land out of agricultural use for camps, training grounds, firing ranges, airfields and many other purposes, and gave rise to localized destruction which occasioned severe complaints in many parts of the war zone. For example, farmers near Fère-Champenoise (Marne) complained that the most fertile part of their land had been requisitioned for an army camp (ADMa 203 M198 Registre des délibérations 03.03.18). Similarly, artillery ranges and an airfield had been sited on the best ground at Sezanne (Marne), despite the fact that poorer farmland was available nearby (Ibid). In French Flanders great efforts were made by local people to ensure that their hop-fields and best pastures were declared out of bounds for British soldiers billetted at Bailleul camp, but troops chose to take their exercise across sown fields instead, to the fury of local farmers (ADN 9R 1098 Extension du Camp de Bailleul, 29.01.17). In Somme posts and signs were installed in a vain attempt to restrict men and horses to specific paths rather than allowing them to wander across farmland at will (Morain 1918: 108). Writing of Meuse *département*, Mgr Aimond focused his criticism on misdemeanours committed by German troops, but his observations would apply to soldiers on either side. He reported: 'Close to the front, the enemy stripped houses of doors, shutters, cupboards and especially bedding, which they carried into the trenches . . . They slaughtered farm animals, taking the best parts to eat and leaving the rest to rot' (Aimond 1922: 117). Poorly supervised army horses damaged crops and civilian buildings, and careless behaviour by soldiers caused fires in fields and farmsteads. Siting munition dumps close to villages gave rise to further damage since explosions inevitably occurred; and, of course, this kind of locational decision made adjacent settlements ready targets for attack from the air (Aimond 1922: 270). Installation by the British army of extensive networks of narrow-gauge railway line (0.60 m) close to the front line further disrupted 'normal' uses of rural land (Naudin 1920: 66).

The Geography of Destruction

As had been the case in earlier conflicts, every feature of physical geography across the northern *départements*, whether it was ridge, plateau, valley, marshy depression or wooded terrain, proved to be of crucial significance for the conduct of the war (Brunhes & Vallaux 1921: 468–82; Brunhes & Deffontaines 1926: 240–53; Hanotaux 1920: 39). As geographer Emmanuel De Martonne insisted, environmental factors were never ignored by those waging war and must be understood by those attempting to explain the pattern of hostilities and to appreciate the challenge of reconstitution (cited in Villate 1925: 9). Exactly the same message was conveyed by Douglas W. Johnson, professor of physiography at Columbia University and lately major in the military intelligence division and chief of the division of boundary geography in the American commission to negotiate peace (Johnson 1917, 1919: 511). At the start of the war the Germans had not headed for Paris across the escarpments, plateaux and northward-flowing rivers of the eastern Paris Basin but had chosen the longer but easier route through Belgium (Figure 2.5). They had streamed across the Belgian frontier into Aisne, Somme, Oise and Marne reaching Meaux, a mere 50 km from Paris, and then pushed toward Senlis and Beauvais, and eastward toward Châlons-sur-Marne and the Argonne. They penetrated to the northern fringes of Aube *département*, and also managed virtually to encircle the fortress of Verdun. After the Battle of the Marne the battle line was pushed north of that river but subsequent engagements produced very widespread destruc-

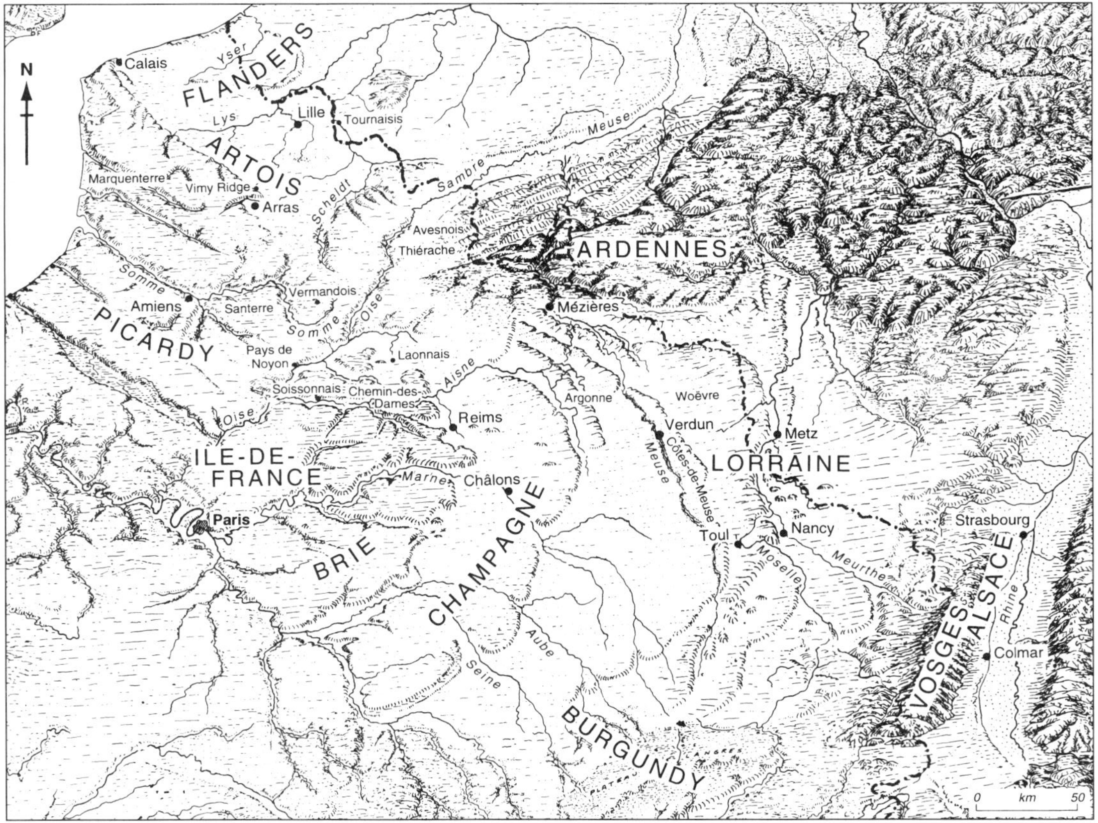

Figure 2.5 Physiography and *pays* of northern France

tion. For four years the German army made full use of 'the tactical assets of the countryside it occupied' and from every range of hilly country observed the movements of its enemies (Brogan 1940: 478–79). The allies duly devoted their energies to trying to dislodge the Germans from the high ground of Vimy Ridge and Notre-Dame de Lorette in Artois, from the Argonne, the Meuse heights and the crest of the Vosges, behind which lay the route toward Germany (Johnson 1919: 512–13).

The pattern of ensuing destruction across the hilly wooded country of north-eastern France and on the broad plains and rolling hills further west was recorded by Guicherd and Maitrot in a series of short articles in the *Journal d'Agriculture Pratique* and summarized in the *Annales de Géographie* by René Musset in the following year (Guicherd & Maitrot 1921; Musset 1922). In the extreme east of the war zone the area of damage had stabilized along a band of largely wooded terrain some 10–15 km broad, which extended from the Vosges to the town of Saint-Mihiel. Forests in the two dozen *communes* of Vosges that had been occupied by the Germans throughout the war experienced clear felling over substantial areas, thereby exposing surrounding trees to wind damage (Deschaseux 1919: 51–52). No regular cutting was undertaken in the narrow combat zone (200–500 m across) where woodland was reduced to a state of chaos during the war, and the surrounding landscape was savagely scarred by trenches, shellholes and military installations (Magre 1923: 103). Conditions were declared to be rather better behind the French lines, for although much felling had occurred, this exploitation had been done in a way that would not hamper future regeneration (Ibid.). This eastern part of the front line had not been the site of long offensives and, with the exception of a narrow strip, experienced what might be described as a kind of 'peace-time warfare' (Lidbetter & Monk-Jones 1919: 181). By contrast, shellfire inflicted serious damage to farmland to the north and east of Nancy, where small areas were duly identified as belonging to the red zone. Indeed, Prefect Mirman spoke of the 'assassination' of groups of villages in Meurthe-et-Moselle during the early months of war (cited in Guillon 1915: 631). Conditions soon calmed in the extreme east of the war zone, and many farmers returned to their ruins and attempted to cultivate their land once again, despite a lack of implements, draft animals, fertilizers and seeds (Ministère de l'Agriculture 1915: 20). The situation proved so stable during 1917 and 1918 that French troops were allocated a range of agricultural tasks to perform between their spells in the trenches. Only a narrow strip, some 3 or 4 km in width, extending between Blamont and Pont-à-Mousson on the river Moselle was left completely uncultivated. In heavily wooded country between the Moselle and Meuse the front was lined by defensive works but military activity proved to be slight.

The same certainly cannot be said for the massively fortified environs of Verdun where the valley of the Meuse had been converted into a veritable 'iron curtain' (Brunhes & Vallaux 1921: 472; Vidal de la Blache 1908). The city remained impregnable but human losses were appalling on both sides, with German soldiers referring to it as 'the slaughterhouse of Germany' (Michelin 1919a: 29). The prolonged impact of heavy shellfire destroyed farming villages along a strip 8–15 km wide extending northwards from Saint-Mihiel and Commercy to Verdun and then southwards to Bar-le-Duc (Figure 2.6). On the 'immense battlefield of Verdun, more than a score of villages were reduced to nothing' (Aimond 1922: 309). As William MacDonald remarked: 'Nowhere in France is there now to be seen a more vivid combination of rugged country dotted with the remains of forts and artillery emplacements, of soil torn by trenches, shellholes, and mine craters, and of forests shattered by shellfire, and towns and villages in ruins. From whatever quarter one approaches Verdun, the ravages of war stand out on every hand' (MacDonald 1922: 6). The whole environment was so devastated in these districts, with their recent history of low agricultural yields and sustained depopulation, that the hope of restoration appeared to pose a virtually insoluble challenge. Guicherd and Maitrot suggested that only small nodes of land should be reclaimed for cultivation and the rest be given over to sheep grazing, or else the whole area should be put under trees (Guicherd & Maitrot 1921: 332). Half of the total cover of oak, beech and hornbeam throughout Meuse was deemed to be damaged as a result of the war (Magny 1928: 123). Over half of the communal woodland in that *département* had been devastated and two-fifths of both state and private woodland had suffered material damage (Forget 1927: 123).

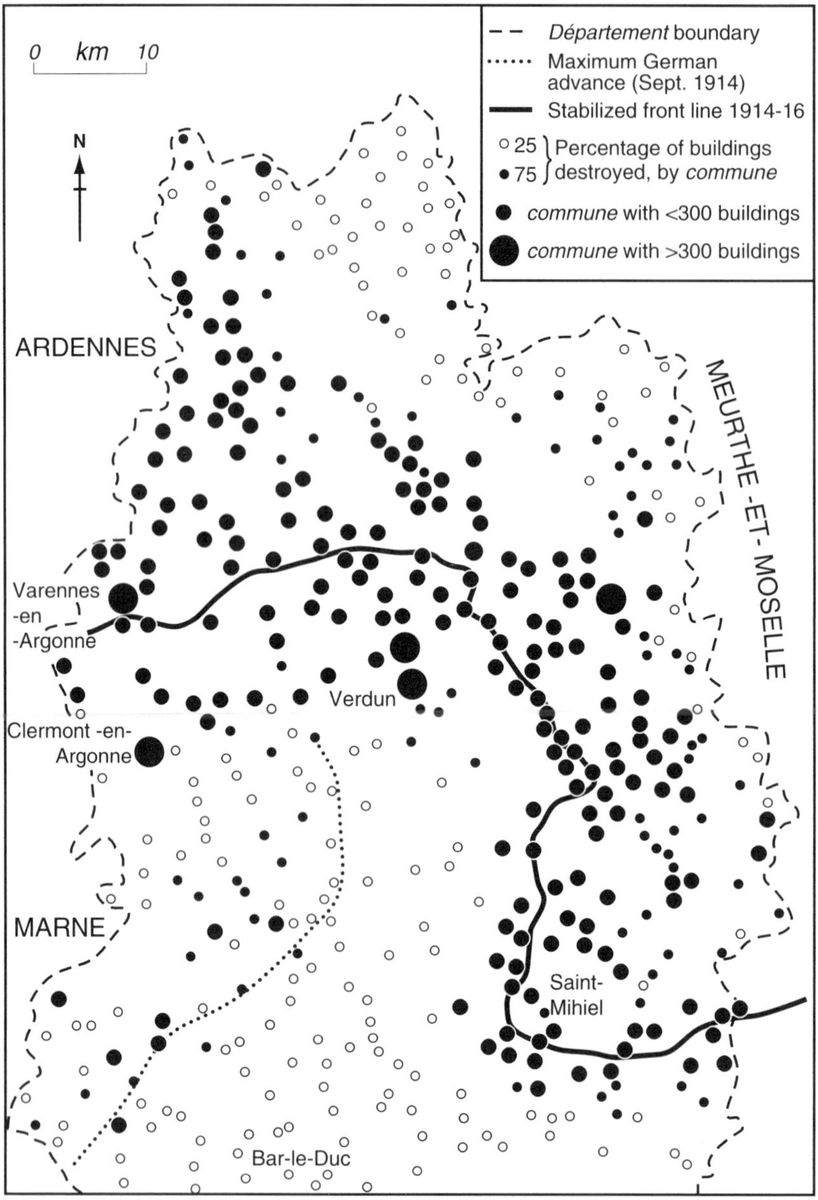

Figure 2.6 Destruction in Meuse

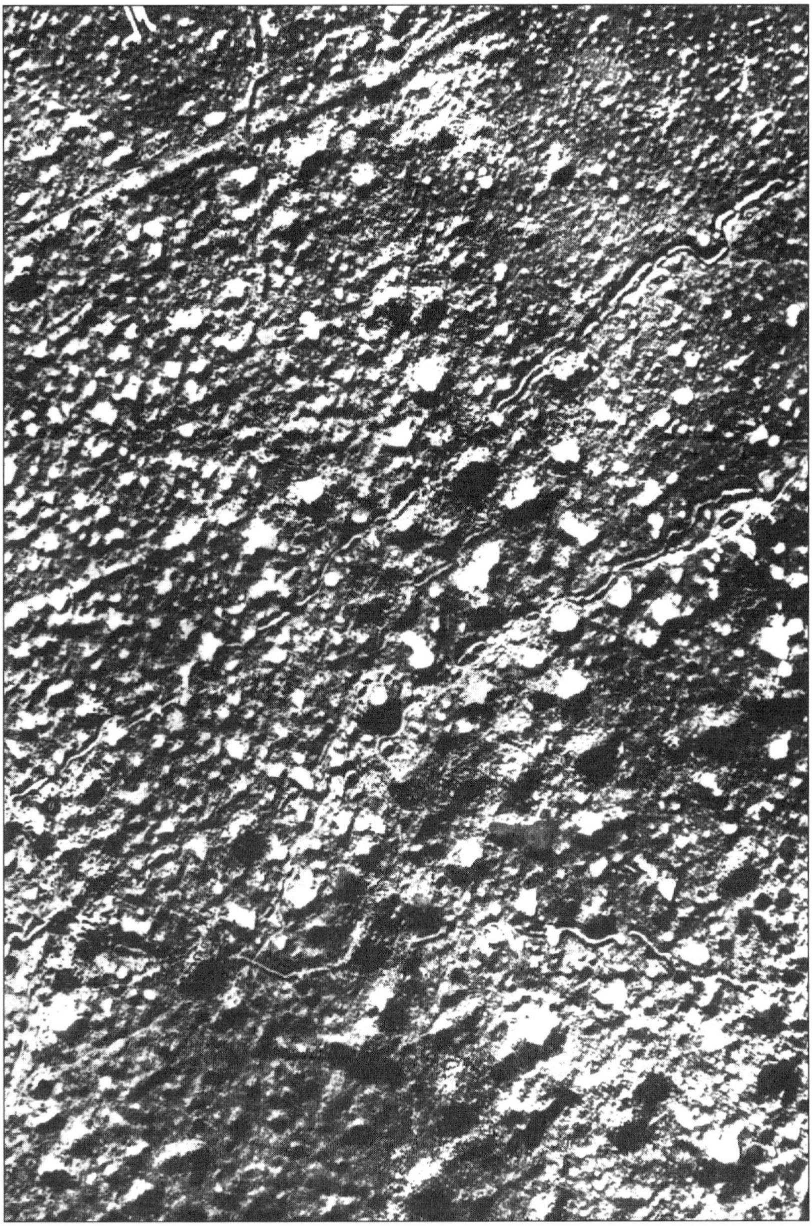

Plate 2.1 Aerial view of the red zone at Douaumont, near Verdun, showing trenches and shell craters

After the Battle of the Marne in September 1914, the Germans dug their first trenches and for four years the front line was fixed across the woodlands of the Argonne and the chalky plateaux of Champagne, from Vauquois westwards to Reims and thence to the plateau of Craonne, south-east of Laon (Laurent 1948: 268). The French offensive of 1915 and the German advance of 1918 did little in these areas to modify the front, which was lined with trenches and all the infrastructure of war, occupying a zone typically 10–15 km in breadth. The broken terrain of the wooded Argonne, with its deep ravines, made movement particularly difficult (Huin 1962: 160). Along the stable front line fighting was fierce and unrelenting, with the French and German trenches often being only 10 m apart. In some places they almost touched. The woodland suffered massive damage because of gunfire and heavy exploitation, with some stretches being cleared completely. Despite reafforestation between 1928 and 1934, the impact of the war may still be read in the detailed biogeography of the area (Ibid.: 162).

Further to the west each natural hollow on the plain of Champagne was used for military installations. Whole villages were blasted out of existence, as were the meagre plantations of pines which had broken the monotony of some stretches of heath. The few trees that survived provided a little shelter for the soldiers. The very topsoil was destroyed in this swathe of red zone (which exceeded 23,000 ha in Marne), with devastation being particularly severe to the east of Reims. Mgr Tissier, Bishop of Châlons, described the scene near Somme-Py in October 1918 as 'absolute desert, without water, people or vegetation . . . a land without colour which we shall call the corpse of a *pays*' (Tissier 1918: 19). The settlements of 'Tahure, Ripout, Rouvroy, Fontaine and Bratreuil have become simply geographical expressions since their very ruins have perished' (Ibid.: 26). So intense was the devastation that he wondered if these villages and their ravaged neighbours could ever be restored. Nine months after the Armistice the north-eastern corner of Marne still could be described as 'a *tabula rasa*, a silent desert with fields split open by shells' (Marne, *JAP*, 10.08.19: 198).

By contrast, the countryside further north, notably in Ardennes, had been behind enemy lines throughout the war. The Germans had arrived in that *département* during August 1914 but only at the end of September 1918 did allied troops set foot in it. Its chief town, Charleville-Mezières, was still being bombarded only a few hours before the signing of the Armistice (Hubert 1923: 11). By virtue of these circumstances, the *département* suffered disruption, loss of livestock and equipment and poor agricultural management rather than widespread material destruction (Fagot 1918: 1087). However, its forests were over-exploited and those in the south of the *département* had sheltered military camps and equipment stores as well as supplying timber (Adam 1937: 90). About one-third of its arable surface had been cultivated for the benefit of the German occupiers, sometimes by tractors and other pieces of large machinery which operated with no regard for the configuration of plot boundaries (Berenguer 1984: 54). As a result of four and a quarter years of occupation, 'uncultivated fields stretched out of sight in all their poignant monotony. Here and there, a few beetroot, cabbages or turnips were being grown, providing the basic food for the wretched *envahis*' whose survival depended on supplies from the Commission for Relief in Belgium (Hubert 1923: 197; AN F12 7808 Ravitaillement du Nord de la France, 1917–18). Namur and Pechenart, writing ten days after the Armistice, described conditions in some detail (AN AJ 25/49 Rapport au Ministre du Blocus et des Régions Libérées, 21.11.18). The area of the German front line in the extreme south of the *département* (the *zone champenoise*) had been bombarded so severely that they judged it to be 'uncultivable'. In the pessimism of the moment they believed that it was 'destined to be transformed into sheep pasture or pine forests, probably under the auspices of the state' (Ibid.). Damage was not so intense in a stretch of country lying between the German front and the river Aisne from which many residents had been evacuated to northern parts of the *département* or across the frontier to Belgium. Most villages in this area were not immediately habitable but the farmland was judged to offer considerable potential for levelling, preferably by tractor. Even less material damage had occurred further north, but livestock, machinery and farm equipment had been removed by the Germans at various stages of the war and especially in their final retreat. As a result, there was considerable opportunity for rapid agricultural recovery across much of the *département*, provided livestock and farm machinery could be brought back (Fagot 1918: 1087).

On the eve of the war, the western sections of what tragically would become the battle zone had supported many of the most productive farms and most efficient agricultural processing works in France, together comprising 'a unique ensemble of rural wealth' (Guicherd & Maitrot 1921: 234). The whole of Aisne fell subsequently into the devastated zone, with the north of the *département* being occupied by the Germans who requisitioned crops and livestock and controlled the activities of the few farmers who remained. Standards of cultivation declined drastically owing to shortages of labour, equipment, livestock, fertilizer and seed, so that Henri Hitier could report that by 1917 only areas adjacent to roads were being worked, with extensive stretches of farmland having fallen into disuse (Hitier 1918: 1082). Intense destruction of land and buildings across the battle zone and major evacuation of residents made this *département* arguably the 'greatest casualty' of the war (Guicherd & Maitrot 1921: 234). At the Armistice the area between Château-Thierry and Saint-Quentin stood completely deserted. Territory along the Hindenburg Line between the Chemin-des-Dames plateau and Vermand had experienced the most horrific loss. Not a village was left standing around Saint-Quentin, and very fertile farmland around Laon and Soissons was scored by trenches and shellholes and was further disrupted by military installations. To the stupefaction of local residents, the German occupying authorities had ordered all the walnut trees in the area to be felled, perhaps because their wood made excellent rifle butts (Lançon & Minon 1921: 61). Conditions were equally appalling in the north-eastern corner of Oise where more than five million fruit trees had been destroyed during hostilities (Augé-Laribé 1923: 52). Intense restoration efforts following the first liberation of Oise in 1917 had been overturned completely during the German advance of March 1918. Large areas of fine farmland around Noyon had been reduced to 'sad wasteland' whose re-cultivation was believed by some to be impossible (De Maricourt 1920: 20).

Further north in Picardy, broad stretches of some of the most fertile agricultural land in the whole of France had been ripped apart by trenches and subjected to bombardment throughout the war (Thierry 1918; Flatrès 1980: 95–96) (Figure 2.2). Vast areas of rich *limon* had been covered with infertile chalk and clay which exploding shells had brought to the surface (Wallon & Gobert 1919: 10). Humble agricultural villages and market towns in the whole of the upper valley of the Somme, from Amiens to Péronne and onward to Saint-Quentin, together with farms on the deep rich soils of the plateau of Santerre and Vermandois and the highly productive areas between the rivers Somme, Scheldt and Scarpe, had suffered the same fate (American Relief Committee 1920). In the words of geographer Douglas Johnson:

> During the war what was merely dreary became the acme of desolation. Four times the contending armies carried the work of destruction forward and backward over the plain [of Somme]. The productive fields were trampled under foot, seamed with an endless network of trenches, and pitted with the shell craters of countless bombardments. Shapeless heaps of stone, brick, mortar, and tiles reveal the site of former villages. (Johnson 1921: 87)

Obstructed watercourses, such as the Ancre, Avre and Luce, flooded surrounding fields (Picard 1922: 1011).

In particular, the quadrilateral between Roye, Bapaume, Albert and Péronne gave the appearance of complete devastation following the battles of the Somme in 1916 and 1918. For Ruth Gaines it was the silence of the devastated countryside that was the most striking, prompting her to refer to the plain of Picardy as 'the land of death' (Gaines 1918: viii). Some settlements, such as Sailly-Salissel (between Péronne and Bapaume) and a line of villages between Bapaume and Albert had disappeared virtually without trace (Cuminal 1918: 3) (Figure 2.2). Any fragments of brick or stone that remained were concealed by luxuriant coverings of weeds. After a tour of inspection in October 1917 Councillor Renaud from Vosges could remark that while whole villages in eastern France 'certainly suffered great losses . . . they have not disappeared totally like some in Somme' (Renaud 1918: 11). However, another inspector on the same tour detected a glimmer of hope along the Albert-Bapaume road, where, near the presumed site of Le Sars, three cabins, 'thrown together from wood and earth, and covered with corrugated iron, were already sheltering farming families' (Loupiac 1918: 17).

Destruction of rich farmland and agricultural settlements formed only part of the devastation in the eastern half of Pas-de-Calais, where ruined coal mines, mining villages and the market town of Arras formed a particularly 'melancholy tribute to the power of modern long-range artillery' (The ruins of Arras, *TS*, 17.06.20: 1138). In April 1917 Prefect Briens was profoundly uncertain how 'this district, formerly so fertile and prosperous, might be reborn. One is overwhelmed by the magnitude of the task' (ADPC R 857 Briens, M., Lettre à M. Pichéry, 1917). Two years later Mlle Elise Guyot recorded the complex social geography of the *sinistrés* who had returned to areas near the front line. She looked forward to widespread recovery which was 'already tearing apart the shroud of death which covers the land, and is hiding the horrific injuries inflicted on the soil beneath its verdure and its flowers' (ADPC 1J 200 Guyot, E., Enquête en Artois, 1919). It was her belief that 'the land only asks to become fertile again, and to be nourished by the peaceful work of mankind' (Ibid.) (Figure 2.1). Areas further west had suffered shelling and bombardment from German aircraft and also had experienced substantial disruption to agricultural activities because of the presence of British army bases, supply depots, hospitals and networks of narrow-gauge railway lines (Conseil-Général du Pas-de-Calais 1918: 390). The slowness with which such installations were to be removed would cause particular resentment among local farmers, with many fearing that this man-made wasteland in Pas-de-Calais and Somme was beyond hope of reclamation and would simply have to be abandoned (Guicherd & Maitrot 1921: 314).

In the densely populated *département* of Nord complete destruction was confined to a narrow belt along the line of the stabilized front on the eastern edge of the Armentières 'peninsula' (Figure 2.4). In November 1918 considerable stretches of newly liberated land were found to have suffered only moderate damage and hence might well be brought back into agricultural use quite soon (AN AJ 25/50 Président de la Société Coopérative, 04.11.18). This was because some districts had been cultivated throughout the hostilities, either by the Germans or by local people forced to work under their surveillance (Lecq 1918: 298).

The American women Corinna Smith and Caroline Hill reported that around Cambrai 'old men, women and children carried on their work, after the farmers had been mobilized. Not only in the back area but in the war zone, often under bombardment, they learned how to use agricultural machinery and acquired a knowledge of farming' (Smith & Hill 1920: 209). However, in some occupied villages the Germans had forced farmers to abandon carefully devised rotations which had been perfected over centuries, and had compelled them to grow wheat every year (ADN 9R 500 Monsarrat, Etat de l'Agriculture, 1916). The occupying forces did the same on land they cultivated themselves, apparently 'impoverishing the soil for their pleasure, and destroying manures' (Ibid.). Thus, 'fields were plowed [sic] constantly, sowed without manure, and used for intensive production of the same crops. They are exhausted and need to lie fallow for a while' (Gibbons 1920: 211). As the Germans retreated in the final weeks of war, they removed or destroyed all remaining animals, machines and crops. Hence Prefect Morain could report that by the Armistice 'all the livestock had gone; what had not been consumed locally during the occupation had been taken during the evacuation; [hence] no agricultural equipment, everything was destroyed or dispersed; no fodder, no seed, no fertilizer, and in many places no housing' (Morain 1923: 30). In addition, orchards containing an estimated 120,000 fruit trees had been destroyed (Ibid.: 40). With the exception of the Avesnois district, which escaped relatively lightly, all parts of the *département* were judged to be in need of important restoration work which often required rebuilding urban housing and industrial plant as well as reconstituting villages and farmland.

Damage to Land and Buildings

According to the official statistics of the Ministère des Régions Libérées (1923), some 1,719,087 ha were judged to need no more than 'simple clearing' once hostilities had ceased (Figure 2.3). This category covered just over half of the total area of the devastated regions and was particularly characteristic of Vosges, which had not been widely damaged, and Ardennes, which had been entirely behind enemy lines save for the very end of the war (Table 2.1). Despite horrific localized devastation to the north of Verdun,

Meuse had almost three-quarters of its surface classified as needing only 'simple clearing'. Some 45 per cent of the whole war zone needed 'important restoration work', but in Nord (75 per cent) and Marne (69 per cent) the proportions were much higher. According to these so-called official figures, only 3.5 per cent of the entire devastated region was recognized as forming the red zone, ranging from a mere 0.6 per cent in both Nord and Vosges, to 8.2 per cent of Marne and 17.3 per cent in Pas-de-Calais. When totals of extreme and moderate damage are summated, the enormous absolute extent of devastation to land in Nord (334,794 ha), Aisne (277,812 ha) and Marne (217,617 ha) becomes readily apparent.

Trenches had been dug along all sections of the battle front but they were particularly widespread and intricate in the western section of the war zone. André Tardieu estimated that a total of 280,000,000 m^3 required filling and levelling, with almost half of that amount being in the two *départements* of Pas-de-Calais (26.0 per cent) and Somme (21.5 per cent) (Tardieu 1921: 392). Official figures presented in 1923 raised the overall total to 333,000,000 m^3. Thickets of staked barbed wire formed another major hindrance to rapid land clearance, covering no less that 375,000,000 m^2 throughout the war zone (or 314,000,000 m^2 according to Tardieu), of which a quarter was found in Pas-de-Calais.

Devastation caused to land was, however, just one expression of the environmental impact of the war. Large numbers of buildings experienced varying degrees of damage, with official statistics (1923) quoting 293,043 private buildings and farmhouses completely destroyed across the war zone (37 per cent), a further 148,948 (19 per cent) having suffered 'grave damage', and 352,049 (44 per cent) having experienced 'partial damage'. Taken together these figures yield a tragic total of 794,040 (Table 2.2). Not surprisingly, reports from prefects and other observers in the war zone cited rather different amounts (Sellier & Bruggeman 1927: 43). For example, in 1924 the Ministre des Régions Libérées Charles Reibel quoted a total of 741,990 (Reibel 1924b: 3) but most enquiries suggested that a higher figure might have been more realistic. Edmond Michel and André Tardieu both advocated 866,844 (Michel 1932: 269; AN 324 AP/62 Reconstitution de la France, 31.03.32). Inconsis-

Table 2.2 Damage to private buildings and farmhouses

	Destroyed	Gravely damaged	Partially damaged
Aisne	51,119	28,506	31,932
Ardennes	14,838	13,946	43,155
Marne	31,258	8,439	18,485
Meurthe-et-Moselle	9,636	14,369	15,092
Meuse	13,625	8,247	13,731
Nord	53,172	40,117	164,626
Oise	8,908	4,661	22,773
Pas-de-Calais	70,852	17,264	16,276
Somme	37,586	12,810	21,502
Vosges	2,049	609	4,477
Total	293,043	148,948	352,049

Source: Ministère des Régions Libérées, 1923.

tencies in classifying farm and non-farm buildings and in recording subsidiary buildings mean that a completely accurate and reliable figure cannot be calculated. Nonetheless, it would seem that the total was likely to have been substantially in excess of 850,000. According to the Ministère des Régions Libérées, 124,024 buildings were razed to the ground in the two densely populated, industrialized western *départements* of Pas-de-Calais (70,852) and Nord (53,172) (Table 2.2). The more 'rural' *départements* of Somme (37,586), Aisne (51,119) and Marne (31,258) also recorded very grave losses. Indeed, complete destruction accounted for two-thirds of all damage to buildings in Pas-de-Calais and over half in Somme and Marne. At the other extreme, 'partial damage' represented more than three-fifths of all damage to built property in Ardennes, Nord, Oise and Vosges.

In addition, a total of 17,466 public buildings (including churches, *mairies* and schools) suffered some degree of damage across the war zone, with 6,525 being razed to the ground, 4,391 experiencing grave damage and 6,550 being partially damaged. For example, 250 churches had 'fallen on the field of honour' in the diocese of Arras alone (Les églises, *BEDA*, 05.19). The highest proportions of complete destruction occurred in Pas-de-Calais and Somme where values were roughly double that recorded for the northern *départements* as a whole (37 per cent). Some 22,900 industrial establishments of all sizes were in need of repair or reconstruction at the Armistice (Ministère des Régions Libérées 1923). Unfortunately no detail is known of workshops that had employed fewer than ten persons apiece. A grand total of 9,355 larger factories had experienced some form of damage, with one-third of that amount involving the industrialized *département* of Nord (3,147), and other large concentrations of damage being found in Ardennes (1,722) and Somme (1,251). Just over one-third of all factories with more than ten workers were razed to the ground throughout the war zone but proportions exceeded one-half in Aisne, Marne, Oise and Pas-de-Calais. Of the 206 sugar refineries in France on the eve of the war, 140 were located in what was to become the devastated zone, and nine-tenths were destroyed subsequently (Smith & Hill 1920: 220). Others were dismantled and their machinery removed for installation in factories in Germany.

Some 4,726 settlements (*communes*) composed the lowest-level administrative mesh of the devastated regions. Of these, 3,524 had been under German occupation at one stage or another and in 3,256 the normal civilian administration had been suspended (Ministère des Régions Libérées 1923). A mere 423 *communes* escaped without suffering material damage (Table 2.3). By

Table 2.3 Damage to *communes* in the devastated regions

	Completely destroyed	Over 50% destroyed	Damaged	Undamaged
Aisne	139	461	235	6
Ardennes	4	77	163	0
Marne	36	124	378	124
Meurthe-et-Moselle	34	92	203	0
Meuse	106	65	239	176
Nord	18	65	526	59
Oise	6	205	381	0
Pas-de-Calais	167	57	68	58
Somme	109	184	88	0
Vosges	1	4	68	0
Total	620	1,334	2,349	423

Source: Ministère des Régions Libérées, 1923.

contrast, 620 (13 per cent) were razed to the ground, with such appalling devastation being widespread in the western *départements* of Pas-de-Calais (167 *communes*) and Somme (109), along the lengthy front line of Aisne (139), and in the shattered environs of Verdun in Meuse (106). As Mgr Aimond noted, 'on the immense battlefield of Verdun . . . some villages, like Fleury, Douaumont and Samogneux, left no trace' (Aimond 1922: 309). Some 1,334 settlements in the war zone were more than half destroyed, with 461 suffering that fate in Aisne alone. In all, 1,954 settlements were obliterated completely or more than half destroyed, of which 600 were in the single *département* of Aisne.

By far the greater share of devastated settlements across northern France involved small farming villages, although numerous towns were damaged and four were completely destroyed or very nearly so (Ford 1919c: 516–21). The coal-mining centre of Lens (Pas-de-Calais) was 'literally wiped out', with the market town of Bailleul (Nord) experiencing an almost identical fate (98 per cent destruction) (Michelin 1920: 1010; Cochin, Bourgeois & De Poncheville 1920: 67). M. Cuvelette, Director General of the coal mines at Lens, reported not only extensive damage to his collieries but the loss of 8,000 miners' dwellings (Cuvelette 1922: 84). He concluded that his company would have to build between 12,000 and 15,000 new dwellings, since over one-third of the workforce had lived in surrounding villages which had also been devastated. The mining settlement of Liévin and the railway centre of Chauny came close behind in terms of damage, both having lost nine-tenths of their buildings (Renaud 1918: 9–10). In the words of the prefect of Pas-de-Calais 'by the Armistice, Lens and Liévin . . . had been destroyed totally and methodically, so that after the rubble had been cleared no foundations remained. Even the trace of some streets had disappeared' (Peytral 1927: 509). Similarly, Chauny had been 'reduced to a spectacle of the most frightening chaos' by the end of the war (Carpentier 1928: 78).

Three better-known towns also suffered very serious devastation: Armentières lost 88 per cent of its built properties, Soissons 83 per cent and Reims 79 per cent (Bernard & Dubief 1985: 79). Taken together, these three urban centres had housed 239,718 people in 1911 and had contained no fewer than 42,649 buildings (Michel 1932: 259). At Arras 4,525 houses had been totally destroyed and 3,881 suffered varying degrees of destruction. Many small market towns, such as Péronne or Albert, throughout the *régions libérées* had been reduced to heaps of rubble and needed to be reconstructed urgently, since they had formed essential elements 'in local and regional life, in the midst of the depopulating countryside and the rapid impoverishment of rural life' (Vallaux 1919: 24; Syndicat des Sinistrés 1917). Expressing the information another way, 109 of the 300 *cantons* in the war zone had experienced the loss of more than half of their built property, in terms of value, by the Armistice (Figure 2.7).

In addition to the destruction caused to these settlements, all forms of communication in the ten *départements* had suffered profound damage. Certainly many new stretches of railway had

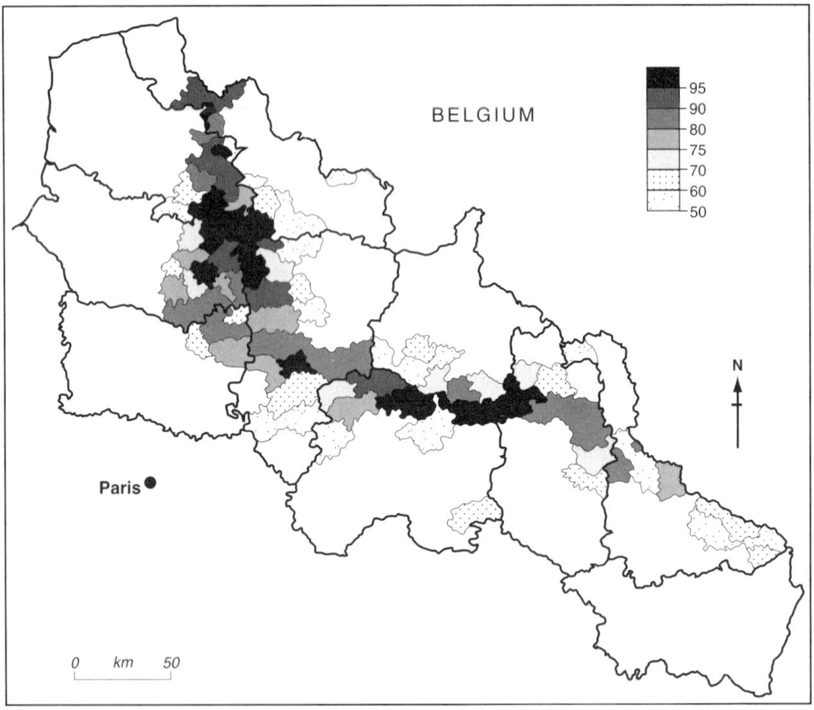

Figure 2.7 Proportionate loss of built property (1913=100%)

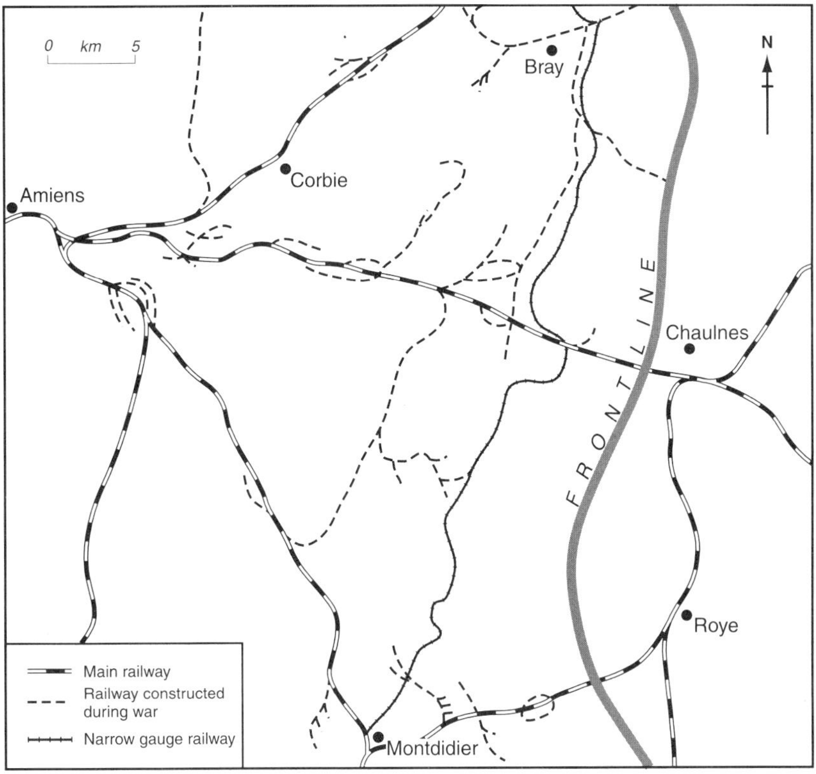

Figure 2.8 Railways on the battleground of the Somme, 1916

been built for military use during the war, as for example on the battlefield of the Somme in 1916, but together with the existing networks (Réseaux du Nord et de l'Est) they were 'worn almost to the point of uselessness as a result of extraordinary traffic and the inability to make ordinary repairs' (MacDonald 1922: 27; Villate 1925) (Figure 2.8). Intense damage was inflicted as the Germans finally retreated so that at the Armistice 2,400 km of railway belonging to the Nord and Est systems needed restoration and a total of 1,503 stations, bridges and tunnels were in ruins (Troller 1919: 248; Javary 1921: 79). Canals and navigable rivers totalling 1,890 km were damaged, as were 2,410 km of local railway and 58,700 km of various categories of road. Nord and Aisne recorded the most extensive disruption in each case. Main supply roads were in an exceptionally poor condition even at considerable distances from the front line, having been eroded by the greatly increased volume of traffic during hostilities. Special teams of military and civilian workers had attempted to keep these routes in a passable state throughout the war but often they had been obliged to use local materials that were not sufficiently resistant to withstand the passage of so many vehicles (Causel 1922: 123). Shellholes were filled as best they could but in Pas-de-Calais Prefect Naudin noted that to drive at more than 15 km/hour proved 'very painful' (Naudin 1919: 68). In the northern section of the war zone the repeated passage of large numbers of German vehicles with heavy metal wheels had made conditions even worse (Ibid.). Yet another aspect of material loss involved many thousands of wells which were damaged, blocked, or polluted throughout the battle areas. For example, in the devastated *arrondissements* of Arras and Béthune (Pas-de-Calais) 17,230 wells needed cleaning at the Armistice, 14,650 required repair, and 7,320 needed to be completely reconstructed (Peytral 1927: 408).

Patterns of Population and Overall Damage

On 11 November 1918 only 2,075,060 civilians were estimated to be present in the narrowly defined 'war zone', equal to just 43 per cent of its total on the eve of the war (AN 324 AP/62 Reconstitution de la France, 31.03.32). This total was 2,715,000 fewer than in 1911 and reflected the fact that large numbers had been removed at various phases by military authorities or had fled as refugees to areas close to the southern and western fringes of the devastated *départements*, to the French interior, to Belgium, or abroad (Huber 1931: 327–79). According to George B. Ford, four-fifths of that total might be considered to be ready to return, provided they could be assured of some kind of shelter and the means of sustenance (Ford 1919a: 166). Refugees started to migrate home as soon as the Armistice was signed. In order to try to regulate these flows, a decree (5 December 1918) was passed which stipulated that intending returnees should obtain prior authorization from the prefect of their destination *département*, but the desire to go home was not easily controlled (Huber 1931: 478). Corinna Smith and Caroline Hill described how

> passport bureaus were crowded with applicants wishing to return north, and a steady stream of refugees flowed back over the highways, not waiting for the formality of papers. It was the same population that had fled in terror before the invading armies. They struggled along, living in cellars, *abris*, huts or ruins, *en attendant*. The goal of all was to reach home, little realizing the scene of complete destruction which awaited them. (Smith & Hill 1920: 3)

In the same spirit, eight days before the Armistice was to be signed no fewer than 380 mayors of liberated *communes* in Somme met at the Hôtel de Ville in Amiens to explore how action might be taken to ensure that their devastated fields and farms would be restored (Augé-Laribé 1923: 96).

Looking more widely, the ten northern *départements* contained an estimated 3,640,000 civilian inhabitants in November 1918, representing the equivalent of 56 per cent of the total inhabitants recorded there in the census of March 1911 (Huber 1931: 490). Aisne contained only 37 per cent of its pre-war total, and for both Marne and Meuse the figure stood at 46 per cent. In

Table 2.4 Estimated population of whole *départements* in 1911 and 11 November 1918.

	March 1911	11 November 1918	1918/ 1911(%)
Aisne	530,226	197,000	37
Ardennes	318,896	175,000	55
Marne	436,310	200,000	46
Meurthe-et-Moselle	564,730	310,000	55
Meuse	277,955	127,000	46
Nord	1,961,780	1,101,000	56
Oise	411,028	300,000	73
Pas-de-Calais	1,068,155	530,000	50
Somme	520,161	300,000	58
Vosges	433,914	400,000	92
Total	6,523,155	3,640,000	56

Sources: Ministère de l'Intérieur, 1912; Huber, 1931: 400.

absolute terms, the population of Nord had declined by 861,000, of Pas-de-Calais by 538,000 and of Aisne by 333,000, with temporary losses of approximately 250,000 in both Marne and Meurthe-et-Moselle (Table 2.4). Four *arrondissements* (Arras, Béthune, Péronne, Reims) were essentially devoid of civilians in November 1918, and around both the fortress city of Verdun (Meuse) and the market town of Montdidier (Somme) the civilian figure stood at a mere 9 per cent of the number recorded in 1911. The *département* of Ardennes, which had been under German occupation throughout the war, apparently contained 55 per cent of the equivalent of its pre-war total. But this figure comprised considerable numbers of *transportés* whom the Germans had moved northwards away from the battle zone which stretched through Aisne, Nord and Somme, and had been installed in buildings that had been vacated by Ardennais families as they fled in August 1914 (La question des transplantés, *JRD*, 18.05.19).

By contrast, a dozen *arrondissements* on the fringe of the devastated zone had the equivalent of over 90 per cent of their pre-war total at the time of the Armistice, while the *arrondissement* of Boulogne contained fractionally more civilians (102 per cent) than at the time of the census seven and a half years earlier. This increase was partly due to the relocation of administrative activities from Arras, with the prefect, the bishop and their associated staff being accommodated in Boulogne, but also reflected the numerous kinds of work that had been created in and around the ports and military camps in the western part of Pas-de-Calais (Hilaire 1988: 345–47). Such figures must be interpreted carefully since the civilian population of the northern *départements* had experienced profound upheaval and relocation, with refugees in their hundreds of thousands having sought 'safe' locations on the outer fringes of the devastated regions and in the interior of France, where they shared accommodation with local residents or occupied property that had been vacated temporarily by its owners until hostilities ceased (Huber 1931: 340). Not surprisingly, returnees would soon be clamouring to move back into their houses and to have the *sinistrés* evicted, even though their homes in the battle zone might well be in ruins (La question des transplantés, *JRD*, 18.05.19). Estimates by the Ministère de l'Intérieur of the location of refugees in September 1918 evoke the temporary redistributions that had occurred and, in particular,

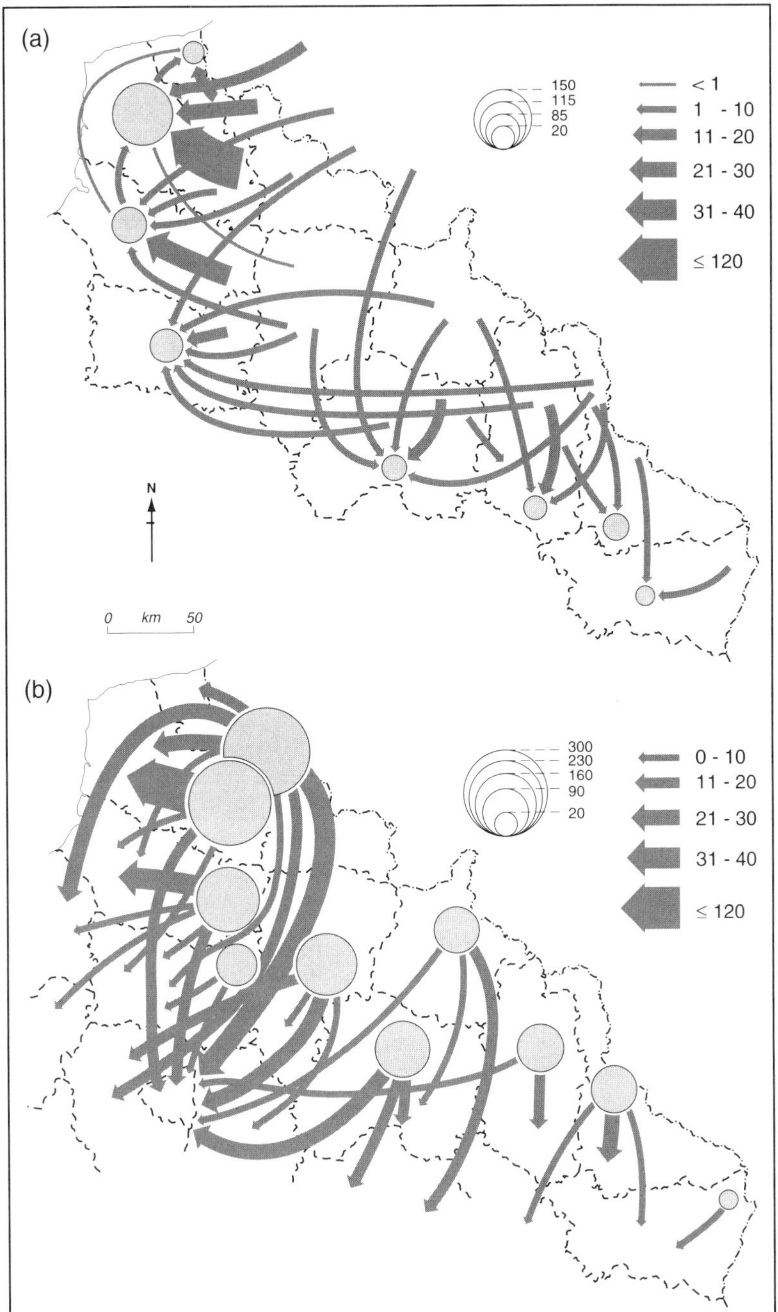

Figure 2.9 Distribution of refugees, September 1918

Table 2.5 Livestock reported missing at the Armistice

(a) Official statistics		(b) Agricultural data		(c) Reparations commission	
Cattle	834,933	Cattle	942,760	Cattle	852,903
Horses etc.	375,393	Horses	343,410	Horses	289,683
Sheep & Goats	890,794	Asses	9,800	Sheep	806,452
Pigs	331,656	Mules	2,830	Goats	36,706
		Sheep	1,285,430	Pigs	337,531
		Goats	53,160		
		Pigs	463,090		

Sources: (a) Ministère des Régions Libérées 1923; Augé-Laribé M. 1925, 96 and 100 quoting (b) Statistiques agricoles annuelles 1913 and 1918, and (c) the Commission Française des Réparations, 1921. Augé-Laribé maintains that the third set of figures is under-estimated.

the enormous absolute losses from the densely populated *départements* of Nord and Pas-de-Calais (Huber 1931: 331–79) (Figure 2.9). However, there is no way of confirming the accuracy of these figures.

In addition to human losses, the northern *départements* had lost very large numbers of farm animals as a result of their removal behind German lines and thence into Belgium or Germany, their relocation into the interior of France for 'safe keeping', or simply because of casualties or slaughter for food during the war. Precise statistics cannot be compiled but the figures shown in Table 2.5, that were quoted by the Ministère des Régions Libérées (1923) and Augé-Laribé using agricultural statistics (1913–18) and estimates by the Commission Française des Réparations (1921), convey a rough order of magnitude (Augé-Laribé 1925: 100).

Perhaps the most comprehensive way to summarize all this information on material loss and disruption is to refer to figures compiled by the *Commissions d'Evaluation* for 1 July 1931, when almost all administrative work dealing with compensation had been completed (Michel 1932: 613). At that time 3,111,441 claims for compensation for material losses of all kinds had been lodged with evaluation commissions in the ten *départements* that had made up the devastated regions (Table 2.6). Not surprisingly,

Table 2.6 Claims for all kinds of compensation lodged with evaluation commissioners, 1 July 1931

	Absolute Number	%	Monetary Loss (%)	Claims Decided (%)
Aisne	439,610	14.1	17.7	99.8
Ardennes	257,277	8.3	8.2	100.0
Marne	231,155	7.4	7.6	98.9
Meurthe-et-Moselle	196,560	6.3	5.3	99.9
Meuse	157,506	5.0	4.2	98.1
Nord	1,116,986	35.6	32.0	100.0
Oise	105,720	3.4	2.9	99.8
Pas-de-Calais	329,366	10.6	13.0	100.0
Somme	221,127	7.1	8.3	100.0
Vosges	56,134	1.8	0.7	99.9
	3,111,441	100.0	100.0	99.9

Source: Michel 1932: 613.

over one-third of those claims originated from the densely populated and partly urban-industrial *département* of Nord. The widely-devastated *département* of Aisne accounted for 14.1 per cent, with a further 10.6 per cent emanating from Pas-de-Calais. At the other end of the scale, a mere 3.4 and 1.8 per cent respectively related to Oise and Vosges. In financial terms, Nord accounted for no less than 32.0 per cent of the 39,000,000 F worth (1914 value) of property of all kinds that had been declared to have been lost (*perte subie*). Aisne (17.7 per cent) and Pas-de-Calais (13.0 per cent) followed on, with Oise (2.9 per cent) and Vosges (0.7 per cent) once again commanding only tiny fractions. By the summer of 1931 virtually all of the claims had been decided but in some instances, presumably because of administrative adjustments, the statistics quoted by Edmond Michel on the number of decisions that had been taken slightly exceed the number of cases lodged (Ibid.).

Despite the enormous gravity of loss and the sense of hopelessness that had overwhelmed some politicians and northern countryfolk at the Armistice, George B. Ford reported that there soon developed 'a very general feeling that almost everyone from the intact parts of the liberated regions will return to their homes; and to the destroyed parts of the liberated regions, where some 2,500,000 people had lived before the war, it is estimated that from 80 to 85 per cent of the original inhabitants will go back' (Ford 1919a: 18). Just how that devastated farmland was to be restored and its ruined settlements to be rebuilt forms the substance of the following chapters.

3
The Start of Emergency Action

Attempts at Administration

Emergency action to restore war-torn northern France did not begin in November 1918 but in fact spanned the period of hostilities and the early months of peace, when shelter was desperately needed and dangerous legacies of war had to be cleared from the land before normal economic activities might recommence. Indeed, almost as soon as the war had begun, efforts had been made by a variety of agencies to harvest standing crops near the battle zone, to cultivate land that was not actually under fire, and to provide some kind of temporary accommodation for brave farmers returning to devastated areas that had been liberated from enemy occupation. As William MacDonald remarked, 'the beginning of reconstruction is almost identical with the beginning of the war' (MacDonald 1922: 40). In the rather exceptional case of Seine-et-Marne, which was occupied for only a short time in 1914, the state assisted the rebuilding of devastated farms in eleven *communes* to ensure that fertile farmland would be brought back into cultivation (Dautresme 1919: 36). Early in 1915 farmers in eastern districts of the war zone, whose villages had been burned, were reported to 'have almost all returned to their land and to be making ready for spring sowing', but they lacked almost everything and 'very few would be able to obtain the means of production without the help of the public services' (Ministère de l'Agriculture 1915: 11). Such 'pioneers who returned to the desert' attempted to bring their farmland back into production but, in so doing, they created great difficulties for both military and civilian authorities, since they needed to be supplied with food, clothing, shelter, equipment, seeds and livestock (Ford 1919a: 73). With the help of prefects and sub-prefects the Ministère de l'Intérieur sought to arrange for the distribution of emergency supplies as best it could and the Génie Rural attempted to provide temporary shelters, livestock and equipment, as well as helping with the harvesting of crops (Ringelmann 1914: 955–61, 1915: 296). But for many returnees the promised housing, food and other supplies failed to materialize, and they were condemned to extreme hardship, having to sleep in 'tents or in army huts amidst their ruins' for months on end (Hitier 1917a: 587).

Farmers in eastern Somme had been obliged to abandon their livestock and possessions under fire as the Germans moved rapidly into the *département* in 1914. After the front line had stabilized in October 1914, military labour was used during 1915 across territory recovered from the Germans in order to collect abandoned machinery, to round up livestock wandering near the battle zone, and to harvest standing crops from areas judged to be safe (AN F2 2103 Objets abandonnés, 27.12.15). At a later phase of the war, government agencies installed almost 4,000 portable houses in sections of Aisne, Oise and Somme, following the German retreat in the spring of 1917 (Ford 1919a: 187). Unfortunately almost all this accommodation was destroyed when the enemy re-advanced during the subsequent spring. Emergency activities such as these were performed by civilian contractors and by groups of French and allied troops, wherever and whenever lulls in the fighting allowed. In addition, a range of foreign agencies operated well away from the front line. By constructing temporary housing and re-starting cultivation, they did more than simply provide welfare for the many thousands of *sinistrés* who took every opportunity to crowd back into their home areas, with or without official permission, once fighting had ceased in their locality.

Despite an abortive attempt in 1915 to establish a special department within the Ministère de l'Intérieur with responsibility for the invaded areas, traditional bureaucratic prerogatives held firm and the task of assisting the war-torn *départements* remained distributed among several ministries, often having overlapping responsibilities and each following its own course (Gibbons 1920: 192–93; MacDonald 1922: 50). Thus the Ministère de l'Intérieur cooperated with military authorities and voluntary organizations to help returning refugees, to construct temporary accommodation, and to undertake repairs. The Ministère d'Agriculture assisted farmers to work their land once again, and the Ministère du Travail implemented numerous regulations on social matters, with the ministries of Commerce and Travaux Publics also being involved with emergency work in the countryside. On 13 April 1916 the Ministère de l'Intérieur took measures to accelerate the provision of temporary shelters, and a government decree of 18 May 1916 set up an inter-ministerial commission to oversee the fragmented responsibilities for rural recovery (Rogers 1920: 11). At the start, this commission was divided into six specialized sections, and subsequently was re-organized several times during 1917. Unfortunately, but perhaps not surprisingly, it offered little prospect of effective coordination. During August of that year a law was passed to open an agricultural credit of 300,000,000 F to facilitate the resumption of agricultural life in liberated sections of the *régions dévastées*, and prefects were authorized to make financial advances to returning *sinistrés*, so that they could obtain food and some kind of shelter, and start to work their land again, even though they had not lodged formal declarations of loss, the critical *dommages de guerre* legislation had not been passed, and, of course, the war was far from reaching an end (see Chapter 8).

One hundred western *communes* were liberated when Hindenburg executed his 'genial retreat' in March 1917 but official preparations for promoting resettlement in that released territory proved to be of little use, to the anger of politicians and *sinistrés* alike (Gibbons 1920: 192). Eventually the government responded to the widespread opinion that a single ministry should assume responsibility for coordinating essential tasks in parts of the northern *départements* that were not under enemy control (Ford 1919b: 222). Thus on 16 November 1917 the curiously-titled Ministère du Blocus et des Régions Libérées was created in order to deal with all aspects of reconstitution, with M. Lebrun at its head (Comité d'Action pour les Régions Dévastées 1925: 14; Couedelo 1991: 211). Its work in the northern districts was to be organized by four sections. The administrative office, placed under M. Bluzet, was responsible for all matters relating to the revival of local life, the eventual payment of war indemnities, and the attempted coordination of work by voluntary relief agencies.

A technical section, supervised by Colonel Suquet, was entrusted with providing temporary shelters, repairing roads, filling trenches and shellholes, repairing farm buildings, and restoring the soil for agricultural use. The section with special responsibility for farming activity was headed by M. Le Seigneur, while its particularly active industrial counterpart was admininstered by M. De Boisson. Initially the four sections operated from different premises in Paris but after one year of dispersed activity their headquarters were brought under a single roof at 223 rue Saint-Honoré on 15 November 1918.

During the subsequent decade and a half the agency with official responsibility for state involvement in the *régions libérées* was to undergo a great deal of organizational change and experience considerable disruption. After being attached initially to the Ministère du Blocus, it was passed to Travaux Publics, then Finances, and then Pensions, before being passed back to Travaux Publics and ultimately again to Pensions (Héricault 1934: 163; Guérin 1930: 33). Over the same period no fewer than forty-five ministers and secretaries of state were concerned with heading the state agency concerned with the recovery and *reconstitution* of northern France. By virtue of their diligence and the quality of their work, some earned a certain respect among *sinistrés*, but others held the post for such a short time that they had little chance to prove themselves, or displayed such little commitment to the job that they did not command respect (Dessaint 1922: 754). Given such inconsistency of responsibility it is hardly surprising that *sinistrés* were to be suspicious of government action on their behalf, or that the archival record of the process of rural reconstruction should be so incomplete and inconclusive. The 'young ministry' had to recruit staff 'in haste and at random from the swarm of demobilized soldiers seeking a position in society' and according to some its activities were 'soon to be worse than the most pessimistic predictions' (Dessaint: 1922: 755).

Nonetheless, as the war was coming to a close, the state assembled a number of special services to help tackle the urgent tasks of clearing debris from agricultural land and of enabling farming and other rural activities to recommence. Understandably, these services were viewed with great suspicion by *sinistrés*, who recalled how inefficient the state had been in its attempts to assist the recovery of districts that had been liberated after the German retreat of March 1917. Roughly 400,000 ha had been released by the start of 1918 of which, it was estimated, perhaps half could be brought back into cultivation (Ford 1919b: 225). With the encouragement of the technical section of the Ministère du Blocus, civilian contractors assembled about a thousand German prisoners of war and an equal number of civilian labourers to undertake essential work in Somme, Aisne and Oise early in that year (Ibid.: 223). Prefect Morain reported that an intricate array of organizations was in place in Somme at the start of March 1918 to repair buildings, level damaged land, assemble temporary housing, plough land by tractor, distribute supplies of livestock, clean out wells and distribute water by wagon (Morain 1918: 66–68). In addition, considerable help was provided by both French and British armies to collect and repair farm equipment and to engage in many forms of agricultural work (see below). The German advance of 21 March meant that many of these initiatives in Somme had to be evacuated rapidly away from the combat zone and regrouped in preparation for a more sustained but nonetheless controversial programme of emergency work that would operate once the Armistice had been signed (see Chapters 4–7).

Sinistrés who returned to their property in many parts of the devastated *départements* before the end of the war were anxious to bring their land back into cultivation without delay. Many judged the various arrangements made by the state to be inadequate, involving agencies that had been set up in haste and whose responsibilities were poorly defined and insufficiently coordinated (AN F12 8030 Warren, De. E., Réorganisation des régions libérées, 27.03.19). As William MacDonald recalled:

> the volume of laws, decrees, and official pronouncements was out of all proportion to the work actually accomplished, and the array of functionaries was excessive in comparison with the record of their achievement. What with a complicated and ineffective personnel, an insufficient theory of indemnity for war losses, and only the beginnings of war credits, more than one *sinistré* felt that he had been left to work out his own salvation for the present and, for the future, to rest in hope. (MacDonald 1922: 56)

Nonetheless, the majority of returning farmers remained desperate to bring their farmland back into use (Augé-Laribé 1923: 96). Not without reason, many of those who would return in the early months of 1919 would be highly critical of past achievements of the state's emergency services and would be profoundly suspicious of their future involvement.

The Military

Throughout the war the resources of the French and allied forces had been used to cultivate farmland that lay beyond the line of fire and was not strewn with dangerous war debris. For example, during 1915 French troops had loaned horses to farmers, worked in the fields, and helped repair damaged farm buildings in Marne, Meuse and Meurthe-et-Moselle (Guillon 1915: 630–32). Similarly, they were involved in various forms of agricultural work in Seine-et-Marne which had been occupied by the enemy for only a brief period in 1914 (Dautresme 1919: 61). In the winter of 1916–17 Capitaine Guicherd and Captain Thomassin, for the French and British armies respectively, were charged to explore all possible ways of making use of military resources to bring more land into cultivation in areas in the shadow of the battle zone (AN F12 8025 L'effort agricole). Thus, equipment and men were 'particularly abundant' in unoccupied territory south of Verdun but unfortunately the extreme fragmentation of land-ownership in this part of Meuse made the use of large machines very difficult and hindered agricultural revival (Alphand 1917: 196). Nonetheless, the armies became involved in the task of rural recovery, even though they were not charged with the complete rebuilding of devastated houses and farmsteads.

Legislation of October 1916 permitted mayors to requisition land whose owners had declared themselves unable to work it, and to arrange for some method of cultivation to be undertaken with financial assistance from the Crédit Agricole (Moreau-Bérillon 1921: 121). Indeed, enabling France to produce more food was described in December 1916 as 'the agricultural offensive' of the war effort (AN F12 8025 Programme de l'offensive agricole, 1916). It was presented as 'one of the conditions for propelling the war to victory, alongside production of cannons and munitions' (AN F12 8025 Note présentée au

Comité d'Action, 15.01.17). Following the decree of 2 February 1916, *comités d'action agricole* had been established at *département* and *commune* levels to help cultivate land that had fallen out of use because of war or any other reason (ADMa 140 M17 Rapport, 12.02.16). These committees provided advice to farmers on how and where they might obtain animals, seeds and fertilizers (Sagnier 1918: 515). They served as clearing houses for complaints and for requests from farmers that needed to be transmitted to the military or civil administrations; and they even attempted to organize the necessary labour and equipment for the re-cultivation of abandoned land. Committees from neighbouring *communes* were urged to assume responsibility for re-working farmland in *communes* that had been evacuated completely (ADMa 140 M 17 Lettre du Préfet, 18.09.17).

As well as these civilian initiatives, it was argued that 'the army must participate as much as it can, by bringing the most effective help to farming in the areas it occupies' (AN F12 8025 Travaux agricoles, 10.03.17). Such participation in any particular location would, of course, be affected by the intensity of military activities at any moment in time as well as the official status and material condition of sections of land at varying distances from the front line. Changes in the position of the front with the passage of time complicated the situation by modifying the precise arrangement of the 'supply zone' and the 'reserved zone' on which differing kinds of agricultural initiative might be attempted (Dautresme 1919: 103). The supply zone (*zone des étapes*) comprised large stretches that had been withdrawn from agricultural use when artillery depots, training camps, aviation fields, firing ranges and other military installations had been established, but it did retain at least some of its civilian population (ADMa 203 M199 Rapport sur le recensement des terres, 24.11.16; Le Mamer 1991: 153). The supply zone was divided into a number of agricultural sectors, each of which was entrusted to a 'farming officer' who had normally been a farmer or a professor of agriculture in civilian life. He would liaise among local farmers, to determine the type and volume of work they wished to be undertaken, and among members of the military command, to ascertain how many men, horses and machines might be released for farmwork for particular periods within specified areas (ADMa 203 M199 Rapport sur les résultats, 25.12.17). Edouard De Warren, who was charged with promoting agricultural cooperation among the *sinistrés*, praised the dedication of such farming officers, insisting that 'no-one is more knowledgeable about local rotations, equipment and the real needs of the country people' (AN F12 8030 Warren, De. E., Note sur la remise en culture, 24.01.18). As well as drafting groups of soldiers to undertake such tasks as hay cutting, harvesting, threshing, or cutting wood, some military units placed individual soldiers for longer periods on farm holdings where labour needs were acute, as a result of workers having been mobilized or because widows were struggling to manage on their own (ADMa 203 M199 La mise en culture, 07.02.17). These efforts were generally appreciated, but it was obvious that available military labour was insufficient to meet all the demands expressed and was always subject to immediate recall because of the changing circumstances of war. The latter condition could, of course, prejudice harvesting, sowing and other pieces of work, which needed to be undertaken according to the agricultural calendar rather than simply as the unfolding events of war could allow. A further problem was produced by particularly harsh weather, for example during the winter of 1917, which could immobilize military workers just at the time when they were available for manual work on the farms (ADMa 203 M199 La mise en culture, 07.02.17).

Closer to the front line the 'reserved' zone was divided into 'back' and 'forward' areas. Civilian authorities continued to operate in the back areas where military labour was used to support civilian farmworkers whose numbers had been reduced severely by virtue of mobilization into the armed forces and by workers fleeing to less vulnerable areas. The farming officers encouraged mayors to stimulate local farmers to work the land as best they could and to requisition temporarily abandoned patches so that these might be cultivated by neighbouring farmers or, if need be, by the army (ADMa 140 M17 Letter 18.11.17). Civilians had to take extreme care as they worked fought-over land and were advised to call on the military to remove any shells or dangerous materials that they might notice (ADMa 140 M16 Lettre du Sous-Préfet, 11.10.18). Problems resulted from the fact that soldiers were often billeted in farmhouses and their horses were housed in barns and other farm buildings, thereby leaving the farmers who remained no storage space for their hay or harvested crops (ADMa 153 M21 Lettre du Maire, 23.05.15). By contrast, no civilians were allowed to remain in the forward areas and hence the armed forces were required to supply everything that might be needed for agricultural work in terms of men, animals, implements and machinery. Wherever possible, abandoned farm equipment was numbered and labelled to indicate where it had been retrieved, prior to being put into store or pressed into service by the soldiers (ADMa 140 M17 Letter, 18.11.17). Blacksmiths from the cavalry corps provided valuable help by turning their hand to repairing equipment for use in the fields.

The relationship between the armies and what remained of the civilian farming population was not always comfortable. Local people complained that some teams of soldiers allotted to farming duties had failed to live up to expectations, preferring to rest up or to ride horses rather than to work in the fields as was expected of them (ADMa 203 M199 Rapport sur le recensement des terres, 24.11.16). In January 1918 M. De Warren reported to the *Ministre de l'Agriculture*, M. Clementel, that there was insufficient continuity of contact between the farming officers and the ordinary military labour which had been allocated to agricultural tasks. He complained also that many soldiers lacked any knowledge of equipment, rotations or other aspects of farming, and hence completely failed to appreciate the real needs of local people (AN F12 8030 Warren, De. E., Note sur la remise en culture, 24.01.18). In addition, coordination of effort between the army, local mayors, civilian administrators and welfare groups was often poor. Thus, large areas had been ploughed by soldiers during 1917 but these had not been sown, since the military labour force had been withdrawn at the critical moment but had not been replaced. The French army acknowledged that it sometimes failed to supply workers with the specific skills required, at the right moment, and for the appropriate duration. However, it alleged that some farmers had refused firmly the offer of military aid, or else having accepted it, turned it away on the pretext that the land was not ready for the particular job for which it had been demanded. Other farmers expected unreasonably large amounts of work to be undertaken by the soldiers in very short periods (ADMa 203 M199 Rapport sur les résultats, 25.12.17). More seriously, some farming officers alleged that many civilians in the back areas, for example around Reims, had simply become camp followers, preferring to devote their time to trade and to leave responsibility for agricultural work to the soldiers.

Prisoners of war were used to help with agricultural tasks but never less than 30 km from the front line (AN F12 8030 Warren, De. E., Note sur la remise en culture, 24.01.18). By the end of 1916 35,000 had been employed on farms and in state forests in the French 'interior' well away from the battle zone. During the following year prisoners of war were set to work on large farms in western Somme, in sugar refineries and distilleries, and in land-drainage activities in the Marquenterre (Morain 1918: 171). Difficulties surrounding the organization and size of work teams represented just one of many problems. Le Rouzic argued that groups of twenty prisoners of war, which were the normal size, were too large to be deployed on small farms and that teams of between five and ten were to be preferred (AN F12 8026 Le Rouzic, M., Main d'oeuvre agricole, 18.12.16). In addition, greater discretion should be granted to local *communes* to devise ways of using this labour efficiently. In his view, too many guards were being used to watch each prisoner-of-war team. Initially, 'families in mourning' were not willing to use prisoners of war but 'once accepted, this source of labour was appreciated in the majority of cases' (Morain 1918: 171).

As the war approached its final stages, the Ministère de l'Agriculture reiterated its requests for soldiers to be allocated to harvest work and threshing (ADMa 140 M16 Lettre du Ministre, 30.07.18). At the same time, the military authorities urged prefects to treat with great caution all requests from civilians for permission to return to their devastated farmlands, since so much dangerous material remained on the ground (ADMa 140 M16 Lettre du Général Commandant, 27.07.18). On 10 August 1918 General Pétain instructed all commanders of divisions, regiments and companies to contact the appropriate local engineer in charge of reconstruction whenever they were due to be based in a devastated settlement for more than a few days, so that they could determine exactly what practical tasks their men might perform (Ford 1919b: 224). These might include clearing debris, repairing roads, or undertaking agricultural work. A month later (6 September 1918) the Ministre des Régions Libérées instructed local engineers and mayors to make emergency plans for using military labour should it suddenly become available in their area. Once the Armistice had been signed, Foch instructed that military installations should be evacuated as soon as possible so that the territory they occupied could be brought back into cultivation (ADMa 140 M16 Tatier, M., Letter, 20.11.18). Armed forces were encouraged to quit buildings that might be of use to farmers or other local residents; and civilian authorities were given the right to start removing barbed wire and filling in trenches.

British forces also played a part in agricultural activities during the war, with the French mission attached to the British army liaising between local farmers and the armed forces, thereby enabling British military labour, machines and horses to be directed to where they were needed (Morain 1918: 95–99). Designated agricultural officers, with their interpreters, organized the distribution of these resources on the ground, and also assumed the difficult task of trying to prevent British troops and their horses from damaging fields that were under cultivation (Thomassin 1917: 625). From its bases near Abbeville and Montreuil, the British cavalry helped with ploughing and threshing, and transported large quantities of manure to fields nearby (Ibid.: 626). British forces were particularly interested in tractor driving and threshing, even using their own machines. They also recovered abandoned farm equipment for repair and redistribution, with collection centres operating at Arras, Péronne, Nesle, Albert and Roye (Ibid.: 627). According to Thomassin, at one stage in 1917 'every day fifty British lorries bring farm equipment to the single collection centre of Arras' (Ibid.). British soldiers also undertook hay-making and planted vegetable gardens in evacuated villages in Somme that were awaiting resettlement (Morain 1918: 100). With the help of 'Chinese' workers in the British labour corps, they cleared large quantities of debris from farmland in Pas-de-Calais and Somme during 1917 (Sagnier 1917a: 471). In addition, over 15,000 Australian troops and 3,300 horses were involved in numerous agricultural tasks in Somme (Morain 1918: 100). Initially the French farmers were very sceptical about using British labour 'because of the differences in language and customs, and the limited aptitude of British soldiers for working in the fields. But the goodwill of the tommies served to break the ice, and now', reported Thomassin, 'everyone recognizes the valuable services performed by them' (Thomassin 1917: 625–26).

Late in 1917 a scheme was devised to bring back into cultivation an area of 20,000 ha which, at that stage, lay safely away from the front line (Fox 1920: 136). In January 1918 an Agricultural Directorate was formed under Brigadier-General the Earl of Radnor, and soldiers started to plough land around Roye and Nesle in eastern Somme. In mid-March they were working 100 ha each day and a total of 2,000 ha had been prepared by the time the Germans readvanced. Some of the British machinery had to be abandoned but most was saved and transported away from the combat zone (ADS 332.252 O'Hanrahan, R.M., Letter, 15.07.18). The Agricultural Directorate changed its plan and directed soldiers, between their turn in the trenches, to harvest crops from 4,000 ha which had been evacuated by French farmers as the front line advanced (Fox 1920: 136). The fields to be harvested were under observation by the Germans and sometimes were under fire. In such circumstances, harvesting had to be done at night, with the soldiers wearing gas masks since gas shells were fired to attempt to prevent their work (Ibid.: 137). Despite performing much valuable work, British military labour was always liable to recall from farming activities at a moment's notice. Prefect Morain noted sadly that 'the direct intervention of the [British] army can only be really useful when it is able to complete agricultural tasks, but that is rarely the case' (Morain 1918: 96).

As the front line moved eastward during August and September 1918, so additional numbers of British troops were employed to harvest cereals from land freshly recovered from the Germans (Ford 1919b: 225). In the autumn another project was started with the intention of using British tractors to plough 8,000 ha near Corbie, but work proved exceptionally difficult since shellholes repeatedly opened up across the supposedly levelled fields. The scheme was abandoned when the Armistice was signed. These courageous failures emphasized the enormity of the work that would have to be undertaken before the once-fertile fields of Picardy could be brought back into use. The end of hostilities opened the way for the emergency services organized by the French state to play a vital, but not uncontroversial, role in restoring the farmlands of northern France (see Chapters 4–7).

Foreign Voluntary Organizations

Throughout the conflict and during the immediate post-war years numerous voluntary organizations involved themselves in welfare activities and in rural reconstruction across areas that were no longer being fought over. Many French associations, most notably the Croix Rouge, played important roles in this work but so too did several foreign voluntary organizations (Smith & Hill 1920: 56). In some instances they busied themselves with the welfare of returnees in individual villages or clusters of settlements set in countryside that was 'in mourning' (Deschamps 1918: 694). Thus from the spring of 1917 to the German invasion one year later sixteen American members of the Smith College Relief Unit, based at the *château* of Grécourt, attended to needs expressed in fifteen villages between Ham and Nesle (Somme) and sold provisions to the *sinistrés* (Ford 1919a: 98; Deschamps 1918: 694; Gaines 1918, 1920: 46). With the help of French workmen, members of the American Red Cross repaired between thirty-five and forty houses and barns in five villages to the north-east of Nesle, and the French Wounded Emergency Fund collaborated with the British Red Cross in fifteen villages between Péronne and Ham (Stephens 1921: 11). In fact, in many devastated settlements, newly released from enemy grasp during 1917, some kind of relief agency was on hand to help returned *sinistrés* with the desperate task of obtaining food, clothing, furniture, bedding and tools (Ibid.: 100). Volunteers from almost of all of these organizations stayed in post during the bitterly cold winter of 1917–18 and were able to help the evacuation of refugees when the Germans advanced rapidly in March 1918. After the Germans withdrew in August and September the refugees began to return and were accompanied by French, British and American relief groups.

Between thirty and forty of these were operating in the devastated *départements* at the time the Armistice was signed and the volume of their activities grew as the number of returning *sinistrés* increased. The American Red Cross started relief work in each of the northern *départements* and collaborated with the American Fund for French Wounded and the Rockefeller family to provide mobile dispensaries and hospitals for children, for example at Toul (Deschamps 1918: 694). The Belgian Relief

Commission erected 360 large huts in Nord and played a truly vital role in assisting the British and French armies and local chambers of commerce to feed some two million people until the French government was able to set up its own mechanisms for doing so (Collinet & Stahl 1928). At a much more local scale, the Smith College Relief Unit returned to Grécourt (Somme) at Christmas 1918 to find that three hundred *sinistrés* had arrived before them and were living in misery, since all surrounding settlements had been destroyed. In the months that followed, the Americans operated a travelling shop, taught local children, and offered the services of a doctor and a nurse (Ford 1919a: 112). Other foreign groups embraced yet more ambitious goals. For example, Mrs Crocker from the wealthy San Francisco family, with the assistance of Miss Daisy Polk, wished to make funds available to accelerate the reconstruction of a devastated village in Lorraine (Lebrun 1922: 3). Following the advice of Prefect Mirman they decided upon Vitrimont, near Lunéville, which had been largely destroyed during the Battle of Lorraine in August and September 1914. *Sinistrés* duly agreed to assign their future compensation claims to the Californian committee so that preparations might be made. Plans were drawn up by M. Charbonnier, the official architect for the *département* of Meurthe-et-Moselle, and fifty workmen started on the site in October 1916 (Ford 1919a: 199). By spring 1919 reconstruction of private houses and public buildings was complete, with the village street being renamed Rue de la Californie.

Quakers in the Shadow of the Battle Zone

Two voluntary organizations, namely the British and American Quakers and the Comité Américain pour les Régions Dévastées (CARD), stand out by virtue of the range of activities they undertook across considerable stretches of territory, rather than concentrating their efforts on single settlements. As early as September 1914 members of the British Society of Friends prepared themselves to work in France and made an offer of practical relief to the French government. This was accepted and in November a group of thirty-two doctors, nurses and helpers arrived in the *département* of Marne (Harvey 1915: 3). In the following month a start was made on medical relief, installing new wells and temporary housing, and undertaking reconstruction work (Guillon 1916: 92–94). A medical centre was opened at the town of Châlons-sur-Marne, which had been occupied for only nine days by the Germans and provided a good base for helping refugees who crowded in from Ardennes and Meuse as well as from Reims and devastated rural sections of Marne (Fry 1926: 6). At this time many thousands of refugees had been sent to the south and west of France but, for various reasons, large numbers of people chose to remain in the southern part of Marne. For some it was a matter of a lack of transport, since the railways were fully occupied with moving troops. Many women refused to leave the neighbourhoods of their ruined homes or the districts where their menfolk were fighting. Others had charge of small children and would not contemplate taking them long distances. Indeed, to provide facilities for mothers and children was to be the main task of the Friends at Châlons during 1914–15 (Pye 1915: 2). By the summer of 1915, 150 Quakers were at work in the *département* (Guillon 1916: 94).

Restoration of housing was their second major activity at that time (Fry 1943: 23). At first the idea had been to concentrate on repair work but soon the initiative was taken to produce completely new wooden houses. These were for installation in villages that had been devastated during the Battle of the Marne and were located around Vitry-le-François and Fère-Champenoise (Pye 1915: 9). At Vitry the English mission commandeered a disused school to accommodate its volunteers and to serve as a base for carpentry work. This was done in full cooperation with the French civil authorities and used timber provided by the *département* authorities as part of the compensation due to *sinistrés* (Bluzet 1916: 1). Wooden shelters were constructed in sections and then taken for erection under the supervision of the Quakers. Paid labour was employed for this task, thereby providing work for a number of male refugees who were neither young nor strong enough for military service. By Christmas 1914 the first wooden house was ready for occupation and applications flooded in from local mayors requesting wooden shelters to be installed amid the ruins of their settlements, since whole villages in this sector of the war zone had been destroyed by bombardment and fire (Fry 1943: 4). The sun-baked clay of the few old walls that remained soon crumbled away, leaving only brick chimneys standing, hence there was no possibility of making use of these ruins as temporary shelters (Harvey 1915: 4). The Friends devoted particular attention to the ruined town of Sermaize-les-Bains which had lost 900 of its 1,000 houses but was, of course, just one of a line of devastated settlements between Vitry and Revigny. Work continued apace during 1915 to enable 'a little garden city' to emerge from the wreckage of Sermaize (Greenwood 1975: 203–04). About one thousand wooden houses were built for those who owned property in the town, with a further two dozen red-tiled houses being erected for landless labourers. The working population returned but 'the comfortably off, the retired and *rentiers* preferred to live elsewhere' (Bluzet 1916: 4). Unfortunately the simple wooden houses proved very cold since they lacked proper ceilings. During 1917 Sermaize came under fire again, but this time the town survived.

Some 65 km to the west, across the main battlefield of the Marne, Fère-Champenoise formed a second focus of activity by the Friends. The town itself had not suffered great damage but many surrounding villages were half destroyed. Relief began in January 1915, involving fewer than twenty Quaker volunteers. From Fère-Champenoise they went out into the villages, organizing the rebuilding of houses, nursing the sick, providing clothing and making furniture to replace what had been destroyed. They also made careful investigations into the needs of the local people, paying particular attention to tenant farmers, many of whom were left almost destitute after their crops, stock and equipment had been lost (Harvey 1915: 5). In this part of Marne temporary shelters were usually built of bricks and other salvaged material found on site, since timber was in very short supply. Local men were hired by the Friends to assist with bricklaying and carpentry. These temporary buildings were installed on the site of outbuildings, leaving the foundations of farmhouses for permanent reconstruction in the years to come. In those instances where rebuilding had enabled farmers to return, the Friends distributed seeds so that some kind of harvest might be gained during 1915.

Given the extreme uncertainty of the time, questions were raised concerning whether it was worth repairing property when heavy gunfire could still be heard in the close vicinity and fighting threatened to return. But Edmund Harvey was convinced that the Quakers' activity gave new hope to local people. In his words:

'They have begun to go about their work again with fresh courage, clearing the wreckage from their farm buildings for the time when permanent rebuilding will be possible, and constructing for themselves little structures here and there, which suffice for the limited farm stock which is left to them' (Ibid.). In the early spring of 1915 Edith Pye commented enthusiastically on the little wooden houses that were springing up 'like mushrooms' in the midst of desolation in this part of Marne (Pye 1915: 12). These houses varied in size from one to four rooms according to the size of the family. They had double walls and good plank floors well raised off the ground. Casement windows and strong doors were provided with locks and every house was covered with tarred roofing felt. Confronted by these examples of success, village mayors presented their requests to the Quakers, whose volunteers then constructed houses on site. Edith Pye believed that 'here family life will begin anew, and when the permanent houses are built, these little shelters will remain for many a year to be used as barns and sheds and serving as symbols of sympathy and goodwill' (Ibid.).

The Friends provided a striking early example of relief and emergency reconstruction, but their efforts were of course at the mercy of fluctuations in the front line. Not until spring 1917 was widespread relief implemented by a variety of voluntary agencies. The Germans were driven back as much as 40 km in some places along a frontier of 240 km, thereby releasing about 4,000 km^2, all the way from Lens to Reims. There were over six hundred *communes* in this area but very few of them were left intact (Ford 1919a: 68). By contrast, such towns as Noyon, Guiscard and Ham had suffered relatively little damage at this time except for places in the immediate proximity of railway lines. This was because the Germans had cleared civilians from the countryside and relocated them in urban areas so that smaller settlements might be obliterated systematically. As Ford explained: 'All along the former front, which the Germans had held for two and a half years, the destruction was complete' (Ibid.: 74).

Once the Germans had been driven out, farmers returned from areas just west or south of the battle front or from the interior of France. The French army clearly did not want them there since they had to be supplied with food and other necessities and their presence interfered with military activities. By contrast, very few people returned to the British army zone located north of the river Somme. This was partly because of the extreme devastation of land and buildings but also because the British forces continued to use the land for military preparation and provisioning. They ploughed about 10,000 ha on which they raised crops, but chiefly for their own use. Not surprisingly the French government did not encourage refugees to return to liberated areas north of the Somme river.

Quakers continued their welfare and reconstruction work in Marne as new campaigns opened. Despite support from the prefect and his staff, they were frustrated repeatedly by lack of timber. The early houses, which they had roofed with tarred felt, proved to be defective and builders changed to using tiles in an effort to prevent leaks. In the summer of 1916 the Friends decided to open a workshop for pre-fabricating wooden houses at Dôle (Jura), which employed up to a hundred men who made use of American water-powered machinery for cutting planks and powering carpentry work (Greenwood 1975: 204). A second workshop was opened soon afterwards at Ornans (Doubs) to undertake this monotonous but important task (Fry 1926: 31). Up to the German offensive of March 1918, the Friends had assisted about 35,000 people, representing 12,000 families in 282 different villages, and had erected 540 temporary houses and three dozen barns (Ford 1919a: 102). They had also distributed numerous packages of clothes and bedding, in addition to furniture, seeds, fertilizers and implements (Fry 1926: 33).

As well as operating in Marne, the Quaker volunteers moved into Meuse *département*, particularly the depopulated district west of Verdun where they undertook some ploughing during 1917 in anticipation of the return of the farming population. At the end of that year the sub-prefect of Verdun, M. Crillon, asked them to concentrate their reconstruction efforts in that area which covered *c.* 500 km^2 (Fry 1926: 90). It was composed of territory that had been fought over, taken and retaken several times, so that only about 5 per cent of its housing stock remained standing at the start of 1918. Even more damage was to be inflicted during the American advance northwards at the end of the war. This area west of Verdun had become a ‘cosmopolitan no-man’s land’ where few French residents remained but where white and black American troops, Chinese coolies, German prisoners of war,

Spanish and Portuguese soldiers and even exiled Russians made up the temporary population (Ibid.: 92; Greenwood 1975: 208). The Friends wrote to about three thousand former residents who were scattered in many parts of France. Barely 5 per cent of the replies 'did not express a strong desire to return at once' (Fry 1943: 31). At the start of October 1918 the new sub-prefect, M. Roimarmier, appealed for funds to assist the Quakers' project which embraced the *cantons* of Clermont-en-Argonne and Varennes, together with a range of ruined *communes* along the left bank of the river Meuse (Society of Friends 1918) (Figure 3.1). Civilians had been evacuated from the greater part of the district since February 1916 and from a small section since August 1914. This zone contained areas of appalling devastation, including Vauquois where 'the whole top of the hill and the village which stood upon it had been blown completely away, and the hill itself . . . was the scene of complete desolation, and bore no trace of the orchards which had formerly been terraced on its sides' (Fry 1943: 30). Once the Armistice had been signed, about a hundred British and American Quakers established their headquarters at Grange-le-Comte (near Clermont-en-Argonne) and proceeded to employ up to five hundred workers in reconstruction and welfare work in sixty villages. The Friends bought up dumps of equipment left by the advancing American army which afforded them supplies that they could use themselves or could distribute in the devastated area (Ford 1919a: 108). German prisoners of war were employed alongside the Friends to install temporary housing and to make furniture. By virtue of their status they could not be paid, but the Quakers sent money to their families in Germany instead (Greenwood 1975: 208).

The role of the Friends in restoring the settlement of Neuvilly-en-Argonne (midway between Varennes and Clermont-en-Argonne) was documented in some detail. The Germans had entered the village in 1914 but for much of the war it was effectively part of no-man's land or was incorporated in the French front line defences. At the time of the Armistice not a single building remained standing and an American army depot had been opened nearby for the controlled destruction of ammunition and captured explosives. During 1919 64 timber houses were constructed, normally comprising three rooms apiece, but ranging from two to five. They were pre-fabricated at Dôle

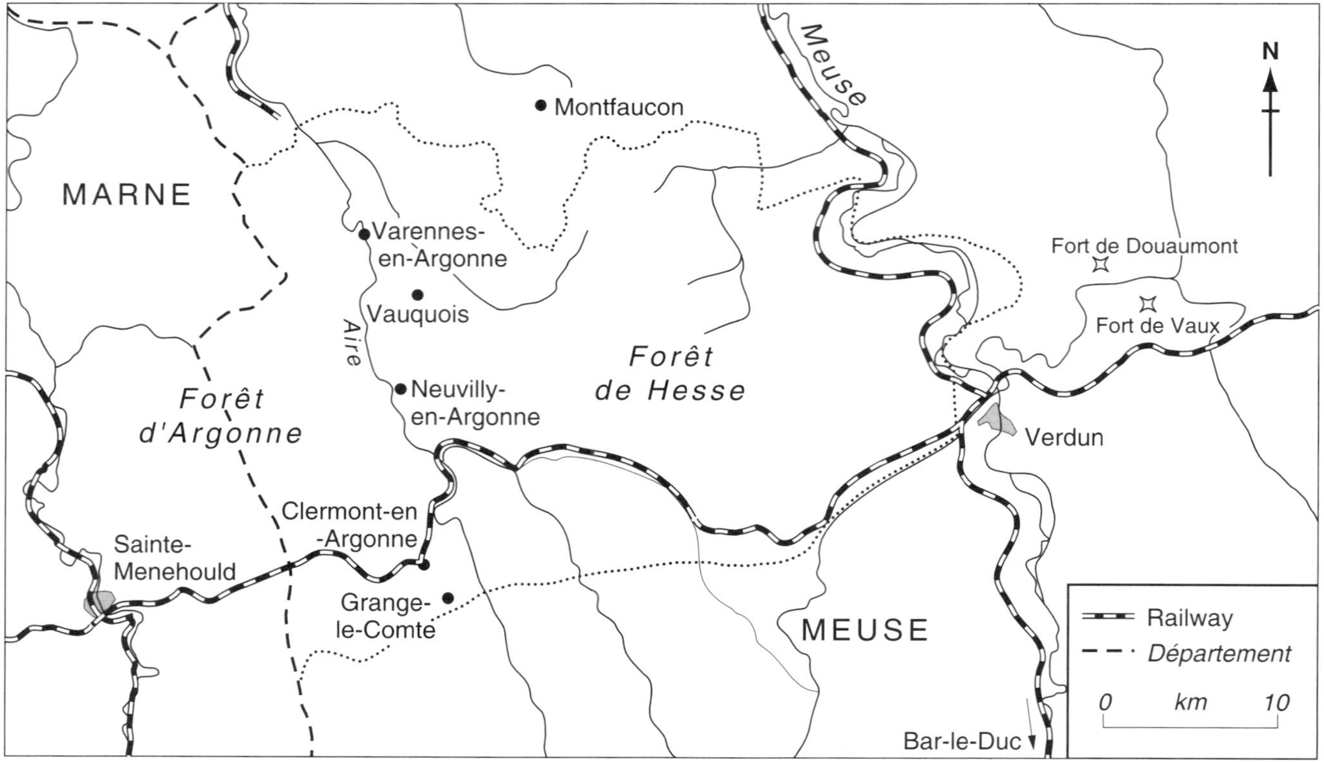

Figure 3.1 Area of Quaker project in Meuse

and Ornans and then sent 300 km by rail to western Meuse. The task had been thought out carefully, and many of the parts for these different-sized houses were interchangeable in order to facilitate assembly and minimize confusion. On site, the Quakers and their civilian and prisoner-of-war workers operated in teams of four in order to make the foundations, lay the floor, assemble the wall and roof sections, and finish off woodwork (Kraus 1944: 62). Reconstruction work of this kind was in progress in about a dozen villages in western Meuse at any one time during 1919. In addition, the Quakers were instrumental in opening over a dozen shops which helped to supply two hundred renascent villages with basic necessities, ranging from bread to crockery, seeds, bedding and tools, some of which had been made in Quaker workshops. These items were not given away but were sold to *sinistrés* at cost price, with travelling shops visiting particularly remote sites. In the spring of 1920 the Friends handed over their retail operation to the local Coopérative Meusienne as they started to withdraw from the *département* in order to concentrate their efforts elsewhere in devastated Europe (Greenwood 1975: 208).

By July 1919 the Friends had constructed nearly nine hundred wooden houses and had repaired a further eight hundred ruined homes, thereby providing shelter for over six thousand people mainly in Marne and Meuse but also in parts of Aisne and Somme (Ford 1919a: 108). Later in the summer the work of the British Friends was merged with that of their American counterparts to form the Anglo-American Friends Mission which comprised more than five hundred volunteers who minstered to the needs of the returning population from forty-five centres in Marne, Meuse, Ardennes, Aisne and Somme (MacDonald 1922: 282; Fry 1943: 31; Smith & Hill 1920: 55). As well as building hundreds of wooden houses, they helped to clear fields and to plant and harvest crops in addition to contributing large quantities of seed and equipment. But as the state and the *sinistrés* themselves began to undertake reconstruction, so the Quakers withdrew, with the Mission ending its work in France in 1921 and dispatching its equipment and stores to Poland and Vienna (Fry 1926: 99).

American Women Volunteers in Aisne

The Comité Américain pour la France Dévastée (CARD) shared

many features with the Friends but, unlike them, it was composed entirely of women volunteers. It was the successor to the Civilian Committee of the American Fund for French Wounded which had been founded in 1917 to assist civilians (MacDonald 1922: 285). The CARD was resourced by funds raised in New York and in two dozen other states, and operated under the patronage of the Ministère du Blocus et des Régions Libérées and the prefect of Aisne (ADN 104J Comités de Secours Américains). Following the German withdrawal, in June 1917 General Pétain accompanied ten American women to the village of Blérancourt, midway between the rivers Aisne and Oise, some 80 km north-east of Paris. Headed by Miss Anne Morgan, daughter of the millionaire banker John Pierpont Morgan, and by Mrs Anne Murray Dike, his sister and friend of André Tardieu, the American women were allowed to establish themselves in the old *château* at Blérancourt (designed by Salomon de la Brosse and François Mansart), whence they offered civilian relief services under the authority of the French army. The *château* was to be purchased by Mrs Dike after the Armistice and in 1929 was donated in her will to the French nation to become the Musée National de la Co-opération Franco-Américaine.

Initially the *sinistrés* were suspicious of these rich foreign women who drove cars through their ruined villages and devastated fields, but the Americans' sheer energy soon erased opposition (Héricault 1934: 37). In the words of Deschamps, hostility to their 'aristocracy' was soon overcome by their 'grace, good humour, enterprise and self denial' (Deschamps 1918: 695). They were allocated thirty villages in the *cantons* of Coucy-le-Château and Vic-sur-Aisne and were charged to assist returning refugees to settle back on their own land. In January the neighbouring *canton* of Soissons was added and the women helped supply food, clothing, equipment and livestock to a total of sixty villages (Figure 3.2). They also opened emergency schoolrooms, dispensaries and small shops, and were entrusted to bring in supplies for sale to *sinistrés* at cost price. With the assistance of the French army, the women established an agricultural cooperative at Blérancourt and with their encouragement a further half dozen were set up in surrounding villages (Héricault 1934: 25). Ploughs and equipment were recovered from abandoned fields, army blacksmiths helped with repairs, and

Plate 3.1 A member of the Comité Américain pour la France Dévastée in the ruins of Blérancourt château, Aisne

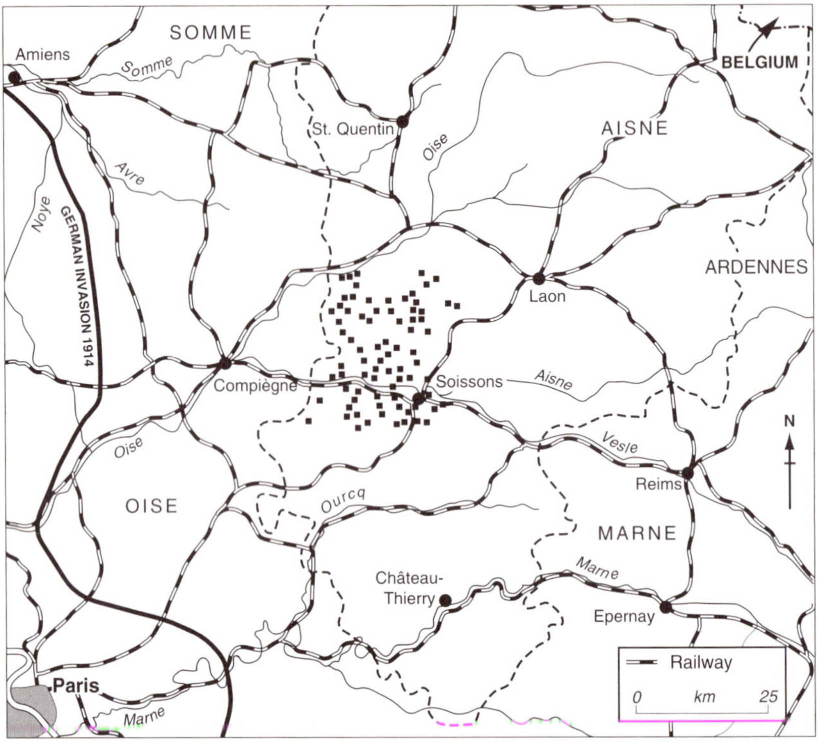

Figure 3.2 Villages assisted by the Comité Américain pour la France Dévastée, Aisne

seeds and draft animals were supplied by the Americans. The cooperatives ploughed and sowed in common nearly 1,000 ha and in February 1918 hopes were high for a good harvest in the coming season (Ibid.: 26).

By early March over eight hundred families had been reinstated and were partially self-supporting in these three *cantons* of western Aisne. Five hundred children had been fed, clothed and provided with medical care. Some seven thousand fruit trees had been planted to replace those cut down by the Germans, and hundreds of local people were given temporary work setting out a million vegetable plants donated by the French army. However, the winter of 1917–18 had proved to be very cold and wet and some returnees had become discouraged and left their ruined houses in order to move back into the interior of France. Those who remained were starting their spring ploughing when the

German offensive in March drove them out again. The French government aimed at complete evacuation of civilians from this area (Ford 1919a: 75).

On 27 March 1918 enemy forces came close to Blérancourt and the American women were ordered to assist in the evacuation. Initial plans to move civilians by train had to be abandoned in the face of intense bombing, so the American lorries played a vital role. The CARD saved all its supplies and livestock, regrouping at Coyelles and Vic-sur-Aisne. The German thrust toward Montdidier and Soissons over-taxed local medical and relief services, so the American women were ordered to provide canteens and rest houses for French soldiers straggling back from the front line. By the end of May the Germans had crossed the river Vesle and had taken Soissons. Once again the CARD helped with the evacuation of civilians, being compelled to fall back to Coulommiers and Viels-Maisons. Refugees streamed toward Paris *en route* for temporary destinations assigned to them in the interior of France.

Early in June came the counterdrive headed by Foch, with French and American troops recovering ground and the refugees from Aisne following in their wake. Soon 29,000 returned to the devastated western *cantons* of the *département*, being for the most part homeless, totally without resources, and with no immediate prospect of cultivating their shell-strewn land. Under legislation which encouraged farmers to recultivate abandoned land and to look to the government for compensation, the Americans requisitioned three large tracts of land which had not been seriously wrecked by shells and trenches. Refugee farmers were employed to raise cereals, vegetables and livestock until their own holdings might be brought into cultivation. A subsidy equal to $30,000 from the French government was granted for the work accomplished.

Following the German retreat, the Americans extended their activities from Blérancourt (in the *canton* of Coucy-le-Château) into the neighbouring *cantons* of Vic-sur-Aisne and Anizy-le-Château. Once the Armistice had been signed they devoted their energies to assisting restoration in these areas, to which the *canton* of Laon was soon added. The women helped to distribute government supplies, provided lorry transport between the *préfecture* at Laon and the *sous-préfectures* of Saint-Quentin and

Vervins further north, organized canteens for civilians and military prisoners released from Germany, and assisted the distribution of clothing throughout the northern part of the *département*. In addition, the CARD turned toward promoting permanent reconstruction in no fewer than seventy-seven devastated villages (MacDonald 1922: 286). Its volunteers played an instrumental role in training tractor drivers and supporting agricultural syndicates, of which twenty-six were created in Coucy *canton* and six in Anizy *canton* (Le Comité Américain, *MI*, 21.01.22: 14). Using forty tractors the syndicates ploughed 9,000 ha during 1919. The material task of rebuilding houses was left to the *sinistrés* themselves but the Americans lent their support to nascent cooperative societies, for example by making loans which enabled their members to pay contractors prior to receiving approval of and first advances on compensation from the government (see Chapter 9).

In a variety of ways, the CARD assisted not only the revival of agriculture, which was judged to be 'particularly successful', but also the reconstruction of farms and villages in western Aisne (Smith & Hill 1920: 36). Its volunteers withdrew during 1924 as local life gradually returned to normal (ADN 104J Comités de Secours Américains). Ten years after his visit to Blérancourt in December 1920, André Tardieu recalled with affection the positive impact that the American women had on the revival of the area, noting how even before the war had ended they had given anxious local people the courage to face the challenge of recovery and reconstruction (AN 324 AP/60 Tardieu A., A Blérancourt, 08.07.30). In contrast with these and many other relatively small, localized examples of rural restoration, the state's own agencies undertook various forms of emergency work throughout the devastated regions. The next three chapters will chart the activities of three services with special responsibility for land, farming and the countryside in general, while Chapter 7 will endeavour to evaluate their achievements. This group of chapters will show that state-directed emergency work proved not only difficult to implement but also highly controversial, and will demonstrate the profound gap between the benevolent pronouncements of the state to support *reconstitution* and the limited ability of its personnel to undertake essential practical tasks that would contribute to that objective.

4
The Service des Travaux de Première Urgence

Objectives and Organization

During the war a wide range of emergency work, such as filling trenches, repairing buildings and clearing wells, had been organized and in part undertaken by the staff of the Génie Rural (Saint 1920: 84). In mid December 1918 its role was modified to dealing with the removal of abandoned military equipment, defining the red zone, and planning the reconstruction of devastated rural buildings. A new organization, the Service des Travaux de Première Urgence (STPU) was set up by the state to assume responsibility for many emergency tasks. By the end of December 1918 the STPU was operating in six *départements* and was on the point of starting work in the remaining four which together composed the *régions libérées* (AN AJ 25/127 Le Service des Travaux de Première Urgence, 31.12.18). It might be called upon to provide various types of assistance, including:

(i) removal of shells and dangerous or suspect equipment, which would then be dealt with by the Service de Désobusage;
(ii) patching of damaged housing to permit temporary accommodation (but not permanent reconstruction);
(iii) installation of temporary accommodation (especially prefabricated wooden buildings and army huts) for emergency workers and returning *sinistrés*;
(iv) filling of trenches and shellholes, levelling of agricultural land and restoring it so that cultivation might recommence;
(v) ploughing and sowing any land that might be immediately available;

(vi) providing advice on re-cultivation through special agricultural officers;
(vii) supplying workers to repair roads, local railways, wells and other damaged features.

Like its immediate predecessor, the Service des Travaux de l'Armement, the STPU was a centralized organization and was run along quasi-military lines, with its senior staff being headed by M. Mauclère and comprising many military officers (Hubert 1923: 128). It functioned at the harshest of times, with some sections of the northern *départements* remaining subject to military administration, transport being in a state of chaos throughout the former war zone, materials of all kinds being virtually unobtainable, and local civilian labour being in extremely short supply (Morain 1921: 94; Gibbons 1920: 217). However, large numbers of prisoners of war still awaited repatriation and they were to form a major source of labour for the STPU (Huber 1931: 464). The Service was to prove controversial by virtue of its organization and its conduct. Some *sinistrés* recalled the lack of official coordination following the German retreat of March 1917, when about a thousand prisoners of war and an equal number of civilians had been taken on by civilian contractors to undertake emergency work (Ford 1919a: 223). Not surprisingly, it was feared that similar chaos might surround the STPU (AN F12 8030 Warren, De. E., Réorganisation des régions libérées, 27.03.19). Its centralized administration in Paris was complemented by a branch organization in each of the northern *départements* where it had its own personnel, transport, and—albeit inadequate—stock of material. Twenty operational 'sectors' were designated across the former war zone and these were subdivided into 'districts' by directors in the ten *départements* whose status was described by Ford as 'virtually autonomous' (Ford 1919a: 175).

Each of the twenty sectors was entrusted to an army officer who, as *chef de travaux*, was responsible for organizing supplies of labour and materials, and ensuring that local contractors were prepared appropriately (Ministère des Régions Libérées 1919). This system made no reference to prefects, sub-prefects or other civilian administrators and hence was to be the cause of considerable irritation (Saint 1920: 139). For example, it was reported that 'in Vosges, as everywhere else, the STPU escapes the authority of the prefect. Its staff members communicate directly with Paris, and receive orders and make changes which the prefect does not know about' (Vosges, *JRD*, 03.08.19:186). In more generous vein, the prefect of Marne acknowledged the 'goodwill and devotion' of some of the staff of the STPU, but was 'struck by the lack of direction, the faulty coordination of effort, and the absence of a single plan for reconstruction to which all schemes should be submitted' (AN AJ 25/47 Rapport sur le fonctionnement des services, Marne, 1919). In principle, weekly conferences should have taken place between the *chefs de travaux* in each *département* and the administrators of the local agricultural service, the Ponts et Chaussées and other organizations, but such meetings were not always held. Critics argued that the STPU was too strongly 'imprinted by its military origins' and displayed 'a certain disdain for local activities' (AN F2 2103 Accambray, L., Mission de contrôle, 1919). As Lucien Hubert observed, it was 'very difficult to direct happily and from such a great distance a machine where detail plays such a great role' (Hubert 1923: 129). In recognition of this problem, the administrative system was modified following a decree of 6 April 1919 and the northern prefects became rather more involved in the local work of the STPU (Saint 1920: 139).

Nonetheless, the delicate and emotive task of organizing emergency work remained largely entrusted to outsiders, whose actions would prove to be rarely in complete accord with the wishes of local people. For example, staff of the STPU in Aisne concentrated initially on removing barbed-wire entanglements and on filling trenches rather than on preparing less disturbed soil for re-cultivation as farmers and staff of the local agricultural services would have preferred (Ibid.). Another source of aggravation was the fact that the STPU often operated in localities where accommodation was available for its workers, rather than where the need for emergency work was greatest. Thus, in the spring of 1919 the prefect of Meuse noted that the local Service 'had to concentrate its efforts in a limited number of *communes* whose choice was fixed not simply by the importance and urgency of the work to be done, but also by the existence of buildings to house prisoners of war, since at present we do not have sufficient means of transporting huts to *communes* where they are not to be found' (Conseil Général de la Meuse 1919: 22).

The work of the STPU was not made easier by the fact that *sinistrés* clamoured to return to their property at the earliest possible moment, and some managed to do so despite instructions from the Ministère des Régions Libérées which advocated 'rigorous control' in conformity with the availability of food and drinking water, the possibility of bringing land back into cultivation, and the likely contribution that returnees might make to the revival of local activities (AN AJ 25/51 Reconstitution des régions envahies, 1919). Thus 'only families assured of finding shelter for the winter and capable of contributing to economic life' should be authorized by the prefect to return (Ibid.). In practice, some *sinistrés* started to come back before permission had been granted, for example to the devastated zone of Nord during November and December 1918. A proportion of those were overwhelmed by the magnitude of the task that awaited them and departed until emergency work had been undertaken, but others remained. Prefect Morain recalled the situation:

> Many at first had despaired, believing the task of reconstruction to be beyond their ability . . . But even if the walls of their farmhouses were in ruins, the fields remained. Their love of the land took hold and thereafter they had but one thought – to make it live again. In the depths of winter they set to work . . . The most favoured found their house and equipped it as best they could. The others built wretched shelters with wood, metal and sheets of iron left behind by the armies. Exposed to the elements, they suffered with resignation, and did not neglect any means of putting their land back into use. (Morain 1923: 30)

But in many instances prefects had 'the painful duty' of turning them away or refusing their request to return (Naudin 1921a: 9). Such apparently heartless reactions were 'dictated by reason' with 'considerable precautions having to be taken regarding hygiene in places where homeless returnees might install themselves alongside camps of Chinese coolies and enemy prisoners' working for the STPU (Ibid.).

Nonetheless, rules and regulations were not employed with

equal rigour everywhere and in some places *sinistrés* managed to return without permission, thereby placing severe strain on emergency supplies of food and water. For example, in Oise and Pas-de-Calais the STPU was trying to patch up damaged houses and to provide as many shelters as possible, but its efforts were overtaken by the ever-growing volume of demand for assistance from returning *sinistrés* (AN AJ 25/51 Service de Reconstitution Oise, 1919; Villey M Pas-de-Calais 1919). In the neighbouring *département* of Somme only 200 wooden buildings had been received by 1 April 1919 which were allocated to house the *commune* office (*mairie*) and other public services. The British army then made available a further 600 huts to assist emergency housing. However, these figures fell disastrously short of the 12,000 requests for temporary housing which awaited resolution in the *département* of Somme alone (AN AJ 25/51 Reconstitution des régions envahies, Somme, 1919). Some prefects encouraged landowners to use their initiative to construct temporary housing rather than wait for the state to come to their aid. In Meurthe-et-Moselle returnees had responded to that advice even before the STPU had started to function (AN AJ 25/47 Reconstitution des régions libérées, Meurthe-et-Moselle, 25.04.19).

The Emergency Labour Force

During the first half of 1919 the STPU assembled its labour force, which exceeded 260,000 by the middle of the summer, comprising 50–60,000 civilians recruited locally, 200,000 prisoners of war, and an unspecified number of colonials, including workers hired from Indo-China who had been engaged for the duration of the war plus an additional six-month period following the conclusion of peace (AN AJ 25/127 Bertrand, F., La main d'oeuvre, 1919; Mauco 1932: 71–72; Gide 1923: 164). The regional press estimated that 25,000 'Chinese', as they were described, had been contracted by the STPU (Hénard 1919: 3). Figures were both imprecise and fluctuating and it is hardly surprising that George Ford quoted rather different numbers and categories from those mentioned above (Ford 1919a: 88). He listed a total of 293,851 STPU employees, made up of 827 officers in charge, 5,197 office workers and foremen, 82,640 French civilian labourers, 8,122

French soldiers, 17,199 colonials and Russians, and 179,906 Germans and other prisoners of war. The payroll for all these workers, together with the cost of transportation and supplies amounted to roughly 200,000,000 F per month. German prisoners of war worked directly under French army supervision and were allocated 40 centimes per day plus food and lodging (Ibid.: 176). Almost all the French civilians worked for contractors who had been awarded work on the basis of submitting the lowest bids. Workers were paid between 8 F and 18 F per day according to their qualifications and the tasks being undertaken. Colonial troops received 6 F per day, with an additional 4 F being spent to feed and house them. Where German prisoners of war were allocated to civilian contractors they were costed at a daily rate of 7 F 90 centimes, all of which was set against eventual compensation claims (Ibid.: 177).

It is not possible to determine the size of the emergency labour force in each *département* but some examples were recorded. At the end of March 1919 Pas-de-Calais had contained 19,316 emergency workers comprising 8,728 prisoners of war, 4,620 Chinese, 1,188 local civilians, 4,700 military workers and 100 explosives' experts (AN AJ 25/51 Villey M Service de Reconstitution Pas-de-Calais, 1919). During the summer the overall total rose to 23,500, including 17,950 prisoners of war who restored land, railways and mines (plus some specialists who repaired houses) and 1,300 North Africans who worked on the roads (Peytral 1927: 296). In March 1919 the STPU in Somme had employed over 14,000 men, made up of 11,310 prisoners of war, 2,380 civilians and 350 military workers (AN AJ 25/51 Reconstitution des régions envahies, Somme, 1919). Two months later, slightly higher figures were noted but trench filling had not been started in many areas, and abandoned machines and debris littered the soil (Les sinistrés, *JRD*,25.05.19: 26).

The STPU in Aisne had employed 18,000 at the start of March 1919, comprising 9,450 prisoners of war, 6,732 civilians, 1,816 military workers and an unspecified number of Russians and 'yellow workers' (AN AJ 25/51 Bonnefoy-Sibour, A., Rapport sur le fonctionnement, 25.04.19). The number of prisoners of war in its employ rose to 20,370 at the start of April and 35,000 at the end of the month (AN F2 2103 Accambray, L., Mission de contrôle, 1919). At that time 22,525 prisoners of war, organized in fifty-three groups, were working in Meuse, and in Meurthe-et-Moselle forty-five groups of prisoners and five groups of colonial workers comprised an emergency workforce of 20,000 (Conseil Général de la Meuse 1919: 23; Conseil Général de la Meurthe-et-Moselle 1919: 7). By June 30,000 civilians and an equal number of prisoners of war were engaged in emergency work in Nord (Conseil Général du Nord 1919: 3). At the other extreme, the STPU workforce for Vosges had been only 2,000 civilians and 350 prisoners of war in April 1919 but this total was soon increased by a further 2,600 Germans (AN AJ 25/47 Laporte, M., Réorganisation de la vie locale, 1919).

Employing prisoners of war was an essential but sensitive matter, as was revealed by the tense atmosphere in Nord during the spring of 1919 (AN AJ 25/47 Naudin, A., Reconstitution du sol, 08.05.19). Prefect Naudin noted that German labour was much sought after in some districts but was strongly rejected in others whose elected councillors stressed the high level of local unemployment among local workers in many parts of the *département* because so many factories lay in ruins. He urged caution, arguing that it would be 'politically unwise' to employ prisoners of war and civilians on identical tasks, since the administration might be accused of depressing civilian wage levels (Ibid.). He argued that prisoners were probably best suited to clearing rubble and barbed wire and to levelling *régions désertiques* that had been ravaged by shells. In practice, their work gave rise to considerable complaint, with Frédéric Bertrand maintaining that they accomplished only two-thirds of what reasonably might be expected (AN AJ 25/127 Bertrand, F., La main d'oeuvre, 1919). This, he alleged, was partly due to poor supervision but was largely attributable to malingering, illness, or being directed to unproductive activities. For example, Bachelet complained that STPU staff in Pas-de-Calais used prisoners of war to plant and tend their gardens rather than to undertake repairs or install temporary housing (AN AJ 25/47 Bachelet, M., Rapport au Ministre, 21.08.21). According to Bertrand, only 125,000 of the 200,000 prisoners of war employed by the STPU were involved in productive work on any one day and their work routines left much to be desired (AN AJ 25/127 Bertrand, F., La main d'oeuvre, 1919). Prisoner of war squads allegedly started work late and finished early; much time was lost returning to camp at lunchtime; and surveillance was mediocre, with guards being overpaid and not exerting themselves in order to safeguard their jobs. The columnist of the *Journal des Régions Dévastées* summarized widespread dissatisfaction when he reported: 'Anyone who has seen these companies of prisoners at work in the streets of Reims or in the surrounding countryside can be under no illusion about the yield of their work, which is zero. Some *boches* know all about System D and practise it to the full' (Marne, *JRD*, 15.06.19).

The civilians employed by the STPU comprised demobilized soldiers from many backgrounds, including building workers, craftsmen, and in particular farmworkers who were attracted by relatively generous wages and by what they perceived as not particularly onerous work (Hubert 1923: 129). In the spring of 1919 civilians performing manual work for the STPU in Aisne were paid 70 centimes per hour plus a 30 centimes per hour cost of living allowance, with an additional 2 F each day for those working more than 15 km from home (AN F2 2103 Accambray, L., Mission de contrôle, 1919). These sums attracted farmworkers from the land, indeed some were surprised at the generosity of their pay, but the amounts were below what was being offered by companies contracted to re-build railways and canals (AN AJ 25/127 Bertrand, F., La main d'oeuvre, 1919). Many *sinistrés* were profoundly critical of such manual workers, especially those who had abandoned farmwork. Frédéric Bertrand alleged that the coffers of the state were being 'raided unscrupulously' to pay the emergency workforce and argued for an independent enquiry to investigate the 'scandalous' cost of the STPU (Ibid.). In Somme, Prefect Morain complained that foremen, labourers and clerks alike were 'insufficiently prepared for the task' and 'seemed more concerned with their own affairs than with those of the *sinistrés*, producing only mediocre work for high wages' (Morain 1920: 4). From his practical experience of restoration work in Aisne, Gaston Héricault reported bizarre instances of a band leader, a cobbler and a photographer having been placed in charge of organizing emergency work (Héricault 1934: 50).

Reactions to the STPU

The detailed activity of the STPU across the ten *départements* is not known, but there must have been important local variations.

In Marne, its workers, comprising fifty-five companies of about four hundred men apiece, cleared shells from about 30,000 ha and filled trenches over 18,000 ha in the sectors of Châlons and Reims before 1 April 1919 (AN AJ 25/47 Rapport sur le fonctionnement, Marne, 1919). Some 8,000 ha of land had been ploughed by the STPU but only 173 houses had been repaired and forty-three wooden shelters erected. Not surprisingly, much more had been achieved in the southern sector (Châlons) than in the northern one (Reims) which had been crossed by the heavily fought-over front line and contained large expanses of red zone.

Reactions to the achievements of the STPU were varied in the extreme. Writing when the work was being done, George B. Ford offered a very positive opinion, and argued that 'the whole work is highly organized on lines which combine the best features of the organization of a big contracting company, on the one hand, and the army engineering corps, on the other' (Ford 1919a: 175). He insisted that 'this "army" . . . was getting splendid results'. In a similarly positive vein, Roger Picard also maintained that the efforts of the STPU could not be praised too highly because all the problems that they were called upon to tackle were new, either in character or magnitude (Picard 1922: 1022). Very few *sinistrés* shared these opinions, being frustrated by the apparent slowness and poor quality of much of its work. For example, in Ardennes they protested that tarred felt had been used for makeshift roofs and oiled paper had been tacked across blasted windows, making officially repaired houses 'stifling in summer but freezing in winter' (Hubert 1923: 134). Farmers in Nord complained that the STPU had not filled shellholes and trenches properly, and left barbed wire and metal stakes in the soil, thereby making ploughing difficult and hazardous (Morain 1923: 31). Mechanized harvesting also could be dangerous, since imperfectly filled holes opened up but remained undetected beneath the cover of standing crops (Helot 1920a: 545). Other commentators were even more damning, alleging that the STPU had recorded some shellholes as having been filled but in fact had done nothing to make them safe (Padieu 1925: 156).

For a variety of reasons, administrators and elected representatives throughout the war zone also were critical of the Service. In the experience of Lucien Hubert in Ardennes, the STPU left too much to chance and produced rather feeble results, with some staff lacking fundamental goodwill (Hubert 1923: 125). He alleged that the Service was characterized by 'particularly irritating slowness at a time when everything had to be re-done, and by particularly regrettable wastages at a point when state finances had to be managed carefully' (Hubert 1923: 130). But, despite these objections, he concluded that 'with greater competence and flexibility the STPU could have worked' (Ibid). The columns of *L'Architecte* pronounced that 'the STPU in Ardennes cannot be eternal . . . state intervention and the thousand constraints which strangle all initiative must be done away with, if we wish our region to enter convalescence' (Vers la renaissance, *LA*, 1919: 468). In nearby Aisne, Prefect Bonnefoy-Sibour maintained that clerks and foremen working for the STPU received sufficient wages but rates of turnover were high, since material conditions were so poor, and employees looked for a less harsh existence elsewhere (AN AJ 25/51 Bonnefoy-Sibour, A., Rapport sur le fonctionnement du service, 25.04.19). In Somme, some administrative staff escaped surveillance and recruited labour haphazardly, thereby producing a veritable army of civilians that was 'more concerned with its own affairs than with those of the *sinistrés*' (Morain 1920: 4). Maxime De Sars complained more vehemently of the 'excessive number of "parasites"' employed by the STPU and how they failed to respond to the efforts of zealous agents who 'tried to shake them out of their torpor' (De Sars 1937: 1).

A particularly damning report came from Léon Accambray, deputy for Laon-Nord, who during April and May 1919 examined STPU activity in fifty-six *communes* surrounding the towns of Chauny and La Fère in and around the marshy valleys of the Oise, Ailette and Serre in Aisne *département* (AN F2 2103 Accambray, L., Mission de contrôle, 1919). In 1914 the whole area had housed 49,560 people but at 1 May 1919 the figure stood at only 13,510 (a loss of 73 per cent), with twenty-two *communes* having been destroyed completely. Accambray showed that 'six months after the Armistice the *régions libérées* [were] scarcely coming back to life' (Table 4.1) and many returnees were becoming 'bitter and discontented' (Ibid.). He argued that work by prisoners of war was markedly deficient, with poor supervision (for example, twenty-five French supervisors to four hundred prisoners) and over-large squads coming in for severe

Table 4.1 Results of STPU activity in five *cantons* of Aisne, by 15 April 1919

	La Fère	Anizy	Chauny	Coucy	Crécy
Total area (ha)	18,325	15,797	15,880	25,933	19,343
Cleared of shells (ha)	2,221	40	2,153	7,880	9,200
Area restored (ha)	2,221	220	550	230	11,300
Horses	88	10	60	56	85
Tractors	4	2	4	2	2
Civilian workers	397	99	292	209	809
Prisoners of war	314	370	1,232	1,275	402
'Chinese' workers	1,600	–	–	–	–
Vehicles (various)	23	6	16	10	25

Source: AN F2 2103 Accambray, L., Mission de contrôle dans le département de l'Aisne (1919)

criticism. One procedure was particularly unsatisfactory. It involved prisoners traversing shell-strewn farmland and signalling the location of dangerous debris and unexploded shells prior to removal by military explosives experts to munitions dumps where controlled destruction took place. For example, in nearby Pas-de-Calais, British troops assumed responsibility for disposing of dangerous materials until October 1919, when the task was taken over by the special Service de Désobusage (Peytral 1927: 485). According to Léon Accambray, the prisoners of war were not interested in this kind of dangerous work and some preferred to ignore debris or even to cover over unexploded shells rather than mark them (AN F2 2103 Accambray, L., Mission de contrôle, 1919). He insisted that general supervision was lax, the number of explosives experts was small (only one per *canton*), and inadequate care was taken when shells were removed for destruction. He argued that the only way to obtain a reasonable amount of work from prisoners of war was to place them in small squads and supervise them very closely. It is clear that filling of shellholes and trenches and removal of barbed wire was being done slowly and haphazardly in western Aisne, and such was doubtless the case elsewhere. Nine months after the war had ended, workers, children and visitors were being killed or maimed in the countryside around Reims because fields and ruined settlements remained strewn with live shells, grenades and explosives (Marne, *JRD*, 27.07.19: 167). Such tragic experiences were not unique to this part of northern France and were to occur for many years. In July 1919 the local correspondent of the *Journal des Régions Dévastées* was prompted to ask 'Has the war not claimed enough victims?' (Ibid).

Colonial labourers seemed no more satisfactory than prisoners of war, with the so-called Chinese workers being condemned for exploding any munitions they could lay their hands on, whether by night or by day, and for frequent thefts (AN F2 2103 Accambray, L., Mission de contrôle, 1919). In Marne, Chinese workers roamed around unsupervised once the working day was over, and their behaviour created many problems for local people, as they placed houses under siege and discharged firearms (Marne, *JRD*, 15.06.19: 3). Complaints proliferated throughout northern France against aggravations caused by 'the yellow peril', which comprised not only workers contracted to the STPU but also Chinese deserters from British labour camps with whom they were confused (Hénard 1919: 3). The size of the British emergency labour corps rose from 42,000 in December 1916 to nearly 125,000 at the Armistice, including 90,000 Chinese, as well as Africans, Egyptians, Indians and West Indians (Swinton 1936: II 768). Prefect Morain received many complaints about Chinese deserters in Somme *département* and approached the British military authorities in the summer of 1919 to try to resolve the problem (Hénard 1919: 3). However, a few appreciative comments stand out from the flood of criticism. For example, the STPU supervisor for the district of La Fère (Aisne) made a special point of employing Chinese workers, having spent four years as a railway engineer overseeing the installation of tracks in Indo-China (AN F2 2103 Accambray, L., Mission de contrôle, 1919). His previous experience of Chinese labourers was that they were 'good, flexible, intelligent and hardworking', and he supervised no fewer than 1,600 in spring 1919. In a similar vein, it was reported that Annamites employed in Meurthe-et-Moselle displayed unequalled patience in removing barbed wire (Meurthe-et-Moselle, *JRD*, 07.09.19: 267). Deputy Accambray conceded grudgingly that this state of practical skill would only be reached after considerable training (AN F2 2103 Accambray, L., Mission de contrôle, 1919).

In Pas-de-Calais 4,250 Chinese had been employed by the STPU during much of 1919 but because of scandalous behaviour, which meant that local 'women would not dare to travel alone',

Plate 4.1 Chinese workers employed by the STPU in the company of French girls

'the population asks to be rid of them' (Peytral 1927: 296; AN AJ 25/47 Bachelet, M., Rapport au Ministre, 21.08.21). French girls were advised to have nothing to do with the Chinese labourers, who would be repatriated as soon as their work contracts ended (Le péril jaune, *JRD*, 02.11.19: 3; Nogaro & Weil 1926: 18). It was alleged that these workers were 'undisciplined . . . playing and smoking with the foremen, or being violent, stealing and even killing. [Hence] terror reigns in these areas, and old people, children and adults receive blows from these marauding thieves' (Pas-de-Calais, *JRD*, 24.08.19: 233; Swinton 1936: II 770). *Sinistrés* repeated their complaint that Chinese labourers were 'useless' and late in 1919 they threatened that unless the government removed them from the northern *départements* 'very disagreeable consequences' would result (Pas-de-Calais, *LA*, 1920: 9). In an atmosphere of 'frequent *brigandages*' almost all Chinese workers in Pas-de-Calais were repatriated during the winter of 1919–20, with only 230 staying to work in the mines (Peytral 1927: 296). Alternative supplies of emergency labour were obtained in the form of 2,700 Polish labourers who reached the *département* at Christmas-time in 1919, but 450 were found to be ill or otherwise undesirable and were sent back to Poland (Ibid.). The remainder provided essential labour for erecting temporary housing. *Sinistrés* continued to express their hostility toward the diminishing number of Chinese workers who remained in the devastated areas, and relations deteriorated even further following the so-called Péronne revolt of January 1920 when two hundred Chinese prevented the police from apprehending three of their number who had been accused of theft (Gentlemen colored, *JRD*, 01.02.20: 3).

The work of the STPU was judged by contemporaries to be deficient in other respects, although one can hardly overestimate the difficult circumstances in which it functioned. Items of various kinds that had been abandoned at random by the armed forces provided its staff with some construction materials but fresh supplies were desperately short, and problems were exacerbated by inadequate transport facilities. For example, in spring 1919 quantities of timber could not be moved from Vosges to the neighbouring *département* of Meurthe-et-Moselle for assembly into temporary shelters because the railway line had not been repaired (AN AJ 25/47 Reconstitution des régions libérées,

Meurthe-et-Moselle, 25.04.19). Building materials that did arrive in Lorraine 'came in a rather chaotic and irregular way . . . to areas that were not always the most appropriate' (Ibid.). Adequate storage facilities were lacking in many parts of the northern *départements* and poor surveillance of depots and building sites meant that batches of vital pre-fabricated parts often were stolen or mislaid. In addition, wagons laden with essential wooden parts sometimes went astray on the imperfectly restored railway system. The net result of this disorganization was that the STPU had erected very few temporary shelters by the spring of 1919. In western Aisne wooden buildings usually came in the form of two-roomed huts, which were installed to house the *mairie*, the school and the village teacher, but by May 1919 some *communes* still had received no kind of temporary building (AN F2 2103 Accambray, L., Mission de contrôle, 1919). The story was no better when it came to patching up damaged houses. Essential building materials were simply not available and the prisoner-of-war labour force contained very few skilled woodworkers or builders. Not surprisingly, returning farmers complained bitterly about the rudimentary forms of shelter in which they were compelled to live, but it should not be forgotten that permanent reconstruction was beyond the remit of the STPU.

In September 1919 the socialist Albert Inghels reported to the Chambre des Députés on the widespread housing crisis in northern France and the appalling living conditions that were endured by many returnees, including those who were heaped into cellars and military shelters (Inghels 1919: 2651). For nine months the authorities had talked about providing supplies of wooden houses but very few had materialized. Indeed, the Ministre des Régions Libérées had confided that he anticipated some *sinistrés* having to leave their ruins during the winter months of 1919–20 to search for accommodation beyond the battle zone (Ibid.: 2650). Deputy Inghels argued that the crisis 'must be resolved by a major effort to construct solid provisional housing. The time of promises is over, we have come to the time for action' (Ibid.: 2651). Hygiene conditions were appalling amid the ruins and around many of the makeshift shelters. The STPU had been charged with cleaning out wells and emptying cesspits, which were notorious breeding grounds for mosquitoes, but adequate supplies of disinfectant and quick-lime were not available, and in some places its workers were reluctant to undertake such unpleasant work (AN F2 2103 Accambray, L., Mission de contrôle, 1919). Polluted drinking water, filthy wells, overflowing cesspits, piles of rotting rubbish, dead animals and newly discovered corpses of soldiers and civilians formed a grim list of health hazards that confronted many wretched *sinistrés* (Inghels 1919: 2648).

Shell clearance had to be undertaken several times in many parts of the war zone, partly because of inefficiency but also because additional dangerous materials continued to be turned up. In Pas-de-Calais shells were collected before and after disturbed soil had been levelled out, and again after the first ploughing had been completed. In many places the task would have to be repeated time and time again. By early 1921 77,000 tonnes of munitions had been removed from the fields of that *département*, but great quantities of shells and grenades were still coming to the surface, with no fewer than 200,000 items being recovered during the spring of 1921 alone (Tribondeau 1937: 132). Many shellholes and trenches in the northern *départements* had not been filled properly during the emergency phase, thereby complicating the work of ploughmen and damaging their equipment in subsequent seasons (Morain 1923: 31). They needed to take particular care in the late afternoon when the light was fading, since many holes in the fields concealed unexploded munitions (Smith & Hill 1920: 209). Shoddy in-filling gave rise to other problems, including the subsidence of stretches of re-laid road. Despite several attempts at repairs, the outline of holes and trenches continued to appear on road surfaces up to ten years after the war had ended (Magny 1928: 85).

In May 1919 Prefect Mathieu in Ardennes argued that the 'strongest complaints and harshest criticisms' of the STPU were coming from returnees who had not lived under German occupation or had experienced the particularly difficult times immediately after the Armistice (AN AJ 25/51 Mathieu, P., Reprise de la vie locale, 04.05.19). By contrast, those who had stayed in their home area during the war or had returned at the end of 1918 displayed more tolerant reactions. Six months after the Armistice that fierce critic Deputy Accambray acknowledged that no other official organization had been charged with

Plate 4.2 Unexploded shells gathered from the fields awaiting collection before controlled explosion

restoring *communes* around the Oise and Ailette valleys of western Aisne and confessed to being 'confounded to see the STPU being given such great responsibility but being allocated such ridiculously insufficient resources' (AN F2 2103 Accambray, L., Mission de contrôle, 1919). Farmers' associations added their opposition to that voiced by administrators and politicians, with the *Journal des Régions Dévastées* carrying many articles that were profoundly critical of the STPU. Thus on 29 June 1919 the powerful Société des Agriculteurs de l'Oise charged the STPU with gross inefficiency and with inflating wages, thereby drawing farm labourers away from the land (Oise, *JRD*, 29.06.19: 107). It advocated that the Service should be terminated as soon as prisoners of war had been repatriated and argued that the tasks of recovery and reconstruction should be transferred to cooperatives for individual *communes* or groups of villages.

Deficiencies were doubtless severe and widespread but there were some positive reactions to this difficult emergency work. In Marne the STPU had supplied labour and equipment to assist local farmers with hay-making during the summer of 1919, retaining half of the hay crops as payment. It seemed that 'this combination gave entire satisfaction' (AN AJ 25/126 Reconstitution agricole, Marne, 28.07.19). Likewise in Oise the STPU undertook hay-making on land which had not yet been regained by its owners (AN AJ 25/126 Reconstitution agricole, Oise, 28.07.19). The Service investigated narrow-gauge railway lines which in part dated from before the war but had also been installed by the German and allied armies. It then examined requirements for moving building materials from supply areas to various locations in the former war zone and duly modified the narrow-gauge systems to serve current needs (Ford 1919a: 184). Thus in Meuse the Service installed additional narrow-gauge tracks to supplement lines that had been left by American and German forces (Magny 1928: 52). In neighbouring Marne it offered practical help to newly-formed agricultural cooperatives where, despite their frustrations, many local farmers recognized that 'considerable efforts had been made and some very important results obtained' (Moreau-Bérillon 1921: 131).

But, without doubt, complaints against the STPU were louder and more frequent than praise. Allegations of money being squandered and concern over the conduct of Chinese labourers

Plate 4.3 A narrow-gauge train carrying building materials, operated by staff of the emergency services

were widespread but *sinistrés* were particularly angry over the tardiness and inefficiency with which the Service patched up buildings (AN F2 2100 Etats généraux des régions dévastées, 09.09.19). When Clemenceau visited Somme in July 1919 he faced hostile groups of returnees who clamoured for immediate restoration of their land and buildings before the winter (Ibid.). Some of the responsibility for slowness in the north-western section of the devastated regions must be borne by the British military authorities which took time to assemble their war dead for re-burial and to collect equipment prior to vacating the area, but much blame must be apportioned to the STPU (Picard 1922: 1022). Indeed, Clemenceau contemplated having to order that returnees should be re-evacuated from parts of the northern *départements* where repairs were proceeding particularly slowly (AN F2 2100 Etats généraux des régions dévastées, 09.09.19). He declared that the most urgent task was to provide adequate shelter for 200,000 people in the liberated regions before the onset of the next winter (Ford 1919a: 179). By virtue of the cost and slowness of the STPU, the state encouraged landowners to group themselves into associations for restoring their land in the belief that they could do so more efficiently and cheaply (Ibid.: 177).

Despite severe difficulties, obvious shortcomings and widespread complaints, the results of basic recovery work by the emergency services during the early months of peace were far from negligible. According to George Ford, by mid June 1919 nearly 2,000,000 ha had been restored for cultivation throughout the war zone, some 80,000,000 m^2 of barbed wire entanglement had been cleared, and 33,000,000 m^3 of trenches and shellholes had been filled (Ibid.: 89). About 75,000 houses had received sufficient temporary repairs to render them habitable, and 5,000 huts had been erected. In addition, numerous polluted wells had been cleaned out and mosquitoes eradicated from shellholes. Unfortunately, it is not possible to determine either the geography of such activities or the relative proportions accomplished by the STPU, by other organizations, and by the *sinistrés* themselves.

A Change of Title: The Service des Travaux de l'Etat

As a result of profound discontent and more specifically of Clemenceau's visit to the northern *départements*, the STPU was disbanded in August 1919 and its activities were transferred to the Service des Travaux de l'Etat (STE) for which the prefects were given some responsibility (Magny 1928: 10). In addition, several northern prefects were moved to different *départements* at this time (De Sars 1937: 1). However, what Lucien Hubert called this 'happy remedy' to inefficiency, really just involved a change in name (Hubert 1923: 133). Many STPU personnel were employed in the new organization and the familiar complaints soon started to be voiced again. In Aisne the upper echelons of STE staff were considered to be satisfactory but lower grade clerical staff, foremen and labourers were judged to be too few and regrettably lacking in competence (AN F2 2100 Rapport du préfet de l'Aisne, 31.11.19). As in earlier months, a very real difficulty involved the severe shortage of habitable housing for STE staff throughout northern France. For example, men had travelled to Aisne from as far afield as Algeria and Alsace to take up clerical work for the STE but many moved on as soon as they learned that there was no decent accommodation available for themselves and their families.

During the greater part of 1919 prisoners of war provided a numerous if unsatisfactory supply of manual labour for the state services. In Aisne the total rose from virtually none at the start of the year to 42,123 in early July and 57,402 in November, with figures falling back to 50,000 in January 1920 and plunging to 2,700 in April once repatriation had taken place (Saint 1920: 78; AN AJ 25/127 Bertrand, F., La main d'oeuvre, 1919; AN F2 2100 Rapport du préfet de l'Aisne, 31.11.19). After representing 53 per cent of all 'emergency' labour in the *département* in July 1919, prisoners of war made up only 5 per cent nine months later. During the second half of 1919 and in early 1920 German prisoners in the northern *départements* became increasingly demoralized and inefficient as they awaited repatriation, and hence the STE had to turn to other types of foreign labour (Huber 1931: 501). At the end of 1919 Indo-Chinese workers in Aisne were still judged to be mediocre and Russians were criticized for being disorganized. By contrast, Portuguese workers were praised for their hard work regardless of language difficulties, but Catalans who had been recruited through Perpignan were said to be in poor physical condition. Such sources of foreign labour were tapped for emergency tasks elsewhere in the northern *départements*. For example, Poles and Russians as well as Portuguese and Spaniards provided sizeable contingents in Meurthe-et-Moselle (AN AJ 25/125 Reconstitution agricole Meurthe-et-Moselle, 21.02.20; Conseil-Général de Meurthe-et-Moselle 1920: 18). At the same time as these foreigners were being recruited, large numbers of local civilian workers were abandoning the STE to obtain more generous wages from private building contractors involved in major repair work or permanent reconstruction. The net result of these changes was the disintegration of this emergency labour force. To cite just one example, the number of STE workers of all kinds in Aisne fell from a peak of 79,000 in August 1919 to a mere 24,000 in April 1920 (Saint 1920: 79).

This branch of the emergency services proved no more popular than its predecessor and unfortunately 'appeared incapable of fulfilling its objectives' (Gouge 1920: 1). It seemed to many *sinistrés*, who had to put up with the most rudimentary of temporary shelters including ruins and tents, that STE workers were being housed 'in a princely fashion' even though they behaved like 'vandals' on occasions (Dans nos ruines, *JRD*, 21.03.20: 1). Returnees charged them with wrecking habitable dwellings under the pretence of salvaging scarce building materials, and with stealing carved masonry and decorated fireplaces for installation in their own homes. To the wretched *sinistrés* it seemed as if the STE operated according to the principle of 'L'Etat, c'est moi' (Ibid.). Opposition reverberated around the northern *départements* and once the prisoners of war had been repatriated the whole logic of the inefficient and widely detested STE collapsed. The Confédération Générale des Associations Agricoles des Régions Dévastées alleged that the STE had used its labour in an inappropriate way and had siphoned away large numbers of civilian workers who were needed for farmwork (Réclamations des agriculteurs, *JAP*, 1920: 88). It urged the Ministre des Régions Libérées to disband the Service and to direct any future financial support to associations, cooperatives and individual *sinistrés* who were desperately keen to re-work their land, rather than to fashion yet another state organization. Along with many others, Léon Accambray argued that effective restoration was not possible through the intervention of the state, hence he insisted that 'it is private enterprise that will reconstruct our devastated areas' (AN F2 2103 Accambray, L., Mission de contrôle, 1919).

The burden of complaint against the STE and the other services was summarized in a letter to the Ministre des Régions Libérées in March 1920 in which the Ministre des Finances noted that they 'already gave rise to great expense and, as far as I can judge, produce a very inadequate result' (AEF 1A 385 Services de l'Etat, Letter 1920). A similar criticism was launched by M. Thomas, Inspecteur des Finances, who stressed the need to cut down state expenditure on emergency services in general, singling out the state-run narrow-gauge railway system, which employed over 7,000 staff to operate 2,750 km of track, for particular criticism (AEF 1A 385, Thomas, A., Rapport concernant les économies, 11.06.20). Because of widespread opposition from many sections of society, the direct involvement of the STE in preliminary recovery work was gradually brought to an end, and after the spring of 1920 this kind of activity was handled increasingly by teams of contractors, by local associations of landowners, or in other ways (Morain 1920: 5). Nonetheless, some commentators argued that this decision to rely on private enterprise and initiative would retard recovery around Verdun (Meuse) and in other seriously devastated areas (Guicherd & Maitrot 1921: 332). Indeed, criticisms of the STPU and the STE quietened down once these organizations had ceased to exist and *sinistrés* realized that they were now left entirely to their own devices (Reibel 1924b: 3).

Many drew up private agreements with groups of labourers or with contracting firms. For example, in Meuse some 9,800 arrangements of this kind had been established by the end of 1921 (Magny 1928: 68). In addition, the staff from the *préfecture* advised on drawing up contracts for the restoration of farmland across whole *communes* or, more rarely, for several *communes* at a time. Other *sinistrés* took the opportunity to form cooperatives to finish work that had been started by the emergency services, or in some apparently forgotten places to commence filling trenches, levelling soil, and preparing it for cultivation. Landowners at Villers-Carbonnel near Péronne (Somme) provided a model for this kind of cooperation, having founded such an association as early as May 1919 and having employed civilian workers and prisoners of war to restore 894 ha (L'initiative privée, *JRD*,

21.03.20: 2). By the end of that year all detectable shells had been removed and all the farmland in the *commune* had been levelled. Rye, barley and wheat had been sown on 102 ha and landowners had taken the innovative step of requesting that their fragmented land holdings should be consolidated (*remembrement*) (see Chapter 10). Similar associations were founded elsewhere in Somme and in other northern *départements*, but usually they disbanded once the soil had been levelled, leaving each farmer to work the land individually thereafter (Gouge 1921a: 1). When collective momentum was dissipated in this way, a vital opportunity for establishing cooperatives to reconstruct village housing or for applying for *remembrement* could easily be lost (see Chapters 9 and 10).

Many commentators agreed that 'the STE phase will count among the worst memories of the *sinistrés* and their hostility was also directed to other forms of direct state intervention in rural recovery (Dessaint 1922: 755). Delegates of the Confédération Générale du Travail, who in January 1921 inspected conditions in the former war zone, reported great anger among *sinistrés* toward the state services which they argued 'should never have existed', having been wasteful and staffed by 'parasitic *fonctionnaires* . . . who poison us with their stupid circulars . . . and do not deign to study the fundamental problems of our region' (Confédération Générale du Travail 1921: 11). They maintained that 'far from helping the farmers in their arduous task, the administration has managed to discourage even the most energetic *sinistrés* through its paperwork, its slowness and incompetence, and the illogical decisions it has taken' (Ibid.). As the next two chapters will show, the Service de la Motoculture and the various organizations supervised by the Office de Reconstitution Agricole were to receive very similar reactions.

5
Motoculture

Preparing the Land

As was painfully clear, the events of war had devastated some of the most productive farmlands in France, whose crops and livestock had played a major contribution to the nation's food supplies. Physical disruption was compounded by the mobilization of agricultural labour and the extensive loss of implements, machines and draught animals. However, many farming women continued to work the land even under extremely harsh circumstances (Pitrois 1916). William MacDonald argued that 'the sight of peasants ploughing, cultivating or harvesting within sight of trenches and batteries, undisturbed by shells which occasionally exploded nearby, was not at all uncommon in localities close to the front' (MacDonald 1922: 153). Material damage was only slight in some sections of the war zone where the real problem was that land had simply been abandoned, involving an invasion of weeds and pests, a failure to work the soil, and a complete absence of fertilization for several years (Troupeau-Housay 1927: 395). At least some of these problems might be overcome by employing various forms of mechanized technology (Théry 1918: 25). For example, caterpillar tractors would prove particularly useful on terrain where imperfectly filled shellholes gave rise to subsidence hollows (Padieu 1925: 156).

In order to promote mechanized restoration of war-damaged land the centralized Service de la Motoculture was established in conformity with the Law of 7 April 1917, which sought to bring abandoned farmland throughout France back into cultivation, and was reinforced by legislation of 4 May 1918 (Bros 1924: 47; Laurent 1919: 28). As part of a broad policy to encourage cultivation in the war zone, the Service was charged with undertaking first ploughing, hoeing, harrowing and other vital operations in districts where land had not been severely disturbed or strewn with shells, but where the real problem was that returning farmers lacked sufficient resources to commence cultivation. To overcome this handicap essential tasks were to be undertaken by groups of tractors that were owned by the state and were operated by its employees. At the start the Service possessed only 111 tractors but a further 290 were on order from suppliers in the USA (AN F12 8025 La mise en culture des terres, 1917). Later in 1917 an additional 400 were ordered as a result of André Tardieu's mission to Washington, and American manufacturers produced smaller, lighter models than usual in order to suit the particular circumstances of northern France (Sagnier 1918: 518; AN AJ 25/97 Le Seigneur, J., ORA; matériel, 08.12.17). By the end of the year the total number of Service tractors had risen to 800 and 1,500 more were on order (Ford 1919a: 168). This achievement was simply a modest start when set against the minimum figure of 10,000 tractors which some observers believed would be necessary to restore the devastated farmland of northern France (AN F12 8025 La mise en culture, 1917). Throughout its existence the Service continued to enlarge its stock by placing orders with French suppliers such as Fiat and Renault and with foreign firms, for example John Fowler of Leeds (AN AJ 25/96 Labourage à vapeur, 21.03.19). Some of its tractors were lost during the German advance of spring 1918 but it had over 1,500 available in the spring of 1919 (Ford 1919a: 168).

The pattern of motoculture (mechanized cultivation) activity was to be conditioned by many factors, including land quality, the intensity of damage in each locality, the suitability of terrain for mechanized operation, and the presence or absence of hedgerows and other field boundaries. But until hostilities ceased, the changing location of the battle front played a dominant role in determining where motorized ploughing might be attempted (Hitier 1917b: 239). During 1917 some 24,739 ha in the Zone des Armées were ploughed by the Service, with George Ford offering a higher estimate of 32,000 ha (AN AJ 25/125 Renseignements statistiques; Ford 1919a: 168). The detailed location of activity is not known, but groups of tractors certainly operated from Roye, Noyon, Nesles and Albert on the Santerre plateau of Somme *département* (Hitier 1917b: 239). Further north ten teams were working near Arras on land which had been liberated in April 1917 (Leullier 1918: 142). They ploughed across unoccupied territory with no regard for property boundaries and thereby enabled 1,500 ha in this part of Pas-de-Calais to be put down to cereals. Based at Beaumetz-les-Loges they were in full operation early in 1918 but the German offensive of 21 March brought their work to a sudden halt. With the exception of this example, no record has been traced of what the Service accomplished during the final year of the war.

Once the Armistice had been signed the Motoculture directorate was instructed to continue its work on 'safe' land, but also to expand its activities in areas from which explosives and other debris had been removed recently. In other words, the operation of the Service de la Motoculture was partially dependent on successful achievement of work by the STPU (see Chapter 4). Initial ploughing plus one or two harrowings would be undertaken by the Service at no direct and immediate charge to the landowner, although the cost would be calculated and set against that individual's eventual compensation for war damages (see Chapter 8). In determining where the state-owned tractors should operate, priority was given to best-quality land and to localities where terrain and landownership were not too fragmented (Ministère des Régions Libérées 1919a: 9).

Before the outbreak of war mechanized cultivation had already made considerable progress not only in inner parts of the Paris Basin but also on large, commercial holdings on the plains of Aisne and Somme *départements* (Bailly 1937: 183). Tractors and other machines had been imported from the USA, Canada, Britain, Germany and Belgium, as well as being manufactured in France (AN F10 2185 Lesueur, J., Machines agricoles, 1916). In each *département* in the war zone, tractors of the Service de la Motoculture were grouped into units which operated on farms up to 10 km from base. Approximately 2,000 ha of contiguous land was considered, in the early days at least, to be an appropriate surface to merit the displacement of a tractor unit. Hence motorized cultivation proved possible only on large consolidated farms or across groups of neighbouring holdings whose owners had agreed to set up cultivation cooperatives or syndicates to enable their land to be ploughed collectively (Ministère des Régions Libérées 1919a; Ford 1919a: 173). As a consequence, small farms tended to be ignored by the Service. In the early months of peace first ploughing by family farmers was hampered by a severe lack of implements and horses, and the desperate shortage of fodder for those draught animals that were to be found (AN F2 2103 Accambray, L., Mission de contrôle, 1919). Under such circumstances, small and medium-sized farmers insisted that they were able to do no more than a little 'gardening' and complained that they were deprived of financial and material advances to help them restore their land back to productive use. However, around Blérancourt (Aisne) small farmers formed a *syndicat de défense* in a courageous attempt to protect their interests. By contrast with its success on the flat and fertile plains of Picardy, motoculture proved to be of only small significance in *départements* with more fragmented terrain in the eastern part of the war zone, where land values were also substantially lower than those further west (see Chapter 1).

The Pattern of Activity

In the spring of 1919 the Service operated ninety-nine groups of tractors, one-third of which were located in the *département* of Aisne (32), followed closely by Nord (27) (AN AJ 25/51 Bonnefoy-Sibour, A., Rapport sur le fonctionnement du service, 25.04.19). During the first ten months of that year a total of 184,163 ha were worked over by the Service, which in October 1919 possessed 1,643 tractors (AN AJ 25/125 Renseignements statistiques) (Tables 5.1 and 5.2). By far the largest numbers of these machines were in Aisne (514) and Nord (283). The situation changed as more tractors became available and as the pattern of demand between *départements* fluctuated. For example, in March 1919 the Service had operated seventy-five tractors in Pas-de-Calais which had been organized in five units (Peytral 1927: 791). During the summer months six more units were transferred from Nord, bringing the total in Pas-de-Calais to 141 tractors and five motorized ploughs (Conseil-Général du Pas-de-Calais 1919: 255). Despite this increase, the number of machines was not enough and 20,000 ha in the *département* still awaited first ploughing (Peytral 1927: 790). In addition, heavier tractors were needed to cope with the sticky soils of Béthune *arrondissement*, and a special request was forwarded to M. Le

Table 5.1 Motoculture activity (ha)

	1.1.19–30.10.19	1.11.19–31.3.20	1.4.20–1.3.21	Total
Aisne	53,268	24,504	75,908	153,680
Ardennes	8,469	2,583	9,196*	20,248
Marne	11,152	4,420	11,987	27,559
Meurthe-et-Moselle	**			
Meuse	0	104	1,817	1,921
Nord	38,306	7,814	14,357	60,477
Oise	23,515	4,491	8,522	36,528
Pas-de-Calais	10,349	8,402	23,400	42,151
Somme	39,104	8,631	24,422	72,157
Vosges	**			
Total	184,163	60,949	169,609	414,721

*Dissolved 1 January 1921
**Service de la Motoculture not established

Source: AN AJ 25/125 Renseignements statistiques concernant le Service de la Motoculture (01.03.21)

Table 5.2 Motoculture: tractors and tractor groups

	Tractors 15.12.19	Tractors 11.5.20	Groups 11.5.20	Tractors 1.3.21	Groups 1.3.21
Aisne	514	676	52	370	32
Ardennes	190	96	8	*	*
Marne	14	104	8	192	10
Meuse	69	81	9	81	?
Nord	283	264	11	186	3
Oise	130	160	10	135	4
Pas-de-Calais	195	364	26	356	18
Somme	180	315	21	208	15
Total	1,643	2,060	135	1,528	82

*dissolved 1 January 1921

Source: AN 25/1 Rapport au Ministre des Régions Libérées sur l'organisation et le fonctionnement du Service du Matériel Agricole; AN AJ 25/47 Service de la Motoculture, (11.05.20); AN AJ 25/125 Renseignements statistiques concernant le Service de la Motoculture, 1921

Rouzic for such equipment (Conseil-Général du Pas-de-Calais 1919: 256). By mid-1920 the total had risen to 398 tractors organized in twenty-seven units and involved an important repair depot at Arras (Peytral 1927: 790). The total staff of the Service in that *département* stood at 600 (Ibid.: 791).

At the end of 1919 Aisne contained no fewer than 422 petrol-powered tractors (organized in over forty Motoculture units), seventy-five steam ploughs (in fifteen groups of five) and seventy-two motorized ploughs that had been delivered from Germany (AN F2 2100 Rapport du préfet de l'Aisne, 31.11.19) (Figure 5.1). Steam ploughing was no innovation around Soissons and Saint-Quentin, where Fowler steam ploughs and other makes had been in use before the war. Nonetheless, their operation proved difficult in the early months of peace, with trained labour as well as coal being in very limited supply. Likewise the operation of petrol tractors was plagued by shortages of labour, fuel and spare parts. Heavy rain and snow in the winter of 1919–20 made working conditions extremely harsh on sticky claylands, and hence breakdowns and other stoppages were very numerous. Even in the spring of 1920 adequate supplies of petrol were simply not reaching the parts of the *département* where they were needed (AN AJ 25/47 Lettre du Préfet, 13.04.20). By June 1920 the number of tractors owned by the Service in Aisne had risen to 790 but about half of those machines were out of commission at any one time (Saint 1920: 136–37).

Very similar problems were encountered in neighbouring Somme, where in the first half of 1919 farmers had purchased 150 tractors for their individual use and had also acquired an unspecified quantity of agricultural equipment from the British military authorities (La Somme, *JRD*, 15.06.19: 74). Within the *département* the number of tractors belonging to the Service de la Motoculture rose from 180 in December 1919 to 274 early in 1920, which were grouped into twenty-two tractor units (Morain 1920: 14). Ten very heavy and powerful tractors not only consumed large quantities of fuel but were also extremely difficult to manoeuvre on sticky soils. The forty-three motorized ploughs in the *département* were no more satisfactory to operate because of fragmented landownership and the very disturbed state of sections of war-torn farmland that urgently needed to be ploughed. As Prefect Morain noted, smaller and more manoeuvr-

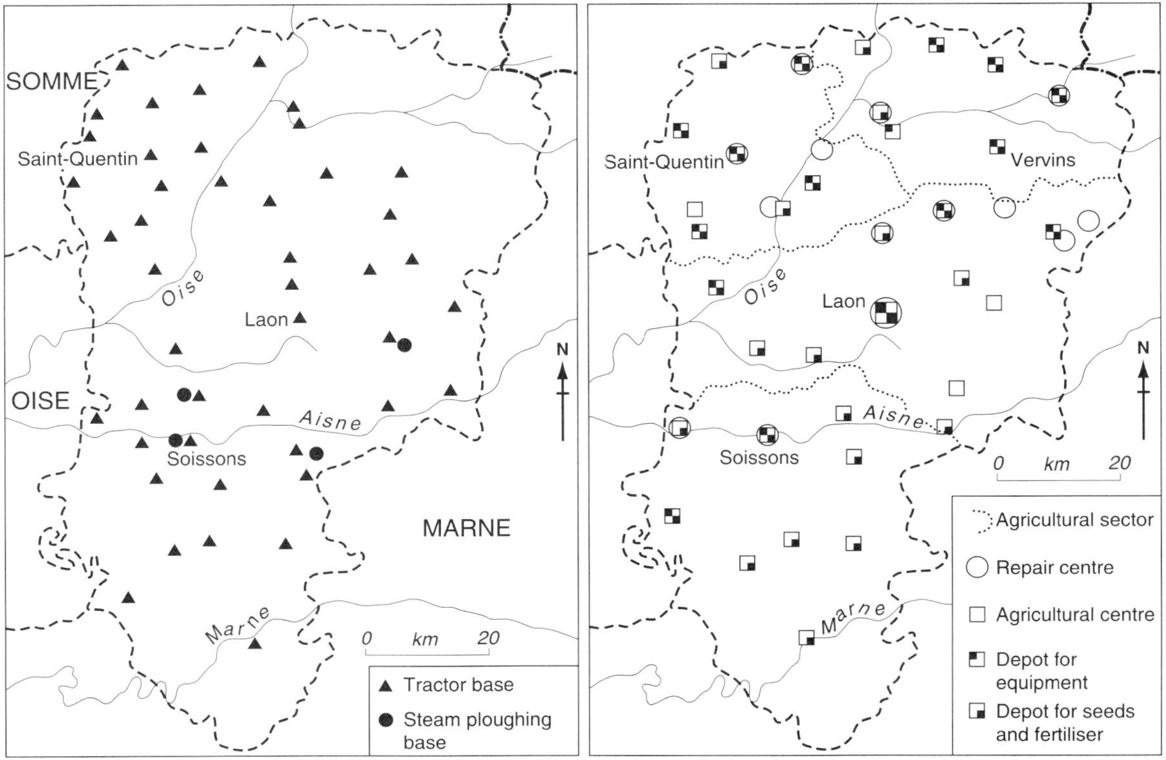

Figure 5.1 Motoculture units and machine repair stations, Aisne

able tractors would have been far more helpful, and he requested that eighty such machines should be supplied (Ibid.). He also made the case for local repair facilities to be improved (for example at Chaulnes) rather than having to depend so much on repair shops in Paris.

Centralization of the Service on the capital inevitably contributed to operational difficulties, as did the need to rely on the STPU for identifying shells and other dangerous objects and summoning experts to deal with them before ploughing could take place (Saint 1920: 137). The usual practice was for grass and weeds to be burned off to help reveal any shells that remained on the surface (Peytral 1927: 790). In order to reduce accidents the chief tractor driver was required to obtain a certificate of *désobusage* (shell clearance) before his workforce might commence ploughing. In addition, an explosives expert had to be in attendance whenever work was undertaken in reputedly dangerous fields. Despite the achievements of the Service in the western half of the war zone, no fewer than 425,000 ha were estimated as being in need of first ploughing in late 1919, even when the supposedly unreclaimable red zone (then believed to be 147,000 ha) had been subtracted from the total (AN AJ 25/1 Action exercée, 15.04.20).

In order to accelerate the pace of restoring land back into cultivation, financial compensation for first ploughing was introduced in November 1919 and special subsidies were made available to encourage individual farmers to purchase their own tractors through approved agents (Sociétés Tiers-Mandataire) (Ibid.) (see Chapter 6). In Somme many of these private machines could not be put into full use because of the triple problem of petrol shortage, lack of spare parts, and the downright incompetence of many drivers. Even in the progressive *département* of Aisne, recruitment and training of staff for motoculture proved to be ongoing problems (AN AJ 25/51 Bonnefoy-Sibour, A., Rapport sur le fonctionnement, 25.04.19). In an attempt to improve operations the administration of the Service was reorganized in November 1919 with general direction passing to the Ministère des Régions Libérées and provision being made for the northern prefects to become more involved in day-to-day matters, but this transition proved to be far from easy and took several months to become effective (Saint 1920: 139).

The Service de la Motoculture worked over a further 60,949 ha during the winter months from November 1919 to the end of March 1920 (AN AJ 25/1 Action exercée, 15.04.20) (Table 5.1). At the latter date the number of tractors in its employ stood at 2,060, grouped into 135 units of which no fewer than 52 were in Aisne (AN AJ 25/47 Service de la Motoculture, 11.05.20) (Table 5.2). Achievements were very slight in *départements* with fragmented terrain, such as Ardennes, and not surprisingly the bulk of activity was concentrated on the rolling farmlands of Aisne where 24,504 ha were ploughed (Hubert 1923: 200). This represented two-fifths of the total worked throughout the war zone during those five winter months. Rates of work slackened because of severe frosts and heavy rain, and many ancillary staff were laid off in order to reduce the wages bill, but experienced drivers were retained and were directed to maintenance work and other jobs (Peytral 1927: 793). The onset of better weather in the spring months of 1920 raised hopes of greater efficiency but petrol shortages continued 'to paralyse' the activities of the Service in the Somme and elsewhere (Morain 1920: 11). Prefect Saint worked to rationalize its operations in Aisne by removing inefficient staff, improving tractor repairs (which he believed would enable the volume of work to be maintained with half as many machines), and ensuring that tractor units were directed to localities where they were especially needed (Saint 1920: 137).

Opposition and Appraisal

Over the eleven months from April 1920 to March 1921 the areas worked over by the Service rose to 169,609 ha and its activities included the provision of help with harvesting (Table 5.1). Unlike achievements on the openfield plateaux of Pas-de-Calais, Somme, and especially Aisne, only quite small areas were worked over by the Service in the enclosed farmlands of Thiérache in Nord *département*. Prefect Naudin reported results in Nord to have been 'feeble' around Avesnes and Valenciennes, where landholding was fragmented, but far more satisfactory around Lille, Douai and Cambrai (Naudin 1920: 50). Results were generally poor in the eastern *départements* of the war zone. For example, in Meuse state-owned tractors were available from the Service Aéronautique de l'Armée and facilities were provided to instruct drivers at Bar-le-Duc but, after unsuccessful attempts at working in hilly country, motoculture was employed in only a limited way across small stretches of relatively flat land in the Woëvre and near Commercy (Magny 1928: 70).

Conditions were no more promising in neighbouring Meurthe-et-Moselle, where many landowners were opposed to the whole idea of a state-run service, preferring tractors to be made available to individual farmers who might wish to purchase them. Indeed, the Service de la Motoculture does not seem to have operated on a formal basis in either Meurthe-et-Moselle or Vosges. Nonetheless, batteries of state-owned tractors had been supplied during 1919 under another scheme to plough devastated farmlands surrounding Nancy and Longuyon (Meurthe-et-Moselle), as well as around Verdun and Saint-Mihiel in Meuse (AN AJ 25/126 Reconstitution agricole, 1919). The absence of official Motoculture activity in these *départements* is confirmed by the information in Table 5.3. This also shows that, at the other extreme, 35.3 per cent of all allowances to *sinistrés* made in kind by the Service between 1918 and the end of 1920 were directed to Aisne and sizeable quantities to both Somme (17.4 per cent) and Nord (15.0 per cent) (AEF 1A 386 Valeurs des avances, 1920).

Table 5.3 Value of advances received by *sinistrés*, via the Service de la Motoculture, 1918–20 (Francs)

	1918	1919	1920	Total	%
Aisne	341,751	3,945,433	7,273,486	11,560,670	35.3
Ardennes	8,740	681,419	987,823	1,677,982	5.1
Marne	38,740	865,920	1,264,613	2,169,273	6.6
Meurthe-et-Moselle	**				
Meuse	**				
Nord	59,111	3,024,215	1,840,740	4,924,066	15.0
Oise	704,079	1,016,170	1,280,624	3,000,873	9.2
Pas-de-Calais	90,767	774,603	2,871,630	3,737,000	11.4
Somme	394,662	2,505,151	2,800,792	5,700,605	17.4
Vosges	**				
Total	1,637,850	12,812,911	18,319,708	32,770,469	100.0

**no information given

Source: AEF 1A 386 Valeurs des avances en nature effectivement reçues par les sinistrés au cours des années successives, 1920

Opposition to the Service de la Motoculture was strong in Oise where *sinistrés* wanted the equipment to be managed by *département* authorities, thereby avoiding complications attributable to the expensive centralized administration in Paris, and to be directed more effectively to the most devastated districts (Le Congrès, *DA*, 02.10.20). Also there was great hostility in Ardennes, where the organization was disbanded as early as 1 January 1921 (Hubert 1923: 200). By that time substantial reductions in the number of state-owned tractors had also occurred in Nord (with the number of tractor units declining from twenty in 1919 to only three in March 1920) and in Aisne. In March 1921 the total stood at 1,528 Motoculture tractors throughout the war-torn zone, with surplus machinery being sold by the state to local farmers (Morain 1923: 31).

With considerable justification, the charge of inefficiency was levelled against the Service. Table 5.4 shows that after a promising period during the first ten months of 1919 Motoculture activity slumped from working on 18,417 ha per month to only 12,189 ha per month during the subsequent five harsh winter months from 1 November 1919 to 31 March 1920. In the

Table 5.4 Motoculture: monthly rates of activity (ha)

	1.1.19–30.10.19	1.11.19–31.3.20	1.4.20–1.3.21	Overall average	Tractors 1921	Work/tractor/month
Aisne	5,327	4,900	6,900	5,911	370	18.6
Ardennes	847	517	1,022	844*	96	10.6
Marne	1,115	884	1,090	1,060	192	5.7
Meurthe-et-Moselle	**	**	**	**	**	**
Meuse	0	21	165	120	81	2.0
Nord	3,831	1,563	1,305	2,326	186	7.0
Oise	2,352	898	775	1,405	135	5.7
Pas-de-Calais	1,035	1,680	2,217	1,621	356	6.0
Somme	3,910	1,726	2,220	2,775	208	10.7
Vosges	**	**	**	**	**	**
Total	18,417	12,189	15,604	16,062	1,624	9.5

*dissolved 1 January 1921
**no information given

Source: AN AJ/25 125 Renseignements statistiques concernant le Service de la Motoculture, 1921 following eleven months activity recovered to an average of 15,604 ha per month. The greatest quantity of work was accomplished in Aisne during each of the three periods and conditions were also promising in Somme, Nord and Oise during 1919 but then achievement slackened. By contrast, motoculture activity in Pas-de-Calais had started at a low level during 1919 but then grew in importance. Ploughing accounted for over two-thirds of the total surface worked over by the Service de la Motoculture, with harrowing, other surface work, and harvesting representing the remainder (Table 5.5, Figure 5.2).

When expressed in terms of mean area worked per month it is not difficult to appreciate why the Service was held in such ill repute, but unfortunately there is no way of knowing how many tractors were out of operation at any one time. In the eleven months following March 1920 notional activity rates ranged between 5.7 ha and 7.0 ha per machine in Marne, Oise, Pas-de-Calais and Nord, slumping to a miserable 2.0 ha in Meuse but rising to 10.7 ha in Somme and 18.6 ha in Aisne (Table 5.4). If the assumption were made that about half of all tractors were out of action these values would, of course, be doubled. Despite continuing problems of labour, fuel and spare parts, such a poor

Table 5.5 Surfaces worked by the Service de la Motoculture, 1919–21

	Surface ha	Ploughing %	Other surface work %	Harrowing %	Harvesting %
Aisne	153,680	64.6	18.6	7.8	9.0
Ardennes	20,248	69.4	22.2	0.0	8.4
Marne	27,559	76.9	13.2	0.1	9.8
Meurthe-et-Moselle	**				
Meuse	1,921	73.0	27.0	0.0	0.0
Nord	60,477	79.5	12.7	7.8	0.0
Oise	36,528	59.5	20.4	8.8	11.3
Pas-de-Calais	42,151	80.7	14.2	0.0	5.1
Somme	72,157	66.1	13.5	10.4	10.0
Vosges	**				
Total	414,721	69.3	16.4	6.6	7.6

**no information given

Source: AN AJ 25/125 Renseignements statistiques concernant le Service de la Motoculture, 1921

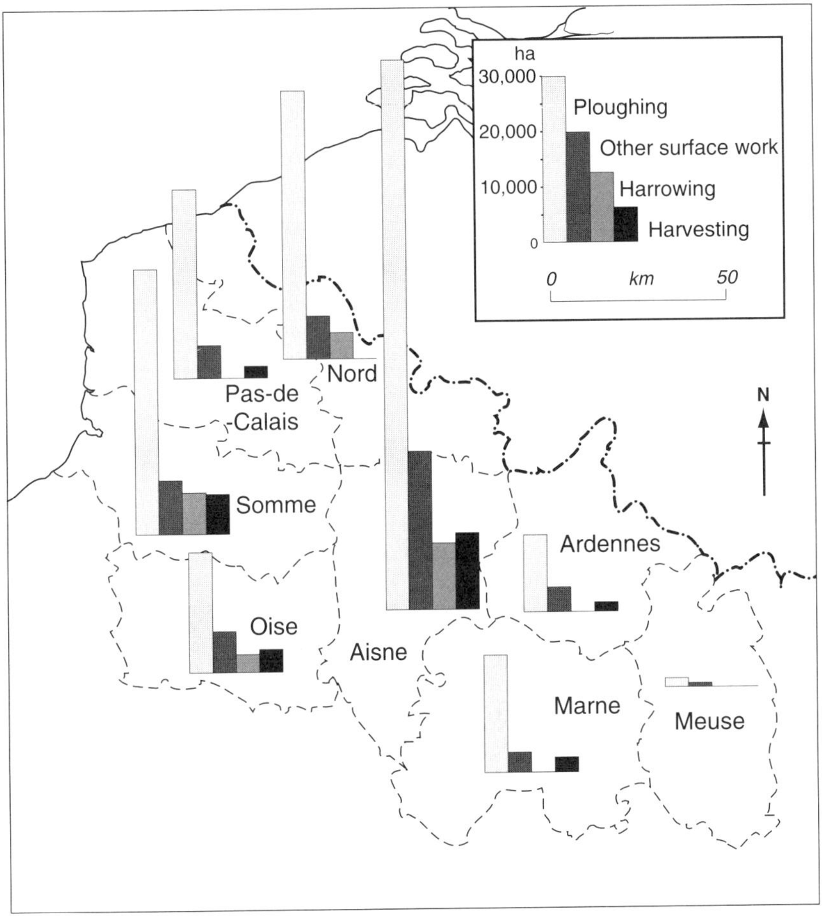

Figure 5.2 Motoculture activity, January 1919 to March 1921

record provided ample ammunition for opponents who argued that the Service should be terminated and the machinery be made available to cooperatives or sold to individual farmers. Several attempts were made to do just this in Pas-de-Calais but to no avail (Peytral 1927: 794).

Early in 1920 the Confédération Générale des Associations Agricoles des Régions Dévastées demanded that the Service be closed down, alleging that 449 tractors in Aisne had worked an average of only 30 ha apiece during 1919 (AN AJ 25/127 Bertrand, F., La main d'oeuvre, 1919; Réclamations des agriculteurs, *JAP*, 1920: 88). Prefect Saint was not much more complimentary, stressing diplomatically that since only a portion of the tractor units in his *département* had 'fulfilled their mission' the overall achievements of the Service de la Motoculture could be described as no better than 'satisfactory' (Saint 1920: 136). The very high cost of the whole venture was stressed in Pas-de-Calais and in Meuse, where motorized ploughing of all kinds had 'not given the expected results [since] the price was too high and landownership too fragmented' (Tribondeau 1927: 125; Magny 1928: 70).

On 26 May 1921 the decision was taken by the government to terminate the Service throughout the northern *départements* at the start of June (Peytral 1927: 794). However, since much land still required first ploughing, it was allowed to operate in a limited way until the end of the year, when all remaining members of its labour force were released (Comité d'Action des Régions Dévastées 1925: 158). For example, in Pas-de-Calais equipment was being sold to *sinistrés* from July 1921 onwards, and in the last quarter of the year the Service had been reduced to just forty-five tractors which worked three of the least favoured areas in the *département* (Causel 1922: 21). The final date for disposing of those machines was fixed at 31 May 1922. Motoculture activities in Somme were terminated in a similar way to the dismay of Prefect Morain, who would have preferred the Service to survive somewhat longer so that it could plough additional land which had formerly been classified as belonging to the red zone (Morain 1922a: 15). In full recognition of the impressive pace of agricultural recovery across much of Santerre and Vermandois, he had already directed tractor services to the seriously devastated *cantons* of Péronne, Chaulnes, Albert and Combles, where he insisted 'agricultural reconstitution would have been impossible' without them (Morain 1921: 17; 1920: 11). He concluded that, despite inefficiencies, motoculture had proved 'extremely useful' in his *département* and had enabled work to be undertaken that was far beyond the capabilities of individual farmers (Morain 1922a: 15).

In the adjacent *département* of Pas-de-Calais Prefect Peytral argued that 'without it, vast stretches would remain uncultivated since ordinary ploughs and ploughteams would not have been able to work across badly levelled shell-holes with soil that was far from stable, and areas containing fragments of barbed wire and other debris could not have been tackled by ordinary ploughmen with horses' (Peytral 1927: 790). In the autumn of 1921 many *sinistrés* and mayors in Somme and Pas-de-Calais voiced the opinion that the Service was being disbanded too soon since plenty of first ploughing still needed to be done (Hénard 1921a: 1; Peytral 1927: 790). By the end of the year 37,700 ha had been worked over by the Service in Pas-de-Calais and it had also helped with harvesting over several thousand hectares (Tribondeau 1937: 124). Many critics changed their appraisal of the Service once they themselves were faced with undertaking the task of first ploughing, and Prefect Morain remarked solemnly that complaints frequently gave way to regrets (Morain 1923: 31). Arguably, much of the earlier opposition had been voiced by farmers who failed the comprehend the numerous difficulties with which the Service had to contend (Tribondeau 1937: 122).

6
The Office de Reconstitution Agricole

Broad Objectives

The Office de Reconstitution Agricole (ORA) was created by legislation of 3 August 1917 with the broad aim to help promote agricultural recovery in the northern *départements* where sections of land became available for re-occupation in response to the shifting location of hostilities (Bros 1924: 46; Illaire 1991: 107). After just a couple of months its management was reorganized and placed under a council which comprised representatives from a variety of agricultural associations (MacDonald 1922: 155). As has been noted, the return of farmers to their ravaged land during wartime gave rise to numerous administrative problems and social frustrations which many people in the devastated areas feared would be repeated in a more substantial way once peace was restored (AN F12 8030 Warren, De. E., Note sur la remise en culture, 24.01.18). Confusion reigned over the precise responsibilities of prefects, sub-prefects and directors of agricultural services, all of whom were overworked and had to cope with new tasks such as allocating foodstuffs and petrol to returning farmers. Despite initial goodwill, liaison between civilian and military authorities was often lacking. Edouard De Warren believed that too many non-producers had been allowed to return to the newly liberated districts and that 'their idleness and wretched trades demoralized well-intentioned local people' (Ibid.). By contrast, some farmers who were desperately keen to bring their land back into cultivation were denied official authorization to return to their home locality.

The state placed great faith in the ORA, which was charged with collecting, repairing and distributing farm machinery and was also given the responsibility for obtaining and distributing seeds, fertilizers and livestock which were vital if devastated land were to be re-cultivated (Saint 1920: 132). An initial budget of 300,000,000 F was allocated and this was to be raised to 400,000,000 F in June 1919 (AN AJ 25/1 Guerin, R., Rapport, 21.03.20). In October 1917 inventories were prepared which listed the various commodities that were needed, but supplies only started to arrive four months later. This process occurred much more slowly than had been hoped since manufacture of equipment needed for warfare took precedence over producing farm machinery (Lebrun 1918: 492). A central depot was planned for the ORA at Le Bourget immediately north of Paris, where appropriate rail links would be readily available. Practical aspects of distribution in each *département* were to be undertaken by approved agents (Sociétés Tiers-Mandataire) (La reconstitution, *ASA*, 1919: 209). The ORA was also given the responsibility of spreading information to assist the agricultural recovery of liberated areas and, in particular, to encourage cooperatives and other agricultural associations as a means of boosting food production (AN AJ 25/3 Richard, M., Délibérations du Conseil, 18.10.17). At the first weekly meeting of the reorganized administrative council of the ORA (18 October 1917) attention was drawn to the availability of supplies of agricultural machinery at Vierzon, Niort, Châtellerault and other provincial towns far to the south of the battle areas (Ibid.). Successive meetings of council were largely concerned with arranging for particular machines to be dispatched from suppliers to liberated destinations on the fringe of the war zone.

The ORA sought to encourage northern farmers to return to their land as soon as possible and to provide them with prisoner-of-war or military labour (Ford 1919b: 225). These objectives proved over-optimistic, at least during the early months of its existence. Labour remained in short supply, draught animals were almost unobtainable, and supplies of oats and fodder were required by the allied armies to feed their horses and were thus not available to the ORA. Given these difficulties, the importance of agricultural mechanization became all the greater. Despite these profound problems, the ORA did manage to accomplish some notable achievements during its first eight months of existence, but at least part of this was managed by bringing several existing organizations under its supervision.

Cooperatives, Equipment and Distribution

The first of these was the Service de Propagande pour la Création des Coopératives de Culture under the direction of Capitaine De Warren, who had established agricultural cooperatives in Tunisia before the war and was responsible for founding over a dozen farming associations in northern France before the ORA was inaugurated (Sagnier 1917a: 322). Cultivation by each cooperative was organized according to a common plan but farmers retained ownership of their plots and were at liberty to work them individually if they so wished, provided that their activities conformed to the cooperative's overall scheme (AN F12 8030 Warren, De. E., Note sur la remise en culture, 24.01.18). The Service de Propagande was made responsible to the ORA in November 1917 following the decision of M. Clementel, Ministre d'Agriculture (AN AJ 25/3 Le Seigneur, J., Rapport des activités, 24.04.18). Edouard De Warren had to work against the 'intense individualism and independent temperament' of many northern farmers which made any kind of cooperation very difficult (MacDonald 1922: 153). He insisted that cultivation cooperatives were essential if the nation's dependence on imported foodstuffs were to be controlled. The need for reducing imports was unquestionably great, since toward the end of 1917 3,500,000 qx of wheat and 500,000 qx of oats were being sent across the Atlantic to France each month (AN F12 8030 Warren, De. E., Note sur la remise en culture, 24.01.18). Many farmers who returned to the liberated fringes of the battle zone soon became discouraged and talked of leaving their land once again. Voluntary cooperation among farmers, De Warren insisted, might be the only way of re-introducing a sense of community to farming settlements whose fabric had been devastated by the events of war. Put rather grandly, it was his wish that 'the association will become the protector and the servant of all private initiatives for agricultural recovery' (Ibid.).

By mid-January 1918 a dozen groups of farm cooperatives had been formed by the Service de Propagande, involving farmers in eight-five *communes*, especially in Somme (41) and Pas-de-Calais (24) but also in Aisne, Marne and Oise (Ibid.). Two months later this Mission des Associations Agricoles had promoted the creation of no fewer than 120 farm cooperatives whose membership reached almost 8,000, and had started to cultivate over 40,000 ha at various points along the liberated fringe of the devastated *départements* (AN AJ 25/1 Programme d'action, 19.07.18; Ford 1919b: 225). Abandoned farm equipment had been collected, repaired and redistributed, with some cooperatives being assisted by overseas voluntary organizations such as the CARD which was based at Blérancourt (Héricault 1934: 25). In De Warren's words, each cooperative was like an 'oasis [in the] desert of these ravaged areas' and its members were the 'real pioneers of agricultural recovery' (AN F12 8030 Warren, De. E., Note sur la remise en culture, 24.01.18). He continued optimistically, anticipating that 'little by little each village or each group of *communes* will have its farming cooperative. But it is not enough to establish cooperatives; they must be helped to survive and overcome the thousand difficulties against which they struggle' (Ibid.).

In such hard circumstances, with so many farmers mobilized or transported behind enemy lines, there is some evidence that traditional individualism seemed to wane, if only for a while (Héricault 1934: 23). Money and agricultural labour were in desperately short supply and the notion of cooperation appeared to offer at least a temporary solution for the many farming women who remained in charge of their family holdings. In this way, remarkable progress in wheat planting during 1917 was reported on the plateau of Santerre (Somme), where members of cooperatives had risked life and limb as they worked land within range of enemy fire (Berthault 1918: 153). Unfortunately, most of their efforts were erased by the German advance in the spring of 1918. Some farmers managed to evacuate livestock and equipment from the plateau but their land and buildings were exposed to devastation once again. Subsequently, De Warren, nicknamed 'the apostle of the cooperatives', tried to reorganize them on holdings in the interior of France and to ensure that his Mission should provide them with implements, machinery and animals so that they might restart operations 'in exile' until their home areas became available for cultivation once again (Ford 1919b: 225).

After the Armistice, cultivation cooperatives were re-formed and benefited from labour supplied by the STPU (and later the STE) for clearing land and for other emergency tasks, since finding and keeping a suitable workforce often proved difficult

(Moreau-Bérillon 1921: 135). Equipment, seeds and animals were obtained either from Sociétés Tiers-Mandataire (which will be discussed below) or from commercial suppliers. In Aisne, De Warren delegated a young officer called Frédéric Jacquemart to persuade farmers around Laon to group together to work their land and to defend their compensation claims, thereby laying the foundations of the Union des Syndicats Agricoles de l'Aisne (Petit 1986: 65). Further to the east, in Marne, the mayor of Witry-les-Reims gave his energetic support to agricultural cooperation, which led to requests for plot consolidation *(remembrement)* and the eventual reduction in the number of plots of farmland in his *commune* from 6,262 to 1,320 (Moreau-Bérillon 1921: 135) (see Chapter 10). However, such enthusiasm was rare and some cooperatives were dissolved very soon after the Armistice, partly because of poor administration and inadequate staffing, but also because *sinistrés* wished to return to working their land in their own individual way. Other difficulties included absentees, large landowners who were often unwilling to provide labour commensurate with the size of their holdings, and the fact that *sinistrés* devoted excessive amounts of time to their private plots that were not worked in a cooperative way (Ibid.: 137). Once the chaotic revival of 1918–19 had passed, it proved very unlikely that additional cooperatives would be set up for working the land.

The second organization that came under the supervision of the ORA was the Service du Matériel Agricole which was charged with obtaining necessary machinery and equipment for recultivation to take place in safe locations in the devastated *départements* and with promoting agricultural mechanization in general (AN AJ 25/1 Rapport au Ministre des Régions Libérées). Large farms in many sections of northern France had suffered shortages of agricultural labour for many years before the war and had recourse to imported machinery from the USA, Canada, Britain, Germany and Belgium (Klatzmann 1955: 408–45; AN F10 2185 Lesueur, J., Machines agricoles, 1916). It was argued by M. Ringelmann, professor at the Institut Agronomique in Paris, that mechanization was vital to maximize cereal production during wartime and would be essential to facilitate agricultural recovery in northern France when peace was restored (Ibid.). In 1916 the exiled prefect of Ardennes obtained the promise of a government grant for new farm equipment in his *département* for use at the end of the war, and other prefects attempted to estimate the likely needs among their farmers for agricultural machinery. Faced with this mounting demand, the Ministre d'Agriculture, Jules Méline, had established a commission to supply agricultural equipment to northern France and had begun to investigate the volume of demand in each *département* and the location of possible sources of supply. A start was made on delivering machines to *départements*, *communes* and to agricultural societies, taking advantage of a subvention which equalled half the purchase price. During May 1917 local authorities and agricultural societies were authorized to sell tractors to individual farmers in the northern *départements* on condition that each beneficiary would undertake to plant at least 50 ha of wheat or 100 ha of other cereals during the following year (MacDonald 1922: 154). In July 1917 prefects were instructed to advance sums of cash to northern farmers in relation to the area capable of cultivation that each possessed (Ibid.: 155). When the ORA was created in the summer of 1917, this commission was taken under its wing.

By March 1918 the ORA had managed to obtain 50,000,000 F worth of farm equipment and 1,400,000 F worth of seed and fertilizer, some of which had reached northern farmers successfully (AN AJ 25/3 Le Seigneur, J., Rapport des activités, 25.04.18). Regional depots had been opened at Ham, Noyon, Nesle and Beaumetz-les-Loges and, by agreement with the Ministère de Guerre, the ORA was operating two types of centre in the northern *départements* for the recovery and repair of farm equipment. So-called military centres were sited in the shadow of the front line and were staffed by army personnel, while civilian centres were managed at greater distance from the front by members of the local agricultural service and other civilian employees. The most notable repair centres were at Péronne, Villers-Saint-Christophe, Blérancourt and especially Arras, where part of the military citadel had been transformed into a vast repair works for thousands of agricultural implements (Sagnier 1917a: 471).

Finally, the ORA worked with special agencies (Sociétés Tiers-Mandataire) in the northern *départements* which were charged with distributing seeds, fertilizers, machinery and livestock to farmers along the liberated fringe. Some of these were already operating in March 1918 and others were on the point of doing so. Much positive achievement could be recorded, but the ORA was very aware that 'the situation will remain precarious for as long as the war lasts' (AN AJ 25/1 La reconstitution agricole, 1918). The German offensive of spring 1918 undid all these initiatives and many recently re-installed farmers, operating as individuals or in cooperatives, were obliged to leave their properties once again, often at only a few hours' notice (AN AJ 25/3 Le Seigneur, J., Rapport des activités, 25.04.18). Many carried nothing with them; others took horses and cattle but in so doing ran the risk of retarding their flight from the invading forces. M. Le Seigneur, Secrétaire-Général of the ORA, received hundreds of letters which described this exodus in 'the most distressing details' but also testified to the farmers' 'courage, their wish to stay as close as possible to their home village and their confidence in a prompt return' (Ibid.). Most of the ORA's depots and equipment centres fell subsequently into enemy hands and, despite efforts to move as much as possible, equipment valued at 125,000 F had to be left behind, together with seed and fertilizer worth 700,000 F. ORA establishments at Beaumetz-les-Loges, Arras and Blérancourt were not overrun but were located so close to the line of fire that they had to be evacuated.

Revised Priorities

Under these harsh circumstances in the spring of 1918, the ORA established a new set of priorities (Ibid.).

- (i) It sought to direct evacuated farmers to vacant holdings beyond the invaded zone and to provide them with equipment, livestock and other goods so that they might commence farming, albeit on a temporary basis. In due course, the value of these materials would be deducted from each family's allocation of war damages (see Chapter 8).
- (ii) The Mission des Associations Agricoles was deemed to have a particular role to play in these harsh conditions, with efforts being made to regroup evacuated farmers alongside neighbours from their home village.
- (iii) The ORA would organize the recovery and stockpiling of

farm equipment that had been abandoned in freshly evacuated *communes*.

(iv) The location of depots had to be rethought, with a main site being sought beyond the Seine in preference to Le Bourget. Places were considered as far south as La Chapelle-Saint Ursin (Cher) adjacent to the railway between Bourges and Montluçon.

The urgent needs of northern farmers, coupled with the fact that legislation for the payment of war damages had not yet been passed, required substantial credit to be extended in those sections of the devastated *départements* that remained safe to cultivate. For example, on 8 February 1918 advances to agricultural societies were authorized according to a sliding scale (200,000 F if the society covered a *canton*, 400,000 F if it covered an *arrondissement*, and 800,000 F if its activities extended across a *département*) (MacDonald 1922: 155). Further arrangements of his kind were to be made in the future.

The loss of additional productive farmland during the spring offensive led to the passage of special legislation (4 May 1918) to encourage cultivation of abandoned farmland, both in the interior of France and in safe *communes* located relatively close to the battle front (AN AJ 25/127 Instructions, actes officiels, 1918). Abandoned land might be requisitioned if owners were unwilling to assist the war effort; supplies of fertilizer and seed would be provided by the state; and interest-free loans would be made available. A sum of 100,000,000 F was allocated to help farmers and evacuees, whether operating as individuals or as members of agricultural associations. Up to 250 F would be loaned for every hectare brought back into cultivation and up to 1,000 F/ha was available where complete holdings were being returned to productive use. These rates could be doubled in the case of evacuees. This system of loans continued to function until after the Armistice had been signed.

During the first twelve months of operation 1,617 loans were allocated, totalling 57,204,586 F and involving undertakings to cultivate 101,644 ha (AN AJ 25/125 Ricard, J.H., Rapport sur l'application, 18.06.20). Individual loans averaged 35,300 F apiece and involved 62 ha being recultivated. The regulations were duly revised on 22 August 1919 in order to assist farm cooperatives and farmers who had been demobilized. Between mid-May and the end of 1919 a further 1,046 loans were granted, amounting to 27,379,568 F and relating to 37,218 ha. During this period the average loan was 26,100 F and involved only 35 ha. Of the 3,168 borrowers, 1,450 were refugees or farmers in the war-torn *départements* and they received two-thirds of the total sum allocated. The four largest areas that were to be restored to cultivation were in the liberated *départements* of Aisne (18,000 ha), Ardennes (10,794 ha) and Oise (10,282 ha), together with the neighbouring *département* of Seine-et-Marne (10,455ha) which had been invaded briefly during 1914 (Ibid.).

The question of providing farm equipment to assist recultivation was tackled by the ORA in three ways: collection, repair and sale of abandoned equipment; ordering of new items; and receipt of equipment from Germany. The Service du Matériel Agricole placed orders with agricultural engineering firms and with companies that had manufactured military equipment during the war (AN AJ 25/1 Rapport au Ministre). In addition, military arsenals turned part of their productive capacity to making farm equipment. The Service advised on which models of machine had proved especially satisfactory and even recommended copying some German equipment 'in order to avoid, as much as possible, being reliant on our enemies in the future' (Ibid.). During the war French agricultural experts had visited North America to discover what kinds of farm machinery might be available for purchase. For example, Jacques Lesueur (*ingénieur agronome*) had spent the winter of 1915–16 visiting agricultural engineering works in the USA and lodged a formal report with the Ministère de l'Agriculture on his return (AN F10 2185 Lesueur, J., Machines agricoles, 1916). Once peace was restored, orders were placed in the USA and Canada for the supply of 13,000 reapers/binders and 10,000 mowing machines (AN AJ 25/1 Action exercée, 15.04.20). These pieces of equipment were judged to be of high quality by French standards but the cost of shipping them across the Atlantic inflated their price alarmingly. Slowness of delivery provided another irritant to French farmers who were impatient to start working their land without further delay.

Faced with such problems, the ORA opened additional repair centres in each liberated *département*. Wherever possible, these centres were placed under the direction of *ingénieurs agronomes* who were charged with organizing the collection and repair of abandoned farm equipment, either by using their own staff or by enlisting the help of local engineering firms. In due course, a third objective was added to the remit of the repair centres, namely to assemble harvest machinery that was needed desperately for the summer of 1919 as well as various types of new machine that were shipped over in knocked-down form in crates. This equipment would eventually be distributed through the Sociétés Tiers-Mandataire.

Shortages of raw materials and severe transport difficulties gave rise to a 'double crisis' which greatly hindered the activities of the ORA during the spring of 1919 (AN AJ 25/127 Office de Reconstitution Agricole, 25.03.19). Important contracts were not being met and provision of ploughs was particularly deficient. The only solutions were to supplement purchases by repairing items that had been abandoned by French farmers or by the enemy, and to bring back machinery that had been carried off to Germany. In fact, by 4 July 1919 about 27,000 agricultural machines of various kinds had been returned to French soil from Germany and were being distributed to farmers in the northern *départements* (Ford 1919a: 172). Furthermore, the conversion of motorized ploughs left behind by the Germans allowed some of the shortfall in conventional ploughs to be overcome (AN AJ 25/127 Office de Reconstitution Agricole, 25.03.19). Not surprisingly, tractors were being requested from the ORA 'in ever growing numbers each day' (Ibid.). For example, in Nord 700 wagon-loads of agricultural equipment were recovered during the second half of 1919, coming from many parts of the *département*, from adjacent areas in Belgium, and even from Germany (Morain 1923: 36). The material was collected at Lille, Douai and Cambrai prior to sorting and dispatch to eleven repair shops. The unit at Lille was by far the most important of these, involving 150 civilian workers and up to 200 prisoners of war who unloaded material that had been recovered and helped unpack new equipment (Conseil Général du Nord 1919: 22).

Unfortunately, operations were not always undertaken efficiently and Guerin argued that some collection stations were not being managed with sufficient diligence (AN AJ 25/1 Guerin, R., Rapport, 21.03.20). Equipment collected from the fields was often dumped in heaps without inventories being prepared, and pilfering from the unguarded piles of rusting but potentially useful ironwork was rife. The administrative council of the ORA had noted serious problems in finding competent directors and personnel to work at its repair centres. It attributed these difficulties mainly to the low pay that was offered and to living conditions in the northern *départements* (AN AJ 25/4 Office de Reconstitution Agricole, 25.09.19). Local directors were allowed considerable flexibility in managing repair work (AN AJ 25/1 Guerin, R., Rapport, 21.03.20). In some *départements* most activity was undertaken by the ORA's own staff (Nord, Pas-de-Calais, Marne, Ardennes), while in Somme and Meurthe-et-Moselle it was largely entrusted to private contractors (Figure 6.1). In the remaining *départements* work was shared between the two systems (AN AJ 25/1 Action exercée, 15.04.20). Guerin noted that the cost of undertaking repairs at state-run centres (as in Nord) was greater than in private engineering works (for example in Meurthe-et-Moselle) (AN AJ 25/1 Guerin, R., Rapport, 21.03.20).

By December 1919 thirty state-operated repair shops throughout the northern *départements* had restored some 45,000 pieces of agricultural equipment, to which should be added an unspecified amount repaired in fifty-two private or semi-private establishments (MacDonald 1922: 161). The 45,000 items were valued at 6,526,280 F and were duly sent to authorized agents (Sociétés Tiers-Mandataire) for sale to farmers (AN AJ 25/1 Action exercée, 15.04.20). The thirty repair shops also assembled 6,431 mowing machines, 4,915 harvesting machines, and a large variety of American ploughs, seed drills, weeding tools, rollers and other equipment. Some repair shops even operated their own foundries to manufacture wheels for ploughs and to make a range of basic parts. Other centres converted pieces of military equipment that had been abandoned by German and American forces for subsequent agricultural use. Despite their shortcomings, the repair centres provided an essential emergency service in northern France at a time when the transport system was still under repair and many private industrial plants were very far from recovery.

In favoured sections of the war-torn zone the state-run Service de la Motoculture was able to undertake first ploughing (see Chapter 5) but at this time, when labour and draught animals

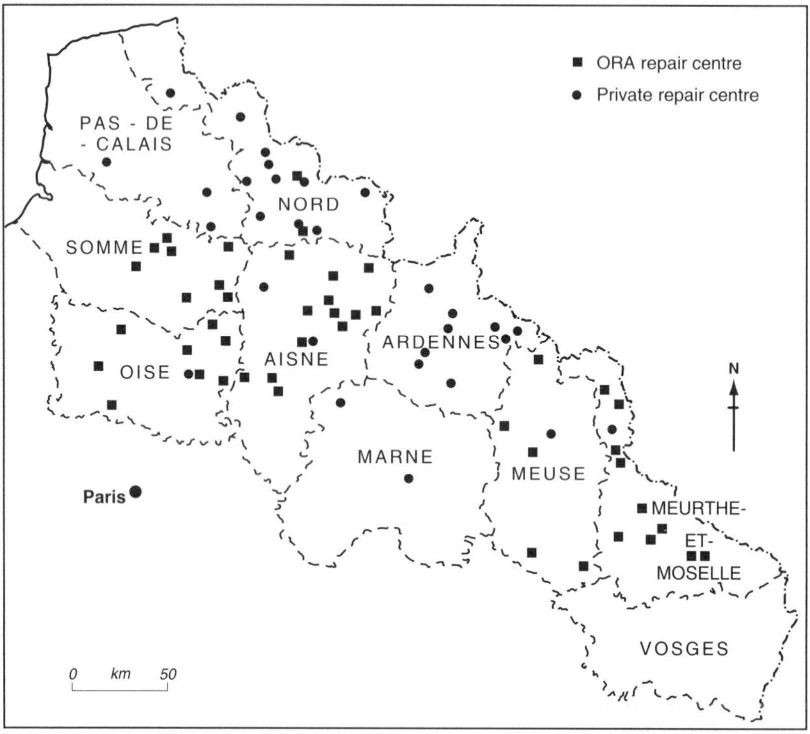

Figure 6.1 Repair centres in the northern *départements*, 1920

were in short supply, some returnees needed to acquire their own tractors if they were to continue to work their land. The ORA, acting on their behalf, purchased machines in bulk and the Sociétés Tiers-Mandataire made them available for down payment of approximately half the normal price, with the remainder of the sum being set against war damages that were being claimed by individual *sinistrés* (Ibid.). By mid-1919 880 tractors had been bought through government agencies, 120 of which had been purchased by farmers in Somme (Ford 1919a: 173). By the early summer of 1920 the ORA had received 13,500 reapers/binders and 9,960 mowing machines from North America, together with 5,000 mowing machines of French manufacture, and had made them available to northern farmers through the official agents (AN AJ 25/47 Ogier, M., Lettre à l'Académie, 24.06.20). By far the largest numbers of these machines were distributed to farmers in Nord (2,000 and 3,130 respectively) and Aisne (1,640 and 2,620).

In addition, the ORA was responsible for receiving farm equipment from Germany, as agreed in accordance with the Armistice protocol of 16 January 1919 (AN AJ 25/1 Action exercée, 15.04.20). Unfortunately the first batches of German machinery were so unsatisfactory that French farmers refused to accept them. Some pieces of equipment were of poor quality, others were very different from what local farmers had used before. For example, farmers in Ardennes judged them to be of the wrong weight, and cultivators in Aisne complained that German ploughs were too large for them to use, arguing that no thought had been given to how spare parts might be obtained (Berenguer 1984: 56; Aisne, *JRD*, 25.05.19: 23). In response to these difficulties, the ORA negotiated for early supplies to be replaced by equipment that had been manufactured according to its own specifications and was due for delivery before 1 June 1920. The first deliveries were deemed to be 'susceptible of giving satisfaction' to northern farmers (AN AJ 25/1 Action exercée, 15.04.20). Not surprisingly, demand for tractors and other farm machinery outstripped supply at this time when very little agricultural labour was available in the liberated *départements*. The situation was not eased by what were seen as 'outrageous formalities' which hindered farmers seeking to obtain financial assistance from the state for purchasing their own machines (AEF 1A 386 La question des subventions, 03.10.20).

Livestock for Northern Farmers

Another major task of the ORA was to oversee the provision of livestock to northern farmers who had suffered serious losses during the war. For example, Prefect Peytral reported that 50,000 cattle, 35,000 horses and 27,800 sheep had been removed from Pas-de-Calais by the Germans (Peytral 1927: 799). As shown in Chapter 2, estimates varied of the total numbers of farm animals missing from the ten *départements* at the time of the Armistice. For example, the Ministère des Régions Libérées quoted the loss of 523,000 cattle, 367,000 horses and 469,000 sheep and goats, while André Tardieu estimated a surprisingly close total of 1,360,000 head of livestock having been 'carried off' (AN AJ

25/125 Animaux enlevés, 17.07.20; Tardieu 1921: 377). Four main sources were available to assist restocking. These comprised horses that were released from military use; recovered livestock that had been removed by the Germans to Belgium or Germany, or had been evacuated to the interior of France; supplies that might be purchased from other parts of France or from Algeria; and livestock imported from other countries (AN AJ 25/1 Action exercée, 15.04.20; AN AJ 25/125 Etat du bétail, 15.06.20).

In the first category, some 15,000 horses had been released by the French forces for use by farmers at the start of December 1918 (Ford 1919b: 226). During the next twelve months a further 165,500 horses were made available from the French (75,000), British (55,500) and American (35,000) armies. Initially some of these animals were supplied on loan, with the armies reserving the right to recall them should future military necessity require (Hubert 1923: 207). Eventually they were allocated to farmers on a permanent basis and were set against future compensation payments. Their quality was very variable and some of those delivered in Nord were declared to be very poor, even suffering from scabies (Morain 1923: 37). Despite the willing assistance of Belgian officials it was not surprising that it proved very difficult to identify exactly which animals had been driven by the Germans across the border and were liable to be returned. Similar problems in identifying and attempting to recover livestock were encountered in northern Lorraine where farm animals had been placed behind German lines for the duration of the war (MacDonald 1922: 159).

In 1919 an urgent start was made on recovering livestock that had been seized by the German occupiers for delivery back to France, but activity during 1919 and the first half of 1920 resulted in the return of only 8,000 cattle and 1,500 horses, mainly to Nord and Aisne (Hubert 1923: 505). These small deliveries provoked discontent among *sinistrés*, who complained that cattle had been returned to the northern *pays* of Thiérache but little had been done to satisfy the needs of farmers elsewhere in Aisne (Aisne, *JRD*, 25.05.19: 23). As well as losses to Germany and Belgium, pure-blooded livestock had been evacuated to the interior of France when the Germans advanced in the spring of 1918 and also had to be recovered. During 1919 10,375 head of cattle and 2,676 sheep were duly returned to their owners

(MacDonald 1922: 159). In addition, small numbers of cattle were purchased in France (12,000) and Algeria (1,750) during that year to supply northern farmers, but shortage of fodder in the northern *départements* hampered these early efforts.

Replenishment of the stock of sheep from distant sources proved particularly complicated, partly because of uncertainty about which breeds would prove appropriate to the pastoral resources of northern France. Despite high freight costs, 22,796 sheep were brought over from Algeria in the summer of 1919, but lack of suitable fodder in northern France led to many being butchered before they reached their intended destinations in the war-torn zone. In April 1919 the ORA had signed contracts with Luxembourg to import 6,000 head of cattle, and similar agreements were made with Switzerland (4,000), the Netherlands (7,000), and the USA (10,700) (AN AJ 25/127 Boret, V., Observations, 23.05.19). In fact, 6,128 cattle were purchased from Luxembourg at an average cost of 1,100 F per head for distribution among farmers in five *départements* of north-eastern France (MacDonald 1922: 158). In May and June 1919 7,261 cattle were imported from Switzerland for the same destinations. During the next two months 6,997 head were purchased in the Netherlands and were allocated this time to western parts of the devastated zone. American cattle started to arrive in mid-August and during the following eight weeks 7,912 were sent to Ardennes, Nord and Meurthe-et-Moselle. A case had been made for elaborate health checks on these trans-Atlantic imports but, in practice, transportation proved very difficult and farmers in the northern *départements* found these animals to be not very satisfactory (AN AJ 25/127 Boret, V., Observations, 1920). For example, the health of American cattle delivered to Nord had deteriorated during the ocean crossing and the beasts arrived in France in poor condition (Morain 1923: 37).

Finally, under the terms of the Treaty of Versailles, Germany was required to deliver a quantity of livestock to France (AN AJ 25/1 Action exercée, 15.04.20). Commissions of reparation visited Germany and included veterinary staff and livestock experts from both nations (Hubert 1923: 205). The animals offered to the French were of variable quality and, although many horses and sheep were acceptable, the cattle and goats proved to be problematic. Nonetheless, the first livestock convoys organized by the ORA were deemed to be generally satisfactory when the change of climate and rigours of the journey were taken into account (Conseil Général du Pas-de-Calais 1921: 24). Some of the animals arriving from Germany were diseased, but it was hoped that the process of reparation would provide an effective way of restoring livestock numbers in northern France. Unfortunately this was not to be the case and by the autumn of 1922 only a low level of recovery had been achieved, with neither the number nor the composition of livestock supplied corresponding with what had been requested (Augé-Laribé 1925: 205). When animals brought back from Belgium and Germany are added to those that were purchased or donated, the total introduced to the war-torn *départements* stood only at 120,263 cattle, 121,164 sheep and goats, and 96,303 horses (MacDonald 1922: 167).

Throughout the early months of peace the Mission des Associations Agricoles continued to preach the virtues of farm cooperatives, which offered a means for the state to reduce its direct intervention in cultivation without greatly damaging the recovery effort. In practice, cooperation proved particularly challenging for farmers who returned to land that had been left uncultivated for several years (Ford 1919a: 171). During early 1919 the Mission met with little success in encouraging new cooperatives, whereby members pooled their land, cultivated it in common, and divided up the profits *pro rata*. By contrast, agricultural syndicates proved to be more popular. Under this arrangement individual farmers cultivated their own property and made their own profit or loss but collaborated with other members for purchasing livestock, implements, seeds and fertilizer (Ibid.: 172). In fact, the notion of cooperation was to prove more acceptable as 1919 and the early months of 1920 elapsed, and by the spring of 1920 2,000 farm cooperatives had been created or revived as a result of De Warren's Mission (Smith & Hill 1920: 217; AN AJ 25/1 Action exercée, 15.04.20).

Since 1917 the ORA had been purchasing fertilizer and seed to distribute to farmers returning to the *régions libérées*. At first these purchases had been fairly insignificant but they acquired considerable importance after the Armistice. Thus the ORA spent 6,500,000 F on fertilizers for the spring of 1919, 20,000,000 F for the autumn and 50,000,000 F for the spring of 1920 (Ibid.).

Much of this expenditure involved imports from the Saar, Algeria, Belgium, the United Kingdom, and Chile. Rather less energy was devoted to purchasing seed, since once the first crop had been grown, farmers returning to the *régions libérées* usually saved enough seed for the next season. Nonetheless, quantities were brought in from England, Belgium, Luxembourg and the Netherlands.

Distribution Agencies

Sale of equipment, livestock and other commodities from state-managed stocks was undertaken by the Sociétés Tiers-Mandataire (STMs) which acted as agents for the ORA in nine of the northern *départements* (AN AJ 25/48 Sociétés Tiers-Mandataire, 1919). The exception was Vosges where the challenge of agricultural recovery was considered too small to require a special agency. By contrast, the curiously shaped *département* of Meurthe-et-Moselle was provided with two agents, based respectively in Nancy and Briey (AN AJ 25/1 Action exercée, 15.04.20). In the final weeks of 1918 STMs were functioning in five *départements*, with those in Nord and Somme being particularly active and other agencies were to be created. The collective volume of business for all ten agents stood at 372,000,000 F in 1919.

An immediate task was to collect and redistribute farm equipment that had been abandoned as the events of war unfurled. Thus the newly-founded STM for Nord acknowledged that while the British army had managed to return much farm equipment to its owners there was still more to be done (AN AJ 25/48 Notices sur la récupération du matériel, 31.10.18). Parallel agencies in Pas-de-Calais, Somme and Oise immediately set about collecting machinery but stressed that depots needed to be guarded effectively to prevent pilfering. As for all other state services, operating conditions were harsh. On 6 June 1919 the Ministère des Régions Libérées was informed that the STMs suffered from shortage of staff and inadequate storage space, and hence were unable to fulfil their duties in a satisfactory manner (AN AJ 25/128 Sociétés Tiers-Mandataire, 06.06.19; Peytral 1927: 811). In particular, each director needed to have access to a fast vehicle for several occasions each week in order to supervise activities throughout his *département*. Also, more lorries were needed if fertilizers, seeds and other goods were to be distributed effectively since many local railway lines remained out of action.

The activities of the STM for Aisne during September and October of 1919 give an indication of the work being undertaken. Seeds and fertilizers were received and sold from various depots to members of the agricultural community (Figure 5.1). Horses from the French (156) and American (2,533) armies were sold to farmers, and three convoys of German horses were received, each of which contained approximately 300 animals (AN AJ 25/49 Sociétés Tiers-Mandataire, Aisne, 18.10.19). The STM noted sadly 'even setting aside the extreme thinness of the animals . . . we are obliged to indicate that it is impossible to use one-third of these horses for farmwork because they are so small' (Ibid.). STM depots received from the American army 130 wagons, fifty-five carts, and a range of machinery including forty-six motorized ploughs *(motocharrues)*, all of which were distributed to local farmers. Additional pieces of equipment that were received were of German origin or came from the STM's repair centres at Guise, Soissons, Laon and Château-Thierry. A third category of equipment was received new from factories in Nantes and Vierzon, and sometimes needed to be assembled at the STM's workshop at Saint-Quentin. The STM handled thirty-five sets of steam-ploughing equipment which were then directed to the Service de la Motoculture and to farming syndicates (*syndicats de culture*), and were promised to individual farmers who worked large areas of land (Ibid.). To the fury of intending purchasers, the steam ploughs that were destined for the private sector remained in the warehouse and could not be released for several months since the STM had not been informed of the appropriate price to charge (Aisne, *JRD*, 25.05.19: 23).

Like the other emergency services, the Sociétés Tiers-Mandataire provoked severe criticism from northern farmers. The experience of Aisne, recounted by Prefect Saint in December 1919, was particularly difficult (AN AJ 25/49 Saint, L. Lettre au Ministre, 08.12.19). Staff of the agency were criticized for allegedly supplying goods of inferior quality, not knowing their correct prices, and of being unaware of when machinery and fertilizers were due to arrive. Deputy Léon Accambray added two further complaints (AN F2 2103 Accambray, L., Mission de contrôle, 1919). The local agents had advised *sinistrés* that particular supplies would be available on specific days, but when intending purchasers arrived, often after lengthy journeys, they discovered that the goods already had been sold to others. Some *sinistrés* reported having made up to five or six fruitless trips in this way. Farmers from the south and centre of the *département* alleged that the agents had sent cattle exclusively to the pastoral area of Thiérache in the north and argued resentfully that it would have been useful if *communes* elsewhere in the *département* had received a few dairy cows to provide milk for children, the sick and the elderly. Not surprisingly the Société Tiers-Mandataire of Aisne maintained in self-defence that it was working in very difficult circumstances, with poor transport by both rail and road, inadequate storage facilities, and a shortage of rolling capital from the ORA. Such conditions, it insisted, prevented it from functioning properly (AN AJ 25/49 Société Tiers-Mandataire, Aisne, 18.10.19). It noted that it had failed to obtain appropriate buildings and staff in the *chef-lieu de département* at Laon and had been obliged to transfer its book-keeping activities to Paris, although it did operate a number of local branches in various towns in Aisne (AN AJ 25/48 Rapport sur le fonctionnement). Faced with a mounting barrage of local opposition, the Société Coopérative de Reconstitution Agricole de l'Aisne threatened to go into liquidation. As befitted a local representative of the state, Prefect Saint sought to save the situation, arguing that despite its shortcomings it would be very harmful to lose the STM at such a vital time when seeds, fertilizers and machinery were needed desperately (AN AJ 25/49 Saint, L., Disparition de la Tiers-Mandataire, 12.12.19). However, it seems that the STM broke its contract with the ORA in late December 1919 and the prefect had to assume responsibility for setting in place an alternative system for distributing these commodities (Saint 1920: 139). This involved the director of agricultural services for the *département* and a range of local administrators (AN AJ 25/1 Action exércée, 15.04.20).

As general conditions improved during 1920, so did the volume of business handled by the Sociétés Tiers-Mandataire which reached a peak of 580,000,000 F in that year (AN AJ

25/126 Cessions de toutes natures, 1921). It then declined to 169,000,000 F in 1921, partly as a result of the private distribution sector functioning effectively once again. By far the greatest financial turnover during the years 1919–21 involved the Société Coopérative Agricole du Nord (255,000,000 F) and the much-criticized Société Coopérative de Reconstruction Agricole de l'Aisne together with its replacement organization (238,000,000 F). At the other extreme, a mere 48,000,000 F of business was handled by the Société Coopérative de l'Union Agricole, Horticole et Viticole de la Marne. The detailed structure of commercial activity for the ten agencies is not known, but in Nord livestock sales accounted for 42 per cent of transactions, followed by agricultural equipment (25 per cent), seeds (20 per cent) and fertilizers (13 per cent) (Naudin 1922: 5).

As the volume of business increased during 1919, so the flow of complaints about the STMs continued to grow and financial irregularities were alleged in both Meurthe-et-Moselle and Marne in that year (AN AJ 25/49 Sociétés Tiers-Mandataire, Meurthe-et-Moselle, Marne, 1919). Writing in October 1920 about the Union Agricole de la Marne, the chief accountant of the ORA noted that 'it would be difficult to find a system of book-keeping as badly kept as that of this society' (AJ 25/49 Massol, M., Société Tiers-Mandataire de la Marne, 19.10.20). More financial irregularities came to light when the agencies in Nord and Meuse were being wound up during 1923 and 1924 (AN AJ 25/50 Sociétés Tiers-Mandataire, Nord, Meuse, 1924). In contrast with so much criticism, Minister Reibel argued that the agency in Ardennes seemed to have worked efficiently and well, and on the basis of his experience M. Bachelet maintained that the STM formed 'the pivot of agricultural reconstitution in each devastated *département*' (AN AJ 25/51 Reibel, C., Société Tiers-Mandataire, Ardennes, 11.09.23; Bachelet 1921: 93).

Shortcomings of the ORA

As with other state services concerned with agricultural recovery in the northern *départements*, the ORA was undoubtedly operating in arduous times and without adequately trained personnel. M. Guerin, Inspecteur des Finances, delivered a harsh review in the spring of 1920 and concluded that:

> the general impression which emerges from the ORA as a whole is one of an inefficient organization, whose management is insufficient. The central services have not functioned methodically and have operated in ways that have not always safeguarded the interests of the Treasury. Administration has been less than perfect. Local branches have acted with too much independence and without any real control. Stocktaking of supplies has been almost non-existent. Although belated, financial accounting does, however, display some qualities. (AN AJ 25/1 Guerin, R., Rapport, 21.03.20)

In the following month the ORA reviewed its own work in more positive terms. It noted: 'Many criticisms have been levelled against [our] activities. The ORA has not been free from reproach but the considerable difficulties that it encountered should be taken into account. In the final reckoning it cannot be doubted that its services have aided powerfully the recovery of economic life in the regions that were victims of invasion' (AN AJ 25/1 Action exercée, 15.04.20). This view was certainly shared by the Conseil-Général of Nord which held its official distribution agency 'in high esteem' and appreciated the assistance it had brought to local farmers (Naudin 1922: 5).

The pattern of these much-criticized ORA activities may not be determined in detail, but one indication is provided by the value of material supplied to *sinistrés* via the ORA during 1918, 1919 and 1920 (AEF 1A 386 Valeurs des avances, 1920). Table 6.1 shows that a quarter of all allocations were directed to Nord, with one-fifth to Aisne and one-sixth to Somme. In April 1920 the ORA argued that it would 'have to extend its activities to provide all that is useful for reviving farming operations, notably to supply farmers with sheds, fodder and fuel; it must continue to devote its energies to the creation of farm cooperatives' (AN AJ 25/1 Action exercée, 15.04.20). But by that time, its days were numbered, since all the activities that it supported were soon to be terminated as the state withdrew direct assistance from the practice of agricultural recovery. Thus, as the final repair shop in Nord closed at the start of 1922, the task of rural restoration passed emphatically from the state domain into the cooperative and private sectors (Morain 1923: 36).

Table 6.1 Value of material advances received by *sinistrés*, via the Office de Reconstitution Agricole, 1918–20 (thousand francs)

	1918	1919	1920	Total	%
Aisne	49,500	70,000	80,500	200,000	22.3
Ardennes	36,500	34,000	14,500	85,000	9.5
Marne	8,000	6,000	15,000	29,000	3.2
Meurthe-et-Moselle	6,500	20,000	28,500	55,000	6.1
Meuse	500	27,000	17,500	45,000	5.0
Nord	13,000	46,500	161,500	221,000	24.6
Oise	5,500	25,000	15,500	46,000	5.1
Pas-de-Calais	1,300	22,000	51,200	74,500	8.3
Somme	30,500	79,500	30,000	140,000	15.6
Vosges	100	1,400	700	2,200	0.2
Total	151,400	331,400	414,900	897,700	100.0

Source: AEF 1A 386 Valeurs des avances en nature effectivement reçues par les sinistrés au cours des années successives, 1920

The inadequacies of direct state involvement in organizing and implementing rural recovery were harshly evident throughout the *régions libérées*. Michel Augé-Laribé noted that 'strong criticisms . . . were thoroughly justified, especially when they related to the failure of ministries to co-ordinate activities or to individual shortcomings among hastily recruited administrative personnel' (Augé-Laribé 1923: 96). The sustained criticisms of *sinistrés* were echoed by the budget commission of the Chambre des Députés which condemned the excessive number of functionaries and services and proposed that thorough-going reforms should come into operation in 1921 (D'Aubigny 1921: 1135–40; MacDonald 1922: 191–95). It recommended that the remaining state services should be halted and individual initiative be encouraged. All aspects of paperwork and procedures relating to compensation should be simplified. Despite the view of some prefects that additional provisional accommodation was still required, the commission recommended that construction of temporary buildings should be discontinued. Instead, more support should be given by the state to groups of *sinistrés* to pool their compensation in the form of cooperative reconstruction societies in order to rebuild whole settlements according to logical timetables (see Chapters 7 and 9). The budget high commission also recommended that regulations on settlement planning, public health and hygiene should be simplified, and rendered more practical and less idealistic (see Chapter 8). Greater call should be made on foreign labour to provide necessary craftsmen and labourers to undertake permanent reconstruction. Finally, investigations should be made to obtain supplies of building materials from Germany.

In the spirit of these proposals, the Ministère des Régions Libérées issued an order on 5 February 1921 to bring all direct state involvement in recovery, except that relating to state property, to a close at the end of the year (Ibid.: 192). By January 1922 the 'emergency phase' had come to a halt, but the new minister, Charles Reibel, stressed his commitment to 'restoring normal life in the towns and villages that fell victim to the invasion' (Le programme de M. Reibel, *LP*, 26.01.22). However, he declared that henceforth he would 'count firmly upon private initiative' and had 'resolved to restrain any form of direct work or purchasing by services of the state' (Ibid.). The government would encourage 'in every way in its power the individual and collective efforts of the brave people of northern France, notably in the form of reconstruction cooperatives' (Ibid.). Those courageous but unfortunate people, who still endured remarkable hardship, knew that reconstruction in Belgium was progressing more rapidly than in their own *régions dévastées*, and were far from convinced by M. Reibel's speech which simply rehearsed the activities of the French state with respect to material recovery during the previous three years (La Belgique qui reconstruit, *LP*, 07.02.22; Déclarations de M. Reibel, *LP*, 08.02.22). These conflicting perceptions of the achievements of the emergency phase will be explored in more detail in the chapter that follows.

7

Achievements of the Emergency Phase

Conflicting Views, Inconsistent Information

The emergency phase of direct intervention by state-run services to assist rural reconstruction in the devastated *départements* was undoubtedly both complex and controversial. Some organizations had come into existence before hostilities had ceased, others were established immediately afterwards. All experienced virulent criticism from *sinistrés* who had managed to return to their home areas and from others who were still waiting to do so. Four months after the Armistice, Edouard De Warren noted how the government's failure to coordinate rural recovery meant that 'refugees are shocked and discontented and their disappointment may grow to such an extent that it will become threatening' (AN F12 8030 Warren, De. E., Réorganisation des régions libérées, 27.03.19). In the opinion of the American observer Herbert Gibbons, 'the first winter of liberation was a cruel deception. So inadequate and dilatory were the steps taken by the military authorities that the people had become bitter', hence 'six months after the Armistice one is tempted to doubt the efficiency, the capacity, and the ability of a government in Paris to undertake and carry through reconstitution in the invaded *départements*' (Gibbons 1920: 189, 191). A full year later *The Statist* reported that some settlements in the devastated regions, especially adjacent to the controversial red zone, still remained 'more or less isolated, because communications by rail, road and telegraph have not yet been fully restored. The assistance provided by the government seems slow in coming, and families decimated in number and deprived of their moveable wealth complain bitterly of the neglect which they endure' (The devastated areas, *TS*, 06.05.20).

In June 1919 the *département* assembly in Somme registered the failure of official organizations to cope with the housing crisis in its ravaged countryside, and asked why the state had allowed *sinistrés* to return to their ruins if they were then simply to be abandoned to their own devices (Somme, *JRD*, 26.06.19: 107). The situation was aggravated by an acute shortage of water on the Picardy plateau, where polluted wells still had not been restored and some returnees were obliged to travel up to 10 km to obtain water for themselves and their livestock. They believed that they had been deceived, and conveyed their distress, discouragement and downright anger to their elected representatives. Such a reaction was not a temporary phenomenon that was unique to Somme; indeed it was to be expressed throughout the liberated regions not simply for months but for years ahead. In such an atmosphere of widespread frustration, all state agencies with responsibilities for assisting rural recovery in northern France were terminated at a variety of dates in the early 1920s following the demobilization of the armed forces and the repatriation of prisoners of war.

In August 1920 Deputy Revault voiced the anger felt by many *sinistrés* when he encountered Alexandre Millerand near Verdun. He accused the government of ignoring the complaints of the *sinistrés* and dismissed the Ministère des Régions Libérées as 'a bastard organization' with too many men whose abilities were less than their responsibilities, and too many administrators 'of whom some possess talent but many are incompetent' (Les régions libérées, *DA*, 29.08.20). He blamed the government for prolonging widespread misery in the northern *départements* and for failing to produce a realistic recovery plan, and urged the minister to allow the *sinistrés* to use their own initiative in reconstruction. In a scarcely more measured way, Louis Marin reviewed the achievements of the emergency phase in a scathing report submitted to the Commission des Régions Envahies (cited in Dessaint 1922: 752). The special services were characterized as having 'too many *fonctionnaires*, poorly chosen, not having sufficient means of action, lacking appropriate links between them, and without well-defined responsibilities' (Ibid.). However, in spite of numerous shortcomings and frustrations, at least some of the most urgent preliminary tasks had been performed. In addition, laws had been passed in 1919 and 1920 which set down the ground rules for claiming financial compensation, planning the reconstruction of settlements, reorganizing field patterns, and setting up cooperatives to facilitate reconstitution (see Chapters 8, 9 and 10). All this legislation would be of vital importance during the subsequent period of replacement during the 1920s.

People

Despite the collection of so-called official statistics by the Ministère des Régions Libérées and the appearance of a shoal of reports of varying length and content from the harassed prefects of the northern *départements*, there are few reliable and consistent figures enabling accurate stock to be taken of the overall achievements of the emergency phase. Instead, information has to be pieced together from a range of sources and for a variety of dates. As mentioned in Chapter 2, George Ford estimated that by early June 1919 over 3,000,000 civilians were present in the *régions libérées* and a further 1,500,000 remained as refugees in the French interior, perhaps 85 per cent of whom were ready to return if they could be assured of a place to live and the means of sustaining themselves (Ford 1919a: 165). André Tardieu stated that by October 1920, the population of the devastated regions had returned to the equivalent of 77 per cent of the 1914 total (Tardieu 1921: 397). A fuller picture is provided by the census of 6 March 1921, but it is not possible to determine how many of those civilians were returnees and how many were recent arrivals, including 'functionaries, traders and workers from all parts of the country', not to mention 'profiteers and undesirables' who had rushed in as soon as the Armistice had been signed to give the northern *départements*, it was alleged, the appearance of 'a new Klondike' (Ministère de l'Intérieur 1922; Dessaint 1922: 749).

According to that census, the civilian population of the ten northern *départements* in their entirety stood at 5,779,132 in spring 1921, equivalent to some 88.6 per cent of the total that had been recorded ten years previously. This figure included 338,734 foreigners, whose numbers had hardly changed (+0.7 per cent) since 1911 (336,303). Increases in excess of 10,000 had occurred in Aisne (+11,914) and Pas-de-Calais (+11,743) but the number of foreigners had declined in Meurthe-et-Moselle, Nord and Vosges (Table 7.1) (Hilaire 1988: 355). In March 1921 the *départements* of Meuse (75 per cent) and Aisne (79 per cent) remained substantially depopulated and, to quote André Tardieu, those who had returned had become 'dwellers in the land of ruins and cemeteries' (AN 324 AP/60 Tardieu, A., Le discours de Laon, 26.03.33). The largest absolute losses were, not surprisingly, from the most densely populated *départements*, namely Nord and Pas-de-Calais (Thumerelle 1979: 256). In complete contrast with the general trend of decline, over two dozen *cantons* housed more people than in 1911 (Figure 7.1). These were located to the south and west of the battle zone, for example in Nord, Pas-de-Calais and Oise, and were surrounded by broad stretches of territory which contained over 90 per cent of the equivalent of their pre-war total. Their numbers held up by virtue of the presence of many refugees who had not yet ventured back to their devastated villages and ruined farmsteads. Elsewhere, the imprint of the battle zone emerged clearly along a line of depopulated *cantons* stretching from Meuse, through Marne to Aisne, and then broadening into a great triangular area representing the battlefields of western Aisne, Somme and Pas-de-Calais, before thinning down to a narrow strip around Armentières in Nord (Demangeon & Matruchot 1926: 501).

Table 7.1 Foreigners in the northern *départements* 1911 and 1921

	1911	1921	% Change
Aisne	7,341	19,325	+163.2
Ardennes	19,973	21,662	+8.4
Marne	9,088	14,929	+64.3
Meurthe-et-Moselle	64,561	43,578	−32.5
Meuse	6,874	11,208	+63.0
Nord	177,100	155,972	−11.9
Oise	11,790	16,968	+43.9
Pas-de-Calais	25,087	36,830	+46.8
Somme	3,610	12,878	+256.7
Vosges	10,879	5,384	−50.5
Total	336,303	338,734	+0.7

Source: Ministère de l'Intérieur 1912, 1922

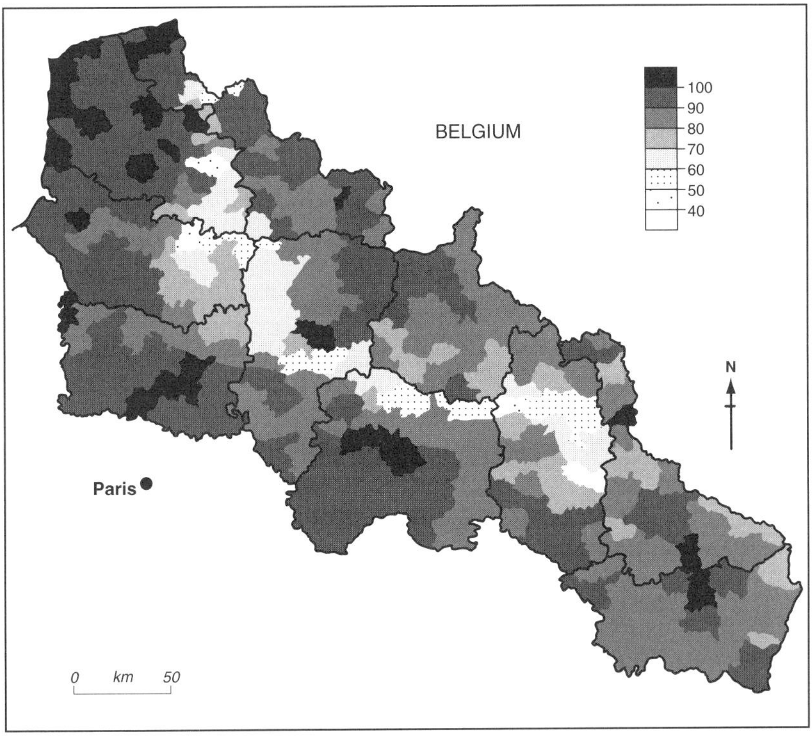

Figure 7.1 Population change, 1911–21 (1911= 100%)

Even though twenty-eight months had elapsed since the Armistice had been signed, and many buildings had been patched up, a sizeable proportion of the northern population still had not gone back to their farms, villages and market towns. Indeed, many 'landless labourers and those living on private income' had decided not to return, preferring to settle away from their devastated home *commune* (ADN M 631(7) Enquête sur l'habitat rural, 26.12.36). By contrast, family farmers were much more likely to have gone back and have risen to the challenge of restoring their land and buildings (Parisot 1939: II 168). Unfortunately, the census summaries provide no specific information on returnees or on those who had relocated elsewhere. Only the bland overall *canton* totals were recorded. The greatest proportionate losses involved areas where devastation had been most intense (Huber 1931: 892; Zimmermann 1922: 37–51).

Thus, in March 1921 the *cantons* of Vimy (49 per cent) overlooking the destruction of Lens and Arras, Albert (47 per cent) in the midst of the Somme battlefield, Varennes-en-Argonne (47 per cent) west of Verdun, and especially Saint-Mihiel (39 per cent) to the south-east of Verdun recorded the equivalent of less than half of their pre-war totals (Figure 7.1).

Restoration of the normal-gauge railway network was an essential prerequisite for most other forms of recovery and had been undertaken at remarkable speed with the help of major building firms during the early months of peace (L'assemblée générale, *Le Parlement et l'Opinion*, 1924: 510). For example, only 25 km of track on the Réseau du Nord had not been repaired by early July 1919, representing less than 1 per cent of what had been damaged or destroyed by the Germans (Ford 1919a: 215). By the same date half of the lines serving the mining concessions of Nord, Pas-de-Calais and Meurthe-et-Moselle had been rebuilt, but 265 km of the Réseau de l'Est remained in ruins, accounting for roughly 10 per cent of what had been destroyed on that system. Not until 1926 would the volume of traffic on lines in northern France exceed what had been carried during 1913 (Labaste 1932: 242). By contrast, repairing narrow-gauge lines, which were necesary for carrying materials to individual building sites, proved to be a much slower operation. However, main roads were restored rapidly and many aspects of land communication were much improved, to the great relief of all who had known the northern *départements* during the war years (Barjot 1991: 231). To quote D'Aubigny's words in 1921: 'travelling has become easy on most roads that were impracticable previously and the railways now work normally' (D'Aubigny 1921: 1135).

Land

According to the statistics of the Ministère des Régions Libérées, 2,301,000 ha had been cleared of shells, trenches and barbed wire by the start of 1920, representing two-thirds of what would be accomplished throughout the ten *départements* by 1931 (Ministère des Travaux Publics 1929; Michel 1932: 612). In Ardennes, Nord, Oise, Pas-de-Calais and Somme more than three-quarters of the surface had been cleared during the first thirteen months of peace, but only half had been treated in Marne and Vosges (51 per cent) and even less in Meuse (46 per cent). By the middle of 1920 some areas of extreme devastation, such as the battlefields north of Epernay, still had 'not been wholly cleared of corpses', and it was reported in *The Statist* that

> along the Ardre valley, isolated detachments of men may be seen at their gruesome work. Exhumation and reburial are going on all over the country. Such details at a time when the War has become a memory to many people in England, show that daily contact with its horrors in their most repellant form is still a commonplace in numerous districts, especially in remote rural areas in northern France. (Epernay, *TS*, 03.06.20)

At the start of 1921 the overall figure for land cleared of shells, trenches and barbed wire had risen to 2,536,500 ha (three-quarters of what would be the 1931 figure) but members of a delegation of the Confédération Générale du Travail could report a truly dismal situation in some localities that were still 'filled with debris of all kinds, equipment, barbed wire, corrugated iron, trenches, and numerous shells which explode and assault the visitor's ear, all recalling memories of the tragic hours of war' (Confédération Générale du Travail 1921: 10). By 1 January 1922 the amount of cleared land had risen to 2,676,500 ha, some 79 per cent of the total that would be cleared by January 1931. Nonetheless, at the start of 1922 the work was essentially complete in Oise, Pas-de-Calais and Somme but lagged distressingly in Marne (57 per cent) and Meuse (53 per cent), both of which contained extensive stretches that had been classified as red zone.

This uneven pattern of achievement was the expression of many interrelated variables, including intensity of damage, pre-war soil productivity and land values (fertile land of course being much more desirable to restore than less productive soil), aspects of land use (woodland being far more difficult and costly to clear than open arable fields), and local variations in the efficiency of emergency services, private contractors, associations of land-owners, and military explosives experts. Once normal agricultural activities started, it became clear to farmers and labourers alike that *désobusage* had to be repeated several times since unsuspected shells continued to be turned up as the soil was worked (Ibid.: 11). Hence, apparently straightforward processes such as ploughing remained fraught with danger across the battle zones for many years. Woodland restoration was entrusted to a special division of the agricultural ministry which established nurseries and planted seedlings as well as clearing debris, filling trenches and levelling land (MacDonald 1922: 169). Donations of seed, for example from the American Forestry Association, were destined for areas of extreme devastation along the Chemin-des-Dames and around Verdun (Ibid.).

Throughout the ten *départements*, 180,000,000 m^3 of trenches had been filled by January 1920, rising to 259,793,000 m^3 two years later (Ministère des Travaux Publics 1929). The official statistics do not contain information on this topic by *département*, but in *The Truth about the Treaty* André Tardieu referred to figures for September 1920 (Tardieu 1921: 392). His estimate of the overall volume needing to be filled would seem to be rather low, hence the completion rates he mentioned may have been rather over-stated. He suggested that two-thirds of all necessary trench filling across northern France had been finished by September 1920, but perhaps a more realistic share would have been just over three-fifths. According to his calculations, over nine-tenths of trenches in Meurthe-et-Moselle, Nord and Oise had been filled, but less than two-fifths had been completed in the wooded countrysides of Ardennes and Vosges and in the seriously devastated *département* of Meuse. Unfortunately, much of the work was not done well and subsidence occurred very extensively. This was a particular problem across stretches of land which concealed underground shelters that were subject to collapse with the passage of time. For example, about a thousand fresh examples of subsidence would occur during 1924 in the fields of Pas-de-Calais alone and would be brought to the notice of its *conseil-général* in 1925 (Peytral 1925: 13).

Thirteen months after the Armistice 222,480,000 m^2 of barbed-wire entanglements had been removed from land in the ten *départements*, accounting for three-fifths of what would be disposed of by 1931 (Michel 1932: 312). At the end of 1921 the area cleared rose to 274,514,600 m^2 (72 per cent). Once again Tardieu's figures differed from the official statistics, but his overall ranking of activity suggests that nine-tenths of the amount that had needed to be cleared had been removed in

Nord, Oise and Marne (Tardieu 1921: 392). However, large quantities of barbed wire still remained in the most intensely devastated districts (L'enlèvement des fils de fer, *LP*, 29.09.21). That fact was drawn to the attention of M. Loucheur, Ministre des Régions Libérées, during his visit to Somme and Pas-de-Calais at the start of October 1921 (Hénard 1921: 1). Returnees complained bitterly and Edouard De Warren, then Deputy for Meurthe-et-Moselle, pressed for ministerial initiatives to be taken to accelerate its removal. Prefects were duly instructed to encourage landowners to clear barbed wire from their own property and to dump it alongside roads or on the margin of their holdings to await collection (Enlèvement des fils de fer barbelés, *JRD*, 02.10.21: 3). Village mayors were given the responsibility of overseeing the work and were informed that any expenses incurred in acquiring land upon which to store it would be reimbursed by the state (Morain 1922a: 9). Official schemes were duly introduced to recover barbed wire by road or by narrow-gauge railway once it was appreciated that money could be made from salvaging its metal content (Peytral 1927: 481).

Rather less is known about the volume of munitions destroyed in each of the ten *départements*, but the total of 14,000,000 tonnes, quoted for the whole of the *régions libérées* in January 1920, suggested a 63 per cent completion rate, which rose to 94 per cent (20,800,000 tonnes) two years later (Ministère des Travaux Publics 1929). Returnees were strongly opposed to shells being exploded *in situ* and demanded that they should be removed to special areas for controlled destruction. In the early months of peace, military munitions experts and prisoners of war had played important roles in this dangerous work, but as demobilization and repatriation occurred so greater reliance for dealing with shells and ammunition dumps had to be placed on civilian contractors (Le désobusage dans la zone anglaise, *JRD*, 22.02.20: 1: Middlebrook 1984: 306). A new workforce had to be recruited and trained hastily (Philippot 1921: 16). Dealing with munitions was, of course, a highly dangerous operation and from the Armistice to early 1922 eighty-three people were killed and 203 injured in Pas-de-Calais alone as they removed shells (Peytral 1927: 485). A further thirteen were killed and fifteen injured by hidden munitions as they worked the fields, and more deaths involved people who tried to remove shells in order to recover their copper content (Peytral 1927: 487). Such sad results doubtless occurred throughout the former battle zones.

Just under half (49.7 per cent) of the farmland in the ten *départements* that was to be levelled, ploughed and brought into cultivation by 1931 had been tackled by January 1920. Progress was particularly marked in Nord (70 per cent) and Pas-de-Calais (67 per cent) which, of course, had also distinguished themselves by having cleared large proportions of shells, trenches and barbed wire. In their desperation to produce crops once again, some *sinistrés* had sown portions of land during 1919, but for a variety of reasons results were universally poor (Morain 1923: 33). Seed was often of miserable quality and was not always sown at the correct time; the land was inadequately prepared, with much still being infested with weeds; and voles, mice and other vermin, which had flourished during the hostilities, had not been destroyed. From the point of view of agricultural output, 1919 proved to be a 'lost year' in northern France, to the sorrow and disquiet of many *sinistrés* (Stapathi 1919: 99).

The following season was very different and an immense effort was made to restore land to cultivation throughout northern France during 1920. Farmers were reported as ploughing by 'lantern light, far into the night [so that] almost all of the fields will be ready for spring planting' (Smith & Hill 1920: 197). After a visit to the *régions libérées* in the second half of June, Henri Hitier reported widespread recovery, and he anticipated a fine harvest, with some war-torn areas possibly having surplus wheat to send to other districts (Hitier 1920: 81). On behalf of the Académie de l'Agriculture, MM. De Lapparent and Thomassin also visited each of the devastated *départements* in June and wrote an account which sought to be 'as exact and impartial as possible' (cited in Hitier 1920: 80). They reported that in most areas the great majority of farmers had regained their holdings and had made great progress in clearing and cultivating land 'before thinking about rebuilding their homes' (Ibid.). Their efforts had been helped by favourable weather conditions during the previous winter and spring (Helot 1920b: 491). With the exception of the extreme devastation in the red zone, only a tiny minority of farms remained unoccupied and this was explained by some families having chosen to remain on properties in the interior of France or having suffered so many fatalities that working their farms would not be feasible (Hitier 1920: 80). Progress was generally impressive in the western parts of the devastated regions. Even in areas where 'not a single house or farmstead was left standing, one often finds that all the fields have been ploughed and sown' (Hitier & Pluchet 1920: 342).

The achievement of local farmers was all the more amazing since many had no practical alternative to spending the winter of 1919–20 in ruined cellars or makeshift shelters dug into the ground (*cagnats*) (Ibid.: 343). For example, in Somme no less than 120,000 ha had been restored to agricultural use during 1919 and three-quarters of this total was being cropped in 1920 (Hitier 1920: 81). Intense activity was also reported in Nord, where farmers anticipated a harvest which they believed would compare favourably with those recorded pre-war. However, in nearby Pas-de-Calais stretches of land still needed to be levelled in 1920 and farmers regretted that the state's emergency services were no longer in existence to undertake that task. Agricultural recovery was generally slower in central and eastern parts of the devastated zone, and De Lapparent and Thomassin reported that no progress had been made in the heart of the battlefields of Verdun, the Monts de Champagne, the Chemin-des-Dames, or indeed the Somme, since farmers had not been allowed to return to the red zone, even though many courageous families were desperate to start working what remained of their land (Ibid.) (see Chapter 10).

By the start of 1921, 1,097,200 ha were reported to be ready to be cultivated throughout northern France, but since state motoculture services continued to operate in some *départements*, the figures for January 1922 are perhaps the more telling. By then 1,474,800 ha had been prepared, namely 72 per cent of what would be completed by 1931. The task was all but finished in Nord; indeed Prefect Morain declared that uncultivated land had 'disappeared' from his *département* by the end of 1920 (Morain 1923: 33). To be more precise, only 2,500 ha remained uncultivated in Nord at that time and by January 1922 the total had fallen to a mere 700 ha, embracing a collection of particularly devastated patches (Ibid.: 32). At that date, Oise, Vosges, Pas-de-Calais and Somme also recorded above average proportions of land preparation, which was all the more remarkable since the two latter *départements* had experienced widespread trench warfare.

During the first full year of peace 2,883,000 ha were recorded as being in arable use across the ten northern *départements*, representing four-fifths of the pre-war total, and doubtless being an improvement on the 1918 season which cannot be quantified because of the absence of information for Ardennes (Michael 1928: 26). The pattern of agricultural recovery was certainly uneven and appeared all the more so by virtue of the variable geography of devastation and its relation to administrative boundaries. For example, in Marne, Somme and Pas-de-Calais the arable area noted for 1919 exceeded 90 per cent of what it had been on the eve of the war, but in Aisne and Meurthe-et-Moselle it was only just over half. Restoration of farmland during the next two years raised the total to 3,375,000 ha (94 per cent) in January 1921, with Somme, Oise, Marne and Pas-de-Calais each achieving above-average recovery rates. Slow restoration of war-damaged land in Meuse and further conversion of arable to permanent grass in Ardennes and Vosges kept arable recovery rates below 90 per cent in those *départements*.

Production

Wheat production in the northern *départements* reached only 7,718,000 qx during 1919, representing one-third of the 1910–13 average (Ministère de l'Agriculture 1911–14). Virtually nothing was harvested in Aisne or Ardennes, with each of these *départements* producing a mere 7 per cent of its annual output pre-war. By contrast, Oise, Pas-de-Calais and Vosges managed to generate over half the volume of their pre-war production. Extensive areas throughout the *régions dévastées* were left fallow during 1919 to enable weeds to be removed thoroughly after four years of abandonment or poor cultivation (Vezin & Vandamme 1937: 394). Output for 1920 (13,630,000 qx) across the ten *départements* was almost double that of the previous year and increased substantially during the following season to yield 21,915,000 qx in 1921, which amounted to 94 per cent of the pre-war total. Wheat production in Pas-de-Calais, Marne and Meurthe-et-Moselle in 1921 actually exceeded the 1910–13 average but remained below 85 per cent of that level in three *départements*, because of slow recovery in Meuse and the conversion of former arable land to pasture in Ardennes and northern Aisne.

Profound devastation of intensively cultivated farmlands in the western parts of the war zone had dealt a severe blow to the production of sugar beet and in 1919 Aisne and Marne achieved only 1 per cent of their pre-war average output. For all ten *départements* the figure stood at a feeble 7,548,000 qx, just one-sixth of what it had been for 1910–13. In the first year of peace only 37 sugar refineries were operating in place of 172 in 1912, with just a single factory functioning in Aisne compared with 51 in 1912, and large reductions characterizing Nord (9 instead of 41), Pas-de-Calais (6 instead of 21) and Somme (4 instead of 32). Two years later the northern sugar-beet harvest rose to 12,277,000 qx but this was only one-quarter of the pre-war level and was processed in only 44 sugar refineries. Aisne and Marne were yielding only one-eighth of their earlier output, while Pas-de-Calais and Somme were producing less than one-quarter, and in Ardennes the cultivation of sugar beet had not yet recommenced (Anon. 1937: 61).

Like property owners elsewhere in the *régions dévastées*, the vine-growers of Marne returned as soon as possible to their plots, seeking shelter among ruins or in temporary accommodation (Moreau-Bérillon 1924: 293). Initially a sum of 3,000 F was advanced from the state to help compensate for each hectare of vines that had been destroyed or damaged. This sum was soon increased to 5,000 F and then to 8,000 F for vineyards which had to be re-planted completely (Brisac 1922b: 864). Conditions were so deplorable that the manpower committee for Marne requested that 200–300 enlisted *vignerons* with experience of grafting vines might be made available by the army to assist with restoration work (ADMa 203 M204 Commission de la main d'oeuvre agricole, 12.03.19). During 1919 land was cleared and dug over, trenches and shellholes filled, dead vines removed, living ones pruned, and necessary chemicals applied to try to control disease. Indeed, 10,000 vine-growers in Marne belonged to over a hundred syndicates which sought to tackle phylloxera (De Polignac 1920: 16). Encouraged by the Syndicat Général des Vignerons de la Champagne Délimitée and assisted financially by the Association Viticole Champenoise, vine-growers prepared the soil and made six million grafts in 1919 and a further fourteen million in 1920. During that year Marne contained 10,325 ha of vines, including 3,184 ha which supported grafted stock. But vine-growers experienced severe difficulties, including an acute shortage of labour which had been attracted to other forms of recovery work, notably the reconstruction of the devastated city of Reims (The wines of France, *TS*, 27.05.20: 1000). Implements, chemicals and other materials necessary for viticulture were much more expensive than before the war. It was estimated that to restore a hectare of vineyard now cost 25–30,000 F, compared with 7–8,000 F seven years previously. Not surprisingly, the grape harvest of 1921 was insignificant, but that of 1922 proved to be very abundant. Ironically, prohibition had been introduced in the USA but during 1923 the Champagne trade revived and consumption both at home and abroad picked up (Chappaz 1951: 111; Brisac 1923: 737). By spring 1923 only 590 ha of vineyard in Marne awaited re-planting and a further 468 ha needed to be restored after wartime damage. At a far more modest scale, the vineyards in a score of *communes* along the Moselle valley to the north of Pont-à-Mousson (Meurthe-et-Moselle) were also being restored, with 15,000 grafts and 35,000 rooted vines having been planted by July 1920 (AN AJ 25/125 Meurthe-et-Moselle, 12.07.20).

Despite the efforts of the state services, the armed forces and individual farmers, the number of farm livestock to be found in the ten *départements* during the early post-war years was only a fraction of what it had been before hostilities (Ministère de l'Agriculture, 1911–14, 1920–4). Numbers removed or killed during the war are not known accurately (see Table 2.5), but one estimate suggests that 523,000 cattle, 469,000 sheep and 367,000 horses had been carried away by the Germans and, of course, additional losses had occurred for other reasons (MacDonald 1922: 31). In 1919 only 25 per cent of the pre-war number of sheep were recorded across the northern *départements* and substantial reductions were noted for horses (59 per cent of the pre-war total), cattle (54 per cent) and pigs (44 per cent). Not surprisingly, the lowest proportions for each type of livestock having returned were recorded in Ardennes, which had been entirely behind enemy lines for the duration of the war, and in Aisne which also had been occupied to a large extent. For example, in 1919 these *départements* contained only 1 and 4 per cent respectively of their pre-war sheep totals, and 28 and 17 per cent of their cattle. Attempts to bring back livestock that had been removed from the devastated regions and to purchase additional animals from other parts of France and from abroad increased the numbers of horses, cattle and pigs in the ten *départements* to roughly three-quarters of their pre-war totals by 1921. By contrast, the number of sheep stood at a mere 39 per cent of the earlier figure. Livestock of all types remained most seriously depleted in Aisne, Ardennes and Meuse during the third year of peace (Cepède 1961: 12). In a broad review of agricultural conditions, Michel Augé-Laribé declared 'cultivation has been restored with a speed that surprises anyone who was in these northern areas during the war. But cultivation is still rudimentary. Although the land is ready to be worked, the farm buildings and houses are lacking, and the villages have not been rebuilt' (Augé-Laribé 1923: 100). In the opinion of the Confédération Générale du Travail, agricultural recovery in many districts in the *régions dévastées* was hindered severely by failure to reconstruct dwellings and farm buildings (Confédération Générale du Travail 1921: 7).

Emergency Housing

Statistical information on these matters and on other activities undertaken, at least in part, by members of the emergency services is unfortunately but not surprisingly both sparse and ambiguous. By January 1920 temporary repairs were declared as having been made to 100,600 dwellings across the northern *départements* and two years later that total had risen to 181,100, with building contractors from Paris and the provinces having arrived in large numbers (Anon. 1924: 511). However, in the same month, Lavollée presented a depressing picture of returnees enduring appalling conditions in numerous parts of the northern countryside (Lavollée 1920: 17). Many were living in overcrowded military shelters and 'simple lean-to structures of bricks and planks propped against ruined walls' (Ibid.: 17). Others had lived in tents during the previous summer but for the winter had taken to their ruins and cellars, where they lived 'like troglodytes' (Ibid.: 21). During the summer of 1919 the red zone of the

Chemin-des-Dames had presented 'a spectacle of overwhelmingly painful monotony; uncultivated fields, heaps of ruins that had been villages; none of the sounds that are heard in the countryside, not a cow, a cockerel or a dog. Here and there, amid the ruins, there were human beings, living in wigwams like savages' (Ibid.).

As sections of land had become available for re-occupation at various phases during the war, so temporary housing had been installed by many agencies, although early attempts simply involved layers of planking nailed on to wooden frames for walls and bitumen paper being tacked over wood for roofs (Bluzet 1916: 20). Such shoddy work had to be patched up several times at considerable expense. Renewed efforts were made to increase the number and quality of temporary houses once the Armistice had been signed. For example, in December 1918 the French state entered into an agreement with the British army to purchase as many military huts that had become surplus to requirements as possible and with a minimum of delay. Most were Nissen huts, which had the advantage of being easily dismantled and re-assembled, but the disadvantage of being far from comfortable to live in. However, as Prefect Causel remarked, '*sinistrés* living in unhealthy cellars or cold concrete shelters accepted them willingly' (Causel 1922: 96). During the first nine months after the Armistice the emergency services erected only 8,000 huts of various shapes and sizes throughout the ten northern *départements* (Despagnet 1919: 2). This total included relocated army huts, and cabins that had been assembled from any surplus materials that could be found. Together they accommodated 30–35,000 people, at a time when hundreds of thousands of *sinistrés* needed housing. From August to October 1919 a further 2,000 huts were erected and it was hoped that the total would reach 25,000 by the end of the year (Vincent 1919: 2033; Despagnet 1919: 2). The process of acquiring British huts was conditioned by the speed with which army camps were dismantled. Thus, by the end of July 1920 in Nord 11,363 British army huts had been purchased, relocated and filled with *sinistrés*, and a further 1,000 huts were awaited, but after twenty months of peace a total of 3,500 households still lodged demands for temporary housing in that *département* alone (Conseil-Général du Nord 1920: 4). At that time 13,740 families in Nord were living in huts, 1,915 in semi-provisional housing, and 59,919 in houses that had been repaired to some extent (Ibid.: 38). Unfortunately, surplus huts were not always available where they were needed across the northern *départements*. For example, during the summer of 1919 thousands of army huts were reported as being left to rot in various parts of Meuse even though such emergency shelters were needed desperately in the devastated *cantons* of Charny, Etain and Fresnes (Meuse, *JRD*, 06.07.19: 121). At the end of June the first huts were still awaited in Fresnes, while the dedicated mayor of Etain ran his office in 'truly pitiful conditions' (Vers la renaissance, *LA*, 1919:403).

In the early years of peace new wooden huts were constructed in large numbers throughout the northern *départements* using timber sections that had been sent by rail from the forests of Landes, Jura, Vosges, and Switzerland (Despagnet 1919: 2). The process was hindered by incomplete restoration of local transport facilities and the fact that timber sections for one design of house were not interchangeable with those for others. Had a uniform pattern been adopted then errors in delivery might have been less serious. Many huts were far from sturdy since unseasoned wood was often used, and warped planks and knotholes let in rain and draughts (Lavollée 1920: 17). Attempts were made to render huts and shelters more acceptable during the winter months of 1919–20 by patching cracks and holes with pieces of tarred cardboard (Naudin 1920: 48). Despite these efforts, erecting huts simply 'did not keep pace with the demands of the returning population, and indescribable conditions, due to insanitary housing, resulted. No sooner was a cellar vacated by placing the occupants in better quarters than another family moved into the dank and damp abode' (Smith & Hill 1920: 5). As Lavollée maintained, 'misery, filth and overcrowding were bringing these wretched people to despair' (Lavollée 1920: 28). Embittered returnees compared their current plight with conditions in various parts of the French interior to which they had been evacuated, and threatened to leave their ruins and seek a more acceptable life elsewhere (Ibid.: 35). Alexandre Millerand urged the *sinistrés* to exercise patience, and during a visit to Chauny (Aisne) in 1920 pronounced, surely unwisely, that reconstruction would last 'at least thirty years' (Héricault 1934: 116). Such words did nothing to encourage *sinistrés* throughout the *régions dévastées*, who felt not only condemned to live in makeshift accommodation but also totally forgotten by the state. The great storms that were to be experienced across northern France during November 1921 and March 1922 would cause extensive damage to the decrepit stock of temporary housing and add to the plight of those who had returned to the devastated regions (Après la guerre, l'ouragan, *LP*, 10.03.22).

The three *départements* of Aisne, Nord and Pas-de-Calais each accounted for about one-sixth of the material advances (including provisional housing) that were allocated to *sinistrés* during the thirty-six months following the Armistice (Table 7.2). At the end of 1920 120,000 temporary houses had been erected in the northern *départements*, and by October 1922 the total stood at 136,165, with by far the largest concentrations in Pas-de-Calais (35,570), Aisne (28,560), Somme (26,820) and Nord (22,940) (D'Aubigny 1921: 1136; Ministère des Régions Libérées 1923). Wooden huts represented three-fifths of this overall total and were particularly important in relative – if not absolute – terms in Meurthe-et-Moselle, Ardennes and Vosges. Shelters made of various salvaged materials comprised a further one-fifth (especially in Aisne and Marne), and former army huts accounted for the remainder. Without doubt the period of definitive reconstruction still had not arrived by the end of 1921 and many

Table 7.2 Material advances to *sinistrés*, including provisional housing, furniture and other materials (million francs)

	1918	1919	1920	Total	%
Aisne	6,480	38,957	22,196	67,633	17.14
Ardennes	0	19,478	11,098	30,576	7.75
Marne	3,240	19,478	11,098	33,816	8.57
Meurthe-et-Moselle	3,240	19,478	11,098	33,816	8.57
Meuse	2,916	23,356	13,317	39,589	10.03
Nord	3,240	38,957	22,196	64,393	16.32
Oise	1,208	9,739	5,549	16,496	4.18
Pas-de-Calais	6,480	36,957	22,196	65,633	16.63
Somme	2,956	25,160	14,427	42,543	10.78
Vosges	0	0	0	0	0
Total	29,760	231,560	133,175	394,395	100.00

Source: AEF 1A 386 Valeurs des avances en nature effectivement reçues par les sinistrés au cours des années successives (1920)

returnees were condemned to spend further months and even years in cramped accommodation that let in wind and rain, was too cold in winter and too hot in summer, and was deteriorating rapidly (D'Aubigny cited in MacDonald 1922: 189). The *sinistrés* argued strongly that the northern prefects should take a more active role to ensure that adequate and robust temporary accommodation be provided since permanent rebuilding obviously remained far off in the future (Hénard 1921a:1). For example, in February 1922 Prefect Morain ordered 1,300 new wooden houses and 190 secondhand ones to accommodate *sinistrés* in Somme, having been informed by the Ministre des Régions Libérées that supplies of good quality used housing were available in Meurthe-et-Moselle where permanent rebuilding by cooperative reconstruction societies was making important progress (ADS RL 332.256 Lettre du Préfet au Ministre, 06.02.22). Construction of temporary houses ceased early in 1923, when their number across northern France totalled 150,000 (Ministère des Travaux Publics 1929). In addition, 34,101 temporary farm buildings had been installed by October 1922, with large numbers in Somme (7,047), Pas-de-Calais (5,324) and Meuse (4,823).

Travellers in northern France in the early 1920s were astonished at the diversity of temporary buildings that they encountered. This was partly due to varying availability of materials in different places and at different times, but also reflected the fact that the emergency services in each *département* had worked to their own guidelines (Braibant 1921: 3). Wooden walls were left exposed to the elements in some areas but were protected with layers of tarred paper in others. In some places roofs were covered with tiles, slates or squares of fibro-cement, but elsewhere tarred cardboard was used widely for roofing. This material had been cheap to install but perished rapidly and needed to be replaced frequently if any attempt were to be made to keep the roof waterproof. On Christmas Day 1921 Braibant reported examples of tarred cardboard having had to be replaced three times during the preceding twelve months at a cumulative cost that was proving more expensive than slate or tiles (Ibid.). Quoting an estimate from the Ministre des Régions Libérées, M. Loucheur, that permanent reconstruction might take a further six to eight years to complete, Braibant argued that government funds should be allocated without delay to ensure that all *sinistrés* living in temporary accommodation should be provided with decent roof covering (Ibid.).

By October 1922 181,417 houses had received temporary repairs in the northern *départements*, with the largest concentrations being in Nord (54,628) and Aisne (42,834). Some 21,165 agricultural buildings had been rendered usable throughout the liberated regions, with the largest numbers also in Aisne (4,401) and Nord (4,092). In all, by the autumn of 1922 170,266 temporary buildings were declared to have been installed and 202,582 damaged buildings to have been patched up and made usable on a temporary basis. These activities certainly fell within the remit of the state's emergency services but an unspecified share of the work had been undertaken by the *sinistrés* themselves and by contractors in their employ. Permanent repairs to dwellings totalled 221,533 in October 1922, over half of which (114,945) involved the single densely-populated *département* of Nord, and to 52,933 farm buildings, two-fifths of which were in Meurthe-et-Moselle. The rapid recovery of that particular *département* reflected the concentrated pattern of damage within it, the ready availability of building materials, its dense network of roads and railways which facilitated their transportation, and above all the remarkable spirit of cooperation among *sinistrés* (Picard 1922: 1027) (see Chapter 9).

Continuing Crisis

In complete contrast with repair work, total rebuilding of devastated property made distressingly little headway during the early months and indeed years of peace, and represented the one 'black spot' in the vast activity of reconstitution (Carpentier 1928: 94). This was despite the fact that during 1917 contractors and builders had presented a memorandum to the government outlining measures which they believed should be decided in advance in order to assist reconstruction when fighting came to an end (Gibbons 1920: 213–14). They advocated immediate release of skilled building workers from the armed forces once hostilities ceased, and suggested that factories which had worked for the war effort should be directed to produce essential materials for reconstruction. The state should be prepared to recruit large numbers of builders, masons and carpenters, and make an intense effort to have emergency accommodation ready for them at key locations in the northern *départements*. Despite numerous committees being summoned and enquiries undertaken, 'nothing was done along these lines. The cessation of hostilities found the government unprepared to grapple with the problems of building in the devastated areas' (Ibid.: 214). Indeed, total rebuilding was not encouraged by the government in the early years of peace since labour, transport and materials proved insufficient to cope with the most pressing needs, namely for industrial recovery and for temporary accommodation (Ford 1919a: 190). In addition, legally acceptable claims for compensation had to be lodged, formal plans for village reconstruction had to be prepared and approved, and an appropriate organizational system devised before permanent rebuilding might commence (see Chapters 8 and 9).

Nonetheless, small numbers of individuals and especially industrialists went ahead on their own initiative, drawing on their financial reserves without having to wait for compensation to be agreed (Confédération Générale du Travail 1921: 12). In a very few instances, groups of *sinistrés* also started to rebuild. Sometimes they sought professional architectural advice, as at Vassincourt near Bar-le-Duc, at Vitrimont (where reconstruction was funded by Americans headed by Crocker and Polk), and at Sermaize-les-Bains and a dozen villages west of Vitry-le-François where the Quakers had been active (Ford 1919a: 199). But in other cases early rebuilding went ahead without much official direction or counselling. Thus planner George B. Ford expressed concern for the appearance of Gerbéviller (Meurthe-et-Moselle), where about forty buildings had been reconstructed by autumn 1919. However, he had to agree that the new farms and houses were 'fairly solidly built and serve their purpose as well as the buildings that were there before' (Ibid.: 198). But by virtue of the legal and financial constraints which governed permanent reconstruction and the profound problems of obtaining materials and labour, very little rebuilding was in fact started. In May 1920 the special correspondent of *The Statist* noted that many returnees were obliged still to live in ruins or in huts, 'being herded together in uncomfortable and insanitary dwellings, often open to every wind of heaven' (The devastated area, *TS*,

06.05.20: 5). In his report on the 1921 budget Deputy D'Aubigny described the lack of new housing as '*the* most urgent' problem in northern France (D'Aubigny 1921: 1137). There seemed to be no effective programme for assembling and organizing labour and building materials, and the 'fiercely individualistic' compensation law that had been passed on 17 April 1919 seemed to have overlooked the need for a rational sequence of work (Ibid.) (see Chapter 8). As a result, many returnees to devastated villages had no alternative to lodging in temporary housing and desolate underground shelters as late as the final months of 1922 (Picard 1922: 1025). In that year the historian Gabriel Hanotaux recounted the story of the mayor of his ruined home village in Aisne having lived for seven years in the cellar of his wrecked house from which he tried to administer his *commune* (Hanotaux 1922: 4).

By 1 March 1922 clearance had been completed in only 737 of the 2,874 settlements which had required debris to be removed (Augé-Laribé 1923: 100). Work was in progress in a further 1,270 *communes* but had not even started in 837. However, according to the evidence presented to the Confédération Générale du Travail delegation, clearance contractors sometimes piled bricks and building stone back on to the site of ruined buildings since the intentions of the *sinistrés* were not yet known (Confédération Générale du Travail 1921: 7). Once the decision had been taken for rebuilding to commence these materials would have to be removed once again. The total number of rebuilt houses for all ten *départements* stood at the pathetically small total of 5,524 in the official statistics for October 1922, including 1,618 in Nord, 1,160 in Somme and 1,037 in Marne (Ministère des Régions Libérées 1923). Prefect Morain offered a higher total for his *département* of Nord, with 2,948 houses having been rebuilt and a further 5,630 in progress by July 1922, but even when added together those figures represented only one-sixth of the 53,107 houses that had been destroyed (Morain 1922b: 9). Morain was certainly not understating the case when he remarked that attempting to resolve the housing crisis in northern France was 'one of the great problems of the day' (Ibid.: 10). In contrast with this wretched result, reconstruction of agricultural property seems to have been rather more plentiful throughout the ten *départements* with 22,258 farm buildings reported as having been completely rebuilt by October 1922 (Ministère des Régions Libérées 1923).

Out of this confused and imperfectly recorded story emerges the stark fact that as late as autumn 1922 many *sinistrés* had no alternative to living in makeshift housing or in accommodation that had undergone only summary repair. MacDonald argued that the situation of many countryfolk was 'unquestionably distressing. One may still find many small villages which stand today in almost the same condition of ghastly ruin in which the war left them' (MacDonald 1922: 199). Some of the most striking examples were regularly shown to tourists taking automobile excursions between Paris and London. However, most of these untouched villages were small, and even if the settlements had not been rebuilt the farmland that surrounded them had usually been brought back into cultivation. One table in the statistics circulated by the Ministère des Régions Libérées in 1923 is tantalizingly ambiguous. It lists no fewer than 2,098,372 people living in 'repaired houses and temporary shelters' (*maisons réparées et abris provisoires*) in October 1922, but there is no way of determining whether this statement referred to temporary as well as permanent repairs, and if so what the quantitative relationship between the two categories might have been (Ministère des Régions Libérées 1923). Nonetheless, in the devastated sections of Meuse, Somme and Pas-de-Calais, more than 90 per cent of residents were in repaired houses and temporary shelters at that time.

Many *sinistrés* were repeatedly frustrated and angered by the inefficiencies and disorganization of the state services, their mounting bureaucracy, and the complicated and sometimes contradictory instructions issued by the Ministère des Régions Libérées (Gouguenheim 1921: 181). Despite a proliferation of staff and an avalanche of rules and regulations, there seemed to be no clear plan or method for restoring the countryside (La CGT va exposer son plan de reconstruction, *LP*, 20.03.21). Throughout the northern *départements* ordinary family farmers had tolerated appalling living conditions in order to exercise their patriotic duty by working their land once again and producing food for the nation, but the vast quantities of seemingly incomprehensible paperwork that assailed them simply filled them with fear (Gouge 1921b: 1). With the exception of rich property owners who enlisted professional help in the form of lawyers and accountants, most individual *sinistrés* were incapable of presenting their claims for compensation in an acceptable format and, since they had no financial resources on which to draw, were unable to start permanent reconstruction (Dessaint 1922: 752).

The plight of the returned *sinistrés* was reported regularly in the pages of the trades unions' daily newspaper *Le Peuple*, whose columns convey a much more harrowing picture of life in the northern *départements* than that reported by the prefects to their *conseils-généraux*. The misery and distress endured by many *sinistrés* emerged forcefully in January 1921 during a visit to the devastated regions by members of the council of the Confédération Générale du Travail (Confédération Générale du Travail 1921: 3). 'What', asked the columnist of *Le Peuple*, 'can be more sad to see, two years after the war has ended, than so many people obliged to live in makeshift houses deprived of basic comforts in the midst of whole areas deprived of normal transport for bringing in food supplies' (Une enquête de la CGT dans les régions dévastées, *LP*, 11.01.21). Many clusters of temporary housing were reported to be in a disgusting condition. At Chauny wooden huts were provided with such primitive sanitary facilities that urine overflowed from makeshift latrines and ran into rutted, muddy tracks that passed for roads (L'état déplorable de Tergnier et des cités construites à Chauny, *LP*, 19.01.21). Piles of household rubbish five or six metres in circumference stood close to these wretched huts, and pools of stagnant water contributed to outbreaks of fever. Temporary housing made of concrete that had been erected by the emergency services near Lens was 'almost uninhabitable' (La délégation syndicaliste, *LP*, 23.01.21). Huts and other forms of provisional housing had been installed at Albert but with no regard for drainage or other hygiene requirements (Albert, *LP*, 25.01.21). Numerous *sinistrés* were condemned to live in 'intolerable misery' and they expressed their anger at 'the great disorder' which surrounded the whole issue of reconstruction (Une enquête de la CGT, *LP*, 11.01.21; Après l'enquête de la CGT, *LP*, 05.02.21). Their voices were added to the allegation that the state's emergency services had been disorganized, unmethodical and excessively bureaucratic, and to the demand that an alternative means of ensuring reconstruction needed to be found without delay (La CGT va exposer son plan, *LP*, 20.03.21).

Early in April 1921 representatives of the Allied Commission for Reparations travelled through the countryside between Soissons, Reims and Château-Thierry and, in similar tones to those used by the Confédération Générale du Travail delegation three months earlier, reported a 'state of chaos' for a distance of over 90 km in the red zone along the Chemin-des-Dames, on the plateau of Craonne, and in nearby localities (La commission des réparations visite nos ruines, *JRD*, 17.04.21: 1). It seemed that nothing had been done to remove debris from fifty devastated villages whose inhabitants were condemned to live in ruins or in wretched wooden huts, and often were deprived of adequate supplies of food or water since local roads had not been restored. At precisely the same time, Gouguenheim described the *pays libérés* as 'still three-quarters devastated' and warned that an effective method of reconstruction needed to be devised, otherwise 'in twenty years from now these areas still will not be restored' (Gouguenheim 1921: 186). By October 1921 nothing appeared to have been done in many areas where intense destruction had occurred. In such places there were 'no villages, no houses and no shelters' (Philippot 1921: 16). Even explosives experts experienced great difficulty in gaining access to such seriously disturbed land. Following its visit in January 1921 the Confédération Générale du Travail pleaded the cause of international workers' solidarity and urged that teams of German building workers should be recruited to restore selected parts of northern France (see Chapter 8). Such a controversial suggestion was, of course, unacceptable to the French government which instead placed its faith in another form of cooperation, namely general purpose reconstruction cooperatives (see Chapter 9). Despite the work of the emergency services, northern France remained *une grande mutilée* which was 'returning painfully to health and to life' (Dessaint 1922: 749). Their energies had not, of course, been expended equally, with the restoration of industries that were vital to the national economy being favoured at the expense of agriculture, and rebuilding of factories being given precedence over ordinary housing (MacDonald 1922: 98). To many observers it seemed as if the interests of country people were being brushed aside in favour of those of industrialists (Ibid.: 196). In April 1921 several thousand *sinistrés* assembled in

Paris to give vent to their anger at the unbearable slowness of rural revival in many northern areas, demanding that compensation claims be settled and a start be made on permanent reconstruction (Comité d'Action des Régions Dévastées 1930: 5). Their frustration gave rise to the Comité d'Action des Régions Dévastées which emerged from the profound concern of the Conseil Economique du Travail of the Confédération Générale du Travail at the general delay in rebuilding, the widespread devastation still to be found in the red zone, and the human misery encountered within it and on its margins (Comité d'Action des Régions Dévastées 1925: 5). With the prime objective of safeguarding the interests of *sinistrés* (as specified in the law of 17 April 1919), the Comité worked to promote solidarity among them by providing information and support, to facilitate reconstruction, and to serve as an intermediary between them (whether in groups or individually) and the various levels of administration. It lobbied forcefully for the reclamation of the red zone, for bringing in German labour to rebuild devastated settlements, and in defence of the *sinistrés* during the remainder of the decade (Comité d'Action des Régions Dévastées 1930: 5).

8

Principles of Compensation, Rules of Reconstruction

Compensation and Compromise

The law of 17 April 1919 providing the mechanism for claiming compensation for war losses was 'the essential charter of reconstitution', without which permanent reconstruction could not have taken place (Reibel 1924a: 7). It emerged only after long controversy in the Senate, the Chambre des Députés and in the country at large. No previous government had committed itself to the notion that the state should reimburse war losses or to the proposition that it was the financial responsibility of the whole nation to make good the losses suffered by *sinistrés* in the war zone (Toulemon 1921). Previously, war losses had not been compensated systematically and restoration costs had to be borne by those who experienced loss. As William MacDonald explained: 'Where reparation had been accorded by the state it had always been as an act of grace, a favour by which the state acknowledged the sacrifice which the citizen had made on its behalf; but it had never been recognized as a right which the citizen might claim, either politically before a legislature or legally before a court' (MacDonald 1922: 59–60).

The general principle of awarding compensation was announced two and a half months after Germany had declared war on 3 August 1914. A circular dated 27 October 1914 was sent from President René Viviani to the prefects of invaded *départements* stating that the government proposed to assist, with every means at its disposal, all those suffering directly because of the war (Benns 1930: 348). It also stressed the principle of national solidarity and announced that *départements* in the French interior, far beyond the invasion zone, would be required to help in this major task (Reibel 1924b: 7). Parliament would be called upon to allocate financial resources but before this could happen mayors in the war-torn areas should submit to their local prefect detailed reports indicating clearly what damage had been sustained. A circular dated 28 October 1914 specified a wide range of agricultural losses that mayors should record, ranging from damage to soil and buildings, to loss of crops, fodder, grain, livestock and personal property. Such investigations were, of course, only possible in districts from which the Germans had withdrawn. Then the prefect would call upon staff of the Ponts-et-Chaussées, professors of agriculture and other local experts in order to prepare a report for the Ministère de l'Intérieur.

Louis Marin, deputy for Meurthe-et-Moselle, took the initiative to argue for legislation that would provide widespread compensation for war losses (Illaire 1991: 106). On 22 December 1914 the government stated its position more explicitly:

> Under the pressure of invasion *départements* have been occupied and ruins have accumulated. The government takes before you a solemn engagement, which it has already executed in part, in proposing to you a first opening of credit of 300,000,000 F. France will restore those ruins, counting confidently upon the proceeds of the indemnities which we shall exact and, in the meantime, upon the help of a contribution which the whole nation will pay, gladly, in the distress of a part of its children, to fulfil the role of national solidarity. Further, repudiating the form of relief which indicates favour, the state itself proclaims the right to reparation for the benefit of those who have been victims, in the matter of their possessions, of acts of war, and it will fulfil its duty to the largest limits which the financial capacity of the country shall permit and under conditions which a special law, designed to avoid all injustice and all arbitrariness, will determine. (cited in MacDonald 1922: 62–63)

The law of 26 December 1914 demanded payment of damages from the enemy and announced that precise conditions for allocating compensation would require further legislation (Augé-Laribé & Pinot 1927: 123). However, a preliminary sum of 300,000,000 F was set aside to meet very urgent needs in the war zone. On 4 February 1915 evaluation commissions were set up for *départements* and for *cantons*, and were instructed to start enquiries and to tackle particularly urgent questions. A subsequent decree (24 February 1915) enabled funds lodged with the Ministère de l'Intérieur to be disbursed.

During March 1915 a special commission was selected by the Ministère de l'Intérieur to determine the conditions whereby war damages might be allocated. It contained about forty members, including a range of senators and deputies, representatives of ministries, chambers of commerce, agricultural societies, and architects. It argued that the task of compensation was within the jurisdiction of Parliament and hence its report, issued on 27 May 1915, was concerned entirely with evaluating material damages that were the result of war. Two theories of evaluation were examined. One started from the cost of replacing specified property, from which an amount would be deducted for depreciation; the other took as its starting point the value of property at the time of its destruction. In fact, the second approach was favoured by a majority of the commission. If the amount of damages allowed under this principle should prove inadequate to permit restoration then legislation would have to be passed for additional sums. The datum plane for valuation should not be the precise date of destruction but rather the date immediately before the outbreak of war. Public records and documents held by insurance companies and other financial institutions should be employed to prepare such valuations. With respect to losses of personal property, *canton* commissions required detailed lists to be presented which would have to be supported by insurance policies and other documents wherever possible. The commission did not favour employing professional evaluators but recommended that lists should be prepared of advisers to whom *canton* commissions might turn.

On May 11 1915 the government placed a proposal for legislation on war damages before the Chambre des Députés. Reparation was to be made for war losses that were 'material, certain and direct' (MacDonald 1922: 63). Entitlement to compensation should be conditional upon its use to produce results that would be similar to those that had characterized the damaged property. Further legislation would be required to deal with compensation due to *communes*, *départements* and public enterprises. Finally, the right of recourse to the courts for recovering proposed compensation was denied. Indemnity was recognized as a right, but compensation was not expected to be paid immediately nor would the state pledge itself to financial promises beyond its means. Detailed financial arrangements would be made in due course but 300,000,000 F were made available to cover immediate needs. *Sinistrés* would not be entitled to compensation unless the sum was to be re-employed to make good specified losses in the war zone. In this way, the state claimed a right to determine the format and composition of the claims of each *sinistré* and to define conditions for re-employment of compensation on reconstruction.

Further progress on this legislation was blocked, and several ministries had to adopt pragmatic ways of providing assistance in the northern *départements*. Thus at the end of April 1916 the Ministère de l'Intérieur cooperated with military authorities to help returning refugees to construct temporary shelters and to repair damaged buildings (Illaire 1991: 106). The Ministère de l'Agriculture helped farmers to restart cultivation, and the Ministère du Travail introduced various social laws. An interministerial commission was set up on 18 May 1916 to encourage liaison in order to aid restoration and this was revised several times during 1917. On 29 May of that year the Ministère de l'Intérieur authorized *sinistrés* in liberated districts to ascertain their losses as best they could and then repair housing with any material they could find, on the understanding that their action would not prejudice any later compensation claims. During the summer of 1917 more laws and regulations came into operation but the *canton* commissions operated very slowly and made the *sinistrés* even more frustrated. In William MacDonald's words: 'The volume of laws, decrees and official pronouncements was out of all proportion to the work actually accomplished, and the array of functionaries was excessive in comparison with the record of their achievement' (MacDonald 1922: 56).

Meanwhile debate continued in the Chambre des Députés and the Senate over a definitive law on financial compensation. Members of both houses wished to ensure that the devastated *départements* should be fully repopulated but they placed differing emphasis on the means of achieving that end (Sauvy 1965: I 201). Progress was blocked by members of the Chambre des Députés who insisted that re-employment of compensation should be compulsory if sums exceeding the original value of the property were to be allocated. Their argument was based on a suspicion that many *sinistrés* might claim and obtain their compensation but then would not return to the northern *départements*. The fact that some *sinistrés* had already relocated commercial and industrial businesses in other parts of France was used as evidence for what might happen more widely. The deputies argued that compulsory re-employment would guarantee that population would return and hence avoid considerable numbers of *sinistrés* migrating to other areas. MacDonald insisted: 'That this fear had any substantial foundation is not apparent, but it seems to have been genuinely entertained' (MacDonald 1922: 67). Deputies continued to voice their concerns, and provisions regarding re-employment were duly modified. After more than a year and half of discussion, the proposed law was adopted by the Chambre des Députés on 23 January 1917. *Sinistrés* opposed both the notion of any tribunal being empowered to adjudicate on re-employment and the requirement for private financial affairs to be divulged. Amid this controversy the Senate rejected the idea of obligatory re-employment on 3 August 1917, after having heard a critical report from Senator Raynauld (Toulemon 1921: 45).

A compromise was suggested attaching a premium to re-employment but allowing each *sinistré* the choice to re-employ or not. If re-employment was favoured then compensation would incorporate not only the 1914 value of loss but also an additional amount to cover the cost of reconstruction or replacement which had increased through inflation during the war (Illaire 1991: 109). This modified law was adopted by the Senate on 22 December 1917 but the Chambre des Députés continued to demand that re-employment should be an obligation that could be waived only after special dispensation. Agreement still had not been reached when the Armistice was signed, but at the start of April 1919 the Chambre finally agreed to a workable compromise. They accepted the principle of individual choice with regard to re-employment, and the provision of a financial supplement when compensation was to be re-employed. They also agreed that *sinistrés* should not have to be authorized by a special tribunal if they chose not to re-employ their compensation. Three years and eleven months had passed since the law had been first proposed. As MacDonald remarked: 'Whatever defects the law might contain, no-one could say that it had not been long and carefully considered, that every argument had not been repeatedly weighed, or that the *sinistrés* and their representatives had not had abundant opportunity to be heard' (MacDonald 1922: 70).

Essential Legislation: The Sinistrés' Charter

The resulting law of 17 April 1919 was effectively a compromise between the Senate's judicial conception of the rights of the *sinistrés*, and the more emphatically economic concern of the Chambre des Députés that the northern *départements* should be restored and repopulated (Sauvy 1965: I 201). Under the legislation all certain, material and direct damages to real or personal property that resulted from acts of war were entitled to compensation following the promises of the law of 26 December 1914 (Bernard & Dubief 1985: 131). Compensation was not to be based on heavier taxes but on the critical assumption, so briefly yet powerfully enunciated by Clemenceau's finance minister M. Klotz, that 'l'Allemagne paiera' (Brogan 1940: 589). Five classes of damage were recognized:

(i) requisitions or other exactions made by the enemy or allied troops, including damage caused as a result of lodging troops;
(ii) moveable property that was damaged, destroyed or stolen (including losses during evacuation or repatriation);
(iii) real property that was damaged or destroyed (including forests and commercial, agricultural or industrial property);
(iv) losses under any of the three headings which occurred in the military zone (regardless of ordinary questions of legal liability);
(v) damage caused to fishing boats (Toulemon 1921: 55).

Sinistrés were entitled to compensation for losses caused by French or allied troops as well as those resulting from enemy activities. The right of compensation applied not only to individuals (and their heirs) but also to associations, public corporations, *communes* and *départements*. Following the passage of this crucial legislation the Belgian law on war damage and compensation was passed one month later in mid-May 1919

(Ford 1919a: 127; Mahain 1926; Chevalier 1919; Huysmans 1919).

In France, compensation for losses of real property was fixed at its value on the eve of mobilization, with due allowance for depreciation and supplements being added to permit reconstruction or repair, bearing in mind the cost differential between 1914 and whenever each particular case was evaluated (Reibel 1924a: 9). If compensation were not to be used for reconstruction or repair, then only the amount of the actual loss sustained would be allocated (Toulemon 1921: 44). Re-employment of compensation was to be used either in the *commune* where the loss had occurred or within a 50 km radius from that point, provided that it was not beyond the limits of the devastated zone (Parisot 1923: 66; Sellier & Bruggeman 1925: 51). Because of this ruling, critics feared that some ruined villages in the environs of towns might never be rebuilt or only partially so, since *sinistrés* might well choose to invest their compensation money elsewhere (Toulemon 1921: 154). For example, it was feared – and not without reason – that recovery of ruined villages around Verdun might well be hampered in this way. Depreciation of farmland, vineyards and forests was to be taken into account, together with the cost of restoration if compensation were to be re-employed. Where compensation was not to be re-employed, the amount due to the *sinistré* was to be paid by means of a bond bearing interest at 5 per cent, inalienable for five years, and payable in cash after five years in ten annual instalments. Losses of personal property were to be calculated from the baseline of values on 30 June 1914, but farm products were to be evaluated as of the date when the crop would have matured.

A commission comprising five members would be set up in each *canton* to evaluate damages, with the possibility of a second commission being convened if the local volume of work were deemed excessive (De Lubersac 1926: 2). Each commission would be nominated by the local prefect (Illaire 1991: 111). It would be presided over by a lawyer or a judge, and would include a delegate of the Ministère des Finances and the Ministère des Régions Libérées; an architect, building contractor or engineer; an expert in valuation of property and household goods; and a farmer, industrialist, merchant or craftsman depending on the economic characteristics of each particular area. These commissions would be assisted by a technical committee in each *département*, with special commissions examining questions relating to mines and woodlands. A Tribunal des Dommages de Guerre would operate in each *arrondissement* in order to revise evaluations and adjudicate in cases of dispute. It would be presided over by a magistrate and comprise two members with legal training (for example, lawyers or retired magistrates) and two citizens drawn at random from a list prepared by the *conseil-général* of each *département* (Hubert 1923: 21). At a later date (May 1921) *comités de préconciliation* were to be established in each *département* to review claims of between 500,000 F and 1,000,000 F before they were submitted to the *canton* commissions, and a *comité central de préconciliation* would assemble in Paris to review all claims exceeding 1,000,000 F (De Lubersac 1926: 4–5).

Claims for compensation, together with necessary documentary evidence, would have to be submitted by *sinistrés* to *cantonal* commissions which would have the power to view damaged property, examine witnesses, and reconcile disputes. Final decisions would normally reside with the *arrondissement* tribunal, whose conclusions, however, would be subject to review by the Commission Supérieure des Dommages de Guerre working alongside the Conseil d'Etat. If agreement could be reached, payment of compensation would be initiated by delivery of a certificate which would have to be exchanged within two months for a bond covering the main sum plus interest calculated at 5 per cent from the date of loss. In cases of re-employment, the *sinistré* would be entitled to an initial advance (ranging from 3,000 F to 100,000 F depending on the estimated value of the property in 1914 or its date of loss) and to advances on the balance in proportion to the rate of re-employment. Additional sums might be advanced to meet urgent needs. The state reserved the right to allocate to *sinistrés* material of similar nature and equal value to what had been lost; to replace personal property; and to carry out repair work or supply necessary materials (for example, through its special services). The state was empowered to take over any property if the cost of restoring that portion of land could be shown to exceed its value. *Sinistrés* were accorded priority in obtaining and transporting materials and having access to labour. The entire cost of clearing away debris, removing explosives, re-establishing public roads, and compensating for accidents resulting from explosion of shells was to be borne by the state.

Thus in the spring of 1919 the regulations and procedures for financial compensation were set in place, however their complexity formed a source of great frustration among *sinistrés* throughout the *régions libérées*. Indeed, in the late spring and early summer of 1919, when returnees were experiencing the most pressing needs, many *canton* commissions were not yet working and those that did operate were doing so very slowly (Hubert 1923: 201–03). In order to circumvent these problems, small financial advances were allocated to farmers in order to encourage them to get land back into cultivation. These advances might not exceed 2,000 F/ha nor be greater than double the amount of real loss (*perte subie*) declared for livestock, equipment and crops in store. Two-fifths of the advances might be allocated in cash to provide farmers with some ready money; the remaining three-fifths would be made available in the form of material supplies to be obtained from Sociétés Tiers-Mandataire (see Chapter 6). In addition, an indemnity of 300 F/ha was allocated to enable farmers to re-cultivate land which had fallen out of use because of wartime action. Of this sum, 120 F was allocated for the first ploughing and the remainder came in instalments as other work was completed in the fields.

The formalities involved in declaring wartime losses and claiming compensation gave rise to widespread misconceptions among *sinistrés*. Many believed that a preliminary declaration of loss, rather than a legally acceptable dossier, was all that was required of them, and others assumed that a brief evaluation by a technical expert would satisfy the *canton* commission (MacDonald 1922: 92). For the majority of ordinary *sinistrés* the most effective solution to these bureaucratic demands was to be found through membership of a reconstruction cooperative (see Chapter 9). In due course, over 3,100,000 compensation claims were lodged and the *canton* commissions, which reached a total of 665 at peak activity, were simply overwhelmed with work (Damade 1924: 9). They were answerable to the Ministère de la Justice and not to the Ministère des Régions Libérées (D'Aubigny 1921: 1138). Methodically, they scrutinized the bulky dossiers which 'piled up in mountains' in the order in which they had been received (Dessaint 1922: 751). There was no mechanism for classifying them in terms of urgency. In a speech in the devastated town of Albert on 24 April 1921 Minister Loucheur announced that only 800,000 claims had been adjudicated, but he hoped that by January 1922 a further 1,400,000 cases might be decided – three full years after the Armistice (MacDonald 1922: 89). Where decisions had been reached, first advances were often allocated promptly but every other element of compensation came very slowly, to the frustration and fury of the returnees. It seemed to many *sinistrés* that the bureaucracy of reparation had 'taken on the form of a colossal trial where *sinistrés* . . . are required to claim their rights before improvised tribunals' (Dessaint 1922: 751). In the words of M. D'Aubigny, reporter of the budget commission of the Chambre des Députés in 1921, 'every *sinistré* complained of the army of functionaries, the lack of uniformity or co-ordination and the overwhelming mass of dossiers' (cited in MacDonald 1922: 191). Further requirements were to slow down the rebuilding of complete settlements, since according to the legislation of 14 March 1919 architectural schemes had to be reconciled with formal rules of reconstruction and translated into village plans which then had to receive official approval before definitive work by cooperative reconstitution societies might commence. In addition to the vital issue of compensation, fundamental questions had to be resolved regarding material aspects of reconstruction in the countryside.

Rules of Reconstruction

As war raged and population returned to ruined houses and temporary shelters during phases when the enemy retreated, the challenge of planning the rebuilding of individual houses and of whole settlements in the devastated zone was being faced by architects and engineers working from Paris and from the unoccupied fringe of the war-torn *départements*. As explained above, less than three months after the declaration of war the government had expressed the principle of compensating citizens for material losses suffered as a result of hostilities (27 October 1914) (MacDonald 1922: 41). At the same time M. Georges-Risler, president of the Section d'Hygiène Urbaine et Rurale du Musée Social, was formulating a proposal that the government should require the municipality of each devastated settlement to draw up a blueprint (*plan d'aménagement*) to guide reconstruction and, if necessary, to prepare a document to steer future growth (*plan d'extension*) (Agache 1917: xx). This proposition was received by M. Léon Bourgeois and was presented to members of the Conseil de l'Alliance d'Hygiène Social who accepted it unanimously.

In a similar vein, the Ministère de l'Intérieur established a special service in 1916 to encourage reconstruction and reminded prefects that the task of recovery would involve rebuilding whole settlements as well as restoring individual properties. They were instructed to investigate how villages and towns in their *départements* might be improved, with respect to streets, sanitation, public health, and aesthetic character (Ford 1919a: 192). The architect J.M. Auburtin warned that to delay reconstruction could lead to social agitation as well as prejudicing the revival of the national economy (Auburtin 1916: 2). In his opinion, immediate reconstruction was simply an 'absolute necessity' (Ibid.). Accommodation built on the model of barracks or army huts could provide only a short-term solution to an extremely urgent problem (Agache, Auburtin & Redont 1916: 112). Indeed, some architects argued a case for direct, permanent reconstruction, that would employ pre-fabricated parts assembled to a number of standard designs (Lill 1916: 176). They acknowledged that the appearance of such new villages would be very different from the old settlements but stressed that 'the aesthetic point of view would not be neglected' (Ibid.: 177).

To facilitate permanent reconstruction a special section of the Ministère de l'Intérieur published a report on 22 October 1916 which indicated the distribution of quarries in the northern *départements* and showed where building materials might be sought (Ford 1919b: 225). Good building stone was available in each of the devastated *départements* except Nord and Somme. Clay for bricks was found in many *départements* and especially in Nord, but the limited availability of coal gave rise to severe problems and hampered industrial brick-making. Building sand could be obtained in most *départements* and cement could be produced in Pas-de-Calais, Marne, Meuse and Meurthe-et-Moselle, provided that supplies of coal and labour were made available (Hersent 1919: 150–51). Large quantities of tiles could be made in many parts of northern France, and roofing slates obtained from quarries in Ardennes and Meurthe-et-Moselle, and to a lesser extent also from Nord and Pas-de-Calais (Hubert 1923: 153). Ironware was made in traditional workshops in Ardennes, ceramic ware was produced in Nord and Pas-de-Calais, and glass was manufactured in Nord, Aisne and nearby Belgium. There was little timber available in the western half of the devastated regions but considerable supplies could still be obtained in the north-eastern *départements* (Auburtin 1919a: 194). Of course, the disruption and devastation of the war and the destruction of land transportation meant that widespread use of these resources would be impossible until peace had been restored.

On 14 March 1919 Parliament adopted a town planning law which applied across the nation and preceded by one month the long-awaited legislation on compensation (Reconstruction des agglomérations rurales, *JAP*, 33, 1920: 89–90). Its main principle was that each town with more than 10,000 inhabitants should draw up a comprehensive plan to guide future construction, dealing with the road pattern, open spaces, building heights, sewerage and public health (MacDonald 1922: 269). The expense of preparing such a document would be borne by the state. Similar arrangements were required not only for settlements of 5–10,000 inhabitants that were undergoing very rapid growth as resorts or industrial towns, but also for all settlements that had suffered destruction or damage as a result of war. The Ministre des Régions Libérées, M. Lebrun, enlisted the help of the Compagnie Aérienne Française to take aerial photographs of what remained of ruined settlements to assist the compilation of comprehensive plans (Roussilhe 1920: 197; Dupuy 1919: 611). The period allowed for preparing such plans was three years for areas that escaped devastation, but only three months for towns and villages in the war-torn zone (Cart de Lafontaine 1921a: 259). In practice, the latter period proved to be far too short and would have to be extended in almost every case. A special commission was created within the Ministère de l'Intérieur to supervise the execution of this law, and commissions in each *département* subsequently gave hearings to interested parties as well as to mayors of individual *communes*. Until such a land-use plan had been approved, no permanent buildings could be erected to replace ruins in war-torn settlements without the specific authorization of the prefect (MacDonald 1922: 299;

Couedelo 1991: 212). Temporary shelters were exempted from this ruling. Once the land-use plan had been adopted, all building operations would be required to conform to it and would need approval by the local mayor (MacDonald 1922: 270). The great *dommages de guerre* legislation of 17 April 1919 also stressed that all reconstruction should conform to general regulations regarding public health and sanitation being laid down by the Conseil Supérieur d'Hygiène Publique (Ford 1919a: 130). The state would bear the cost of clearing unexploded shells and ruins, making surveys, drawing up town and village plans, and improving public sanitation. It would also expropriate and pay for any property required to implement a public improvement specified in the local settlement plan.

Four Themes in Rural Reconstruction

Not surprisingly, the bulk of contemporary architectural writing on reconstruction was concerned with determining principles for the renaissance of ruined towns and cities rather than for the reconstitution of rural areas. Some authors believed that reconstruction of farms and rural housing could be left to the initiative of individual property owners, but others insisted that countryside planning needed serious forethought simply because it 'ran the greatest risk of being neglected' (Rosenthal 1918: 233). Thus, *communes* of all sizes should produce some kind of reconstruction plan (Couturaud 1915: 347). Four main themes permeated the surprisingly sparse literature written on planning the reconstruction of rural settlements.

The first involved the fundamental question of timing. As was abundantly clear, farmers were desperate to return to their land in order to restart cultivation once shells had been removed, trenches filled, and land levelled. However, permanent reconstruction of farmhouses and other rural dwellings was not allocated top priority, given the poor transport conditions, desperate shortages of labour and building materials, and ultimately the requirement for village rebuilding to conform with land-use plans. Such definitive reconstruction did not, of course, fall within the remit of the state-run emergency services (see Chapter 4). Partly as a result of the legislation of 14 March 1919, temporary shelters and wooden huts would be required to play a vital role during the first few years after the Armistice. Such accommodation entailed much inconvenience for the returnees and, once established, 'threatened to survive for many years, to the great detriment of the villages and their hygiene' (Joyant 1923: I 71). But, on the positive side, its use enabled time and thought to be given to the requirements of definitive rebuilding. Even if it had been possible, hasty reconstitution exactly as before would have carried the threat of merely replicating the deficiencies of pre-existing housing and settlement layout.

The second theme involved the realization that a more considered approach would offer an opportunity to improve living conditions in the countryside, whose shortcomings had been widely recognized as having played a major role in contributing to rural depopulation in the past. The message was proclaimed by the philanthropists, politicians, economists and administrators who belonged to the Société d'Hygiène Sociale which had been created in 1907 (Couedelo 1991: 211). Ten years later Georges-Risler asserted that doctors knew that hygiene in French villages was 'deplorable' and Léon Rosenthal used the same adjective to describe living conditions on many agricultural holdings, especially those where farm families lived in close proximity to their animals (cited in Agache 1917: xxix; Rosenthal 1918: 235). It was believed that they became 'intoxicated' at night by the odours from dung heaps, with sunlight and fresh air rarely penetrating their squalid accommodation (Agache 1917: xix). Civil engineer Georges Hersant was sweeping in his condemnation, arguing that 'with only rare exceptions, our hamlets and villages have remained much as they were two or three centuries ago' (Hersant 1919: 216). He alleged that many rural dwellings were no better than slums, with floors of beaten earth, inadequate windows to let in light and air, insufficient drainage, and often suffering pollution because of the proximity of cowsheds and manure heaps to supplies of drinking water. He insisted that to provide a 'hygienic, light and comfortable dwelling is one of the best ways to keep countryfolk on the land' (Ibid.: 217). Unless this were done, he continued, there would be a very real risk that migration from the countryside would intensify in the years ahead and agricultural labour would become even more scarce and therefore more expensive than it had been on the eve of the war.

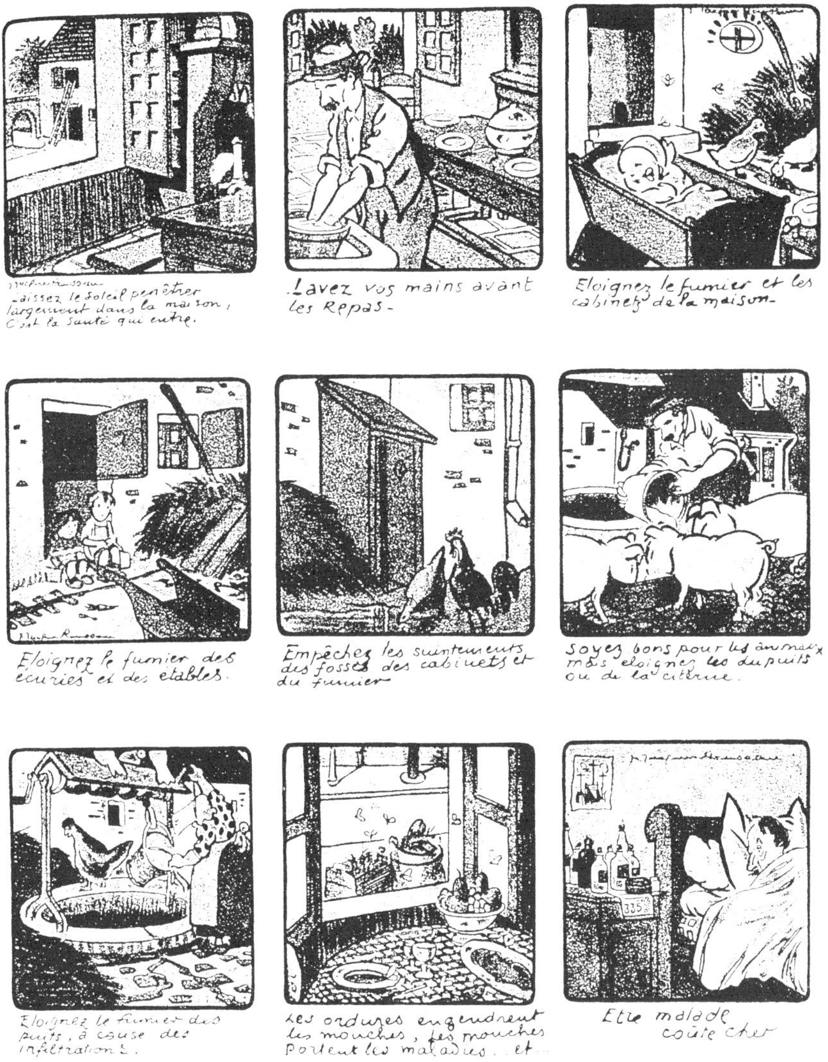

Plate 8.1 Official propaganda encouraging the improvement of hygiene in reconstructed farm buildings

Installation of damp-courses would be a major improvement in reconstructed farmhouses, as would higher ceilings, better lighting, and larger windows (Cellerier 1917: 40; Auburtin 1916: 5). Abolition of the tax on doors and windows on 31 July 1917 opened the way for improvement in this respect and twelve months later the Conseil Supérieur d'Hygiène Publique published two model sanitary ordinances, one dealing with urban areas and the other with villages (Rosenthal 1918: 235; Ford 1919a: 151). The rural ordinance outlined the need for damp-courses and described practical measures for minimizing the threat of damp and fire, and for ensuring that kitchens were well illuminated and ventilated. Rules were also pronounced for disposing of foul water and sewage, and for ensuring that manure heaps be kept clear of wells and piped water supplies. Manure was required to be removed regularly and was prohibited from being piled in the traditional way along village streets or against houses (Auscher 1919: 11). In rebuilt agricultural property, sleeping accommodation was forbidden in cellars, attics, barns and stables, hence special facilities would be required for housing farmhands in the future (Ford 1919a: 151). Thatched roofs were prohibited even on barns, and windows and doors on reconstructed farmhouses preferably should face south or south-east to receive maximum light (Brisac 1922a: 6). Concrete and steel might usefully be introduced to replace timber in some parts of the new buildings (Ibid.). Drawings of 'model' types of farm building were prepared by the Ministère de l'Intérieur and the Génie Rural to assist the reconstitution process (Les types de constructions agricoles, *CM*, 01.06.17: 1). Examples of freshly constructed farms would figure prominently on the pages of the agricultural and architectural press (such as the *Journal d'Agriculture Pratique* and *La Construction Moderne*) during the 1920s. Local prefects had an important role to play to ensure that such ideas also spread among the ordinary *sinistrés* (Brisac 1922a). For example, in Meurthe-et-Moselle several thousand plans for reconstructing farm buildings were scrutinized by the official *département* architect and his staff, and the opportunity was taken to make valuable suggestions for introducing improvements, since many architects were 'unaware of the most elementary necessities of agricultural life' (*L'agriculture dans le département de Meurthe-et-Moselle*, 1927: 82).

The third theme embraced the complicated, interrelated issues of style and appropriate materials to be used for individual buildings. By virtue of the need for widespread reconstruction, a major opportunity presented itself for fundamental changes to be made. Architectural opinion was effectively divided between modernists who favoured new designs and materials, and improvers who preferred constructing better versions of traditional rural housing. Dassonville argued that there should be no false archaism or pastiche employed in reconstruction (Dassonville 1919: 69). Likewise, Emile Gavelle, Directeur de l'Ecole des Beaux-Arts de Lille, insisted that the exigencies of the time precluded any 'cramponning' on to historic features simply for their own sake (Gavelle 1920: 7). As early as November 1915, M. Revault, Deputy of Meuse, had urged the use of cement components to accelerate reconstruction (Auburtin & Blanchard 1915: 17). Preparation of plans for model buildings and for whole settlements by members of the Société d'Architectes Diplômés par le Gouvernement (SADG) gave ample opportunity to explore the possibilities offered by pre-fabrication in reconstructing rural housing, as well as urban tenements, at a time when building workers were in desperately short supply (Auburtin 1919b: 324; Bousquet 1919: 23).

At a finer scale, the Ministère des Régions Libérées emphasized that time would be saved by using standardized doors, windows, locks and other fittings, which relatively unskilled builders could install (Delaire 1919–20: 89). An exhibition of cheap housing was mounted in the Tuileries Gardens in Paris during the summer of 1916 to inform architects and building contractors of what might be accomplished (Ford 1919b: 226). However, transport difficulties loomed large and made the use of a variety of local building materials all the more necessary during the war, to the relief of commentators who were opposed to mass-produced housing being constructed across the northern countrysides (Lecq 1918: 312; AN F21 2904 Hermant, J. Les conseils, 1917). Nonetheless, some young architects employed their imagination to the full and produced 'more or less strange' designs for new farmhouses which made abundant use of concrete and iron (Quénedey 1920: 10). Not surprisingly, the majority opinion eschewed radical innovation and favoured forms of reconstruction that respected traditional styles, made full use of local stone or brick, and employed slate or tile as roof covering. It was, however, agreed that great efforts should be made to improve facilities inside all reconstructed housing while, as far as possible, economizing on the use of building labour (Léon 1918: 208).

This broad line of thinking had been evolving since the start of

Plate 8.2 A farmhouse in Fossieux, Lorraine, before and after reconstruction in a completely different style; the views are dated December 1919 and July 1920.

the century under the guidance of Jean Lahor (also known as Dr Cazalis), who founded the Société pour la Protection des Paysages in 1901 and the Société d'Art Populaire et d'Hygiène three years later (Vigato 1983: 33; 1994: 75–137). He sought to avoid excessive urbanization and industrial development, and argued that construction in rural areas should be inspired by traditional examples. Through the pages of *L'Architecte*, which was founded in 1906, students of the Ecole des Beaux-Arts were encouraged to sketch building styles in the provinces. In September 1916 the SADG published a brochure on model dwelling types and in January 1917 organized an exhibition on 'L'architecture régionale dans nos provinces envahies' under the patronage of the Sous-Secrétariat d'Etat aux Beaux-Arts (Boussard 1991: 194). The catalogue which accompanied it was prefaced by art critic Léandre Vaillat from *Le Temps* who was to express strong opinions on rural reconstitution during the war and in the early 1920s (Bédarida 1991: 265). Particularly notable among the work displayed at the 1917 exhibition were eighty designs by André Ventre, an architect of the Service des Monuments Historiques, who had been sent by Paul Léon, chef des services d'architecture au Ministère des Beaux-Arts, to sketch traditional houses in Artois, Picardy, the Pays de Noyon, Soissonnais, Champagne, Lorraine and Alsace (Vaillat 1917; L'exposition de l'architecture régionale dans les provinces envahies, *LA*, 1917: 30). Improved versions of regional styles figured very largely among the submissions to the competition that was launched in May 1917 for designing three types of rural dwelling in sample settlements in the devastated *départements* (Exposition du concours pour la reconstruction, *LA*, 1918: 9–13).

Many authors stressed the need to take local agricultural practices as well as variations in building material into account when preparing architectural drawings for new housing to be constructed in the war zone (Ringelmann 1920). Paul Léon insisted that 'housing, like flora or fauna, is a geographical element that is linked closely to the nature of terrain, to climatic conditions, to landownership, and to the nature of farming' (Léon 1918: 204). Quénedey contrasted the restricted use of timber in the traditional buildings of Flanders and Picardy with its more abundant presence in the vernacular architecture of

Champagne and Argonne, and stressed the widespread use of Jurassic limestone in Lorraine and of the Tertiaries of the Paris Basin in Soissonnais, Laonnais and Brie Champenoise (Quénedey 1920: 14–19). With the help of André Ventre's drawings, Léandre Vaillat also explored variations in geology and local building material throughout the northern *départements* and enunciated the compromise that rural reconstruction should 'fully respect tradition but also innovate in a modest way' (Vaillat 1917: 37). For example, architect Déville, working in Meurthe-et-Moselle, was praised for examining the detail of ruined buildings and studying their principles of construction before commencing reconstruction (Ibid.). Vaillat argued that there was no need to look beyond northern France to establish guidelines for restoration, and maintained that 'from this kind of enquiry we can easily deduce the type of house for tomorrow, that is adapted to climate, customs, local resources and landscape. It exists already: why invent another?' (Ibid.). Nonetheless, respect for traditional styles certainly did not require manure to be heaped beneath windows, demand rooms to be poorly ventilated, or the basic rules of hygiene to be ignored (AN F21 2905 Rapport présenté par M. Léon Rosenthal). In this way, 'regionalism became . . . the official doctrine of reconstruction' in the countryside, not only evoking pre-war conditions before the impact of the technology of mass destruction but also permitting scope for improvements in the internal organization of housing and the external arrangement of farm buildings (Vigato 1983: 35). Early reconstruction of Vassincourt, near Bar-le-Duc, was quoted as a successful example which combined 'all the charm' of pre-war buildings with all the convenience and efficiency subsequently required (Ford 1919a: 198). In their various ways each of these initiatives echoed a willingness to reconstitute *la France profonde* as it had existed before the conflict (Bédarida 1991: 266).

What might constitute appropriate advice on the reconstruction of whole settlements formed the fourth main theme of debate. Rosenthal argued that 'to rebuild at random would be criminal folly. All the progress that we have envisaged can and must be realized' (Rosenthal 1918: 244). Expressing his thoughts in more grandiose terms, Holliday insisted that 'the most destructive of wars has given the world a magnificent opportunity

Plate 8.3 The village of Vitrimont, Meurthe-et-Moselle, rebuilt with an American loan

for creation' (Holliday 1921: 5). In the dark days of conflict and in the initial enthusiasm of peace, architects dreamed of rapid rebuilding in the countryside and of creating model villages that would be devised according to the best rules of hygiene and settlement planning (Joyant 1923: I 71). A sample of their ideas was conveyed by the drawings that were submitted to the competition launched in May 1917 for planning the reconstruction of three specific localities, which characterized differing types of settlement in the northern *départements*. Thus, Vailly (Aisne) had housed 2,000 people before the war; Templeuve (near Lille, Nord) had contained 3,000 and had supported a range of industrial as well as agricultural activities; while Sommedieu (Meuse), with a pre-war population of 1,400, had occupied an isolated site close to extensive woodlands which had provided much local employment (Agache 1917: 9). Almost one hundred architects submitted their drawings to this competition and their ideas were presented in a sequence of chapters in *Nos agglomérations rurales* by the *rapporteur-général*, Alfred Agache. A few years later Quénedey echoed the progressive mood of the moment and went so far as to argue that village reconstruction and other aspects of rural recovery provided an excellent opportunity for also undertaking the consolidation (*remembrement*) and reallocation of agricultural land holdings (Quénedey 1920: 23) (see Chapter 10).

From Principles to Practice

In fact, *remembrement rural* was to take place rarely and most northern householders were opposed to radical changes being introduced to the morphology of villages requiring reconstruction (Héricault 1934: 108). It was, to quote Héricault's analogy, as if 'a new dress, of simple and harmonious design, had to be fashioned from a complicated old one' (Ibid.: 109). Hence in only in a small proportion of cases were the sites of settlements modified and completely new villages constructed away from the ruins of the old (see Chapter 11). Although popular in theory, model villages proved to be very much in the minority in terms of practical reconstruction. Far more generally, it was a question of improving a settlement's layout by judicious widening of roads, avoiding blind corners, removing narrow alleys, and providing communal open space around the points where the village school, church and *mairie* were to be re-built (Auburtin 1919b: 324). Reconstruction afforded an opportunity to ensure that the school had a proper playground and that the cemetery would be relocated on the margins of the village (Agache, Auburtin & Redont 1915: 105). In addition, a range of communal facilities, such as a meeting room, a library and a dispensary, might be introduced, as well as piped water supplies and mains drainage (Auburtin 1919b: 325). It was hoped that the provision of *salles communes*, where talks might be given and films shown, would 'combat the pernicious influence of the bars [*cabarets*] on the physical and moral condition' of the rural population (Ministère des Régions Libérées 1919: 4). An unusually comprehensive example was to be built at Fargniers (Aisne) where a donation of $150,000 from the Carnegie Foundation for International Peace enabled a new *mairie*, two schools, a library, public baths, cinema, market hall, sports facilities and gardens to be installed around the appropriately-named Place Carnegie (Fondation Carnegie 1922: 3). The ensemble was designed by two Parisian architects, MM. Nenot and Bigot, and work began in July 1922 (Figure 8.1). The building which contained the public baths now houses the Musée Départemental de la Résistance et de la Déportation en Picardie.

Implementation of the law of 14 March 1919 was not easy and progress proved slow. Before permanent reconstruction might be authorized, architects were required to produce comprehensive plans at a scale of 1: 1,250, 1: 1,000 or sometimes in more detail to show both the morphology of the old village and the proposed arrangement of streets, public buildings, housing and other features that would replace it (ADMe 976.Rp.2705 Plans d'alignement). These documents needed to be accompanied by detailed written proposals for scrutiny by staff of the local *préfecture*. Examination of a small sample of submissions in four *départements* suggests that the officials paid particular attention to matters of hygiene, water supply, drainage and the location of cemeteries (Ibid; ADMM W1312 Plans d'aménagement; ADA 12J 15 Collection Marlier; ADN 10RA Plans Généraux d'Alignement). Not surprisingly, village plans that had been drafted by, or had received advice from, the staff of the Ponts-et-Chaussées or another official body were more likely to be

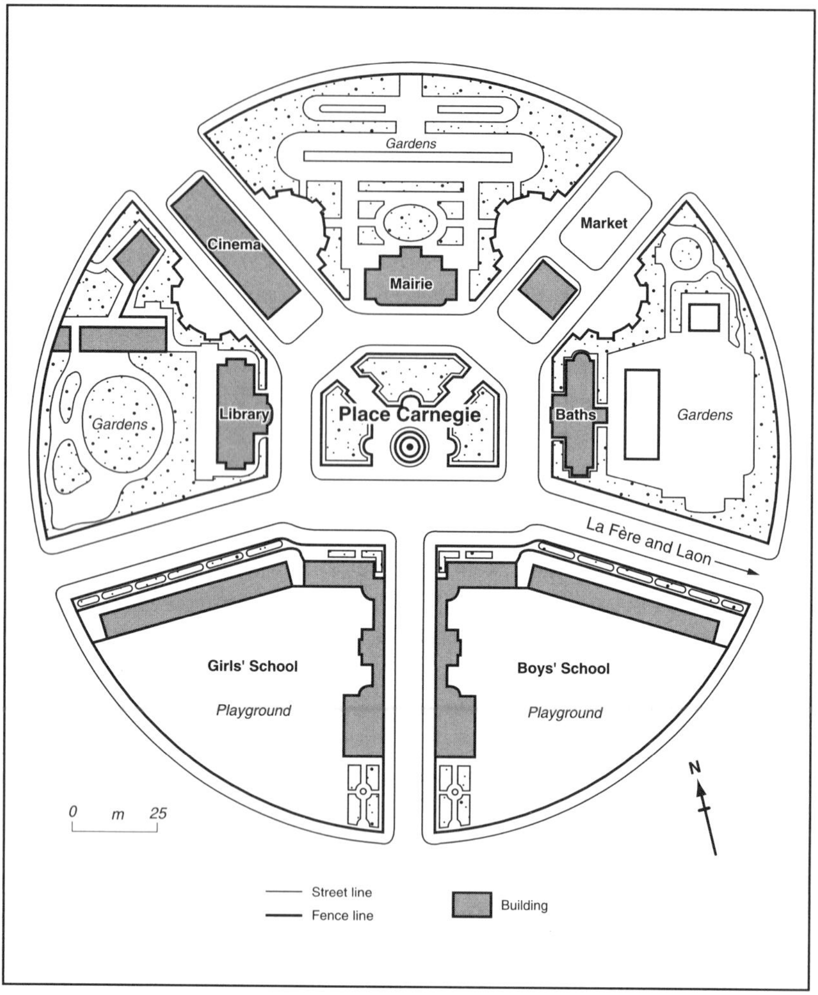

Figure 8.1 Reconstruction of Fargniers, Aisne

approved than those which had been submitted by architects who had worked without consultation. A circular from the Ministère des Régions Libérées dated 23 June 1921 informed prefects of the need to accelerate their methods for reviewing and approving settlement plans if their task of appraisal was to be completed by the extended, three-year deadline of March 1922 (MacDonald 1922: 271). A major complication proved to be the ambiguity of whether the costs of expropriation to enable road widening would be met by the central state or had to be borne by each *commune*. A circular of 23 June 1922 urged that changes to street lines should be kept to a minimum, and reinforced that message by stating that the expense involved in unnecessary changes to village morphology would have to be carried by the *commune* in question (Ibid.: 272). Many of the bold ideas for village planning that had been proposed at the time of the Armistice proved both impractical and expensive, and hence much simpler plans were drawn up in many instances (Carpentier 1928: 68). Long and delicate negotiations regarding property rights would be necessary if a village were to be remodelled, but such deliberations were scarcely possible in ruined settlements whose administrative services might not be functioning normally, whose archives and cadastral maps and registers might be lost, and a proportion of whose landowners might not have returned. As Carpentier remarked, 'almost everywhere the desire to do well was sacrificed to the desire to build fast' (Ibid.: 67).

After the harsh experience of working as a *directeur départemental des services de reconstitution* in northern France, M. Joyant provided realistic advice on rural reconstruction in his *Traité d'Urbanisme*. Problems of labour, materials and cash flow forced him to recommend that 'projects for rebuilding villages should not be too ambitious. They should be reasonable and, as the circular of 5 March 1920 advised, should incorporate old features in order to improve rather than to transform' (Joyant 1923: I 71). He argued that architects should be fully aware of the cost implications of their designs (and of the grandiose ideas held by some village mayors) and should avoid trying to install the most modern features of urban hygiene in every village whose plans they drafted. He recognized that provision of fresh, unpolluted drinking water was essential and that mains drainage and piped water were desirable, but he believed that fountains and cesspits would be both adequate and acceptable in many country places, provided that sensible steps were taken to avoid pollution. Even schemes for modifying road layout, he argued, should be done 'with prudence' (Ibid.). Ruler-straight roads and lengthy un-broken building façades should be avoided since, he insisted, the established 'alignment of houses gives a village its character and picturesque quality; these features must be preserved when they do not cause any serious drawbacks to traffic movement' (Ibid.). In some instances, wise suggestions from architects were ignored by contractors so the end result resembled more closely what had been lost than what had been intended (Ibid.: 75).

To assist the reconstruction of northern settlements, the Renaissance des Cités organization had been founded in 1916 by two artists, M. Adar Mitrécy and Mlle Tarrade-Page, who foresaw the problems that would attend rebuilding (Cart de Lafontaine 1921b: 1). It was a non-profit making society for the provision of free advice from experienced *urbanistes*, engineers, doctors and lawyers to local mayors and architects in the devastated *départements* (Cart de Lafontaine 1924: 1022). Its executive committee included ministers and leaders of various shades of religious opinion. In addition, specialist committees were set up to deal with technical, social, legal, artistic and archaeological matters. Renaissance des Cités was to play an important role in introducing garden-city and garden-suburb ideas into northern France, promoting such notions not only among local politicians and professionals but also among industrialists, and owners of mines and railway companies (see Chapter 11). Its members included many distinguished professionals who devoted their time and abilities to such work in an entirely honorary capacity. At first the organization had to rely on voluntary subscriptions, but the French government eventually allocated a small annual grant toward running expenses, and subscriptions were received from *départements*, municipalities and banks. Funds were also obtained from the USA, including an annual grant from the Rockefeller Foundation (Cart de Lafontaine 1921b: 3). Its experts were keen to ensure that improvements took place but they also sought to avoid the kind of radically intrusive changes that some architectural plans would have produced, thereby 'destroying the personality and picturesque quality' of the villages involved (Joyant 1923: I 72; Smith & Hill 1920: 199).

Through the generosity of the American Red Cross and with assistance from other benefactors, the Renaissance des Cités acquired the services of Major George B. Ford, the American town planner who would become well known for his advisory work on the reconstruction of Reims (Holliday 1921; Clout 1989; Joyant 1923: I 72). He was charged by the organization to examine many village plans in order to recommend sensible modifications before rebuilding might commence and he visited a large number of devastated *communes* to enable him to do this effectively (Cart de Lafontaine 1921b: 3). It was his belief that the greatest challenge was trying to persuade villagers that they needed the services of an expert adviser (Ford 1919a: 197). Despite difficulties of this kind, Renaissance des Cités helped more than two hundred rural and urban settlements across the northern *départements* to prepare the final version of their reconstruction plans (MacDonald 1922: 269). Several examples of Ford's suggestions, which were reproduced in the first volume of Joyant's *Traité d'Urbanisme*, indicate that he was particularly concerned with adjusting street alignments and the location of individual buildings, with taking local variations in terrain fully into account (especially with regard to traffic, water supply and drainage), and with ensuring adequate provision of public open space (Joyant 1923: I 73–5). Figure 8.2 shows the distribution of ruined buildings in the village of Emberménil (Meurthe-et-Moselle), together with Ford's revised alignment of the village street along which new houses would be built. Public buildings were to be grouped around an enlarged village square, with new service roads to be installed behind each row of dwellings. Sewer pipes were to be laid beneath the two main roads, draining to the south-west and south-east respectively.

The German Option?

In order to reconstruct whole settlements it was necessary not only to produce plans, ensure effective organization, and secure finance and building materials, but also to obtain adequate supplies of qualified labour. The Confédération Générale du Travail, the Union Syndicale des Techniciens de l'Industrie, du Commerce et de l'Agriculture, and related trades-union organizations saw the latter challenge as a means of using labour to promote international reconciliation and repeatedly argued a case for bringing German craftsmen to restore devastated French villages (Toulemon 1921: 181). This idea of using German specialists had been discussed by French and German trades unions soon after the Armistice and had been explored in discussions in July 1919 which preceded the Treaty of Versailles (La participation allemande, *LP*, 13.01.21). It was examined

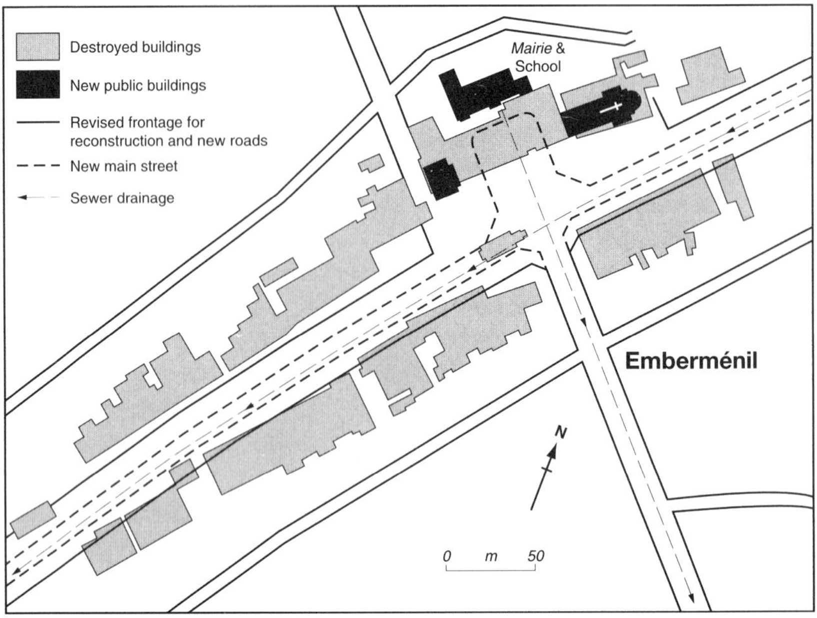

Figure 8.2 Reconstruction of Emberménil, Meurthe-et-Moselle

cautiously by M. Loucheur, Ministre des Régions Libérées, early in 1921 and he argued that *sinistrés* would not wish to have German workers living among them (Loucheur dit: Il faut que l'Allemagne paye! Pas de main-d'oeuvre allemande, *LP*, 25.04.21). Like their compatriots elsewhere in northern France, *sinistrés* in Somme wished to reconstruct as soon as possible but their views on German workers were clouded by memories of wartime occupation and many urged that rebuilding should be 'an essentially French operation' which might call on labour from colonies and friendly European powers if need be (Morain 1921: 45). However, if there proved to be no alternative to German skilled workers, Prefect Morain believed that the *sinistrés* of Somme might agree to make what he termed 'this last sacrifice' to ensure that their homes were rebuilt (Ibid.). The issue was put to the test in November 1921 when members of the Confédération Générale du Travail and other trades unions organized a visit by their German counterparts to a dozen ruined villages in the devastated *canton* of Chaulnes in the red zone of eastern Somme in order to propose a reconstruction strategy (Figure 8.3). Before the war about 3,740 people had lived in these villages, which had contained 750 houses (Une délégation ouvrière franco-allemande, *LP*, 31.10.21). It was estimated that reconstruction might require a workforce of 2,500. The area was served by two railway lines and was close to the Canal de la Somme (Carpentier 1928: 50). The German delegation offered to supply craftsmen but not to provide building materials or finance (Le recours aux allemands, *JRD*, 06.11.21: 1).

Claiming to speak for the *sinistrés*, Marcel Hénard argued in the *Journal des Régions Dévastées* that, should 'the *bocho-communiste* building site be allowed to open, other Germans will follow' and the they 'will colonize, coming in droves, they will submerge the *sinistrés*. They will operate an invasion plan' (Hénard 1921: 1). By contrast, the trades-unions newspaper *Le Peuple* insisted that the delegation and its proposals had been received warmly across the former battle zone (La délégation ouvrière franco-allemande, *LP*, 01.11.21). M. Loucheur demanded that the views of all *sinistrés* in the dozen villages should be sought, and that at least 80 per cent of households would have to be in favour before he would grant his approval (Meissel 1986: 171). An unofficial enquiry undertaken rapidly by local councillors indicated that 86 per cent of local households were favourably disposed to the idea, but the minister insisted that an official referendum would have to be organized and that additional information be made known with regard to German workers (Où en est la question de reconstruction par la main-d'oeuvre allemande?, *LP*, 04.12.21). First, the *sinistrés* would be required to form an association which would hire the labour and organize the programme of work. Inhabitants would, however, be able to appoint their own architects. Second, the German craftsmen would be housed in camps, but not in conditions reminiscent of prisoner-of-war accommodation, and would be at liberty to move around the area in their free time. Contrary to widespread rumours, they would not be billeted on *sinistrés*, many of whom were living in appalling makeshift conditions (see Chapter 7). Considerable hostility toward Germans coming to work in the area was voiced in and around the town of Péronne (Meissel 1986: 173).

Prefect Morain duly conducted meetings in the dozen *communes* and obtained the impression that their inhabitants were

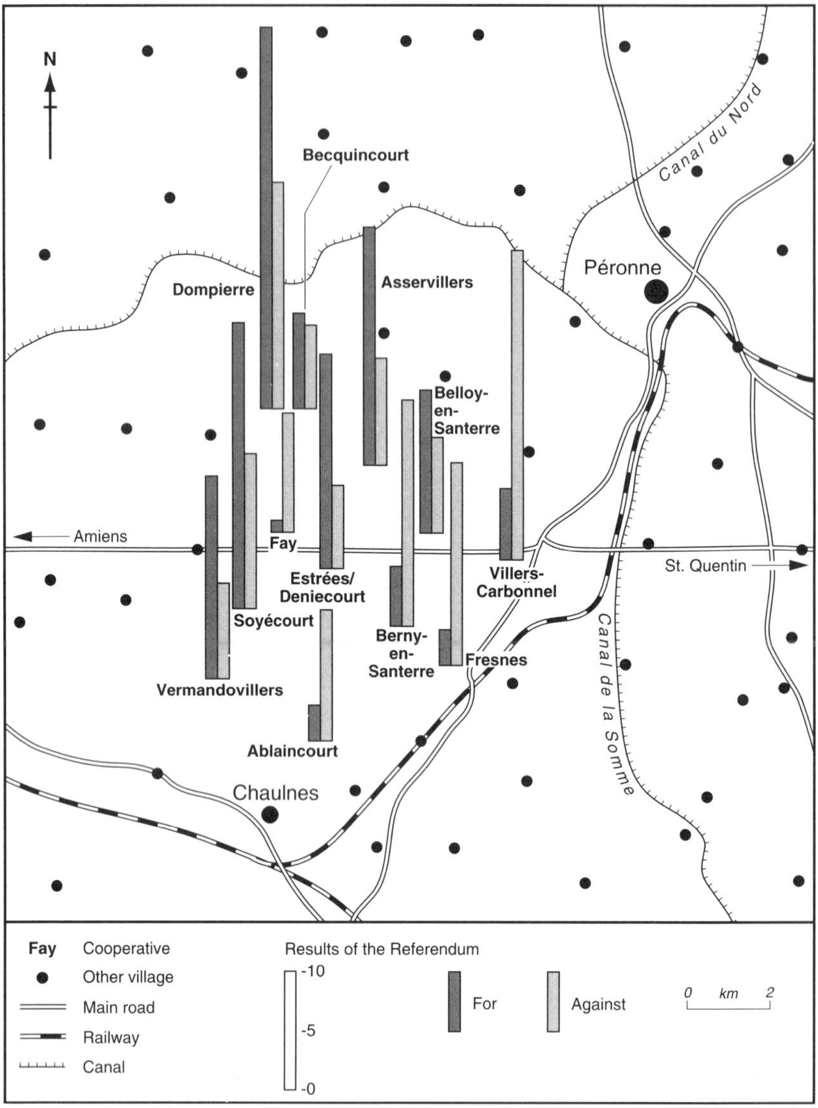

Figure 8.3 Results of the referendum in Chaulnes *canton*, Somme

not opposed to German workers as such but were strongly against the German *system* being allowed to operate in their home area (Morain 1922a: 121). A total of 303 households expressed their opinion. Only 149 (49 per cent) declared in favour and hence the proposal was rejected summarily by the Minister (Carpentier 1928: 52) (Figure 8.3). As a result, contractors and craftsmen would have to be sought wherever they could be found and, to the chagrin of the Confédération Générale du Travail, the ruined villages of Somme would not be used as a test case to promote Franco-German solidarity, nor would German labour be brought in to restore isolated parts of the red zone as others had advocated (Toulemon 1921: 183). As Denis Brogan argued later, it might indeed have made more economic sense to have used German labour as a method of payment in kind rather than to hope that financial and material reparations would be recoverable from Germany (Brogan 1940: 599). However, the objection that it would be intolerable to have invaders working alongside their recent victims carried greater emotional force. This sentiment was allegedly stronger among French building firms, which feared that they might lose their contracts, than among ordinary labourers and *sinistrés*. Hence, specialist bricklayers, masons and carpenters were duly enlisted from Italy, Belgium and Poland and to a lesser extent from Spain and Portugal, with this pattern of recruitment being repeated throughout the *régions dévastées* (La main-d'oeuvre allemande dans les régions dévastées, *LP*, 08.02.21).

In fact, during 1923 thirty craftsmen from the German Rhinelands were brought to work on short contracts on two building sites near Montdidier (Somme) and gave complete satisfaction to their employers by virtue of their diligence, professionalism and rapid work (Emery 1924: 107). They were housed on the building sites and were not permitted to visit Montdidier or surrounding villages unless accompanied by a French supervisor (Carpentier 1928: 53). The uneven flow of compensation money from the state for reconstruction meant that the number of building workers of all kinds and origins fluctuated considerably during the 1920s. For example, by April 1923 16,958 building workers were employed on reconstruction work in Somme, but twelve months later the figure had fallen to 11,119 as a result of serious cash-flow problems (Emery 1924:

102) (see Chapter 9). Neither the French state nor German workers would provide the mechanism for permanent reconstruction, hence the *sinistrés* had to organize themselves and look to their own resources.

As the early paragraphs of this chapter have shown, the whole issue of lodging claims for compensation was the responsibility of individual *sinistrés*. However, by insisting that a comprehensive blueprint be prepared for the reconstruction of each devastated settlement, the law of 14 March 1919 lent its support to the idea that there might be some form of collective approach. Even before the Armistice had been signed, modest initiatives had been taken to promote the creation of reconstruction cooperatives. The role of these organizations was to prove of fundamental importance in rebuilding the devastated villages of northern France.

9
Reconstruction Cooperatives

Collective Responses to a Fiercely Individualistic Law

The fundamental principle behind the legislation of 17 April 1919 on war damages involved the individual *sinistré*, who was responsible for declaring and evaluating material losses in a form that would be acceptable to the *canton* commission prior to lodging claims for compensation from the state. Rich property owners and industrialists could employ legal and financial advisers to steer them speedily and profitably through this bureaucratic morass but, as Deputy Albert Inghels argued with great force, such assistance was unthinkable for the great number of family farmers in the war zone who had few if any resources behind them. It was as if 'for some, everything is permitted . . . for others, everything is taken away, so that ordinary *sinistrés* have nothing left, having been squeezed like lemons' (Inghels 1924: 13). Many *sinistrés* were overwhelmed by the magnitude of the task of evaluation and fell into despair, believing that they would have to abandon their ruins and their land (De Mahuet 1927: 5). As André Tardieu stressed, the law of 17 April 1919 was 'fiercely individualistic' but nonetheless it contained two articles (49 and 58) which stressed the merits of *sinistrés* grouping together to confront the challenge of reconstruction (AN 324 AP/63 Tardieu, A., Ce que demandent les régions libérées, 01.09.20). It also offered more generous financial advances to associations which lodged claims for compensation than to *sinistrés* who operated individually (Caraud 1924: 70). Within days of the passage of the law, the Ministre des Régions Libérées instructed prefects to encourage the creation of reconstruction associations in their *départements*. A few weeks later, the Belgian government similarly favoured the establishment of cooperatives to assist rebuilding (Willaert 1930).

Farm cooperatives and associations for the sale and purchase of agricultural commodities had been well established in some parts of northern France before the war and offered a model that might be adapted to the reconstruction of built property (Brethe 1923: 6). Other approaches might be developed in localities where associations for constructing workers' housing, for levelling out war-damaged land, or for working the devastated soil had been set up. In a more general sense, the idea of cooperation was partly derived from the growth of industrial trades unions and the corresponding rise of syndicates of employers, as well as 'the new sense of common effort, common sacrifice and suffering, and personal comradeship born of the war' (MacDonald 1922: 207). Thus, during the summer and autumn of 1917 the ORA had encouraged the creation of cooperative associations for working abandoned farmland, which involved 40,000 ha and nearly 8,000 farmers in the *départements* of Aisne, Pas-de-Calais and Somme (see Chapter 6). Reconstruction of housing did not, of course, figure in the remit of these farming associations, which in any case were virtually all wiped out during the German advance in the subsequent spring (Ford 1919b: 220). In a similar vein, the staff of the Génie Rural had taken the initiative to group *sinistrés* into associations to work stretches of farmland in Nord at various stages during the war (Morain 1923: 131).

In fact, a cooperative approach to rebuilding had already been promoted in two parts of northern France. The first involved engineers of the Génie Rural encouraging property owners to group together in order to permit rational reconstruction of settlements in the *département* of Marne that had been damaged in 1911 by floods in the Marne valley (Fiel 1935: 10; Morain 1923: 131). The second embraced a dozen farming villages, to the south of Châlons-sur-Marne and around Vitry-le-François, which had been destroyed during the first Battle of the Marne (1914) and where the government, through the staff of the Génie Rural, encouraged the creation of four cooperative reconstruction societies in 1916 (Rodolphe-Rousseau 1920: 2; AN F21 2904 Hermant, J., Les conseils à donner, 1917). Almost all local property owners joined these societies which were able to employ a single architect and contractor for each cooperative to rebuild whole settlements at a time. By so doing they saved a great deal of time and money and were able to approach the government to secure the services of German prisoners of war for manual work. They also received special dispensation from the army for obtaining the necessary supplies of timber, lime, cement and transport facilities for rebuilding. In each case, members of the cooperatives were allocated the maximum advance on the eventual indemnity for their losses. Initial attention was devoted to rebuilding grain barns but by the end of 1918 the four cooperatives had constructed about 150 buildings, which represented roughly a quarter of what would be needed to make good their total losses (Ford 1919b: 220). In late March 1919 George Ford was able to report that these villages were 'nearly completely resurrected from their ruins', with new buildings having been designed to be far more practical than the ones they replaced (Ford 1919a: 225). The success of these organizations provided a fine object lesson to groups of *sinistrés* elsewhere in northern France who were contemplating setting up reconstruction cooperatives at the time the Armistice was signed (Brethe 1923: 6).

Throughout 1918 the cooperative approach to reconstruction had been advocated in a series of circulars emanating from the Ministère des Régions Libérées, and following the Armistice the Génie Rural organized meetings throughout the northern *départements* to encourage the creation of cooperatives (Caraud 1924: 9). Rather than risk chaotic, piecemeal rebuilding, it was argued that cooperation offered at least six advantages.

First, it was hoped that rebuilding whole villages or groups of villages would attract architects and contractors to come to work in the devastated zone, since they showed little interest in reconstructing individual houses 'of little importance, lost in the countryside, several kilometres from a railway line' (Ernest 1919: 90). They would be able to order building materials in bulk and thereby keep costs down. In addition, they could hire an appropriate quantity of labour and take measures to accommodate their workers in huts or patched-up buildings on their construction sites. Recent experience had shown that architects, in particular, found it virtually impossible to operate drawing offices in wet and windy ruins (Dupuy 1919: 615).

Second, by employing lawyers and technical experts, the cooperatives could guide individual *sinistrés* through the numerous formalities involved in declaring and evaluating war damages and in preparing dossiers for presentation to *canton* commissions in order to claim compensation. This service was perceived as a very real advantage by many humble rural folk (MacDonald 1922: 207).

Third, the cooperatives offered the potential of ensuring that reconstruction should proceed in a logical order, rather than simply responding to the selfish concerns of individuals. Thus, in farming villages agricultural buildings were usually allocated higher priority than communal or commercial premises, with individual residences coming toward the bottom of the list (Naudin 1922: 4). On the other hand, belonging to a cooperative meant sacrificing one's independence and hence jealousies could arise among members when the schedule of building work had to be defined (Hubert 1923: 176).

Fourth, the staff of cooperatives would be aware of changes to the intricate planning rules and other regulations which impinged on reconstruction and which might easily escape the attention of individual *sinistrés*. Guerin wrote scathingly of the 'deluge' of official papers that assaulted the *sinistrés* each week, and he wondered if it really were the intention of the Ministère des Régions Libérées that northern France should be rebuilt of paper (Guerin 1930: 32).

Fifth, the *sinistrés* believed that membership of a cooperative would safeguard their interests. As Guy De Lubersac was to argue: 'these societies would not be so numerous if the *sinistrés* had not felt that it was absolutely necessary to protect themselves from the activities of the STE and the manoeuvres of swindlers and crooks' (cited in Caraud 1924: v).

Finally, while not producing completely replanned model villages, the cooperation formula offered a very real chance that settlements would be rebuilt in a more hygienic and spacious way than if reconstruction were left entirely to individual enterprise (Confédération Générale du Travail 1921: 36).

Local Initiatives

At the same time as official encouragements were being delivered, local initiatives for cooperation were taking root in Lorraine, in Aisne and elsewhere in northern France (*Les coopératives de reconstruction en France*, 1948: 4). In Meurthe-et-Moselle this movement emanated from the combined forces of socially committed priests and administrators (Caraud 1924: 8). Abbé L. Thouvenin (1868–1934) was the prime mover, having been involved since 1898 in schemes for providing decent housing for growing numbers of industrial workers in this rapidly changing section of north-east France, and latterly having devoted considerable energies to the welfare of refugees. After a visit in January 1915 to his birthplace, the devastated village of Sainte-Geneviève 8 km south-east of Pont-à-Mousson, Thouvenin became convinced of the great potential of general-purpose reconstruction cooperatives (De Mahuet 1927: 6; Rolin 1950–3: 162). During the early months of 1918 he, Abbé Fiel, and M. Dupan of the Génie Rural encouraged the creation of such associations in a handful of devastated *communes* which had been abandoned by the Germans since 1914 (Caraud 1924: 8). Another Lorrainer, Albert Lebrun, Ministre du Blocus et des Régions Libérées, advocated the idea of reconstruction cooperatives during October 1918 and presented it to the Chambre des Députés in January 1919. An active campaign was set to begin, being supported by a pamphlet entitled *La coopérative de reconstruction* that had been written by Francis Delaisi and published jointly by La Renaissance des Cités and the American Red Cross (MacDonald 1922: 208)

Spurred on by the minister's approval, Abbé Thouvenin succeeded in founding the first reconstruction cooperative in Meurthe-et-Moselle at Norroy-les-Pont-à-Mousson in February 1919 (Rolin 1950–3: 162). He continued his campaign in the devastated villages of the *département*, with the blessing of his bishop and the prefect, and the material assistance of a car and a sheaf of printed papers which provided specimen regulations for general-purpose cooperatives. During the next few months their number rose rapidly in the *département* from seventeen in late March to sixty by early May (Caraud 1924: 8; AN AJ 25/47 Reconstruction des régions liberées, Meurthe-et-Moselle, 25.04.19). It did indeed appear that the cooperative movement was 'ready for a great extension' (Ibid.). The work of Thouvenin and of other advocates of cooperation was facilitated by a suite of encouraging communications sent to northern prefects by the minister and by the content of the general law on war damages (17 April 1919). By the start of August 1919 a further ninety-two cooperatives had been created in Meurthe-et-Moselle and by 1 January 1920 the total had reached 180. During this early phase it soon became clear that individual cooperatives needed higher-level coordination if they were to be truly effective, and be able to overcome the problem of being directed by men who did not always have sufficient time to devote to them or whose competence sometimes did not 'live up to their goodwill' (Caraud 1924: 26). The first *union* of reconstruction cooperatives was founded in Meurthe-et-Moselle in June 1919 and soon would be emulated throughout the liberated regions.

A second almost contemporary nucleus of cooperative innovation was formed in Aisne. This involved a very early example on the Plateau de Passy-en-Valois (December 1918), and also the much better known example which developed around Blérancourt in Soissonnais (De Busscher 1983: 16; Héricault 1934: 48). This area had already witnessed the welfare work of the Comité Américain pour les Régions Dévastées (see Chapter 3) and the creation during 1917 of eight farming cooperatives which had enabled 1,000 ha to be re-cultivated. Unfortunately, the German advance of March 1918 had erased these initiatives and led to the population being evacuated until after the Armistice. Then the task of recovery started once again, with continued support from the American women volunteers. During October 1918 Gaston Héricault had proposed that a general-purpose cooperative be set up at Blérancourt and this was duly inaugurated on 20 March 1919. With the vigorous encouragement of the Génie Rural, mayors and landowners from surrounding *communes* and from nearby Oise *département* travelled to Blérancourt to learn how they might establish their own cooperatives (Saint 1920: 97). The next one in Aisne was set up at Soissons and by September of that year the *département* contained no fewer than seventy-three (Caraud 1924: 8).

Reconstruction associations in Nord were inspired by the experience of agricultural cooperation earlier in the century and by a series of lectures delivered by staff of the Génie Rural during wartime, in which the merits of cooperatives were extolled and particular praise was devoted to their ability to organize the reconstruction of whole settlements in a coherent way once peace had been restored (Devaine 1922: 123; Morain 1923: 131). By

June 1919 thirty-five associations, representing over eight thousand *sinistrés*, had been set up and others were being organized to bring the total to 233 by the end of July 1920. However, at that time only fifty were functioning fully and a further 120 had only just started their work (Conseil Général du Nord 1920: 25). Six months later their number had risen to 272, representing more than one-third of the damaged non-industrial property in the *département* (Ibid.). These cooperatives covered the interests of 31,000 *sinistrés* in 294 *communes* (Morain 1923: 131).

Two other mechanisms for setting up reconstruction cooperatives were reported by Lucien Hubert in Ardennes (Hubert 1923: 171). In some *communes* groups of *sinistrés* approached architects and surveyors for help with evaluating damages and preparing claims, and then decided that it would be advantageous to remain together to undertake reconstruction. In other instances, the initiative came from the professionals who appreciated the great opportunity for work that was offered by taking on the rebuilding of whole villages in the liberated regions. However, such contracts did not always prove beneficial to the *sinistrés*.

The Need for Cooperation

Passage of the law of 17 April 1919 and the subsequent opportunities for reconstructing complete settlements heralded the arrival in the northern *départements* of large numbers of architects and building contractors from Paris and the provinces (L'assemblée générale de l'Office du Bâtiment, 1924: 511). Experience in the first few months of peace had shown that local builders were willing to tackle repair work but were quite unable to cope with the challenge of rebuilding whole villages, hence external help was needed (Hubert 1923: 165; Parisot 1939: II 121). In their desperation to have their homes rebuilt, the impressionable *sinistrés* formed easy prey. Unscrupulous businessmen descended 'like locusts on the ruined countryside' and used persuasive arguments to gain their confidence but then demanded high rates of commission for helping them lodge their compensation claims (De Busscher 1983: 14). The *Journal des Régions Dévastées* headed one article with the warning 'Beware vampires!'

(Sinistrés, méfions-nous des vampires! *JRD*, 19.10.19: 1). In similar fashion, swindlers arrived with lorries full of equipment and persuaded local people to part with what remained of their meagre savings before moving on to operate similar confidence tricks in other villages (Héricault 1934: 49). The northern *départements* attracted their share of 'false contractors, fake architects, go-betweens of all kinds, "manufacturers of compensation dossiers", specialists in risk, as well as dubious suppliers and financiers' who appeared to demonstrate 'the most praiseworthy of intentions and the purest of sentiments' (Hubert 1923: 52). Individual *sinistrés* were 'weakened by their isolation' and urgently needed the kind of protection from such operators which, it was hoped, membership of a reconstruction cooperative would afford (Carpentier 1928: 63).

After their frustrating experience of counting on the state to undertake emergency work, groups of *sinistrés* turned to their own resources and began to set up reconstruction cooperatives throughout the northern *départements*. This occurred even in Somme where family farmers had a reputation for fierce individualism (Les oubliés, *JRD*, 06.07.19: 122). Ministerial speeches continued to extol the virtues of cooperation as the best means of reviving whole villages. For example, on 29 December 1919 André Tardieu, then Ministre des Régions Libérées, argued that if reconstruction were to be achieved successfully three major tasks would have to be achieved (Caraud 1924: 9). Village plans would have to be drawn up, landownership boundaries be re-established, and cooperative reconstruction societies be organized in a serious and efficient way. Unfortunately, very few of the early cooperatives functioned properly.

These groups were voluntary associations that were allowed to receive, on behalf of their members, the advances granted by the government for preparing claims' dossiers and also the first 20 per cent advance toward the cost of rebuilding (MacDonald 1922: 207). If architects were to be employed, a circular of 22 December 1919 required them to be chosen from lists for each northern *département* that had received ministerial approval. None of these early cooperatives possessed any capital of its own and hence immediate expenses had to be met by their members. *Sinistrés* could allocate all or part of their anticipated compensation to their local cooperative which would direct and pay for any work undertaken, and would then recover compensation from the state. As Prefect Magny noted, 'the great inconvenience was that members could leave at any moment, even when the cooperative had entered into considerable expenditure. There was no guarantee' (Magny 1928: 40). André Tardieu observed that even 'one member . . . who is defiant and legalistic, can halt the operation of the whole cooperative' (AN 324 AP/63 Tardieu, A., Ce que demandent les régions libérées, 01.09.20). These proto-cooperatives were on a weak legal footing, simply being in receipt of certain delegated powers from their members. The government recognized them because they were obviously useful, and official circulars attempted to ensure that they should be non-profit making and be composed of *sinistrés* rather than speculators (MacDonald 1922: 209).

Despite their laudable objectives, many early cooperatives proved to be far from satisfactory. The most frequent difficulty involved conflicts between the nascent associations and the contractors whose services they were attempting to engage. Writing in 1920, Jacques Rodolphe-Rousseau insisted that 900 of the 1,600 early cooperatives throughout northern France were 'paralysed', having only 'theoretical existence', and hence were 'lacking any vitality' (Rodophe-Rousseau 1920: 7). Despite the goodwill of their founders, he believed that the majority had been 'reduced to almost absolute impotence' (Ibid.: 11). The groups possessed no consistent legal status, owing their existence to a wide range of laws and decrees. For example, some were defined as associations under legislation of 1901, while others were commercial societies established according to a law of 1867. Many were poorly organized and badly administered, with practices of book-keeping being rudimentary or non-existent. They lacked credit facilities and could be used simply as instruments for speculation or exploitation. Thus, in some instances unscrupulous businessmen had moved into devastated villages where they had themselves nominated as directors, administrators or managers of cooperatives (Ibid.: 14). In such capacities they engaged contractors with whom they were in collusion and from whom it was alleged they received large commissions.

Some architects failed to honour their agreements in a variety of ways, for example by taking on too much work, making rare or cursory visits to the reconstruction sites, failing to resolve problems when they did appear on site, or being slow in preparing plans and financial estimates. Difficulties of this kind certainly hindered reconstruction in some parts of Meurthe-et-Moselle during 1919 and 1920 (Préaud & Fiel 1922: 19). Conversely, some *sinistrés* drew up very restrictive contracts with their architects and builders, allowing them no reasonable leeway in the way they operated (Michel 1932: 294). For these and other reasons, several prefects became suspicious of the whole concept of cooperative reconstruction. Financial uncertainties were legion in these early days and some *sinistrés* grew so discouraged that they quit their infant associations in the hope of achieving better results on their own (Saint 1920: 98). Not surprisingly, a number of early cooperatives foundered (Rodolphe-Rousseau 1920: 12). Other *sinistrés* hoped, unrealistically, that the process whereby some devastated villages were adopted by settlements in other countries would provide sufficient donations for reconstruction (Magny 1928: 21; Peytral 1927: 358).

Approved Cooperatives

By means of a circular dated 25 May 1920 attempts were made by the Ministère des Régions Libérées to improve the situation. This specified future conditions under which cooperatives would be entitled to financial support from the government (MacDonald 1922: 209). The ambiguity that surrounded them was removed subsequently by the law of 15 August 1920 and the decree of 9 October 1920 which defined the status of approved cooperatives and elaborated proposals that had been made in March 1920 by M. Ogier, then Ministre des Régions Libérées (Ibid.: 67). These formalities were complemented by further legislation of 12 July 1921 and by the decree of 29 August 1921. In order to achieve approval from the government, a reconstruction cooperative needed to have statutes that conformed to models prepared by the Ministry. Normally, there should not be more than one cooperative per *commune*, except in cases where very large volumes of damage had been incurred. Existing associations were, of course, open to reorganization in order to conform with the new regulations.

(i) Approved cooperatives were to be composed of *sinistrés*; to exist for the reconstruction of buildings; to prepare dossiers and evaluate damages; to execute, supervise and pay for reconstruction work, normally through the re-employment of advances from the state; and to exist only for as long as necessary for these objectives to be met.

(ii) They were permitted to make use of rights of compensation which the law of 4 April 1919 had directed to individual *sinistrés*. However, each *sinistré* was still entitled to compensation for loss of personal items. In addition to payments from the state to *sinistrés*, the funds of approved cooperatives might include contributions from members, as well as gifts and legacies. Each cooperative was required to open an account with each of its members and with the Crédit National in order to receive payments from the state.

(iii) The precise legal relationship between *sinistrés*, the cooperative, and professional staff was defined. Architects, surveyors and contractors had to figure on authorized lists and needed to receive approval from the staff of the local prefecture if they were to be employed by cooperatives.

(iv) Each cooperative needed to elect a council of administration every year, which chose from among its members a president, one or several vice-presidents, a secretary and a treasurer.

(v) The council of administration was entrusted with wide powers for the general management of the cooperative which had to be executed in line with the law of 1920 and subsequent amendments.

(vi) Auditors would be appointed to examine the financial dealings and general activities of each cooperative. This was in conformity with the fact that the state was the creditor of the cooperatives and would exercise some surveillance of their activities (Magny 1928: 40).

(vii) Each cooperative should determine for itself the order in which reconstruction work would take place. Normally repairs were undertaken before permanent reconstruction was started, and then farm buildings were rebuilt before communal and commercial facilities, and lastly ordinary dwellings (Caraud 1924: 24).

Under the law of 15 August 1920 the state undertook to advance to each approved cooperative, having at least seven members, the sum of 50 F per member. Typical advances per cooperative were to prove to be in the range of 500–3,000 F. These and other funds were deductible from war indemnities which related to the cost of reconstructing built property (Michel 1932: 293). In addition, the state agreed to allocate, after approval of each reconstruction scheme by the relevant prefect, up to a quarter of the total credit allowed for the reconstruction work. These payments were not made directly in cash but were transmitted to the relevant branch of the Crédit National. Despite this arrangement, the fundamental rules controlling payment emanated from the law of 17 April 1919 which stressed the rights of individual *sinistrés* to receive compensation. Hence every cooperative functioned to manage and advance the claims of each of its members, but did so on a collective basis. Payments to individual members therefore ceased.

Given these new circumstances, prefects and agricultural advisers mounted campaigns to ensure that existing associations reconstituted themselves to conform with the new law. The majority did so rapidly, being encouraged by a flood of printed guides and handbooks (De Mahuet 1927: 9). For example, prior to August 1920 Marne had contained 147 associations which operated in 210 *communes* (Sociétés coopératives de reconstruction, *JRD*, 03.7.21: 3). These were duly reorganized to satisfy the new requirements so that by autumn 1922 the *département* had 142 approved cooperatives representing 11,566 *sinistrés* in 237 *communes*. Similarly in Nord, Prefect Naudin was able to report in 1921 that 272 associations were in the process of reorganization to satisfy the new law (Naudin 1921b: 10).

Uneven Responses

The degree of enthusiasm for creating completely new cooperatives varied considerably both within and between *départements*. Delegates of the Confédération Générale du Travail visiting the northern *départements* in January 1921 encountered a great deal of frustration among *sinistrés* who 'forcefully expressed their discontent at the inadequacy of the state services and the disorder that reigned within them' (Confédération

Générale du Travail 1921: 3). Many *sinistrés* and their mayors were unable to comprehend the fundamental compensation law of 17 April 1919, the numerous qualifying circulars that had been produced, or the notion of a *plan d'aménagement* (or blueprint) (Ibid.: 5). In such an atmosphere of confusion verging on despair, many *sinistrés* declared their willingness to group together so that work might begin and that they might defend themselves from swindlers. But others still held the illusion that donations from overseas would allow them to retain their prized independence (Ibid.: 4). The delegates quoted Nord and Meurthe-et-Moselle as examples of particularly effective cooperation in order to encourage stubborn individualists in other *départements* to pool their resources (Ibid.: 3). Thus, during the spring of 1921, M. Loucheur, then Ministre des Régions Libérées, encountered a spirit of optimism and self-confidence among *sinistrés* who belonged to cooperatives in Meurthe-et-Moselle where they were 'growing from strength to strength' (Monsieur Loucheur et les coopératives à Nancy, JRD, 10.04.21: 1). Members of recent cooperatives in this part of Lorraine were enthused by the demonstrable success of some earlier associations (Figure 9.1).

A good example was provided by the village of Ancerviller which had straddled the front line near Lunéville and was well on the way to being rebuilt in November 1921 (Un succès coopérateur, *JRD*, 13.11.21). Forty-two of its 170 houses had been destroyed and the remainder had been seriously damaged. Some 950 ha of ploughland and meadows and 250 ha of woodland had been devastated. On the advice of Abbé Fiel, the villagers had formed an association in February 1919 and engaged a building contractor who brought in 200 workers. A proper reconstruction cooperative was established in June. Thirty months later the settlement had been resurrected and comprised thirty-nine new houses, a completely new church, and a set of public buildings, all with piped water supply. The village's population stood at 552, representing a sizeable increase on the pre-war figure of 513. By November 1921 all its meadowland had been restored, 90 per cent of the arable was back in cultivation, and the remainder was being prepared for cropping in 1922. The success of this pioneer venture was crucial in convincing seven neighbouring *communes* to set up reconstruction cooperatives of their own.

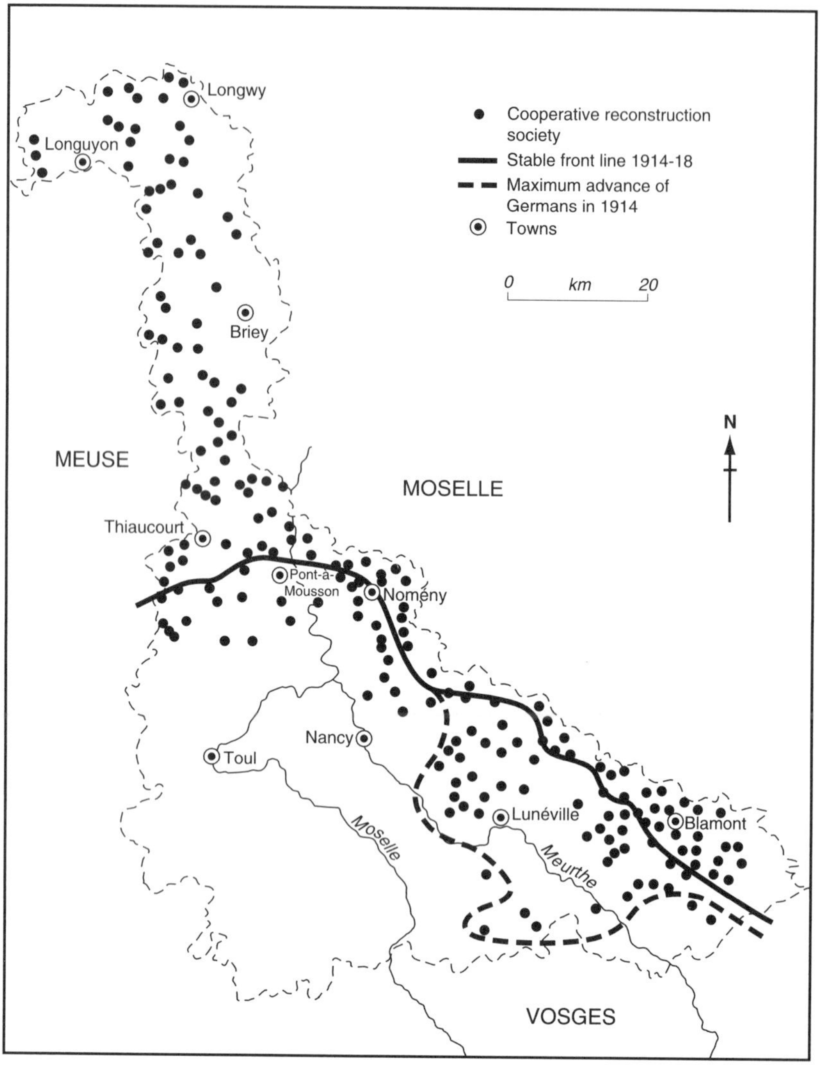

Figure 9.1 Cooperative reconstruction societies in Meurthe-et-Moselle

This kind of demonstration of self-confidence in Lorraine was very different from the complaints and pleading by *sinistrés* that were encountered in other *départements* (Monsieur Loucheur et les coopératives à Nancy, *JRD*, 10.04.21). For example, reconstruction was said to be 'lagging lamentably' in some parts of Aisne and Somme (Confédération Générale du Travail 1921: 4).

But attitudes began to change even in these areas during 1921 and a number of cooperative initiatives were launched in the most seriously devastated parts of the red zone around Combles, to the east of Albert (La reconstitution dans la Somme, *JRD*, 19.02.22). Likewise in Marne, cooperatives had been often 'challenged rather than supported' by local *sinistrés* (Clause 1975: 405). In the *département* of Meuse, Prefect Emery reported a profound contrast between rapid reconstruction by cooperatives in the Meuse valley and a very slow pace of recovery in the hilly country to either side, adjacent to extensive stretches that had been classified as red zone (Emery 1922: vii). Cooperatives were being established very slowly in these areas, with poor transport and a long history of depopulation and low agricultural yields adding to the understandable sense of uncertainty for the future in the minds of local people. *Sinistrés* were also reluctant to cooperate and initiate reconstruction in the unrealistic hope that rates of compensation might be higher in the future. To Prefect Emery's great regret, 90 per cent of the finance allocated to assist rebuilding in the *cantons* of Varennes, Clermont, Montfaucon and Fresnes had not been used by November 1921 (Ibid.: viii). His response was to launch a personal campaign to promote cooperation and to allocate his very best staff to supervise the task.

Reconstruction was proceeding in an uneven fashion in many other sections of the northern *départements*, depending on whether or not *sinistrés* belonged to cooperatives and how dynamic those organizations had proved to be. In many areas flourishing new villages built by cooperatives contrasted with individual attempts at piecemeal reconstruction in settlements which lacked any kind of cooperative organization (Confédération Générale du Travail 1921: 12). The survival of ruined villages with clusters of temporary accommodation nearby normally meant that cooperation had been rejected (Bastide 1923: 589). Despite initial doubts and uncertainties, 'with remarkable unanimity the great majority of *sinistrés*, except the industrialists, acquiesced' to membership of reconstruction cooperatives (MacDonald 1922: 207). Hence, the number of approved cooperatives throughout the liberated regions rose from 1,040 at the start of 1921 to 1,720 in November and to 2,160 on 1 October 1922 (Michel 1932: 294) (Table 9.1). By that date the

Table 9.1 Approved reconstruction cooperatives, 1922–31

	Cooperatives	Communes involved	Membership
1.10.22	2,160	2,602	152,779
1.01.23	2,200	2,625	156,756
1.01.24	2,316	2,717	170,100
1.01.25	2,346	2,712	173,323
1.01.26	2,325	2,722	176,290
1.01.27	2,323	2,766	175,595
1.01.28	2,267	2,740	163,984
1.01.31	1,783	2,210	155,218

Sources: Ministère des Régions Libérées 1923; Ministère des Travaux Publiques 1929; Michel 1932: 612

great publicity campaign was over and the number of cooperatives was to rise only slightly in subsequent years to reach a peak of 2,346 at the start of 1925.

The creation of so many cooperatives reinforced the role of the northern *départements* as 'a kind of magnet, of great attractive power' drawing in labour from many parts of France and from elsewhere in Europe (Hubert 1923: 46). According to Georges Mauco, in mid-1922 no fewer than 310,000 workers were employed on building sites run by reconstruction cooperatives, individual companies, the state and other agencies in northern France (Mauco 1932: 89). For the summer of 1923 a not greatly dissimilar figure of 280,000 was put forward by the Office du Bâtiment et Travaux Publics (L'assemblée générale de l'Office, 1924: 516). Hubert believed that 'every worker, even those without specific skills, will find a job on the building sites' (Hubert 1923: 210). He reported that this movement involved 'a mixture of all races, all languages and all customs. It is almost a new invasion, a peaceful one, that is destined to repair the ravages of the first' (Ibid.: 47). In his *département* of Ardennes, French building workers were only half as numerous as the diverse contingent of foreigners, originating especially from Italy and Spain, but with much smaller groups coming from Belgium, Poland and Portugal (Ibid.: 157). In general terms, foreign workers were willing to accept poorer living conditions than their French counterparts. Accommodation was far from good for the majority of building labourers and technical staff, who were housed in patched-up ruins, in rented rooms in the already crowded homes of returnees, and in every conceivable form of temporary accommodation (Ibid.: 122).

The complete size of the workforce employed by the reconstruction cooperatives in the ten *départements* is not known, but in Nord it included 450 architects, 2,000 building contractors and averaged 60,000 workers during 1921–2, to reach a peak of 72,000 at the height of the summer of 1922 (Morain 1923: 139; Naudin 1922: 21). Two-thirds of this total was made up of French nationals, with Belgians (11,270) and Italians (6,180) being the largest foreign groups (Morain 1923: 139). In February 1924 an estimated 7,000 architects were at work across the *régions dévastées* and employed a further 43,000 technical staff for drawing plans, supervising work and auditing accounts (L'assemblée générale de l'Office du Bâtiment, 1924: 508). However these figures were lower than their peak in the middle of 1922 because of the worsening financial situation during which the Office du Bâtiment et Travaux Publics estimated that some builders would be 'obliged to practise a demobilization operation' (Ibid.: 516).

Partly for external reasons, the second half of 1922 had proved to be a particularly difficult phase in the restoration of the northern *départements* since the government had been unable to allocate the expected volume of funds through the Crédit National either to cooperatives or to individual *sinistrés*. During the first two and a half years of peace the French state had distributed compensation money from its special budget of recoverable expenditure, on the assumption that Germany would pay up soon (Benns 1930: 349). Since reparation payments could not be recovered immediately, the budget was funded from loans floated by the French government which would be repaid once the money started to arrive from Germany (Bury 1972: 56). For example, by May 1921 the special budget had allocated 20,000,000,000 F in compensation to those who had submitted their claims promptly, but had received virtually nothing from Germany on the reparation account (Benns 1930: 349). Small amounts of reparations had been recovered during the summer of 1921 but these fell far beneath the levels of expenditure. Essentially, the French Treasury was not able to obtain sufficient funds from Germany, nor was it particularly effective in distributing among reconstruction cooperatives and other *sinistrés* the small sums that had been recovered. In addition, some enthusiastic cooperatives had launched very costly programmes of work which were greatly in excess of available credits (Caraud 1924: 81). This was an expression of 'the fever of getting started, without knowing what would come from the risks being run, and reflected confidence in the promises from on high . . . *Le boche paiera!*' (L'assemblée générale de l'Office du Bâtiment, 1924: 511). Because of the worsening situation in the second half of 1922, many contractors remained unpaid for several months, and some of their labour force had to be laid off. By contrast, and with considerable irony, cooperatives which had functioned with rather less dynamism managed to enter 1923 on a sounder financial footing than their more ambitious counterparts. Unfortunately, the cash-flow problem was to prove to be a recurrent one, so that during the summer of 1924 many cooperatives had 'reached an impasse' (L'impasse, *JRD*, 17.08.24). In some villages no work was taking place and teams of building workers had to be reduced greatly. Only those cooperatives that had reserves of credit could continue to operate.

Cooperation at a Higher Level

The need for a level of organization above that of the individual cooperative, in order to study laws and decrees, to defend the interests of local societies, and to facilitate links between them, had been recognized very early in Meurthe-et-Moselle, where the first *union* was established by fifty-four reconstruction cooperatives on 9 June 1919. This was placed under the presidency of Abbé Thouvenin and had the blessing of the Bishop of Nancy (De Mahuet 1927: 9). By the end of the year a hundred associations had joined it. On 31 August 1919 Gaston Héricault established a consortium of thirteen reconstruction cooperatives in the *canton* of Coucy-le-Château (Aisne) in order to overcome the problem of finding appropriate managerial staff for each of them (Héricault 1934: 53). During the next few weeks a similar but larger organization, the Union Soissonnaise des Coopératives de Reconstruction, was voted into existence in Aisne under the stimulus of the Marquis Guy de Lubersac (who had just been elected to the Senate), Louis Brunehant (Membre de l' Académie d'Agriculture and owner of a large sugar refinery), and Comte Jehan de Hennezel d'Ormois, who worked to centralize the accounts of the component cooperatives rather than leaving them in the hands of unskilled treasurers in every village (De Sars 1937: 6). Five unions in Aisne brought together the interests of 249 cooperatives (De Busscher 1983: 22–25). These and subsequent initiatives of the Union Soissonnaise were studied with great interest, and comparable unions were soon established in the other northern *départements*. They were duly reorganized to conform with the law of 15 August 1920 and special legislation of 12 July 1921. Only approved unions could qualify for financial support from the state. They needed to be made up exclusively of approved cooperatives, to have statutes that were acceptable to the Ministère des Régions Libérées, and to keep financial accounts that were open to scrutiny by state auditors.

Approved unions offered four main types of service to their constituent cooperatives. First, they provided information on changing legal formalities and compensation facilities. Second, they improved methods of book-keeping. Third, they assisted cooperatives in devising logical programmes of work for groups of villages and in ensuring that building workers might be redistributed when individual reconstruction projects were completed, and thereby continue to be employed in an efficient manner (Caraud 1924: 28). Finally, they offered opportunities for bulk purchase of building materials at trade prices. At the start of 1923 a total of thirty-five unions had been established in the ten *départements*, with Vosges and Pas-de-Calais having only one apiece, but Nord containing no fewer than eight.

Useful though the unions proved to be at the local scale, there was no way of operating an efficient channel of communication among them or between them and the *préfectures* of the northern *départements*. This shortcoming was resolved during the summer of 1920 by the Marquis De Lubersac, who proposed that a *fédération* be created which would represent the five unions and all constituent cooperatives in Aisne (Ibid.: 49). He was elected president, with Gaston Héricault as treasurer and Jacques Rodolphe-Rousseau as secretary-general. The presidents of the five unions became vice-presidents of the new *fédération* (De Busscher 1983: 32). Nine other *fédérations* were soon created across northern France and provided effective mechanisms for representing the interests of the *sinistrés* and their cooperatives in each northern *préfecture*. They held meetings and published regular bulletins dealing with a wide range of practical and financial aspects of reconstruction.

Within a few months the whole hierarchy was crowned by the Confédération Générale des Sociétés Coopératives de Reconstruction, which was founded in Paris by De Lubersac on 1 March 1921 and voiced the interests of over 150,000 *sinistrés* from all thirty-five unions (Héricault 1934: 75). It sought 'to supervise the strict application of the law on war damages and to respond to all the difficulties emerging from reconstruction' (Comité d'Action des Régions Dévastées 1930: 48). It liaised with the appropriate ministries, the Union de Syndicats d'Architectes Agrées des Régions Dévastées, and the Fédération Nationale du Bâtiment. The well-informed general confederation of cooperatives initially was 'greeted with mistrust, if not to say hostility' by the Ministère des Régions Libérées (Caraud 1924: 54). De Lubersac took steps to ensure that an effective working relationship was soon established, stating quite simply in a letter to the minister, 'We do not set ourselves up as adversaries of the administration. We wish to collaborate; we must collaborate' (Ibid.). The Confédération subsequently was recognized by law on 31 March 1922 and its officers entered into frequent meetings and exchanges of correspondence with the Ministry (Héricault 1934: 54). The Confédération consistently lent its very considerable support to the unions to attack the slow and dilatory behaviour of the *canton* commissions which held back the drive for permanent reconstruction, and it also exposed unfair practices and excessive charges among architects and contractors (MacDonald 1922: 217). In addition, the Confédération assisted individual cooperatives in the task of raising loans to ensure that reconstruction might take place without delay (Confédération Générale de la Marne 1923: 27). As Dessaint remarked, it was 'making an energetic effort to pull reconstruction out of the mud of bureaucracy' (Dessaint 1922: 757).

The pattern of reconstruction cooperatives that emerged across the northern *départements* was complicated, reflecting variations in the degree of destruction as well as the effectiveness of campaigns for promoting their creation, and a host of other factors. At the start of October 1922 northern France supported

Table 9.2 Approved reconstruction cooperatives by *département*, 1922, 1928, 1931

	Cooperatives			Communes involved			Membership		
	1922	1928	1931	1922	1928	1931	1922	1928	1931
Aisne	443	488	431	633	670	610	33,498	26,748	33,587
Ardennes	156	157	121	208	210	167	9,163	10,513	9,315
Marne	142	145	120	237	254	198	11,566	12,964	12,083
Meurthe-et-Moselle	200	160	94	232	170	101	13,000	9,564	9,200
Meuse	242	244	69	271	273	69	10,455	12,870	3,948
Nord	262	276	242	282	312	312	26,530	39,597	35,665
Oise	94	106	96	113	165	163	4,022	4,750	5,057
Pas-de-Calais	296	299	295	265	266	266	32,212	29,301	28,373
Somme	302	372	306	288	320	281	11,140	16,380	17,021
Vosges	23	20	43	73	60	43	1,193	1,297	969
Total	2,160	2,267	1,783	2,602	2,740	2,210	152,779	163,984	155,218

1 October 1922; 1 January 1928; 1 January 1931
Source: Ministère des Travaux Publics 1929; Michel 1932: 295, 612

2,160 cooperatives which were responsible for repair and reconstruction in 2,602 *communes*, containing three-fifths of all settlements that had experienced war damage (Table 9.2). Together, they involved a membership of 152,779 *sinistrés*, the largest numbers of whom were found in Aisne (33,498), Pas-de-Calais (32,212) and Nord (26,530) (Ministère des Régions Libérées 1923). Not surprisingly, these *départements* headed the league in terms of financial commitment. Although all seventy-three war-damaged *communes* in Vosges belonged to the twenty-three cooperatives that operated in that *département*, the number of *sinistrés* involved was only 1,193. Very high proportions of war-damaged *communes* participated in cooperatives in Pas-de-Calais (90.8 per cent) and Ardennes (85.2 per cent), but at the other end of the spectrum only one-fifth of all war-damaged settlements in Oise belonged to them, compared with an average of 60.5 per cent throughout the devastated *départements*.

Repairs and Reconstruction

Not surprisingly, cooperatives began by repairing damaged buildings and clearing debris before starting to cope with complete reconstruction (Naudin 1922:4). While adhering to a general formula which commenced with farm buildings and ended with individual dwellings, some cooperatives placed particular emphasis on providing solid accommodation for the elderly (Héricault 1934: 96). By virtue of the necessary programming of reconstruction, some members in each cooperative had their homes rebuilt before others and this fact sometimes gave rise to animosity among neighbours (Hubert 1923: 173). Statistics quoted by Caraud dating from 1 May 1923 give an indication of the work accomplished by cooperatives after just a few years of activity (Caraud 1924: 162–64) (Table 9.3). They were responsible for restoring 144,912 buildings, which represented 27 per cent of all repair work completed or in progress in the ten *départements* by that date. Almost all repairs in Ardennes, Oise and Vosges were being done without the help of cooperatives but, by contrast, they undertook four in every five repairs in Meurthe-et-Moselle where cooperation had made a particularly early start. Some 44 per cent of repairs to farm buildings across northern France were the result of cooperative action, and once again there were marked local variations in activity. Only one-fifth of the repairs to public buildings undertaken by May 1923 throughout the northern *départements* were being done by cooperatives.

Table 9.3 Proportion of repairs and reconstruction work undertaken by cooperatives, 1 May 1923 (%)

	All repairs	Repairs to farm buildings	All reconstruction work
Aisne	43	55	63
Ardennes	13	24	37
Marne	57	60	60
Meurthe-et-Moselle	79	79	76
Meuse	43	55	71
Nord	17	49	35
Oise	12	17	47
Pas-de-Calais	36	40	74
Somme	17	28	53
Vosges	3	2	74
Total	27	44	58

Source: Caraud 1924: 162, 164

A much more emphatic role was being played by cooperatives where complete reconstruction was involved. In William MacDonald's words: 'It is not too much to say that wherever today, throughout the liberated regions, the progress in the reconstruction of non-industrial property is most rapid, an energetic and well-administered cooperative society will be found to be chiefly responsible' (MacDonald 1922: 220). He contrasted the village of Chassemy in Aisne, which was 'two-thirds rebuilt in a solid and attractive style', with the neighbouring settlement of Sarcy which had no cooperative and very little rebuilding in progress, with 'much of that little poorly done' (Ibid.: 222). In the spring of 1923 59,353 buildings were being rebuilt by reconstruction cooperatives throughout northern France, which represented 58 per cent of all reconstruction at that date (Caraud 1923: 164) (Table 9.3). In Meurthe-et-Moselle, Pas-de-Calais and Vosges they were responsible for three-quarters of all rebuilding, but in Ardennes and Nord the proportion was only one-third. Taking the ten *départements* as a whole, some two-fifths of all public buildings were being rebuilt by cooperative associations.

In September 1921 M. Loucheur had expressed the optimistic hope that the *canton* commissions would complete their work in twelve months' time and hence the cooperatives might well be on the point of closing their financial accounts in 1925 or 1926 (MacDonald 1922: 222). Two months later he suggested that six years was likely to be the shortest period within which reconstruction might be completed. Even his revised estimate was greatly over-optimistic. Physical reconstruction and the termination of financial and legal affairs were to prove to be remarkably long-drawn-out processes. For example, at the end of 1924 M. Dalbiez, then Ministre des Régions Libérées, was receiving 'numerous complaints' from *sinistrés* about the quality and cost of reconstruction work being done for the cooperatives and the circumstances in which it was carried out (Lettre de Monsieur Dalbiez, *LA*, 1925: 9). The end of rebuilding was far from being in sight.

Changing Numbers

Between October 1922 and the start of 1928 the overall number of reconstruction cooperatives in northern France rose by just over a hundred to reach 2,267, which involved 2,740 *communes*

(64 per cent of the war-damaged total) and incorporated the interests of 163,984 members (Table 9.1). These global figures mask the fact that new cooperatives were still being founded in the mid-1920s and that a number of associations had completed their work by the start of 1928. Indeed, the prefect of Oise had reported that a few cooperatives in his *département* were approaching completion as early as 1925 (Figure 9.2) (Conseil-Général de l'Oise 1925: 18). Reductions in membership totals provide a further clue that some settlements had been completed, even though the number of cooperatives continued to rise. Table 9.2 shows that the total of cooperatives had started to decline in Meurthe-et-Moselle and Vosges, and membership was dropping in Aisne and Pas-de-Calais, even though additional cooperatives had been established in the two latter *départements* between October 1922 and January 1928. Prefect Peytral noted that thirty cooperatives in Pas-de-Calais were on the point of concluding their activities during 1927 (Peytral 1927: 766).

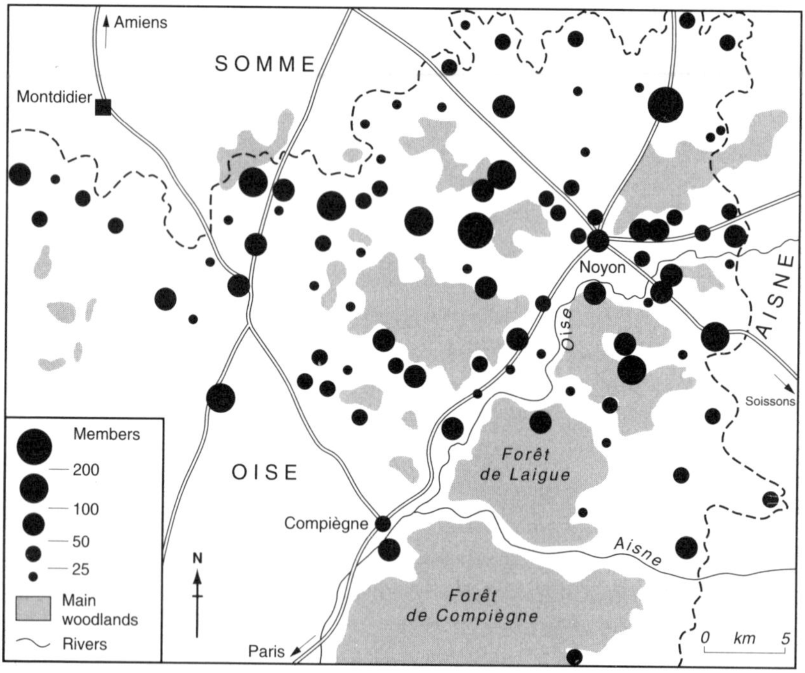

Figure 9.2 Reconstruction cooperatives, north-east Oise, 1925

Between 1922 and 1928 the net total of cooperatives rose by no fewer than seventy in Somme (bringing 5,240 additional members) and by forty-five in Aisne; however total membership declined in that *département* as a result of early completions. Most striking of all was Nord where a net increase of fourteen cooperatives (some of which embraced densely populated areas) raised the net membership total in that *département* by 13,067 *sinistrés*. However, twenty-one reconstruction cooperatives in Nord were reported to have terminated their affairs in September 1928 and a further twenty-six were on the point of doing so (Debus 1928: 24). Further completions occurred in each of the ten *départements* during the next three years and reduced the total number of cooperatives from 2,267 to 1,783 at the start of 1931 (Michel 1932: 612) (Table 9.2). Prefect Catusse reported that 183 of the 246 cooperatives in Meuse *département* had been wound up by 31 August 1931 (74 per cent) and that figure rose to 208 (85 per cent) ten months later; the remaining thirty-eight were stated to be at the point of liquidation (Catusse 1932: 11). Overall membership of cooperatives contracted to 155,218 at the start of 1931 across northern France, although increasing membership in Aisne, Oise and Somme implied that additional cooperatives were still being founded, or at least new members were being allowed to join, in the late 1920s (Guerin 1930: 64).

Tantalizingly little is known about how efficient reconstruction cooperatives really were, but the experiences recorded in eastern Somme and the adjacent district of Blérancourt in Aisne cast some light on the kinds of problem that surely must have also been encountered elsewhere in the *régions dévastées*. Members of cooperatives in Somme voiced numerous complaints about the timetable of work, architects failing to spend enough time on site, building contractors being poorly organized, and accountants and auditors proving inefficient (Emery 1923: 56). Wherever possible, local brickearth was used to supply brickworks near cooperative building sites, but deliveries of bricks and other materials were poorly organized and proved insufficient, especially during the mild years of 1922–3 when reconstruction work was beginning to 'take off' in Somme (Ottavi 1923: 1). Some cooperatives received virtually no deliveries, while others had more bricks than they knew what to do with. Distribution problems were encountered elsewhere in the devastated *départe-*

ments, and in Nord special kilns had to be fired to boost supplies (Naudin 1922: 11). However, the presence of many brick works and tile works in that *département* and the proximity of coal mines, cement works (in Artois) and lime kilns (in Tournaisis) allowed rebuilding to take place rather more cheaply than in other northern areas (Morain 1923: 118).

Subsequent problems were very much to do with inadequate cash flow and the inability of the government both to recover reparation payments from Germany and to distribute compensation to the cooperatives (Les travaux faits depuis six ans, *Bulletin*, 1928: 7). Hence cooperatives throughout northern France were effectively 'paralysed' and work ground to a halt when sufficient finances were not available (Sellier & Bruggeman 1925: 78). Prefect Emery's annual statements on the matter to the *conseil-général* of Somme in the second half of the 1920s make depressing reading (Emery 1925–8). Reports of a ministerial visit to the environs of Montdidier and Roye in summer 1927 reveal that many houses remained half built in surrounding villages (Les travaux, *Bulletin*, 1927). Wooden huts and ruins patched with corrugated iron, planks and tarred paper were still widespread (Alexandre 1928a: 12). By spring 1928 only three out of 373 general-purpose cooperatives in Somme had finished their work and settled their finances (Emery 1928: 9). Even when reconstruction had been terminated, closure of accounts proved a slow and controversial matter, with 240 cooperatives still being in existence in the *département* at the end of 1932, and some still not being dissolved by 1936 (Les travaux, *Bulletin*, 1932, 1936).

Problems such as these were reflected even more sharply in the record of the work of the consortium of the *bas-canton* of Coucy-le-Château (Aisne) by its secretary-general Gaston Héricault, who had been tax inspector at Blérancourt since 1907 (Héricault 1934: 53–99). The consortium was founded on 31 August 1919 and comprised fifteen cooperatives that were responsible for eighteen settlements in the triangle of land identified by Noyon, Chauny and Soissons (Figure 9.3). Earlier experience of cooperation in the area included eight agricultural cooperatives and welfare schemes initiated by the CARD (see Chapters 3 and 6). Indeed, Miss Morgan and Mrs Dike became honorary presidents of the consortium. *Sinistrés* complained that architectural drawings were prepared in Paris, 80 km away from the devast-

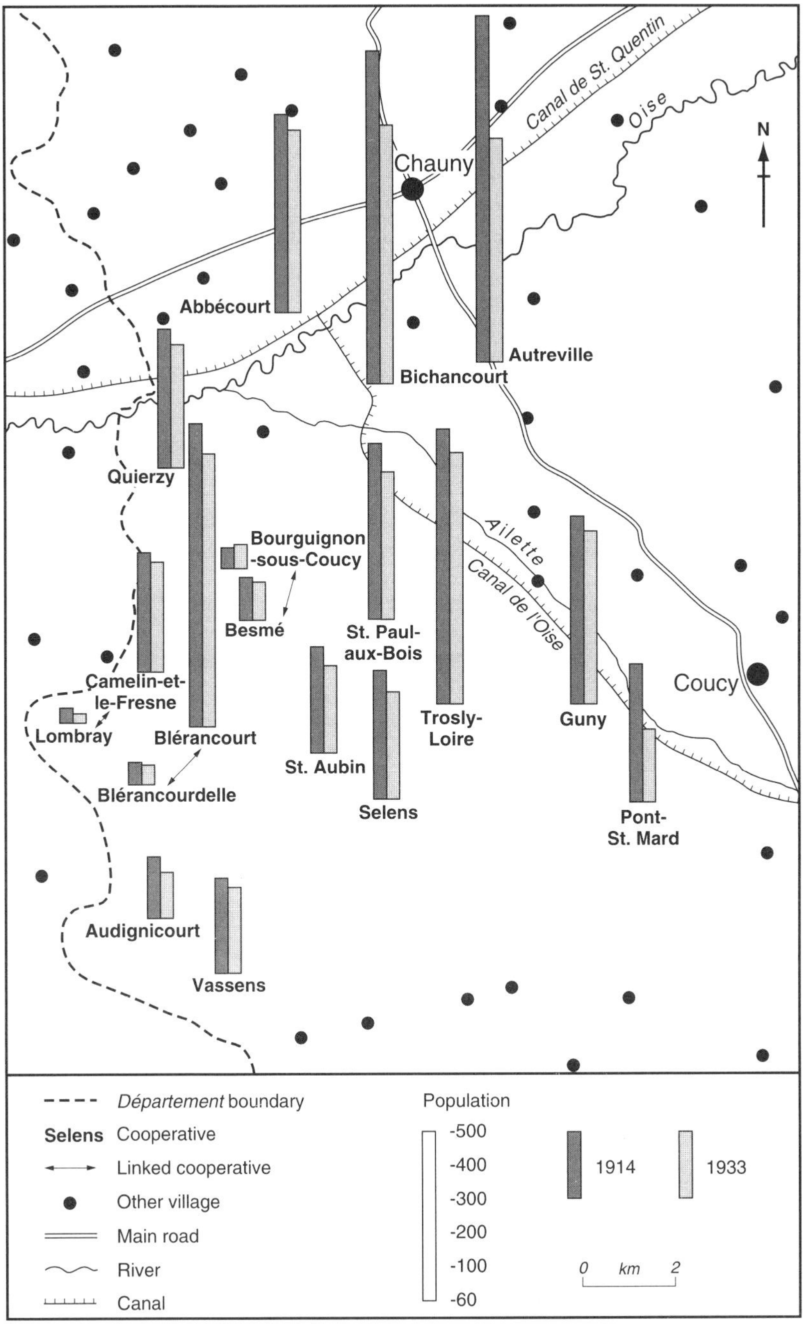

Figure 9.3 Reconstruction by the Blérancourt consortium, Aisne

ated settlements. In response to this criticism drafting work was duly transferred to three temporary offices on the building sites where assistant architects were available each morning to deal with enquiries from local people. *Sinistrés* alleged that the designs for houses were inferior to what might be reasonably expected for the promised sums of compensation money. Random checks by M. Héricault proved these allegations to be unfounded and showed that they were based on an insufficient grasp by the *sinistrés* of the impact of inflation on the work of the building trade.

A contract had been signed for all fifteen villages in the consortium to be rebuilt by a single contractor (Chouard) but the *sinistrés* were greatly dissatisfied with the speed and quantity of work being accomplished and so the consortium entered into a new agreement with a different contractor (Loiseau-Moulinet). After an initial burst of activity in 1923, the new builder declared that local railway links were inadequate for transporting building materials to certain reconstruction sites and he instructed his labourers not to work there. New contracts had to be signed with other firms in order to bring the task to completion, with all thirteen cooperatives in the consortium closing their accounts during the twenty-four months after April 1931. Following numerous practical and financial difficulties, the net result was the completion of forty-six public buildings and 1,800 dwellings and farm buildings which housed 6,674 people in 1933 compared with 8,089 in 1914 (-17.5 per cent). Seven of the seventeen churches that were destroyed in the area were reconstructed directly by the consortium, six by the cooperative for church reconstruction in the diocese of Soissons, and the remaining four by the historic monuments service of the Administration des Beaux-Arts (Ibid.: 102) (see below).

After a decade of recovery in the devastated countrysides it was clear that general-purpose cooperatives had been responsible for reconstructing two-thirds of the war-damaged settlements in the ten *départements*. By the start of 1931 the task had been completed in over 500 *communes* but the continued existence of 1,782 cooperatives meant that work was still in progress or financial matters still had not been settled in 2,210 settlements at that time (Table 9.2). Numerous general purpose cooperatives, together with their superstructure of *unions*, *federations* and the

Plate 9.1 The village of Malaucourt, Lorraine, before (December 1919) and after coordinated reconstruction

Confédération générale, survived into the second half of the 1930s, with, for example, the pioneering Union Soissonnaise not being dissolved until 1935 (De Sars 1937: 6).

Churches, Schools and other Public Buildings

In addition to the broad challenge of reconstructing whole villages, large numbers of churches, schools and *mairies* required particular help. During the hostilities no fewer than 2,675 churches had been destroyed or damaged throughout northern France (Caraud 1924: 159). In many places mass had to be celebrated in the open air even after the Armistice had been signed, to the irritation of many *sinistrés* who requested that wooden shelters should be supplied (Les églises dévastées, *BDA*, 02.06.19). Repair or reconstruction of churches was accommodated by the law of 17 April 1919 which related to religious as well as civil buildings. Thus compensation to be paid on a village church would be restricted to the amount necessary to construct (or repair) a building of the same character and importance, designed for the same uses, and embodying the same durability as the building that had been lost or damaged (MacDonald 1922: 226). In practice, restoration of churches was not accorded particularly high priority when compared with the urgent need to rebuild farms, industrial premises and homes. Hence well into the 1920s religious services in many villages had to be held in makeshift wooden chapels, often erected by local initiative or by a Catholic charitable society known as the Oeuvre des Secours aux Eglises Dévastées to which the faithful throughout France made donations (Oeuvre des Secours aux Eglises Dévastées 1923). By late 1922 the Oeuvre had disbursed some 15,000,000 F, which had been contributed to help pay for temporary buildings, altar furnishings and other religious materials in the northern *départements* (MacDonald 1922: 235).

In October 1920 Abbé Thouvenin had been approached to devise a formula to encourage church rebuilding (Fiel 1927: 7). This was to take the form of a special diocesan cooperative to which each member *commune* would delegate its indemnity for reconstructing the local church, and by using this collective sum as guarantee a loan could then be raised to provide funds to accelerate reconstruction (De Mahuet 1927: 11). With the approval of the prefect of Meurthe-et-Moselle and the blessing of the Bishop of Nancy and Toul, the first church cooperative was established in March 1921 and embraced every *commune* except one in the diocese and included a total of 103 churches in need of restoration or rebuilding (Ibid.: 11). A loan was raised and in just three months the foundation stone of the first new church was laid at Ancerviller. This building was consecrated with all due pomp on 23 November 1923 (Société Coopérative de Reconstruction des Eglises du Diocèse de Nancy, 1923: 1). Three years later fifty-nine churches had been rebuilt completely, a further twenty-nine partially reconstructed, and sixteen repaired in the diocese (De Mahuet 1927: 12).

In accordance with the law of 15 August 1920 on approved cooperatives, the diocesan cooperative model was adopted elsewhere in northern France during the spring of 1921, with almost every devastated *commune* opting to join (Héricault 1934: 101). For example, 227 *communes* participated in the cooperative for Arras diocese which was approved in June 1921 and was entrusted with rebuilding 235 churches that had been destroyed or had suffered very grave damage (Peytral 1927: 652). The nearby cooperative for Soissons diocese (Aisne) worked to reconstruct or restore a total of 306 churches at a cost of 165,000,000 F (De Busscher 1983: 45). Staff of these diocesan cooperatives were concerned with financial matters and also sought to exert a measure of technical control over rebuilding by scrutinizing architects' drawings and by making at least five visits to each site while building work was in progress (Fiel 1927: 21). They also made recommendations on detailed matters such as appropriate furnishings (ADMe 1008 Rp 1–20 La coopérative de reconstruction des églises du diocèse de Verdun). Ordinary village churches were usually designed and rebuilt by the same architects and contractors who were responsible for the other buildings in the settlement. In some instances the decision to rebuild the village church served as a stimulus for creating a cooperative to reconstruct buildings elsewhere in the *commune*.

Not surprisingly, the results varied greatly and ranged from striking examples of modern church architecture to attempts at reconstituting more or less faithfully what had been lost. Diocesan committees usually managed to avoid gross design errors being converted into solid reality, but opinions varied on the merits of the final products (De Sars 1937: 136–37). Many of the results featured on the pages of the periodical *La Construction Moderne* throughout the 1920s and early 1930s. Reconstruction of those churches that were classified as *monuments historiques* needed the expertise of the staff of the Commission des monuments historiques in the Ministère de l'Instruction Publique et des Beaux-Arts, with regard to choice of architect and builder, and detailed plans and estimates (Caraud 1924: 60). It was not surprising that reconstruction of monuments historiques took longer to complete than humble village churches (MacDonald 1922: 223–36; Léon 1923: 115). Thus, faithful rebuilding of the medieval church in the village of Nomeny, which straddled the front line in Meurthe-et-Moselle, was completed in 1928 (Caplain 1928: 223–27). However, church reconstruction as a whole continued well into the 1930s with, for example, the financial dealings of the cooperative for the diocese of Cambrai not being terminated until March 1938 (ADN 10R 5569A Coopératives de Reconstruction des Eglises des Diocèses de Lille et de Cambrai).

The diocesan cooperatives established their own special union and in January 1922 they joined together to form a joint-stock company known as the Groupement des Sociétés Coopératives Approuvées de Reconstruction des Eglises Dévastées, which was masterminded by Cardinal Luçon, Archbishop of the war-torn cathedral of Reims (De Sars 1937: 134). This organization, with headquarters in Paris, solicited donations from Catholics throughout France for use alongside state finances to guarantee funds for accelerating the reconstruction of more than two thousand churches (Groupement des Sociétés Coopératives 1924). The Groupement also had responsibility for allocating these resources among dioceses (Héricault 1934: 101). Early in 1922 it raised its first loan of 200,000,000 F to enable rebuilding to commence (MacDonald 1922: 236).

A third form of cooperative also originated in Meurthe-et-Moselle and was established in October 1921 with special responsibility for rebuilding the 116 schools and *mairies* that were in ruins at the end of hostilities (De Mahuet 1927: 13). A dozen new schools were opened during 1922 and the full total was finished by the start of 1926. A similar cooperative was created in 1923 in Meuse and organized the rebuilding of 143

Plate 9.2 Church reconstruction at Monthenault on the Chemin-des-Dames plateau, 12 km south of Laon, Aisne

schools and *mairies* (Magny 1928: 44). This kind of model was emulated in other northern *départements*, since it was widely recognized that holding classes in damp huts threatened to endanger the health of the pupils (Carpentier 1928: 65). These special purpose cooperatives made a vital contribution to the massive task of permanent reconstruction whose achievements will be reviewed in Chapter 11.

10

Land and Livelihood: Continuity and Change

The Case for Plot Consolidation

Without question, the reconstruction of rural settlement in the northern *départements* brought about detailed modifications in density, layout, design, building materials, and internal features, but above all else it represented a sustained effort by hundreds of thousands of *sinistrés* and the architects and builders in their employ to reconstitute fairly faithfully what had been lost during the war. The same kind of reaction characterized the re-establishment of property boundaries and the restoration of the most devastated portions of land to agricultural uses. Only rarely was innovation espoused; far more widespread was the wish to return to the familiar environmental context of earlier times and, as best as possible, to work the land as before.

On the eve of the war, the agrarian structure of northern France might have been summarized as a predominance of openfield, with an array of enclosed landscapes in Thiérache, Avesnois and Flanders, and considerable stretches of woodland in the northern and eastern sections of what were to become the devastated *départements* (Brunet & Dionnet 1962; Flatrès 1967; Lequeux 1936) (Figure 1.3). Several areas displayed extreme pulverization of land holding because of the traditional practice for each farmer to cultivate a range of land parcels with differing characteristics of soil, exposure, drainage and microclimate. This was accentuated by the custom whereby landed property was divided among heirs. Plot fragmentation was exceptionally pronounced in north-eastern France, although some voluntary exchanges had operated before the outbreak of war (Patrix 1931:

13). This kind of fragmentation had its logic rooted in agricultural systems which had been well supplied with labour and in which mechanization was slight or non-existent. Conditions had changed substantially during the half century prior to 1914, with rural depopulation robbing many parts of northern France of their once-abundant supplies of farm labour and hence mechanization being adopted on some large holdings. By the end of the war the disadvantages and monetary costs of fragmentation were understood by many agricultural experts and market-orientated producers who favoured plot consolidation *(remembrement)*, however such arguments were not heeded by more traditional family farmers (De Mestral 1915: 487). It was widely believed that consolidation would only work to the advantage of large farms and had nothing to offer small holdings (Hoc 1924: 91). Writing about the future role of France in the world, Albert Demangeon regretted that progress occurred so slowly in the French countryside and insisted that plot consolidation and farm enlargement were necessary preconditions for agricultural mechanization, which would be required to counteract the massive loss of farm labour that had occurred in the northern *départements* over the preceding half century and which had been cruelly accentuated by the war (Demangeon 1920: 299–300; Herbette 1918: 428).

In several respects, the impact of war offered an important opportunity for remodelling the agricultural mosaic of the northern *départements* (De Monicault 1915: 23). Trenches, shell-holes, marshalling yards, army camps, munitions depots and many other intrusive features had disrupted the rural landscape, destroying visible property boundaries and obliterating the array of subtle indicators (such as particular bushes, lines of stones or trackways) which distinguished one person's parcel from those of neighbours in areas of openfield. Property boundaries also had been erased in districts where French, British or German military groups had used tractors to work the soil during wartime, or where emergency services and farming cooperatives had employed large machines both before and after the Armistice had been signed. Staff of the Ministère de l'Intérieur, visiting the battle zone in November 1916, had reported that 'Over vast stretches of land all trace of the boundaries of fields and properties has disappeared. Over several hundred *communes*, indeed the whole region, there is complete confusion of landholdings. This situation creates one of the most difficult problems to resolve by normal processes of law' (cited in Morain 1923: 45). In fact, this kind of confusion was to be much more extensive than this interim report suggested. To complicate matters even more, at least one of the two copies of the cadastral maps and registers of landownership in 1,109 *communes* had been destroyed during the war, and the urgent need to produce completely new records provided another incentive for landholdings to be reorganized (Ministère des Régions Libérées 1923).

The case for government encouragement to promote plot consolidation throughout France had been made by Dr Chauveau, Senator of Côte-d'Or, well before the war had started (Hoc 1924: 91). Wartime devastation gave another impetus to the campaign, with agricultural experts arguing not only that *remembrement* should form an essential element in any reconstruction programme, but also that it should take place ideally before cultivation was restarted and farmsteads were rebuilt (Chenevier 1917: 15). For practical, financial and fundamentally human reasons this was not to be the case in the majority of devastated *communes*, despite the fact that *remembrement* had been described as a 'question of life and death for French farming' during a debate on the agricultural budget for 1922 in the Chambre des Députés (cited in Morain 1922: 7).

Limited Experience of *Remembrement*

Unlike parts of the German lands, Denmark and southern Sweden, most sections of France had very slight experience of plot consolidation prior to 1914, with only a handful of examples having taken place in Burgundy, Picardy and the Ile-de-France (Hottenger 1914: 139). By contrast, *remembrement* had occurred in many localities in Lorraine where the term meant originally to 'remember' or 'reassemble' what had been lost as a result of the Thirty Years War (1618–48) (*L'agriculture dans le département de Meurthe-et-Moselle*, 1927: 77). As Jean Peltre has shown, a generation of new villages was built in the north-eastern provinces to replace those destroyed in the second quarter of the seventeenth century (Peltre 1966). Each was surrounded by a carefully restored mosaic of openfields. During the eighteenth century and more especially in the second half of the nineteenth century, *remembrement* in Lorraine acquired the modern meaning of refashioning the pattern of landownership (Morain 1922c: 5) For example, land had been consolidated at Roville and Neuville-sur-Moselle in the 1770s and half a century later Mathieu de Dombasle had argued in favour of *remembrement* in the pages of the agricultural journal entitled the *Annales de Roville*, which first appeared in 1823 (Gay 1922: 250). Twelve years later the *conseil-général* of Meurthe *département* lent its support to the operation (Hottenger 1914: 103). After having gained experience as a railway surveyor and forestry manager, M. Gorce, the cadastral surveyor for the neighbouring *département* of Meuse, was charged in 1859 with revising the cadastral records of Altroff (Meurthe) where landowners wished to reorganize property over an area of 1,326 ha. Four years later the task was complete and Gorce then turned his attention to the *commune* of Lening. As a result of the confidence he inspired, and the propaganda emerging from the success of his schemes, many other landowners sought to consolidate their plots (Chauveau 1918; AN F12 8026 Chauveau, M., Rapport pour faciliter le remembrement, 15.05.17).

In the following half century cadastral surveyors in Meurthe-et-Moselle revised landownership by exchanging parcels and modifying the shape of irregular plots in no fewer than forty *communes* and practised full-scale reallocation (*remembrement*) in half of these. Their operations embraced 140,161 parcels covering 31,517 ha, and involved the installation of 568 km of field track (Hottenger 1914: 140). The overall reduction in the number of parcels was only about 10 per cent, but the new tracks certainly played an important role in improving access to broad stretches of arable land (Peltre 1979: 213). Thirty-five operations were attributed to the activities of M. Gorce, either working alone or in partnership (Hottenger 1914: 107). Some 385 km of new field track were due to his efforts, and reductions in the number of parcels in the order of 15–25 per cent were quoted for *communes* where full-scale reallocation had occurred. By 1913 the Direction du Service des Améliorations Agricoles in Meurthe-et-Moselle had implemented land consolidation over a further 4,571 ha (16,256 parcels) in nine *communes* where 153 km of field track had been installed. Work was underway in eight more *communes* in the spring of 1914, but the impact of war destroyed what had been achieved in three of these. A further five were awaiting consolidation to accompany revision of their cadastral documents. By contrast with these solid results, only three consolidation schemes had to be abandoned because of hostility from local landowners. In 1914 Meurthe-et-Moselle was able to boast a team of experienced and successful land surveyors, but unfortunately this was disbanded as a result of mobilization during the war (Floremont 1983: 117).

Despite such activities in several parts of French Lorraine, Hottenger insisted that consolidation was still necessary across four-fifths of Meurthe-et-Moselle, in an equal proportion of the *communes* of Meuse (where ninety-nine had already experienced modest changes to the structure of their land parcels between 1865 and 1891), and in half the *communes* of Vosges, where a very small amount of *remembrement* had taken place at Mont-les-Neufchâteau in 1908 (Hottenger 1914: 140; Reconstitution et association, *RL*, 15.09.17: 7; AN F12 8026 Chauveau, M., Rapport pour faciliter le remembrement, 15.05.17). By 1914 only two examples of plot consolidation had been attempted in the other northern *départements*, and Hottenger was surely correct when he remarked that at this stage national legislation remained 'mute with respect to land consolidation' (Hottenger 1914: 141).

Laws and Procedures

Under the auspices of Senator Chauveau, a law was passed on 27 November 1918 which enabled landowners to establish two types of association to undertake plot consolidation and other land improvements within specified areas (Loirat 1931: 5). 'Free associations' required the unanimous written consent of landowners in the areas concerned before consolidation might commence. 'Authorized associations' needed to involve either the majority of landowners in the area owning at least two-thirds of the land surface, or two-thirds of landowners holding more than half of the land. In practice, it would often prove difficult to achieve either form of majority (Peltre 1969: 18). In each case a special communal commission would be set up which would be presided by a justice of the peace to arbitrate on contentious issues. The state made a notable financial contribution to such activities, covering all costs involved in establishing the association, providing 80 per cent of the cost of plot consolidation, paying between one-third and one-half of the cost of providing or improving farm tracks, and meeting the whole bill for drawing up new cadastral documents (Gruet 1937: 246). In addition, a portion of the sum that normally would have to be met by landowners could be claimed from the budget of the local *département*.

Two months later a second proposal relating exclusively to the war-torn *départements* was placed before the Senate by Dr Chauveau and duly became law on 4 March 1919 (Morain 1922: 21–24). It enabled the Service de la Reconstitution Foncière in each *département* to approach specially constituted commissions in each devastated *commune* in order to explore two options (Chauveau 1918). The first was to re-establish on the ground all property boundaries that had been erased during the war. The second was to take the much more innovative step of opting for plot consolidation. In no way did *remembrement* change the proportion of land owned by individual landholders or have anything to do with the size of operating farms, but it did offer a range of advantages.

(i) By doing away with excessive fragmentation and dispersion of plots, it rendered the land more desirable for purchase for agricultural use and offered the possibility of enhancing its market value.
(ii) By necessitating a revision of cadastral registers it enabled absentee landowners to be identified and gave local residents an incentive to approach them with purchase in mind so that they might increase the size of their farm holdings.
(iii) Fewer horses were necessary for ploughing less fragmented properties and hence costs of working the land were reduced, at an estimated 250–300 F/ha each year depending on the size and degree of fragmentation of the holding (AN 324/AP 47 Historique de la Société des Agriculteurs de la Somme, 16.05.31.; Emery 1924: 114).
(iv) Absolute output of crops was increased on larger parcels since less land was wasted around the margin of each plot.
(v) Finally, higher rents could be charged for consolidated parcels.

Local commissions were composed of five members sitting by right (the justice of the peace for the *canton*, the village mayor, a qualified land surveyor, and a representative of the taxation service and of the Génie Rural), who then selected a group of six sympathetic landowners, two of whom were required to be resident outside the *commune* in question (Partie officielle, *JAP*, 1919, 147–48). The work of the local commission would be complemented by a *département* commission whose members scrutinized any proposals that were challenged by landowners. Each of these commissions was presided by a magistrate, and comprised nine landowners (three of whom were designated by the *conseil-général* and six by agricultural associations) and the directors (or deputy directors) of the agricultural service, the Génie Rural and the tax service in the *département* in question.

Despite its apparent complexity, the system established under the law of 4 March 1919 proved to be reasonably flexible to operate and offered the attraction of complete financial compensation by the state. However, in order to qualify, projects had to be submitted to the local prefect before the end of July 1922 (Gay 1922: 252). The operation involved several distinct stages. To start with, it was necessary to define the perimeter of action, which could comprise the whole or part of a *commune*, and then to determine whether the *commune* would opt for re-establishing the old pattern, or for redistributing parcels and reducing their number. Then a new detailed map would be prepared indicating the proposed redistribution of parcels and the location of innovations, such as field tracks. Once a desirable programme had been agreed, detailed ground surveys would be started.

In fact, by far the majority of communities in the devastated *départements* rejected wholeheartedly the opportunity for *remembrement*, opting instead to re-establish the old pattern. Such decisions resulted from a complex array of arguments and attitudes. In the latter months of 1919 some villagers simply refused to believe that legislation had been passed to make *remembrement* possible (Gay 1922: 252–53). Many small farmers argued that consolidation would only benefit large landowners and not themselves. Sentimental attachment to specific pieces of ancestral land was widespread, as was jealousy toward neighbours and the feeling that they might gain special advantages from any reorganization. In addition, there was the fear that a re-allocated and hence unknown plot might include unexploded shells or other debris that would cause future complications. Non-farming landowners believed that it would be easier to sell small plots of land for building purposes and to obtain greater profit from such transactions than from disposing of larger, consolidated blocks.

Against this background of resistance to change, agricultural advisers and land surveyors concentrated their initial efforts on *communes* where ownership boundaries had been obliterated rather than just confused during the war (Peytral 1927: 496). However, if consolidation was chosen, the local commission was required to classify the quality of the land in fairly rudimentary terms and to determine the precise areas to be allocated to each landowner in accordance with the following five principles. Attempts would be made: to create rectangular plots; to ensure that all plots would have access to roads or field tracks; to cluster new parcels in proximity to the landowner's residence; to arrange that village-dwelling smallholders would have their plots close to the village; and to ensure that each landholder would have approximately the same amount of land after the operation, although slight modifications were permissable in order to take variations in soil quality into account.

In practice, the effectiveness of the local commissions varied enormously. Those that functioned well investigated the requirements of each landowner and produced schemes which were tailor-made for them. By contrast, less scrupulous commissions left a great deal of the work to the land surveyors, whose youth and enthusiasm was sometimes not matched by an adequate understanding of the detailed characteristics of soil and hydrology. In such circumstances, guidance from local landowners proved essential if serious errors were to be avoided (Gay 1922: 252). Once drawn up, the proposed re-allocation document was placed in the *mairie* for ten days so that reactions from landowners and other interested parties might be lodged. Then the proposal and any objections to it were transmitted to the *département* commission for adjudication and dispatch to the prefect. The next stage involved tracing the pattern on the ground and, provided that no further objection were raised in the following month, the new arrangement was set to become definitive.

Uneven Innovation: Three Examples

Despite the generous provision of finances from the state, most northern *communes* opted to re-create exactly what they had lost and to re-establish the pre-war distribution of landholding (Estier 1976: 412). Only 441 *communes* throughout the devastated regions chose plot consolidation (Table 10.1). According to the agricultural enquiry of 1929, no *remembrement* was recorded in either Marne or Nord, even though the same investigation declared that both contained large areas where property fragmentation was harmful to the rational functioning of agriculture. In Aisne, Meuse, Pas-de-Calais and Vosges the number of schemes was very small, in the latter case being in response to disruption caused by the installation of a military airfield (Mireur 1924: 389). Agricultural advisers in Meuse lamented that fragmentation of holdings was impeding the introduction of machinery but recognized that 'unfortunately, the mistrust and the individualism of the farmers presents an almost unsurmountable barrier' to consolidation (Roche 1931: 54). Only a score or so schemes were completed in the twenty years following the Armistice (Jolivet & Brousse 1959: 55). By contrast, *remembrement* was accepted far more widely in Ardennes (118 schemes), Meurthe-et-Moselle (74),

Table 10.1 Land consolidation in the northern *départements*, 1929

	Area where fragmentation is harmful (ha)	Number of schemes	Area involved (ha)	Parcels exchanged	Area covered (ha)
Aisne	35,500	11	7,139	7,525	6,473
Ardennes	0	118	57,606	44,052	20,296
Marne	420 000	0	0	87,850	29,926
Meurthe-et-Moselle	100,000	74	36,502	26,095	7,830
Meuse	10,000	21	7,395	60,616	18,448
Nord	100,000	0	0	4,503	4,941
Oise	0	61	19,000	16,412	11,794
Pas-de-Calais	100,000	0	0	3,975	5,111
Somme	404,000	154	85,107	11,076	6,228
Vosges	291,000	1	563	23,131	9,003
Total	1,460,500	441	213,312	285,235	120,050
France Total	9,721,018	541	218,972	916,889	447,955

Source: Ministère de l'Agriculture 1936

Somme (154), and the north-east corner of Oise (61). Detailed conditions varied substantially among these *départements* but the common factor was that agricultural advisers were particularly active in each of them (Ovise 1948: 12). Work was to continue during the 1930s, but only 565 communes in the ten northern *départements* had undergone *remembrement* by the outbreak of the Second World War (Schmerber 1949: 55).

In various parts of Ardennes scattered parcels of land had been exchanged on a voluntary basis prior to 1914 (Ministère de l'Agriculture 1909: 28). By virtue of being behind enemy lines throughout the war, farmland in the *département* had not suffered serious or sustained material damage as a result of heavy shelling or other greatly destructive acts of war. Indeed, in some localities the land had been worked intensively by the Germans with the help of teams of civilian and military labour and heavy machinery brought in from Germany (Damuzeaux 1931: 9). Ploughing had been undertaken across large blocks of land, with no regard for patterns of landownership or for field boundaries (Damuzeaux 1933: 14–15). Initially farmers not only resisted but feared plot consolidation which they found 'too radical', hence a report of April 1921 anticipated that only 35,000 ha would be reorganized across the *département* (Adam 1937: 159; ADA 12J 15 Collection Marlier: Roquère, M. Extraits du rapport, 28.04.21). In fact the early examples completed during that year proved so successful that in 1923 Hubert could remark 'little by little the criticisms decline and mistrust falls' (Hubert 1923: 228). Even the fiercest opponents were gradually won over and took the decision for a 'giant step forward' (Adam 1937: 159). Some 314 *communes* were entitled to benefit under the 1919 legislation and 150 of these opted initially for *remembrement*, with the remainder choosing to reinstate the former pattern plus a few small improvements (*rebornement*) (Berenguer 1984: 55–56). Communities in the south-western and north-eastern parts of the *département* proved particularly willing to accept *remembrement* (Figure 10.1). The first 93 consolidation schemes covered 48,688 ha and reduced the number of property parcels by an average of 79 per cent (Table 10.2). According to the agricultural enquiry of 1929, 118 consolidation schemes had been completed over a total of 57,606 ha during ten years of peace (Ministère de l'Agriculture 1932).

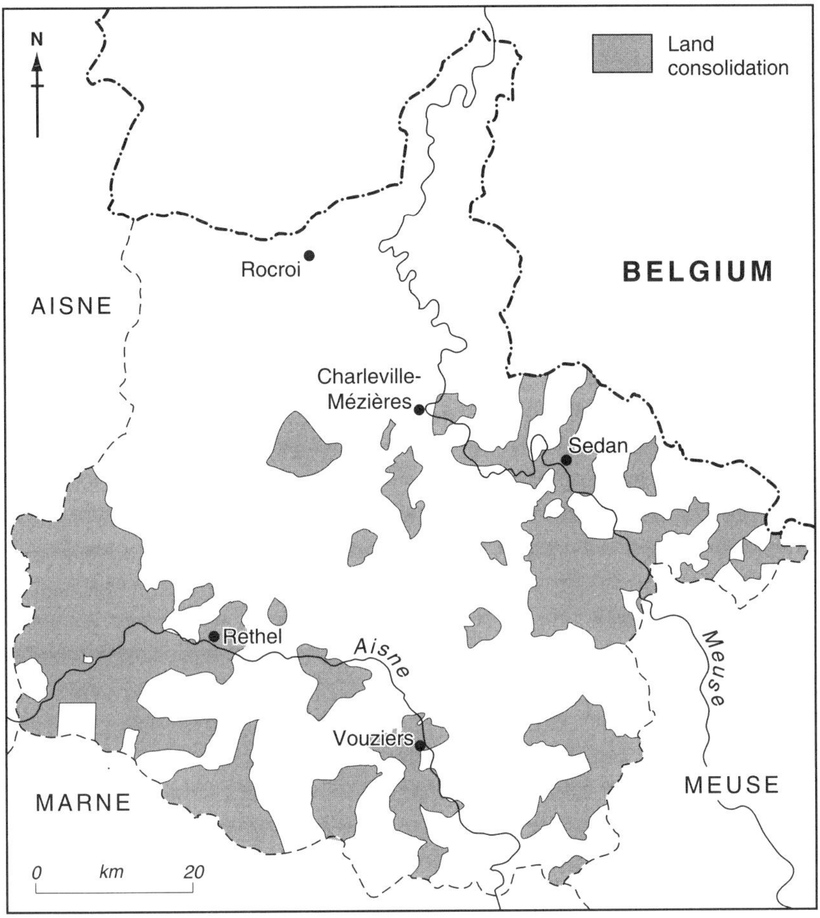

Figure 10.1 Land consolidation in Ardennes

Across the openfields of Meurthe-et-Moselle property fragmentation had been 'pushed to the ultimate limit' and was described by agricultural experts as 'an obstacle to any kind of economic cultivation' (Gruet 1937: 244). For example, the very few large holdings (in excess of 150 ha) in the *département* were composed of an average of 700–800 plots apiece, which were intermixed with the strips of neighbouring landholders. In many places tiny plots were abandoned (*champs perdus*) because they were inaccessible, and throughout the *département* openfield

Table 10.2 Land consolidation in Ardennes

	Before	After
Surface consolidated	48,688	48,688
Number of landowners	8,619	8,619
Number of parcels	179,819	38,136
Number of ilots	99,439	38,136
Average size of parcel, ha	0.27	1.27
Parcels/landowner	21.00	4.40
New field tracks opened, km		900

Source: Damuzeaux 1933: 14

cultivation could only operate with the agreement of adjacent farmers (Floremont 1983: 114). Voluntary exchanges of individual parcels were quite common, as landowners sought to cope with this problem on a piecemeal basis, and doubtless there had been some improvement on the average plot size in the *département* which had stood at a meagre 0.22 ha in 1892 (Dietrich 1954: 85).

The Service de la Reconstitution Foncière for Meurthe-et-Moselle was established immediately after the law of 4 March 1919 and a training centre for young surveyors was opened by the Chambre de Commerce et de l'Industrie at Nancy in order to replace the pool of expertise that had been lost during the war (Gay 1922: 252). Work began early in 1920 and was concentrated at three types of location in the devastated area, namely the battle zone, the northern *communes* where German tractors had erased former boundaries, and specific sites that had been disturbed by the installation of aviation camps or munitions depots (Second 1920: 34; Peltre 1969: 15; Floremont 1983: 118; Minella-Bouchy 1956: 39–54) (Figure 10.2). By the end of July 1922, seventy-four *communes* had opted for complete *remembrement*, thirty-three believed that *rebornement* would be adequate, and nine had failed to reach a decision. Seven years later, consolidation had been completed in those seventy-four *communes*, embracing 36,502 ha which were held by 12,500 landowners. The average size of plot increased from 26 ares to 89 ares and their number decreased by 70 per cent. The process of plot consolidation did not enlarge farm sizes but, as Minella-Bouchy remarked, 'was of enormous importance since it liberated farmers from all communal

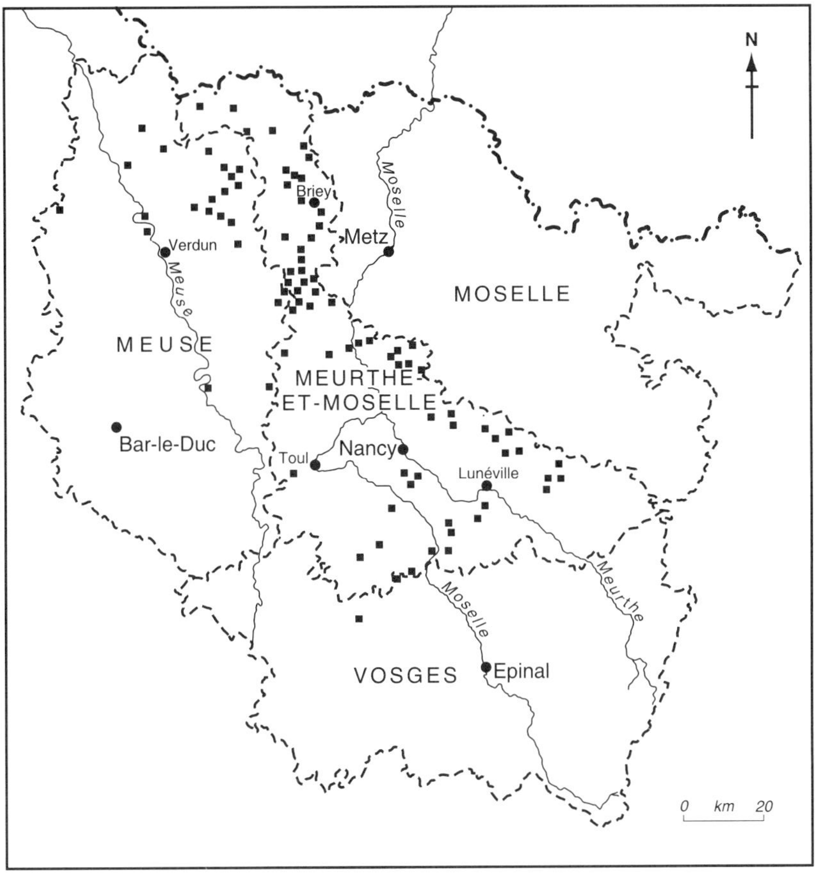

Figure 10.2 Land consolidation in Lorraine

constraints' associated with triennial rotations and enabled them to work their land as they wished (Ibid.: 44; Gravier 1910: 444). By contrast, such traditions continued to survive in *communes* that were not consolidated. The *commune* of Seichamp, 8 km north-east of Nancy, provides a classic example of this phase of *remembrement*. On the eve of the war 1,451 plots had covered 330 ha, with an average plot size of 23 ares (Figure 10.3a). After consolidation the number of plots was reduced to 395, with an average size of 84 ares, and 13.7 km of farm track had been installed which facilitated the movement of agricultural equipment (Figure 10.3b). The sample property (indicated in black) covered

Figure 10.3 Land consolidation in Seichamp, Meurthe-et-Moselle

48 ha and its number of parcels was reduced from 132 to 19 as a result of *remembrement* (Demangeon 1946: 163). As was the convention elsewhere, gardens, orchards and former vineyards were excluded from the operation.

Unlike Lorraine, the *département* of Somme had not enjoyed a history of plot consolidation, with only two schemes having been undertaken by the Service des Améliorations Agricoles immediately before the outbreak of war (Loirat 1931: 5). In addition, Picard farmers had a reputation for being particularly stubborn, but even they acknowledged that the extreme fragmentation of landownership led to considerable increases in the cost of cultivation and that voluntary exchanges of parcels were 'not capable of bringing a rapid remedy to this harmful situation' (AD 324 AP/47 Leroux, M., Agriculture dans le département de la Somme, 13.05.31). The gravity of land disturbance in the battle zone had been investigated in November 1916 when MM. Ogier and Bluzet reported that it would be impossible for individual landowners to recognize, let alone cultivate, their former plots without recourse to lengthy, discouraging and expensive legal procedures (cited in Peytral 1927: 495). When the Service de la Reconstitution Foncière was created in May 1919, under its 'energetic and devoted' director M. Leroy, it acted in the spirit of the earlier report and immediately launched a publicity campaign to ensure that the possibility of opting for *remembrement* was understood widely (Loirat 1931: 10; Morain 1922: 7). The matter was indeed a delicate and time-consuming one and advisers concentrated initially on *communes* that had suffered great devastation and where they believed some shreds of 'enlightened public opinion' to exist (Morain 1921: 32). Opposition was often a matter of ignorance, hence effective propaganda was not only essential but could be decisive (Girault 1922: 100).

Early reactions to the idea of consolidation were particularly positive in Combles *canton* in the north of the *département* (Ibid.: 6). This was in response to three factors: the extreme fragmentation of landholding and scattering of plots which had made cultivation difficult prior to 1914; the experience of some amicable exchanges which softened the traditional hostility to change; and the rarity and high cost of agricultural labour before the war which made some kind of structural change desirable (Carpentier 1928: 38). At Villers-Carbonnel, near Péronne, land consolidation was a logical extension of land-clearance activities which already had been organized on a cooperative basis (L'initiative privée peut sauver les régions libérées, *JRD*, 21.03.20: 2). But in many other parts of the *département* opposition was fuelled by misconceptions, including the belief that savings in time, labour and ultimately money as a result of *remembrement* would accrue only to large landowners. As Deputy Gonnet reported, some farmers perceived consolidation to be an unnecessary complication that would hinder their ability to undertake the urgent task of cultivating the land (Gonnet 1924: 1). By contrast, *remembrement* was supported by the active committee of the Société des Agriculteurs de la Somme and, as time passed, requests for anything less than complete consolidation became increasingly rare, thereby enabling Prefect Morain to estimate in 1921 that about 150 *communes* in the *département* would select this option (AN 324 AP/47 Leroux, M., Agriculture dans le département de la Somme; Morain 1921: 33).

By the spring of 1921 101 local commissions had been set up, of which seventy-two had opted for *remembrement*, twenty-five favoured re-establishment of the former pattern, and four still had not decided between the two options (Morain 1922: 9; Girault 1922: 5–6). Priority was accorded to areas that had been fought over, although landowners throughout the *département* could request *remembrement* under the legislation of 1919 (Loirat 1931: 11). The seventy-two schemes involved about 180,000 parcels and covered a total of 51,670 ha, with work having started in thirty *communes* extending over 21,669 ha. Prefect Morain noted that 'this total might appear mediocre but it is quite favourable when one notes that this kind of work started scarcely a year ago' (Morain 1921: 34). He might well have added that it was all the more remarkable when compared with the widespread rejection of *remembrement* in several other northern *départements*. His successor, Prefect Emery, was more forthright, declaring in 1924 that this was 'an extension that even the most ardent propagandists . . . would not have predicted four years ago' (Emery 1924: 114). The first thirty schemes involved 5,252 landowners who held 16,934 ha (Morain 1922: 13). Their number of plots was reduced from 45,560 to 9,463, with the mean size increasing from 0.37 ha to 1.79 ha. The average

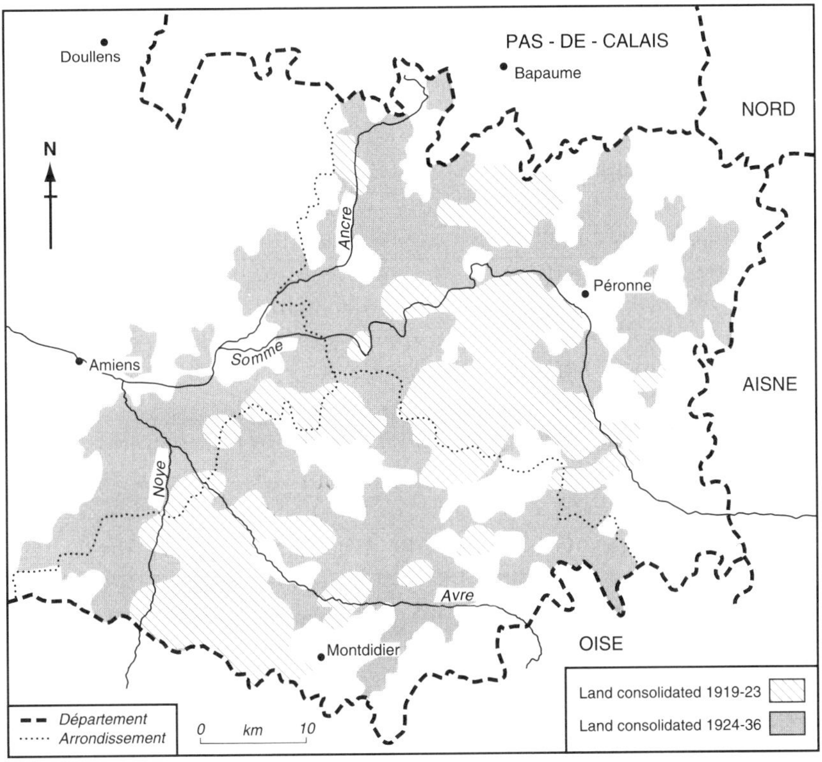

Figure 10.4 Land consolidation in Somme

holding was only 3.22 ha and had been composed of eight or nine plots before consolidation, compared with one or two afterwards.

Although Picard farmers were notorious for being sceptical of new ideas, the practice of *remembrement* overcame their hostility (Morain 1922: 11). Members of the commission of enquiry of the Confédération Générale du Travail mentioned examples of *communes* where no opposition was voiced and 'the landowners congratulated the land surveyors for their dedicated and conscientious work' (Confédération Générale du Travail 1921: 11). By the spring of 1927 ninety-three schemes had been completed and two years later the total reached 154 (Figure 10.3) (Ministère de l'Agriculture 1936). The results of work in 110 of these *communes* are summarized in Table 10.3. Despite some

Table 10.3 Land consolidation in Somme

	Before	After
Surface consolidated, ha	76,621	76,621
Number of landowners	21,778	21,778
Number of parcels	245,670	49,469
Average size of parcel, ha	0.31	1.55
Parcels/landowner	21.00	2.27
New field tracks opened, km		765.00

Source: Loirat 1931: 11

initial resistance, sustained and serious objections proved rare in Somme, unlike the situation in several other *départements*. Writing of his experience as an engineer for the Génie Rural in Somme, Loirat noted that 'In most cases one does not encounter irreducible hostility, but only hesitation regarding this reform, which like all innovations gives rise to certain mistrust. It is relatively easy to exercise persuasion and to create favourable attitudes so that the operation is accepted by almost all interested parties' (Loirat 1931: 7). No objections at all were registered in eighty-six *communes* where *remembrement* was to be undertaken, and the *département* commission had to deal with complaints from only 176 landowners out of the 21,778 whose property was involved. As a rule, consolidation worked 'to the great satisfaction of even those who had been most strongly opposed to the measure' (AN 324 AP/47 Historique de la Société des Agriculteurs de la Somme, 15.05.31). However, on average, only four-fifths of the surface of each *commune* was consolidated and hence many enclaves remained untouched or were re-created much as they had been before the war (Emery 1923: 95). Redistribution was normally arranged by *section* or *lieu-dit*, rather than across a whole *commune,* and this meant that a certain scattering of landownership could not be avoided (Rieucau 1966: 66). In addition, land was simply classified as good or mediocre, which provided a rather blunt criterion for implementing reorganization. The limited impact of mechanization at this time served to keep structural targets low, as did the frequent wish by landowners to retain specific plots with distinctive environmental conditions in particular locations (Loirat 1931: 11). In similar fashion, *remembrement* was accepted very readily in sixty-one *communes* in adjacent areas of north-eastern Oise, with a further 139 opting for the re-establishment of their old cadastral pattern. As the prefect recorded in 1925: 'With the exception of incidents in two or three *communes*, plot consolidation was welcomed by the majority' of landowners in this district (Conseil-Général de l'Oise 1925: 26).

Reconstituting the Familiar

According to the *enquête agricole* of 1929 the war-torn northern *départements* embraced 441 consolidation schemes, accounting for 97 per cent of all *remembrement* undertaken throughout France by that time, and with Somme containing two-fifths of what was achieved in the northern *départements* (Table 10.1). Figures quoted by Vandervynckt for work undertaken under the law of 1919 were fractionally lower, but the overwhelming dominance of Somme and Ardennes emerged clearly (Table 10.4) (Vandervynckt 1936: 273). It was, indeed, remarkable that so much was accomplished on the Santerre plateau in Somme but so little in neighbouring areas where roughly comparable conditions prevailed. For example, only thirteen schemes had been contemplated in adjacent areas of Pas-de-Calais, even though the landownership mosaic of no fewer than 217 *communes* needed to be re-established because of war-time devastation (Peytral 1927: 496). In Aisne only eleven schemes were contemplated, covering

Table 10.4 Land consolidation under the legislation of 17 April 1919

	Schemes completed	Schemes in progress
Aisne	7	11
Ardennes	85	40
Marne	33	1
Meurthe-et-Moselle	39	27
Meuse	18	6
Oise	59	6
Somme	135	37
Total	376	128

Source: Vandervynckt 1936: 273

a mere 7,139 ha. This state of affairs was truly astonishing since hundreds of *commune* commissions had been set up to determine what form the pattern of landholding should take. Ovise argued that the land surveyors employed by the Service de la Reconstitution Foncière in Aisne were young and inexperienced and failed to appreciate the sensitivities of local landowners on this issue (Ovise 1948: 13). He reported that private land agents had advised against *remembrement*, since they were anxious to defend their established role as intermediaries when plots were exchanged on a voluntary basis. They feared, not without some justification, that part of their livelihood would disappear if plot consolidation were to be implemented. In addition, some local politicians encouraged small farmers to oppose *remembrement* in the widespread but misguided belief that it would only be to the advantage of large landholders.

As Alexandre explained 'the reform came up against uninformed opinion and the farmers' hostility led to its failure almost everywhere' across the northern *départements* (Alexandre 1928b: 67). Likewise Prefect Peytral complained that rural opposition led to a very low level of completion in Pas-de-Calais (Peytral 1927: 496). Some of the reason for this reaction, in peri-urban farmlands at least, was given by Prefect Morain in the neighbouring *département* of Nord (Morain 1923: 48). He argued that, by virtue of its potential for house-building, a stretch of fragmented land adjacent to a road could command a much higher price than a single consolidated plot of equal area in the midst of a completely cultivated stretch of countryside. In addition, fragmented landholding was of particular interest to factory workers and miners who wished to acquire small pieces of land to work in their free time. Amicable exchanges were certainly taking place in Nord during the 1920s but no examples of formal *remembrement* were recorded, even though 350 *communes* had qualified for state finances to restore their patterns of landed property (Naudin 1921b: 48).

Despite the fact that the costs of consolidation in the devastated zone were covered by the state, there is no doubt that *remembrement* was both time-consuming and disruptive for farmers who were desperate to start working their holdings once again. However, the soil had to be cleared of shells, trenches and craters had to be filled, and decisions had to be taken on the precise delimitation of the 'red zone' before surveyors might move in. Even when communities reached the crucial decision to opt for consolidation, more time was consumed by commissions and enquiries which further hindered working the land. Mayors complained about the slowness of surveyors and reported the frustration experienced by anxious returnees for whom restoring land to cultivation was the prime imperative rather than re-arranging its geometry (ADS 332.256 Lettre de l'Inspecteur des Contributions Directes, 01.06.22). Had *remembrement* been carried out directly after the Armistice, and had sufficient teams of agricultural advisers and land surveyors been available immediately, then the result would doubtless have been very different (Gay 1922: 297). Short-term interests prevailed and retracing the old pattern of landownership was preferred. Over the great majority of the farmlands in northern France the cultivated landscape was re-created much as it had been on the eve of the war. The opportunity for structural innovation was allowed to slip by, despite the efforts of agricultural advisers to promote its virtues (Chambre d'Agriculture de Meurthe-et-Moselle 1934: 21).

Redefining the Red Zone

In this way the old cadastral pattern of farmland was restored across most of northern France, just as the fundamental patterns of land use and settlement reappeared once the devastation of war had been erased. In the face of fierce opposition from local landowners, who argued that to leave land uncultivated was 'sacrilege', the extensive red zone was revised down from an early estimate of 178,511 ha in 1918 according to the Ministère de l'Agriculture (including a highly devastated core of 55,898 ha) to 116,794 ha in 1922, as depicted in the official statistics of the Ministère des Régions Libérées (Hubert 1923: 198; Michel 1932: 30). In accord with legislation of 24 April 1923, the destiny of the red zone was reappraised and 60,000 ha were released for restoration (Le boisement dans la zone rouge de la Meuse, 1930: 789). But at the start of 1924 Charles Reibel, then Ministre des Régions Libérées, pronounced that 55,000 ha remained too profoundly disturbed to be brought back into cultivation for a long time and he was unsure if this would ever be possible

(Reibel 1924c: 246). He announced that these areas were to be expropriated by the state, in accordance with the compensation law, and would be planted with timber wherever possible (Reibel 1924b: 1). Indeed, it seemed likely that cultivation would be 'forbidden for tens of years and perhaps even for centuries' (Bros 1924: 69). However, the *sinistrés* were not to be dissuaded by such pronouncements and continued to argue their case steadfastly, so that by 1927 the red zone had been revised down to 48,820 ha in 178 *communes* that were located mainly in Marne and Meuse (Gide & Oualid 1931: 172).

In the disruption of November 1918 it seemed that broad stretches of devastated land were beyond any hope of restoration, and the idea of taking those areas into state ownership to form a kind of national shrine gained favour in Paris during the subsequent spring, with the argument being strengthened once the provisions of the compensation law were known (Michel 1932: 207). For example, it seemed that in the eastern half of Somme, 'from Thiepval to Albert, Combles and Péronne, and from Chaulnes to Roye, the ground was so completely upturned as to render it useless for agriculture for many years to come, and a scheme to plant this area with pine trees is now being considered' (Michelin 1919c: 11). A decision to create just such a *forêt sacrée* was taken 6 April 1919 (Michel 1932: 207). The fundamental compensation law was passed eleven days later (17 April 1919) which enabled the state to purchase land that was deemed unworthy of reclamation and to offer compensation to those who would be dispossessed. Strict application of the letter of the law would have produced myriad tiny patches (*îlots*) of red zone whose management would have been impracticable (Magny 1928: 61). Instead, prefects argued the case for delimiting continuous blocks over which some kind of alternative land use might be devised on a more rational basis. In that spirit, the prefect of Meuse insisted that 'the limits of the red zone must be simple, defined as much as possible by roads or along the crest of a hill or through the bottom of a valley' (ADMe 976 Rp.2705 Note du préfet, 07.01.20). An alternative view on the future of the red zone, reported by Strachey in the pages of *Spectator*, was to establish a broad commemorative highway from the Channel to the Alps, that would not only follow the front line but afford it a new symbolic significance in peacetime (Vaillat 1919: 781). It would be spanned by triumphal arches identifying particular phases of the war, be marked by monuments to recall the actions of specific divisions and brigades, and would give access to great cemeteries for the war dead. It would be lined with poplars and bordered with flowering shrubs, which would 'add to the beauty and dignity of the *voie sacrée*', but some stretches would simply be purged of shells and left unreclaimed, thereby 'enabling Nature to do its work and permitting the wind and rain to renew this blood-drenched land' (Ibid.). As well as 'tracing a furrow of memory across no-man's land', it was hoped that the highway would also perform a valuable practical role in reconstitution by giving access to surrounding fields and settlements (Ibid.).

The law of 17 April 1919 provided a controversial mechanism for delimiting broad stretches of red zone, and hence it seemed likely that 'a hundred or more . . . tragic villages' would never be rebuilt (Ford 1919a: 244). During the summer and early autumn of that year staff of the topographic bureau of the Service de la Reconstitution Foncière, assisted by the Génie Rural, undertook preliminary surveys of severely damaged land and assembled consultative committees of *sinistrés* who were desperate to know what fate awaited their land. Without a clear judgement on their devastated property, they had to endure the uncertainty of not knowing whether they would be allowed to return, and hence they were unable to initiate claims for compensation (Proposition de résolution, 1919: 2511). During the autumn, prefects throughout the northern *départements* communicated a depressing message to countless village mayors informing them that part or all of their *commune* would be excluded from reclamation. Thus Prefect Morain argued that large areas in eastern Somme, lying within the quadrilateral bounded by Albert, Combles, Bray and Péronne, seemed suitable only for afforestation or for sheep grazing, and hence he would recommend that the state should purchase a total of 28,000 ha in the *département* (Morain 1921: 26). Some large landowners agreed with this proposal but many family farmers were desperate to restore their land to cultivation with the minimum of delay and insisted that the prefect should reduce his estimate.

A little further north, the authorities of Pas-de-Calais had declared on 6 April 1919 that the *commune* of Roeux was beyond hope of restoration, but on the following day the members of its freshly reconstituted *conseil municipal* expressed the fervent desire to start re-working the devastated land. They managed to gather together forty workers to begin the task, despite a complete lack of shelter (Comité d'Action des Régions Dévastées 1925: 159; Michel 1932: 208). One month later landowners at Villers-Carbonnel near Péronne (Somme) formed an association to bring 600 ha of red zone back into cultivation, and by the end of 1919 they had managed to purge the whole of this area of shells (L'initiative privée peut sauver les régions libérées, *JRD*, 21.03.20: 1). In August 1919 disconsolate farmers in north-east Marne complained that the emergency services had done virtually nothing to help them, and the lack of available temporary accommodation prevented them from starting to reclaim their ravaged fields (Marne, *JRD*, 10.08.19: 198). Similar reactions were echoed in ruined villages throughout the liberated regions as farmers refused to accept the official pronouncement that their devastated soil had been made irrevocably sterile. Instead, they believed that the land could be brought back into use in a comparatively short time, and they even volunteered to bring in topsoil from other areas to assist this task (Ford 1919a: 244).

Faced with such dogged opinions, the northern prefects re-examined the evidence they had collected and duly revised their estimates downwards. Thus in the spring of 1920, Prefect Morain became convinced that over 20,000 ha of the red zone in Somme might be brought back into cultivation leaving only 8,000 ha for compulsory purchase (Morain 1920: 26). This kind of reappraisal was reinforced by the visit of President Millerand to the red zone in August 1920 and his attentive response to 'formal evidence gathered from the mouths of the *sinistrés*, of their willingness to restore their homes and their land' (Morain 1921: 28). In consequence, Morain received presidential instructions 'to put into practice – as rapidly as possible – every measure to enable this unfortunate area to recover from disaster' (Ibid.). In January 1921 the Confédération Générale du Travail noted that great efforts had been made in the preceding months to fill trenches and shellholes in intensely devastated parts of the *département* (Confédération Générale du Travail 1921: 11). By August 1921 the amount recommended for compulsory purchase in Somme had been reduced to 4,500 ha and to 4,027 ha by November. At that stage it seemed to the prefect that this small quantity of very poor soil would have to be left uncultivated, since even before the war areas of such low productivity had started to be abandoned to scrub. Very recent experience confirmed his doubts, since some returning *sinistrés* had tackled exceptionally poor chalky soils, but 'laden with sorrow and regret' had to resign themselves to abandon them after having devoted a couple of years of valiant struggle (Morain 1922: 176). Indeed, in the mid-1920s desolate areas of scrub were still to be glimpsed from the railway line running north from Albert (Alexandre 1928b: 62). However the drive to reclaim the red zone continued, and in 1928 only 526 ha remained in Somme, located almost entirely around Thiepval (Carpentier 1928: 34).

Reclaiming the Red Zone

The desire to restore war-torn land was in evidence throughout the northern *départements* as landowners expressed their willingness to cultivate land afresh and as the heavily criticized emergency organizations removed quantities of unexploded shells and other dangerous material (Confédération Générale du Travail 1921: 10). In Pas-de-Calais Prefect Peytral reported a reduction in the area of the red zone from 26,409 ha (according to the provisional estimate of 1919) to a mere 2,131 ha early in 1921, involving parts of thirty-six *communes* (Peytral 1927: 500). However the cost of bringing red zone land back into cultivation was rising alarmingly, since the easiest sections had been restored already, prisoner-of-war labour was no longer available, and civilian workers were increasingly expensive (Leuillier 1920: 20). Nonetheless, the red zone in that *département* had been reduced to 1,400 ha by the autumn of 1921 and twelve months later had fallen to 484 ha in just five *communes* (Thélus, Vimy, Neuville-Saint-Vaast, Givenchy-en-Gohelle and Souchez) (Tribondeau 1927: 124). By 1925 a figure of 300 ha was being quoted by M. Queille, the Ministre de l'Agriculture (Comité d'Action des Régions Dévastées 1925: 7).

Several proposals for dealing with the red zone were mooted by the prefect of Pas-de-Calais, ranging from total expropriation and afforestation, to partial expropriation with a mixture of land uses, including timber, grazing and arable. These ideas evoked varying degrees of opposition from local landowners, especially in Givenchy and Souchez, even though large numbers of unexploded shells were known to remain buried there (Peytral 1926: 129). Their presence attracted unemployed people and foreigners who risked their lives stripping off the red copper casing (Conseil-Général du Pas-de-Calais 1927: 124). More than twenty people had been killed in this way in Pas-de-Calais during the first nine months of 1927 alone. In the following year the *conseil-général* received information on another set of solutions for the red zone, whereby 174 ha would pass to the Eaux-et-Forêts administration for afforestation, 107 ha would be ceded to the Canadian government for its memorial site and surrounding plantations on Vimy Ridge, and the final 203 ha would be restored, divided and re-cultivated once any remaining shells had been removed and the surface had been worked over thoroughly (Conseil-Général du Pas-de-Calais 1928: 156).

Further to the south-east the initial definition of the red zone in Aisne included broad stretches of the Chemin-des-Dames plateau where large farms had worked soil of 'legendary fertility' before the war (Roussel 1923: v). During the course of 1919 the total was reduced from 19,000 ha to 15,000 ha, with a distinction being made between patches that were only suitable for afforestation and others that might possibly be brought into cultivation, albeit at very great cost (Ibid.: 145; AN AJ 25/51 Bonnefoy-Sibour, A., Rapport sur le fonctionnement, 25.04.19). In June 1921 André Tardieu remarked that, despite thirty months having elapsed since the Armistice, there were still many stretches of the Chemin-des-Dames whose chaotic condition gave rise to great consternation (AN 324 AP/62 Reconstitution de la France dévastée, 31.03.32). Vigorous debate ensued, with those *sinistrés* who had returned to live in makeshift shelters begging that their land should be restored and their farmsteads rebuilt as part of a methodical scheme to revive the district (La visite de Monsieur Loucheur au Chemin-des-Dames, *LP*, 08.08.21). During a visit by Minister Loucheur, the devastated *communes* of the Chemin-des-Dames were awarded the *croix de guerre* but, as M. Doucedame insisted, that honour 'does not bring them bricks or building stone' (Ibid.). Mayor Bezançon from Soupir argued that 'wasteland which recalls the war and all its horrors' should not be tolerated and that abandoned land would simply be a breeding ground for 'vipers, foxes, badgers and boars which would destroy crops up to 10 km away '(Comité d'Action des Régions Dévastées 1925: 45). He believed that if the red zone were not reclaimed a 'major scheme for improving land and public health [would be] necessary within ten years, since life would be impossible in these conditions' (Ibid.). In the spring of 1922 Minister Reibel visited this 'desert-like region' to hear the requests of *sinistrés* and to see for himself that 140 ha of former red zone at Soupir had been restored to cultivation with great success (Monsieur Reibel visite l'Aisne, *LP*, 15.03.22). In the light of this evidence, he pledged his support for measures to further scale down the red zone and to encourage its return to normal use. By 1923 the red zone of Aisne had been reduced to 9,500 ha in thirteen *communes*, of which the state wished to acquire 3,564 ha, much to the anger of a vociferous group of landowners (Roussel 1923: 145). As a result of protracted negotiation it was further reduced to just 750 ha of very poor soil alongside the Forêt de Vauclerc in four *communes* on the Craonne plateau (Ratineau & Gaillot 1928: 132; Conseil-Général de l'Aisne 1929: 10).

By the summer of 1924 the transformation of the Chemin-des-Dames was proclaimed to be nothing short of 'miraculous', with ravaged land having been levelled and ploughed to yield harvests of wheat, barley and sugar beet (La zone rouge, *JDD*, 27.7.24: 1). Four years later the remaining 750 ha had been purchased by the state and were ready to be transferred to the Eaux-et-Forêts administration for planting up with softwoods (Ratineau & Gaillot 1928: 132). Clearance and levelling of land for agricultural purposes continued to operate for several more years from large farmsteads on the Chemin-des-Dames plateau (Brunet 1960: 397). This fundamental reappraisal of land potential satisfied most local farmers, but some agricultural experts adopted the contrary view. They argued that 'it is regrettable that the whole red zone has not been entrusted to the Eaux-et-Forêts' since they believed the churned-up soil was only fit for planting with trees (Ratineau & Gaillot 1928: 135).

Greening the Red Zone

The major exceptions to this trend of restoration and recovery were in Marne and Meuse, where large stretches of red zone

(21,000 ha and 21,242 ha respectively) still survived in 1927 (Michel 1932: 208). The red zone in Marne embraced three dozen *communes* in the north of the *département* which had been occupied by the enemy for the duration of the war (Garnotel 1985: 74). Seven villages had been destroyed without trace and in some places the topsoil was 'pure chalk, completely without vegetation' (Lebrun & Guille 1926: 108). Following a ministerial decision of 24 January 1922, the state proceeded to purchase compulsorily three large blocks of land (Moronvillers, Tahure and La Gruerie) which totalled 24,541 ha (Brisac 1922b: 858). As elsewhere, this kind of action produced severe opposition from local farmers and in consequence the area to be expropriated was reduced; however, the administration believed that over 10,000 ha were too damaged and inherently poor to be cultivated (Brisac 1923: 753). Nonetheless, by early 1926 over 2,300 ha had been returned to their owners and brought back into agricultural use (Conseil-Général de la Marne 1926: 250). In contrast, 8,000 ha were judged to be beyond hope of restoration and were added to the large military training ground at Suippes (Clause 1975: 405; Brunet 1981: 57).

The fate of the red zone in the neighbouring *département* of Meuse was recorded in intricate detail (Amat 1987a; Clout 1992). During 1922 the Service de la Reconstitution Foncière surveyed 21,000 ha in 103 *communes* in order to delimit it accurately (Emery 1923: 82). It was anticipated that the state would purchase all of it and steps were taken to deposit proposed compulsory purchase orders in the *mairies* concerned and to present details to the relevant landowners (Magny 1928: 62). If agreement could be reached, then titles of credit would be prepared without delay. During 1923 lawyers were charged with drawing up letters of intent for compulsory purchase but before this could happen each landowner had to be identified. Obviously the procedure could become unworkable if landowners were unknown or if they failed to reply to communications from the administration. Such proved to be the case in areas of extreme property fragmentation where a multitude of owners possessed only a handful of parcels apiece. Legislation of 24 April 1923 attempted to simplify matters by enabling some areas of the red zone to be divided and returned to agricultural use; a second group to be handed over to the Service des Eaux-et-Forêts for afforestation; and other areas to be recognized as *vestiges de guerre* or to be converted into military camps (Amat 1987a: 229).

Classification of land with a view to its future use was a very complicated, protracted and controversial operation which was undertaken in each *département* by the Service de la Reconstitution Foncière and the Service Technique, after consultation with agricultural and forestry organizations, village mayors and local inhabitants (ADMe 976 Rp.2705 Procès-verbaux de réutilisation da la zone rouge, 1920–3). The procedure proved to be highly contentious and in some instances anomalous situations developed. For example, the inhabitants of Grémilly (8 km north-east of Douaumont) had returned to their devastated village and succeeded in establishing a cooperative reconstruction society which was duly approved by the authorities of Meuse (La zone rouge, *JDD*, 27.07.24: 1). However, part of their village land was classified as being within the red zone and hence permanent reconstruction of farmsteads was forbidden. Almost six years after the Armistice, returnees to Grémilly were still living in temporary shelters 'like a camp of nomads' on the fringe of their ruins (Ibid.). The columns of the *Journal des Départements Dévastés* argued that if the prefect of Meuse were to take the time to visit the Chemin-des-Dames in Aisne he would be convinced that similar miracles could be worked in his own *département* (Meuse, *JDD*, 27.07.24: 1).

Of 6,953 landowners in Meuse who were eligible for compulsory purchase, 5,952 accepted the offer, 257 refused, a further 346 did not reply, and 398 could not be contacted (Magny 1928: 62). Agreements became increasingly rare as time passed and hence expropriation with due compensation was to be carried out, by following the law of 20 April 1922 and using the names of proprietors as they had been listed in the cadastral registers. Some landowners claimed that the offer of compensation was too small, choosing to take their case to the *commission supérieure*, which further retarded a solution to the 'virulent debate' on whether or not the environs of Verdun should be afforested (Amat 1987a: 220). Eventually, actions were taken to expropriate two large blocks of land to either side of the river Meuse and four smaller ones (Argonne, Vauquois, Les Eparges and the Forêt d'Apremont). Those six zones involved forty-six *communes*, eleven of which were expropriated in their entirety. In addition, there were many tiny *îlots de zone rouge* covering 3,018 ha in eighty-six *communes*, which were especially numerous on the Plaine de Woëvre. These were too small and dispersed to be acquired by the state, so instead they were returned to their owners for cultivation (Schmitt 1928–9: 89; ADMe 976 Rp.2705 Procès-verbaux de réutilisation de la zone rouge).

By 1928 the red zone of Meuse was almost entirely classified, with only the Butte de Montfaucon and a number of disputed properties (totalling 684 ha) still awaiting a decision on their fate (Le boisement dans la zone rouge de la Meuse, 1930: 789). Some 3,980 ha had been returned to their owners for cultivation; a part of the Butte de Vauquois devastated by massive shell craters had been classified as a *vestige de guerre*; and 13,404 ha had been transferred to the Eaux-et-Forêts. This latter total involved stretches of land in forty-one *communes*, including two large areas at Morthomme (3,103 ha) and near Verdun (9,270 ha) (Forget 1927, 1928). Very soon work began on clearing military tracks for peacetime use, removing barbed wire and shells, laying out new paths, and preparing detailed programmes of afforestation. Over two-thirds of these areas (8,789 ha) had comprised active farms or land that had fallen out of cultivation before the war. Some devastated areas subsequently had been grazed by sheep brought in from Moselle, even though the animals ran the risk of injury or poisoning (Samson 1931: 49). Most of the remainder (3,414 ha) had supported some kind of timber cover which had been gravely damaged by wartime activity. A mere 171 ha were marshy, as a result of heavy bombardment or disruption of watercourses, and were only suitable for planting with poplars. Elsewhere stretches of sloping terrain were sown with seeds or planted with saplings, often by women workers who had been recruited locally. By the end of the winter of 1929–30 2,500 ha had been planted and it was estimated that a further two or three years would be needed to reach completion. The war zone of Meuse was becoming 'year by year a green area, with green the colour of hope' (Forget 1927: 131). The transformation of what remained of the red zone elsewhere in northern France was in progress also, as was the definitive reconstruction of thousands of farmsteads and hundreds of villages (Amat 1987a). Nonetheless, twenty years after the Armistice the wounds in the landscape had not healed entirely,

Plate 10.1 The ruins of Montfaucon, Meuse, have been preserved: the village was rebuilt on a lower site nearby

with Denis Brogan being able to record that 'even today there runs all across [northern] France a great scar . . . visible to the naked eye' (Brogan 1940: 599).

11
Toward a Balance Sheet

Visiting the Battlefields

Commercial tours to the northern *départements* had begun as early as April 1919 and visitors, duly informed by the *Illustrated Michelin Guides to the Battlefields*, travelled to view the devastation for themselves (Ford 1919a: 254). The following report, which appeared one month later, figured in the volume devoted to the Second Battle of the Marne. 'The ruined villages are as the shells and bombs left them. Everywhere are branchless trees and stumps, shell craters roughly filled in, trenches, barbed wire entanglements, and shelters for men and ammunition. Thousands of shells, shell casings, rifles, and machine guns lie scattered about. Corpses are occasionally seen' (Michelin 1919b: 40). To stray from the road invited trouble, since 'the paths were too often bestrewn with unexploded shells and other missiles', leading one prudent visitor to conclude that the battle zone 'is not yet a land for tourists' (Franklin 1919: 64).

Nonetheless, the two railway companies serving the *régions libérées* ran special trains to numerous ruined towns during the summer of 1919. A day excursion ran twice a week from Paris to Albert, Arras and Lens, returning to the security of the capital in the evening (Chemin de Fer du Nord 1919). At Albert up to a thousand visitors at a time transferred to the open carriages of 'the pilgrimage train' protected only by a simple roof which kept off the rain (Wallon & Gobert 1919: 11). They were advised to dress warmly and to bring their own food, but especially to exercise extreme caution when leaving the train and walking along pathways lined with the debris of war. They were warned that 'already grave accidents have happened to people who have not observed basic rules for their own safety' (Chemin de Fer du

Nord 1919). On an even larger scale, several thousand inquisitive visitors travelled by train from the capital to Reims each day during the first summer after the Armistice, going back to the hotels of Paris for the night. They were surprised that so many residents had returned to the devastated city and that 'there was so much animation in streets bordered by ruins' (Vers la renaissance, *LA*, 1919: 401). Visiting the *régions dévastées* involved serious risks for the foolhardy and the downright unfortunate. Tourists and children as well as workmen were maimed or killed in Reims, in the surrounding countryside, and right across the northern *départements* because of the widespread presence of unexploded shells, grenades, fuses and numerous types of weapon (ADMa 203 M205 Armes et munitions, 25.06.19). In Marne, 'never a day goes by without another violent death being recorded' from such causes (Vers la renaissance, *LA*, 1919: 501).

In these early months of peace motoring was constrained by petrol shortages and a lack of suitable overnight accommodation in the former battle zone. The first American visitors to the ruins of Verdun had to sleep in the streets until hotel huts could be installed (Meuse, *JRD*, 09.11.19). M. Ogier requested that they should be treated fairly by local people, recalling that some shopkeepers 'both during the war and since the Armistice have exploited our American allies unworthily' (Ogier 1919: 118). The Touring Club de France urged existing hotel-keepers to improve what facilities they could offer, recognizing that new hotels could not be built sufficiently rapidly to satisfy requirements, even though the demand for accommodation had been anticipated by some foresighted architects during the darkest days of war (Agache 1917: 110). Despite their emphasis on where to stop in order to obtain 'the best general view of the extensive ruins . . . and absolute devastation', the Michelin Illustrated Guides urged that 'such a visit should be a pilgrimage, not merely a journey across the ravaged land. Seeing is not enough, one must understand' (Michelin 1920:111; Michelin 1919b: 2).

In addition to visitors who were merely curious to see where fighting had taken place and devastation was to be found, the battlefields also received large numbers of bereaved visitors of all social classes and of many nationalities. Once a year, widows, parents and children of soldiers *morts pour la France* were accorded free return travel by rail between their homes and where their husband, son or father was buried (Reynes 1929: 83). Under exceptional circumstances, brothers and sisters might be substituted to receive these travel privileges. Official handbooks, for example those published by the Ministère des Pensions, provided 'useful information for families visiting military graves', including the precise location of each cemetery, details of local public transport, and the availability of accommodation and meals nearby (Ibid.: 1). As M. Revault had reported to the Chambre des Députés in 1920, the nation could not ignore that millions of visitors would travel to the former battlefields, for a variety of motives, in the years ahead (Revault 1920: 587). He believed it was essential that these places, 'where each footstep touches a grave', should retain their dignity but should also provide accommodation, meals and other goods and services so that visitors would make a contribution to the local economy (Ibid.). To help achieve these goals, he argued that hotels and restaurants, which would cater for all financial circumstances, should be constructed as soon as building materials would become available, and automobile tours should be organized as soon as sufficient petrol could be obtained.

The Long Road to Recovery

On Armistice Day 1927 André Tardieu, then Ministre des Travaux Publics, proclaimed that reconstruction was complete in northern France (Bury 1972: 105). In fact, his announcement was somewhat premature since destroyed dwellings would continue to be replaced well into the next decade, but it was true that much had been achieved so perhaps his statement was not too unreasonable. However, just as Richard Kuisel has warned, it seems impossible to draw up a comprehensive balance sheet for the reconstruction years (Kuisel 1981: 293). During the second half of the 1920s the topic disappeared from annual reports presented by prefects and from the periodic proceedings of *conseils-généraux* in the northern *départements*. Official statistics became even more sparse than for earlier years, but Edmond Michel included a few figures for January 1931 in the postscript to his vast analysis of *Les dommages de guerre* which, although completed in November 1928, was not to be published for a further four years (Michel 1932: 612). Like many of the other official statistics that he reproduced, those in the postscript contain their unfortunate share of ambiguities and possible errors of transcription, thereby rendering any quest for accurate and complete statements of achievement all the more elusive. Nonetheless, these scant figures together with the results of the *statistique agricole annuelle* for 1928, the *statistique agricole* of 1929, and the *dénombrement de la population* for March 1931, provide a broad indication of what may have been achieved ten to a dozen years after the war had ended (Ministère de l'Agriculture 1929, 1936; Ministère de l'Intérieur 1932). No trace or even mention of an official statement of the full accomplishments of the reconstitution years has been found.

As earlier chapters have shown, by far the greater share of land restoration had been undertaken during the 'emergency phase' of the early 1920s, with the remainder of the decade being concerned with work in particularly problematic stretches and in areas of red zone which had been re-appraised for cultivation. As was reported in Chapter 7, some 259,793,000 m^3 of trenches had been filled by 1 January 1922 throughout the ten *départements*; nine years later the total had risen by 17 per cent to reach 305,277,055 m^3, by comparison with the official estimate of 333,000,000 m^3 that was noted in 1922 as needing to be filled (Ministère des Travaux Publics 1929). The amount of barbed wire collected rose by 26 per cent from 274,514,600 m^2 (1922) to 345,857,646 m^2 (1931) which differed from the estimated target of 375,000,000 m^2 announced in 1922 (Michel 1932: 612; Sauvy 1965: I 454). The quantity of shells recovered increased only fractionally from 20,800,000 tonnes to 21,162,874 tonnes between 1928 and 1931, no estimate of their recovery having been offered in 1922. But, three-quarters of a century later unexploded shells were still being unearthed, with 23 tonnes being recovered in a six-month period in 1990 along the new route for the *train-à-grande vitesse* (TGV) in the single *département* of Somme (Becker J-J 1991: 22). *Déminage* by state employees continues to this day across the fields and woodlands of northern France. Apparently, three dozen farmers died from encounters with live shells in 1991 alone (Webster 1994: 31).

Taking data at face value, the amount of land purged of trenches, barbed wire and shells rose by a quarter from 2,676,500 ha to 3,367,992 ha over the nine years from 1922 to 1931, producing a rather larger result than the objective of 3,306,350 ha that had been estimated at the time of the Armistice (Michel 1932: 612). In fact, two-thirds of the surface that was to be cleared by January 1931 had already been treated by January 1920, with 85 per cent of the devastated area of both Somme and Oise having been worked over by that date. By contrast, eleven months after the Armistice only half had been treated in Marne, Vosges and Meuse. By January 1924 the proportion had risen to 87 per cent across the northern *départements* as a whole, and was virtually finished in Oise, Pas-de-Calais and Somme, but lagged in both Marne (68 per cent) and Meuse (69 per cent). The curiously high level of completion recorded for 1931 may well have resulted from incorrect estimates in 1922 of what needed to be done or from double counting of what was achieved across areas that had been worked over more than once. Nonetheless, by 1931 land restoration would seem to have been completed in six *départements* but appears to have fallen massively short in Meuse (70 per cent) and fractionally so in Somme (91 per cent) and Ardennes (97 per cent). At this point two statistical adjustments are perhaps advisable. First, the estimate of work needed in Oise appears to be suspiciously high, and hence data for that *département* are best omitted from further calculations. Second, the apparent overstatements of completion in four *départements* may be avoided by replacing these figures with the total areas estimated in 1922 as being in need of restoration. Once these adjustments are made, it would seem that 95.5 per cent of the surface that needed to be purged of shells, trenches and other obstacles in the nine *départements* (omitting Oise) had been completed by January 1931. It comes as no surprise that clearance continued into the 1930s in Marne and Meuse.

According to the official statistics published in 1923, a total of 1,923,479 ha of farmland had needed to be levelled at the time of the Armistice across the ten *départements*. As early as January 1920 half of that total had been worked over and, not surprisingly, every *département* recorded the largest annual volume of activity during 1919. By January 1920 Nord (79 per cent), Oise (67 per cent) and Pas-de-Calais (66 per cent) were substantially ahead of the others. Conversely, Meuse (31 per cent) and Ardennes (39 per cent) were at the bottom of the league, and in Aisne only 41 per cent of disrupted land had been levelled, even though the largest absolute volume of work had been accomplished in that *département* (208,500 ha). Two years later three-quarters of all damaged farmland had been levelled across the ten *départements*, and Nord was only 0.5 per cent short of reaching its objective.

By January 1928 levelling had been completed in Nord and Ardennes but in the subsequent three years extensive activity continued in Marne (16,042 ha) and Meuse (34,000 ha) as stretches of red zone were reclaimed. The statistics reproduced by Edmond Michel imply that very substantial areas were levelled in Aisne (100,521 ha) and Oise (32,302 ha) but those figures are so large and produce results that exceed so greatly the areas initially declared to be in need of levelling that they cannot be accepted at face value (Michel 1932: 612). The high figure for Aisne is probably due to a single typographical error (and probably should have read 515,948 ha for 1931 rather than 615,948 ha) but the statistic for Oise once again looks completely erroneous. When the data are re-worked on the basis of nine *départements* it would seem more likely that 1,846,592 ha had been levelled by January 1931. If one assumes, not unrealistically, that all disrupted land in Oise had been levelled by that date, then the complete total would rise to 1,914,842 ha, representing 99.6 per cent of the surface declared initially as being in need of restoration. Only Meuse (88.7 per cent) and Somme (95.1 per cent) appear to have had notable proportions of land still in need of levelling a dozen years after the Armistice had been signed. But of course, the soil continued to settle into trenches, craters and underground shelters that had been filled imperfectly, thereby making ploughing a hazardous business for many decades to come (Meissel 1986: 153). As a result, the smoothed-out traces of old shell craters can still be glimpsed in many northern fields before the crops have grown (Fussell 1975: 70).

The official statistics, quoted by Edmond Michel and echoed three decades later by Alfred Sauvy, enable the broad trend of reconstruction and definitive repair of dwellings and farm buildings to be identified during the first twelve years of peace (Sauvy 1965: I 454). The greatest volume of achievement was accomplished during 1922 when 140,450 buildings were restored (representing 16.8 per cent of all activity between 1920 and

1931), followed by 96,890 in 1923, with 85,240 having been restored before January 1920 (Figure 11.1). Meurthe-et-Moselle, Nord, Pas-de-Calais and Somme achieved their maximum pace of restoration during 1922, with Marne and Oise peaking one year later. By contrast, in Ardennes, which had remained behind enemy lines throughout the war, one-third of all restoration had been accomplished before 1920. Conversely, maximum restoration was achieved late in Meuse (1926), where so many aspects of recovery lagged, and also in Aisne and Vosges (both 1927). Despite all this achievement, it was possible in 1925 for Victor Dalbiez, then Ministre des Régions Libérées, to note that 'six years after the Armistice many inhabitants are still housed in huts. This is a deplorable situation which must be remedied without delay' (Comité d'Action des Régions Dévastées 1925: 3). This was not to be the case, and a quarter of a century after the end of the war thousands of 'temporary huts' continued to be occupied in many settlements across northern France (Hilaire 1988: 350). Even now a few may be seen around the back or to the side of reconstructed houses. Most are used as garden sheds or for general storage rather than for housing. Without doubt, the survival of ruins for a decade or even more after the end of the war 'must have been one of the most poignant images in French life' (Becker J-J 1991: 22).

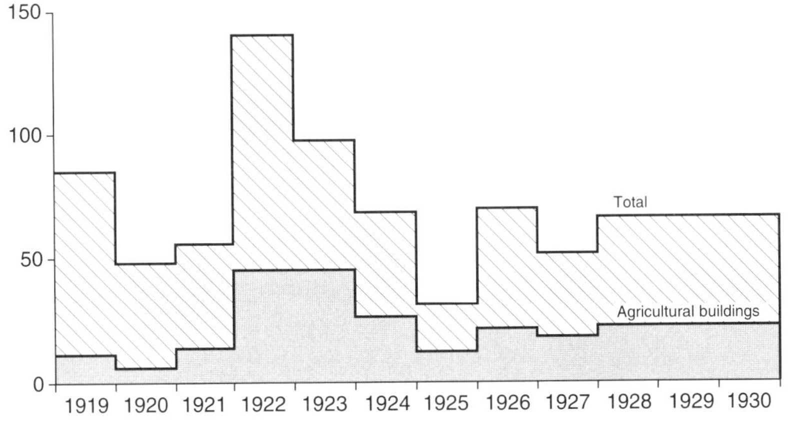

Figure 11.1 Annual volume of repair and reconstruction of dwellings and farm buildings 1919–30

Taking the official statistics at face value would indicate that 834,516 dwellings and farm buildings had been repaired or reconstructed by 1 January 1931, representing a notional shortfall of just 3.7 per cent from the 866,844 that had been declared damaged or lost across the ten *départements*. However, the figure for repair and reconstruction in Oise greatly exceeds the volume of loss declared at the Armistice and once again is best omitted. A revised calculation, excluding Oise, yields an 8.0 per cent shortfall for the nine remaining *départements*. By 1931 the stock of housing and farm buildings in Ardennes, Nord and Vosges would appear to have recovered completely. That of Aisne and Meurthe-et-Moselle was still slightly below the pre-war level (both −4.4 per cent), and restoration in crude numerical terms fell substantially short in Marne (−18.3 per cent), Pas-de-Calais (−18.8 per cent) and Somme (−16.4 per cent). Not surprisingly, Meuse earned the sad distinction of having restored a lower proportion of housing and farm buildings than any other northern *département*, with 36.5 per cent fewer units in 1931 than in 1914. However, in some instances the ruins of two or even three buildings were replaced by a single, more substantial building, and all these figures on housing must be treated with considerable caution (Schmitt 1928–9: 89).

By January 1931 some 20,563 public buildings were reported to have been rebuilt or permanently repaired, but this represented a figure substantially greater than the 17,516 listed as damaged or destroyed twelve years previously. The discrepancy may well result from instances of two buildings (for example a *mairie* separated from a school) replacing a single building on the same site. As was the case for housing and farm buildings, the greatest volume of restoration occurred during 1922 when 2,996 schools, *mairies*, churches and other public buildings were repaired or rebuilt, followed by 2,256 during 1923. Not until the start of 1925 were half the devastated public buildings restored throughout the northern *départements*.

Some 61,382 km of roads were recorded as having been repaired and rebuilt a dozen years after the Armistice, which substantially exceeded the 58,697 km declared to be in need of recovery in 1918. The greatest length (10,588 km) was restored during 1922, which brought the average rate of completion by January 1923 to 53 per cent across the ten *départements*. At that time Oise (68 per cent), Nord (64 per cent) and Marne (62 per cent) were ahead of the northern average, with Meuse (36 per cent) once again lagging behind. Similarly, a greater length of local railway line (2,908 km) had been relaid or restored by 1931 than had been declared damaged in 1918 (2,409 km). By January 1922 roughly half of the total had been completed, but rates of achievement were lagging in Meuse, Vosges and especially Somme, where only 9 km were recorded as having been restored. All main lines had been rebuilt in a matter of months after the end of the war.

Ten years after the Armistice very many aspects of agricultural recovery were complete (Michael 1928: 177–78) (Figure 11.2). The amount of arable land throughout the devastated *départements* stood at 3,228,000 ha in 1928, 90 per cent of the pre-war average, having peaked at 3,415,000 ha (95 per cent) in 1922, but declining thereafter as a result of the long-established trend away from cereal production in favour of dairying (Ministère de l'Agriculture 1911–14, 1929; Auge-Laribé 1945: 56; Braibant 1936: 32). In 1928 the arable surface was very close to the pre-war average in Pas-de-Calais, Somme, Aisne and Nord (each over 95 per cent) but came below 80 per cent of that level in Ardennes, Meuse, Meurthe-et-Moselle and Vosges where pastoral activities were gaining in importance (Adam 1937: 189). The amount of land under wheat throughout the ten *départements* peaked in 1925 at 86.5 per cent of the pre-war average and stood at 82.5 per cent in 1928; however, output exceeded the pre-war level in 1925 and declined somewhat to 97 per cent in 1928. Nonetheless, average wheat yields increased progressively during the 1920s in each of the northern *départements*. Starting at a very low point immediately after the war, by 1928 sugar-beet production rose to 85 per cent of the 1910–13 average and the structure of processing had changed considerably, with only 72 sugar refineries operating in 1928 across the ten *départements* compared with 172 on the eve of hostilities (Michael 1928: 91). Large corporations had purchased the compensation allocated to many small refining firms and thereby managed to restructure the industry in northern France (Inghels 1924: 48–50). For example, between 1913 and 1928 the number of sugar refineries in Aisne, Nord and Somme fell from fifty-one to fifteen, from forty-one to fourteen, and from thirty-two to nine respectively (Carpentier 1928: 30).

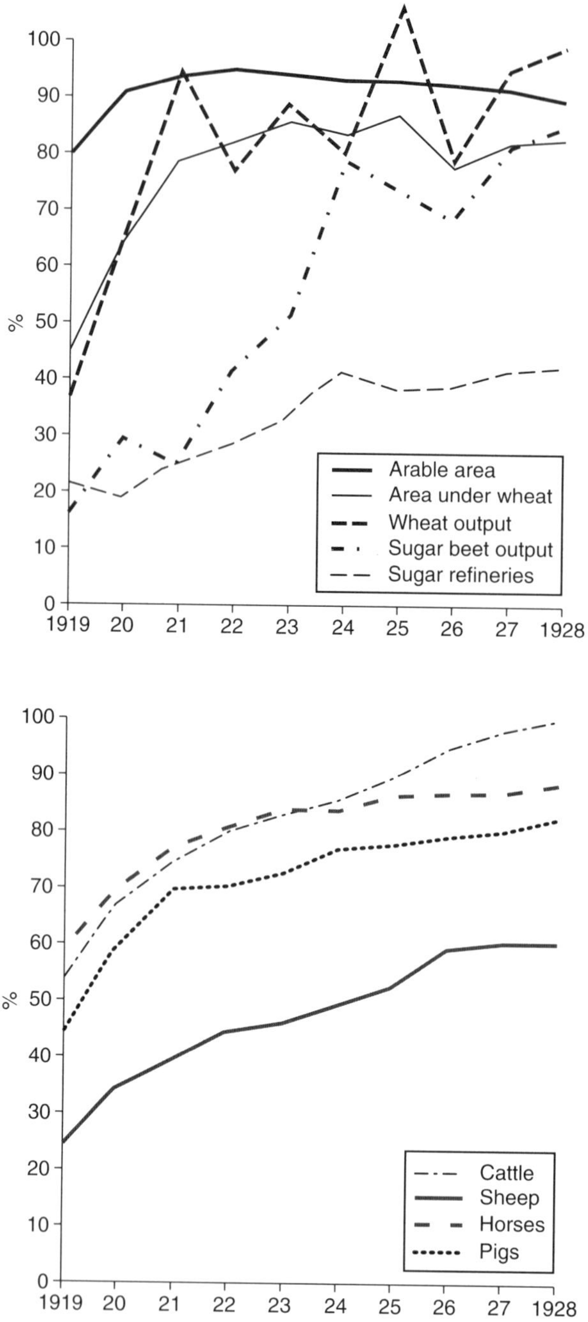

Figure 11.2 Agricultural recovery in northern France, 1919–28

Only one aspect of livestock husbandry had recovered completely by 1928, with the number of cattle in the northern *départements* standing at 99.9 per cent of the pre-war figure, and the most impressive increases being in Aisne and Ardennes (each 111 per cent). Meuse (95 per cent) and Vosges (94 per cent) came at thc bottom of the recovery league. After the war substantially fewer horses were being used for draught purposes, with the overall number in the northern *départements* in 1928 reaching only 88 per cent of the pre-war total. Pigs were also well below the earlier total (79 per cent), and only in Nord was the pre-war figure reached again. However, the largest proportional decline involved sheep, which reached only 79 per cent of the earlier total and were still below the 50 per cent mark in Ardennes and Pas-de-Calais (Augé-Laribé 1925: 259). Such results arguably reflected the changing circumstances of farming rather than a failure to recover from the devastation of the war, with changes in arable practices providing less fallow land for sheep to graze, rural depopulation making it increasingly difficult to recruit shepherds, and livestock husbandry shifting from the traditional production of sheep to the modern, market-orientated raising of cattle for meat and milk (Ibid.: 33; Ogburn & Jaffé 1929: 483).

Uneven Repopulation and Resettlement

The census for March 1931 recorded a combined total of 6,490,000 residents in the ten northern *départements*, which was only 0.5 per cent below the total listed twenty years previously (Ministère de l'Intérieur 1932) (Table 11.1). However this should not be interpreted as an indication that virtually all the pre-war population had returned. Unfortunately there is no way of tracing the spatial relocation of population during the war and in the subsequent dozen years, but undoubtedly important changes did take place. For example, the number of foreigners living in northern France in 1931 (624,429) was almost double the total recorded in 1911 (336,303), with increases in excess of 30,000 apiece in Aisne, Meurthe-et-Moselle and Nord, and a phenomenal increase of 137,000 in Pas-de-Calais, especially as a result of recruitment of workers from Poland (Table 11.2).

Despite the apparent recovery of population for northern France as a whole between 1911 and 1931, net growth occurred

Table 11.1 Population of whole *départements,* 1921, 1926, 1931

	1921	1926	1931	1931/1911 (%)
Aisne	421,515	488,999	489,368	92.3
Ardennes	277,811	297,448	293,746	92.1
Marne	366,734	397,773	412,156	94.5
Meurthe-et-Moselle	503,810	552,087	592,632	104.9
Meuse	207,309	218,131	215,819	77.6
Nord	1,787,918	1,969,159	2,029,449	103.4
Oise	387,760	405,971	407,432	99.1
Pas-de-Calais	989,967	1,171,912	1,205,191	112.8
Somme	452,624	473,916	466,626	89.7
Vosges	383,684	382,100	377,980	87.1
Total	5,779,132	6,357,496	6,490,399	99.5

Source: Ministère de l'Intérieur 1922, 1927, 1932

Table 11.2 Foreigners in the northern *départements* 1911, 1926, 1931

	1911	1926	1931
Aisne	7,341	35,182	38,652
Ardennes	19,973	29,621	29,211
Marne	9,088	21,851	20,619
Meurthe-et-Moselle	64,561	79,774	96,638
Meuse	6,874	16,837	15,336
Nord	177,100	219,153	212,485
Oise	11,790	27,335	32,349
Pas-de-Calais	25,087	146,571	162,086
Somme	3,610	17,680	17,053
Vosges	10,879	9,458	9,959
Total	336,303	594,004	624,429

Source: Ministère de l'Intérieur 1912, 1927, 1932

only in the urban-industrial *départements* of Nord, Pas-de-Calais and Meurthe-et-Moselle, exactly as it had during the years before the war (Table 11.1). The seven remaining *départements* contained fewer inhabitants than on the eve of war, with Meuse recording only 77 per cent of its 1911 total. Population growth characterized the Channel ports and their surroundings, the industrial and mining *cantons* of Nord and Pas-de-Calais, the eastern part of Oise within the immediate orbit of Paris, and the environs of Nancy and the iron-mining and metallurgical district of northern Lorraine, with more isolated cores of growth occurring around Amiens, Laon, Château-Thierry, Reims and Châlons-sur-Marne (Figure 11.3). Perhaps not surprisingly, the spatial arrangement of growth was not substantially different from what had been noted for 1896–1911.

All other parts of the northern *départements* lost residents between 1911 and 1931, and just over a dozen of the *cantons* that had experienced particularly severe damage still failed to reach 70 per cent of their pre-war totals by 1931. This phase of depopulation was partly due to the consequences of war but was also a continuing response to long-established causes of rural to urban migration (Houssel 1960: 126). The most pronounced loss between 1911 and 1931 involved groups of *cantons* to the north

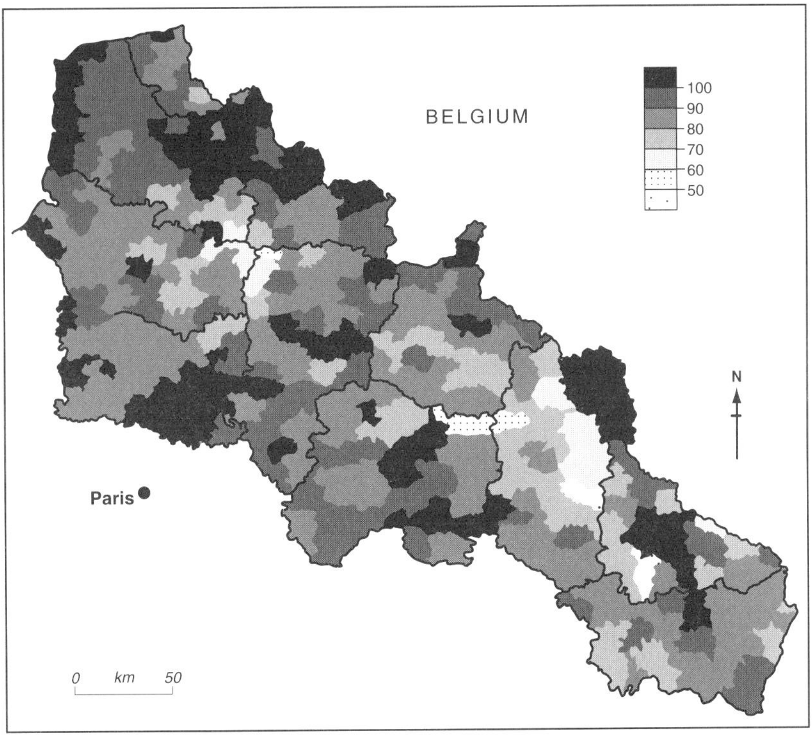

Figure 11.3 Population change, 1911–31 (1911=100%)

and east of Péronne, to the east and west of Verdun, and in two areas near Nancy. In fact, three-fifths of the 379 *cantons* in the northern *départements* recorded a reduction in population between 1926 (when *reconstitution* was well established) and 1931, with four-fifths of the *cantons* in Meuse and Somme and three-quarters of those in Ardennes and Vosges undergoing decline during those five years. In other words, a new phase of depopulation had set in following the initial five or six years of post-war recovery. Higher salaries on building sites and in factories, operation of the eight-hour day in industrial work, and 'the attraction of the town' all encouraged landless agricultural labourers to leave farmwork (Adam 1928: 33). In addition, a regrettably unidentifiable proportion of rural property owners had chosen to use their compensation monies to quit farming and to move to urban residence and employment (Mauco 1937: 493). By contrast, only one-third of the *cantons* in the industrial and mining *départements* of Meurthe-et-Moselle and Nord saw their population decline during those five years, and manufacturing areas in the other northern *départements* also experienced localized population increase. For example, industrial zones along the river Meuse in Ardennes underwent considerable growth, unlike the continuing depopulation of farming districts nearby (Adam 1928: 33).

After ten or a dozen years of courageous effort, almost all fought-over farmland had been restored to agricultural use and devastated rural settlements had been rebuilt (Michael 1928: 178). Driving northward from Senlis toward Roye, Gabriel Hanotaux expressed not only his personal pride but that of his compatriots in what had been achieved across by far the greater part of the battle zone. 'Ahead of us [we glimpse] the first panorama of reconstruction: opulent farms, large haystacks, abundant livestock, red brick walls, and red tiled roofs. The road passes through reconquered riches' (Hanotaux 1931: 9). This *pays rouge* had indeed largely replaced the 'red zone', which had been reduced to a tiny fraction of its former extent (Ibid.). By contrast, in northern Meuse extensive areas of devastated land had not been reclaimed for farming but were being converted to national forest. Complete eradication of the remaining fragments of the red zone was to prove a very long affair, with patches still being returned to farming as recently as 1976 (Becker J-J 1991: 21).

Very few villages disappeared, although nine were not reconstructed in Meuse and a further two in Meurthe-et-Moselle and seven in Marne suffered the same fate (Juillard 1977: 147; Fallon 1986: 42; Amat 1987a: 220). In 1919 their mayors had performed the painful duty of informing inhabitants that their homes would not be rebuilt and that such villages were *morts pour la France* (Becker J-J 1991: 21). In the following year these 'heroic villages' were honoured by the Ministre de la Guerre (Citations à l'ordre de l'armée, 1920: 671). Some ruined villages were rebuilt completely on fresh sites, such as Fey-en-Haye, Reillon and Flirey in Meurthe-et-Moselle, Montfaucon, Forges and Vauquois in Meuse, or Craonne in Aisne, but these examples were very much in the minority (Blache 1938: 152; Gérard 1981: 36; Meissel 1986: 138) (Figure 11.4). By far the greater number were reconstructed on or near their historic foundations, and were provided with more spacious layout, wider roads, improved housing, relocated cemeteries, and new or restored churches, schools and *mairies* (Brion 1935: 8; Harbullot 1977: 31). Modern building materials were used widely with, for example, brick and tile replacing cob and thatch in eastern Somme (Parisot 1939: II 379). Farm buildings made of traditional materials may of course still be found in parts of western Somme which escaped the devastation of the war (Hitier 1903; Dufournet 1943). For the *sinistrés*, and indeed for many observers such as Hanotaux, the bright red bricks, mass-produced tiles and cement-rendered walls were welcome and long-awaited expressions of recovery and renewal, but for others they were intrusions in the landscape which stood in stark contrast with the charm of the local vernacular architecture still visible away from the war-torn zones (Laurent 1948: 268). Twenty years after the Armistice there were still complaints being made about 'new villages that are too white, and roofs that are too red' (Grosdidier de Matons 1938: 261).

In broad terms, the old settlement patterns of northern France were re-created but, despite many improvements, the reconstruction process did not produce 'a revolution' in rural housing (Brion 1935: 29). However, many rebuilt villages contained fewer dwelling houses than before, as a result of compensation money being used to replace two or three buildings by a single improved dwelling (Gérard & Peltre 1979: 86; Gérard 1981: 37). As a result, young couples found it increasingly difficult to obtain

Figure 11.4 Reconstruction of Flirey, Meurthe-et-Moselle

Plate 11.1 The village of Bioncourt, Lorraine, before (March 1920) and after reconstruction

accommodation in these smaller reconstructed settlements (Brion 1935: 17). In addition, some property owners used their compensation money to acquire a house in town rather than in the countryside. For example, some proprietors abandoned Craonne (Aisne) and used their compensation to rebuild in Lille or Saint-Quentin (Meissel 1986: 143). The same trend was reinforced by those who renounced the financial supplement of re-employment and chose to settle in Paris or elsewhere in the French interior well beyond the liberated *départements*. The general arrangement of northern farmsteads was improved, with, for example, traditional Lorraine farmhouses which had the farming family and its animals housed under the same roof being replaced by structures in which dwellings were separated from the livestock quarters (Parisot 1939: II 293). By way of example, the rebuilt village of Brabant-sur-Meuse, 15 km north of Verdun, contained fewer buildings than before the war, with substantial areas of open space remaining between them (Figure 11.5). Several farmsteads were relocated away from the site of the old village to positions along the main road (Brion 1935: 12–13). Contemporaries argued that the progress achieved in the devastated zone should serve as a useful example for modernizing farm buildings in surrounding districts where improvements would have to be made sooner or later (*L'agriculture dans le département de Meurthe-et-Moselle*, 1927: 83).

Despite the idealistic schemes of many architects, only a few carefully designed model villages were built. For example, the village of Pinon north of the Chemin-des-Dames, together with its *château* and surrounding woods, had been destroyed totally by bombardment during 1917 and 1918, and the opportunity was grasped to relocate the settlement a little further north on a site closer to its railway station (Joyant 1923: I 74). On behalf of the Renaissance des Cités organization Charles Abella prepared a comprehensive reconstruction plan. This was greeted with initial hostility by the *sinistrés*, who 'clung . . . to the scarcely recognizable plots where once their house or cottage had stood' (Cart de Lafontaine 1921a: 195). Above all they wished to re-create their gardens just as they had been before. Eventually some *sinistrés* perceived the advantages of having a freshly organized village, and in a referendum forty-three out of sixty households voted in favour of rebuilding on a new site (Abercrombie 1921:

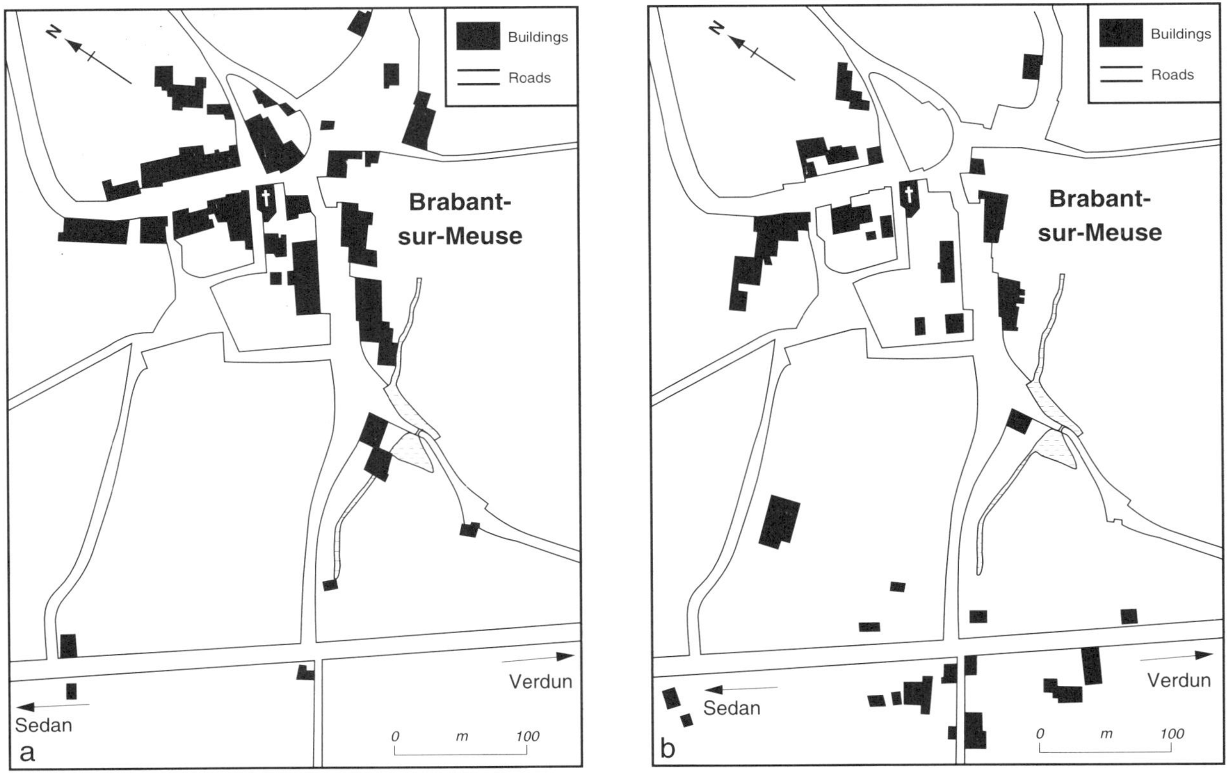

Figure 11.5 Reconstruction of Brabant-sur-Meuse, Meuse

13). The initial plan was modified to ensure that properties would be located on the same side of the new village as of the old. Traditional styles would be retained but new building materials would be used and the settlement would be equipped with communal facilities grouped around a central square, including a village hall, with a library, dispensary and nursery (Figure 11.6). Each house would be set back from the road to avoid dust and mud from passing vehicles, and would be provided with a water supply, sanitation and, of course, a garden (Boussard 1991: 194). The Renaissance des Cités advanced funds for the model village to be built, with the *sinistrés* agreeing to refund their compensation to the organization.

A second model for reconstruction was that of the *cité-jardin* adopted in May 1919 by the Compagnie des Chemins de Fer du Nord for housing its workforce close to marshalling yards and railway works in the suburbs of large towns, such as Arras, Béthune, Lens and Lille, but also at a number of junctions (including Tergnier where 1,112 houses were built on 110 ha) and in much smaller settlements that were really little more than villages (Figure 11.7) (AMS Compte Rendu de l'Assemblée Générale 17.05.25; Goissaud 1925; Anon, 1923–4; Baudoui 1991: 245). The first houses were built of timber, but as more solid building materials became available they were rapidly superseded by brick-built homes (Joyant 1923: I 68). These were surrounded by spacious private gardens which suited many of the railwaymen who had recently moved from work in the countryside. Many of the *cités-jardins* were arranged according to geometrical ground plans, and were equipped with nurseries, schools, dispensaries, playgrounds and other communal facilities, as well as allotment gardens (Sellier & Bruggeman 1927: 72). In June 1925 they boasted nineteen libraries, with 7,742 books and having made 16,211 loans during the previous year (AMS Compte Rendu de l'Assemblée Générale, 17.05.25). On 1 January 1925 their total population stood at 33,727, with 850–900 births being recorded in each of the previous three years. Carefully planned *cités-jardins* were promoted also by other agencies and were installed around the fringe of the war-torn city of Reims (Clout 1989: 23–34).

Such well-equipped social experiments were, of course, exceptions to the rule. Nonetheless, compensation for war damage and

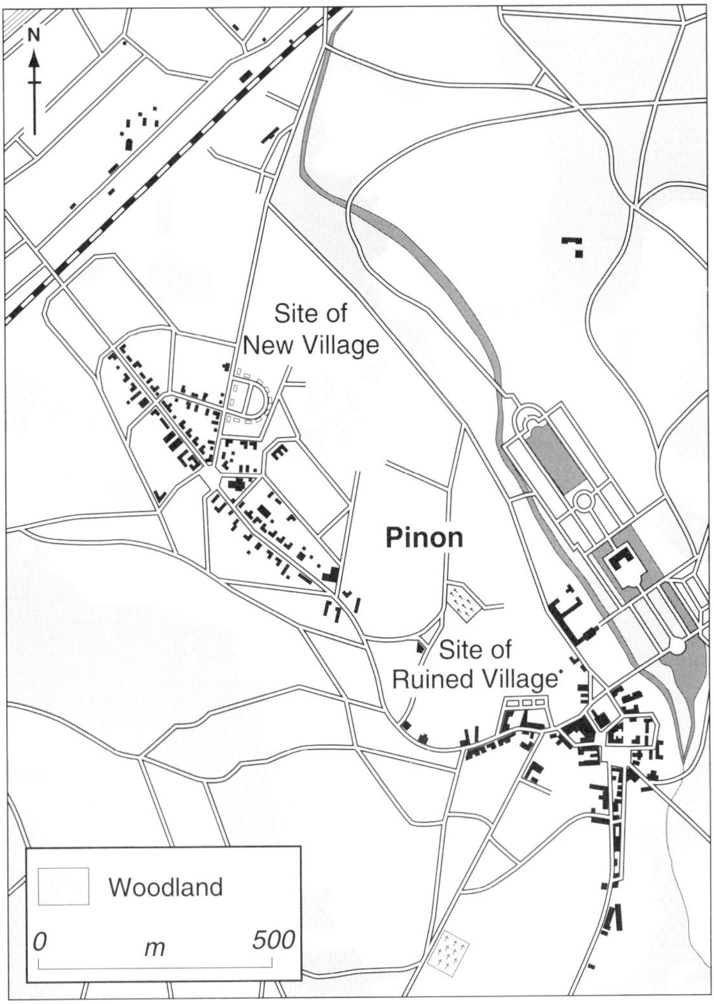

Figure 11.6 Reconstruction of Pinon, Aisne

funds raised through the *pari mutuel* were used to provide piped water and electricity in most of the reconstructed settlements of northern France (Fromont 1925: 385–89; Hubert 1923: 104; Ratineau & Gaillot 1928: 193). Installation of new water distribution networks began in 1922–23, with deep boreholes and large water towers serving clusters of villages (Carpentier 1928: 76). They provided an efficient solution to the problem of

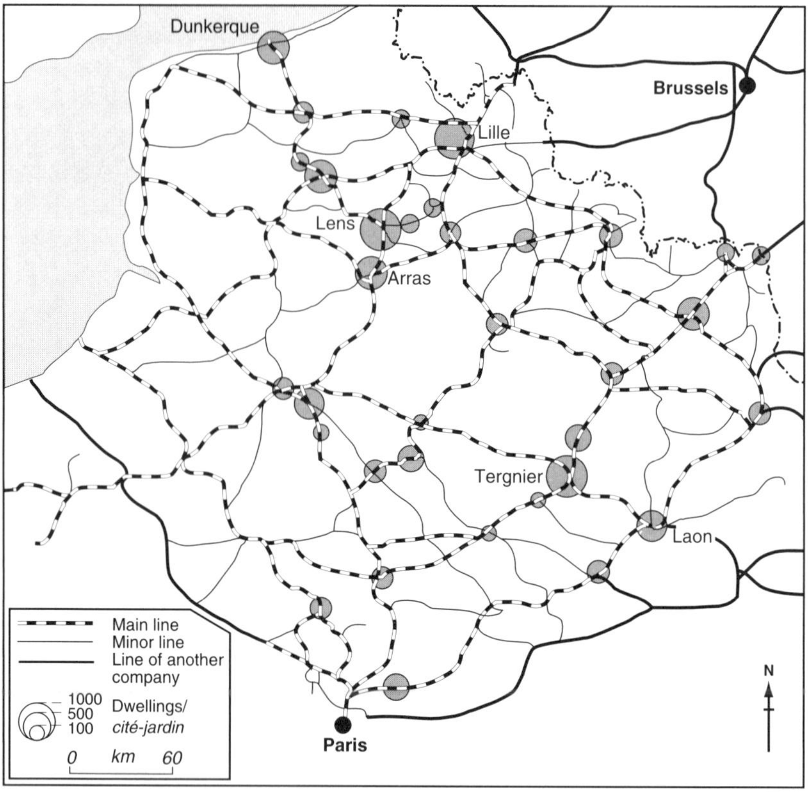

Figure 11.7 *Cités-jardins* built by the Compagnie des Chemins de Fer du Nord

drought which afflicted Santerre and other parts of Picardy when traditional wells dried up, as in the summer of 1921. Despite the loss of historic monuments and 'many touches of quaintness and beauty . . . the reconstructed villages were undoubtedly better places to live in than those that were destroyed' (MacDonald 1922: 274). But as well as villages 'reconstructed with taste', there were others which Hubert described as 'the juxtaposition of various forms of ugliness' (Hubert 1923: 185). Unfortunately one must agree with Denis Brogan's rather sharp observation that 'some of the dreariest villages of northern France had been reduced to ruins . . . but when the time came to rebuild, they appeared again in all their nineteenth-century hideousness' (Brogan 1940: 600). Reconstitution most certainly did not always enhance the built environment, but by 1932 it was 'almost entirely completed' (AN 324 AP/62 Reconstitution de la France dévastée, 31.03.32).

The Commemorative Phase

Gradually the landscape healed, with many of the war dead being assigned more fitting places of burial than mass graves or the spot where they had fallen haphazardly on the field of battle (Dyer 1994: 12). During the war, some military corpses had been collected for burial in provisional cemeteries but many of these 'were disturbed during subsequent combat' (Reynes 1929: 1). Six months after the Armistice, the killing fields of Picardy and many other stretches of the northern *départements* were strewn with graves bearing makeshift crosses 'sometimes grouped, sometimes isolated, some bearing no name' (Wallon & Gobert 1919: 11). The French authorities granted free gifts of land for establishing permanent cemeteries and once peace had been restored, the process of recovering bodies and grouping them, often in very large concentration cemeteries, took place (Middlebrook 1994: 10). The presence of large numbers of German graves reassembled in what could be thought of as 'great ostentatious cemeteries' provoked some hostility, with opponents arguing that in this way Germany was achieving another form of 'occupation' of French territory (AN F23 213 Jacomet, D., Rapport sur les cimetières allemands). Figure 11.8 shows the situation in Somme in early 1922, a time when official searches by military authorities and by staff of the military registration service of the Ministère des Pensions were still in progress (Morain 1921: 88). These searches were completed by September of that year, with Stephen Graham's *The Challenge of the Dead* (1921) providing an eye-witness report of parties of soldiers exhuming bodies (cited in Dyer 1994: 123). Up to six further searches of the major battlefields occurred before the outbreak of the Second World War, by which time the remains of 38,000 missing soldiers had been discovered in northern France and Belgian Flanders (Ibid.: 14). Three-quarters of a century after the Armistice, bodies of the missing are still being unearthed as a result of regular ploughing activity, and a military cemetery near Boulogne remains open to receive British bodies from the Great War. It seems that, on

Plate 11.2 A mass grave containing the remains of fifty British soldiers, the author's uncle being one of them

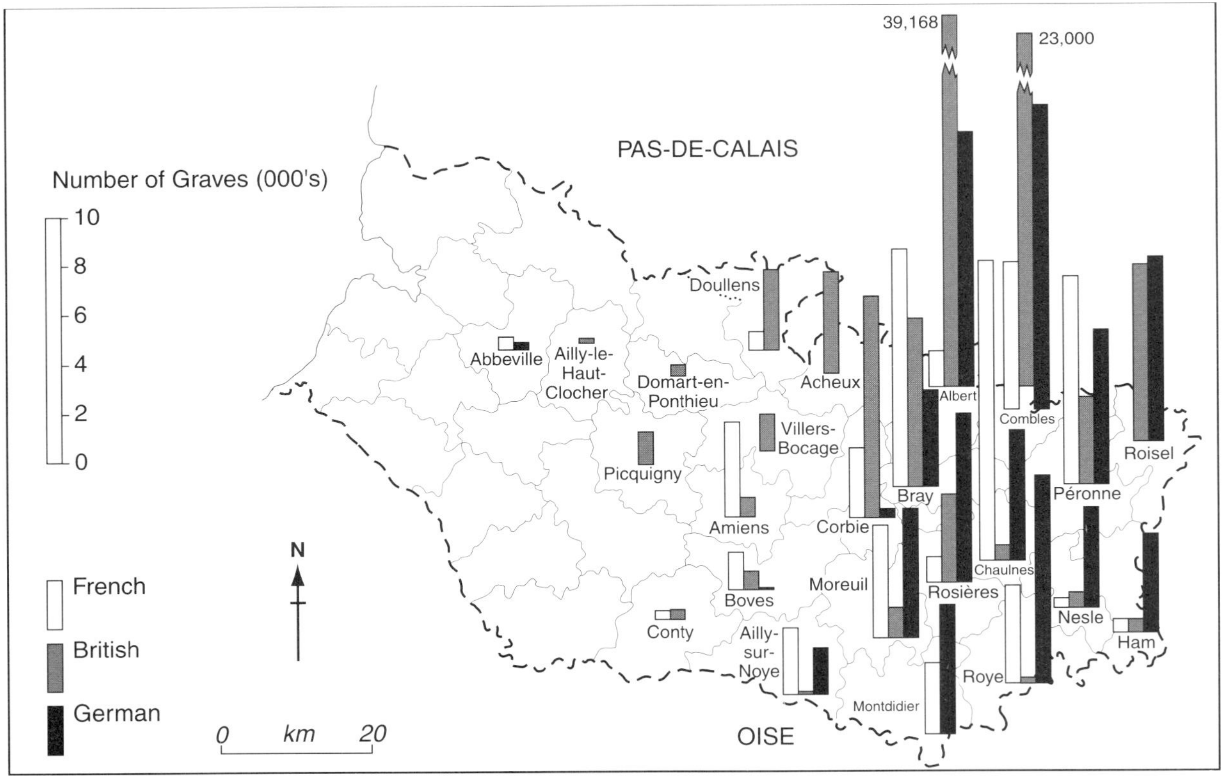

Figure 11.8 Number of graves in war cemeteries in Somme 1922

average, about five are discovered each year (Middlebrook 1994: 10).

National practices of interment and commemoration varied considerably in the 1920s, thereby bringing new aspects of diversity to the rather ordinary countrysides of the northern *départements* (Borg 1991; Winter 1995). The French authorities buried the majority of their dead in vast concentration cemeteries, where each grave was marked by a simple white cross, economically produced from concrete aggregate on a metal frame (Borg 1991: 18). Plain headstones were provided for families not wanting a cross, and Muslim soldiers had their distinctive headstones. In other instances, soldiers were buried in small village graveyards, or relatives arranged for the mortal remains to be returned to their home community. But many dead could not be identified and their anonymous remains were interred collectively. In the 1920s wooden crosses covered the lawns of the great German concentration cemeteries in northern France, but over the past twenty years black metal crosses and stone markers have replaced them (Ibid.: 19).

The US authorities permitted repatriation and 46,284 of the 78,734 members of the American Expeditionary Force who died during the war were returned to America (American Battlefields Monuments Commission 1927: 246). Some 30,592 of the remaining bodies were buried in six main cemeteries in northern France, having been collected from 2,400 burial places in the four years following the Armistice (Ibid.: 247). The largest cemetery, at Romagne-sous-Montfaucon, had been laid out with the assistance of 4,000 German prisoners of war during 1919, taking on the appearance of 'an oasis in a desert' amid the waste and desolation of the Argonne (Elwood 1920: 510; Amat 1988a & b). By the mid-1920s it had received the remains of 14,134 Americans (American Battlefields Monuments Commission 1927: 246). Operating a controversial policy of non-repatriation, the British Army Graves Service and the Imperial War Graves Commission established vast concentration cemeteries but also favoured small secluded burial grounds, leaving some of their war dead close to where they had fallen (Middlebrook 1994: 10). British graves were identified by plain white headstones in Portland Stone of standard design, with each concentration cemetery being marked by a tall white Cross of Sacrifice, whose height varied according to the number of graves, and a Stone of Remembrance (Hurst 1929; Heffernan 1995).

Commemoration was not simply a matter of individual headstones or lists of names on village war memorials which were erected in great numbers (Borg 1991; Troyansky 1987–8; Grailles 1992). Dyer notes that 30,000 memorials, averaging fifty each day, were raised throughout the country between 1920 and 1925 (Dyer 1994: 64). As Bertrand Tavernier's recent film *La vie et rien d'autre* (1989) evokes, it was a veritable golden age for memorial sculptors, headstone engravers and funeral directors. In 1922, 11 November was declared a *fête nationale*, with village memorials providing the formal sites for official commemoration (Becker A 1991: 25). On a grander scale, each nation erected its own monuments, either as focal points in vast cemeteries or as evocative *lieux de mémoire* (Meissel 1986: 189–209). The great *ossuaire* at Douaumont, midway between the forts of Thiaumont and Douaumont, dominates a cemetery of 16,000 graves but more poignantly commemorates some 300,000 French soldiers who died in the defence of Verdun but whose remains could not be identified and claimed by their families (L'ossuaire de Douaumont, 1922–3: 361; *Atlas des nécropoles nationales*, 1994). Fifty or so chambers within the vast structure recall the localities from which anonymous remains were collected. Much further west, the great French national shrine at Notre-Dame-de-Lorette crowns Vimy Ridge and dominates the battlefields of Artois (Le monument aux morts de Notre-Dame de Lorette, *CM*, 1921–2: 238). A few kilometres to the south, the immense brick and stone arch at Thiepval soars above the Ancre valley and the battlefield of the Somme bearing the names of 73,367 missing British soldiers (Whittick 1946: 35; Dyer 1994: 126–28). The fallen of each part of the British Empire are commemorated in distinctive ways. The brilliant white Canadian memorial stands above Vimy Ridge and commands views of the Douai plain (Simson 1943: 410). It was unveiled in 1936, with construction having taken eleven years, and bears the names of 11,285 Canadian dead with no known graves (Dyer 1994: 111). A caribou statue recalls the war dead of Newfoundland, and the Indian dead are commemorated at Neuve-Chapelle (near Béthune) by a memorial evoking a Hindu temple (Whittick 1946: 35). American losses are recalled by a tall stone column next to the ruins of the village of Montfaucon, and the commemorative stone terrace at Varennes which evokes American sacrifice (Amat 1985: 85; Mayeux 1930).

By the late 1920s and early 1930s it was these cemeteries, war memorials and national shrines which attracted 'pilgrims'—like my widowed aunt—to the once more placid countrysides of northern France, which may indeed be said to have entered the 'monumental phase' (Becker A 1988, 1994). The topic of reconstruction faded from the public record, with *conseils-généraux* no longer receiving annual reports from their prefects, just as the brightness of new bricks, tiles, stone and paintwork mellowed and blended into the rural scene. In 1917 John Masefield had written repeatedly to his wife about the horrors of destruction in the Somme, but he also predicted that 'when the trenches are filled in, when the plough has gone over them, the ground will no longer keep the look of war' (cited in Dyer 1994: 124). In 1935 Lieutenant Colonel G.S. Hutchinson wrote concisely of the changed conditions he encountered during his pilgrimage to the former *régions dévastées*:

> Except in their topographical outline, the battlefields have changed. The rebuilded [sic] towns and villages and the re-sown fields, yielding their crop, bear no resemblance to the crumbling ruins, shattered woods and shell-pitted wastes, which marked the War years. And for the pilgrim, revisiting the scene, it may even be difficult to rediscover villages and scenes whose every stone and contour in former years were so familiar as the palm of the hand. (Hutchinson 1935: 2)

The initial fear that land and buildings would not be restored had been dispelled, and some veterans had become concerned that insufficient material evidence remained to evoke what had happened during four and a quarter years of war (Dyer 1994: 124). No such concerns were raised by the millions of *sinistrés* whose memories of the painfully protracted but ultimately joyous experience of recovery sufficed. Their contentment was, of course, to prove short-lived. A quarter of a century after the Armistice, broad stretches of northern France lay in ruins once again, with the challenge of material reconstruction having to be confronted anew (Favier 1991; Minella-Bouchy 1956; Dubreule & Courtassol 1950).

References

Archival Sources

General titles of files that have been consulted are listed below. Specific documents within files that have been cited in the text are also indicated by date order.

Archives Nationales, Paris (AN)

AN AJ 25/1–4 Office de Reconstitution Agricole

AJ 25/1 La reconstitution agricole des départements victimes de l'invasion (05.18).
AJ 25/1 Programme d'action (19.07.18).
AJ 25/1 Guerin, R., Rapport concernant l'organisation de l'ORA (21.03.20).
AJ 25/1 Action exercée et résultats obtenus par l'ORA (15.04.20).
AJ 25/1 Rapport au Ministre des Régions Libérées sur l'organisation et le fonctionnement du Service du Matériel Agricole.
AJ 25/3 Richard, M., Délibérations du Conseil d'Administration (18.10.17).
AJ 25/3 Le Seigneur, J., Rapport des activités (25.04.18).
AJ 25/4 Office de Reconstitution Agricole (25.09.19).

AN AJ 25/47–51 Sociétés Tiers-Mandataire

AJ 25/47 Rapport sur le fonctionnement des services (1919).
AJ 25/47 Rapport sur le fonctionnement des services, Marne (1919).
AJ 25/47 Laporte, M., Réorganisation de la vie locale dans les régions libérées, Vosges (04.19).
AJ 25/47 Reconstitution des régions libérées, Meurthe-et-Moselle (25.04.19).
AJ 25/47 Naudin, A., Reconstitution du sol dans le Nord (08.05.19).
AJ 25/47 Lettre du Préfet de l'Aisne (13.04.20).
AJ 25/47 Service de la Motoculture, Lettre du 11.05.20.
AJ 25/47 Ogier, M. Lettre à l'Académie d'Agriculture de France (24.06.20).
AJ 25/47 Bachelet, M., Rapport au Ministre des Régions Libérées (21.08.21).
AJ 25/48 Notices sur la récupération du matériel agricole (31.10.18).
AJ 25/48 Sociétés Tiers-Mandataire.
AJ 25/48 Rapport sur le fonctionnement de la Société Tiers-Mandataire de l'Aisne.
AJ 25/49 Namur, M. & Pechenart, M. Rapport (21.11.18).
AJ 25/49 Sociétés Tiers-Mandataire, Marne, Meurthe-et-Moselle (06.19).

AJ 25/49 Société Tiers-Mandataire, Aisne (18.10.19).
AJ 25/49 Saint, L., Lettre au Ministre des Régions Libérées (08.12.19).
AJ 25/49 Saint, L., Disparition de la Tiers-Mandataire (12.12.19).
AJ 25/49 Massol, M., Société Tiers-Mandataire de la Marne (19.10.20).
AJ 25/50 Président de la Société Coopérative Agricole du Nord. Lettre du 04.11.18.
AJ 25/50 Sociétés Tiers-Mandataire, Nord, Meuse (1924).
AJ 25/51 Bonnefoy-Sibour, A., Rapport sur le fonctionnement du service (25.04.19).
AJ 25/51 Villey, M., Service de reconstitution des régions libérées, Pas-de-Calais (04.19).
AJ 25/51 Service de reconstitution des régions atteintes par les événements de guerre, Oise (04.19).
AJ 25/51 Mathieu, P., Reprise de la vie locale, Ardennes (04.05.19).
AJ 25/51 Reconstitution des régions envahies, Somme (1919).
AJ 25/51 Reibel, C., STM: Ardennes. Lettre du 11.09.23.

AN AJ 25/96–97 Office de Reconstitution Agricole

AJ 25/96 Labourage à vapeur, Lettre du 21.03.19.
AJ 25/97 Le Seigneur, J., ORA: matériel, Lettre du 08.12.17.

AN AJ 25/125–128 Reconstitution Agricole

AJ 25/125 Reconstitution agricole Meurthe-et-Moselle (21.02.20).
AJ 25/125 Etat du bétail remis aux agriculteurs des régions libérées (15.06.20).
AJ 25/125 Ricard, J.H., Rapport sur l'application de la loi du 4 mars 1918 (18.06.20).
AJ 25/125 Meurthe-et-Moselle, Service de la reconstitution agricole (12.07.20).
AJ 25/125 Animaux enlevés et introduits (17.07.20).
AJ 25/125 Renseignements statistiques.
AJ 25/126 Reconstitution agricole, Marne (28.07.19).
AJ 25/126 Reconstitution agricole, Oise (28.07.19).
AJ 25/126 Reconstitution agricole (1919).
AJ 25/126 Cessions de toutes natures faites aux sinistrés (1921).
AJ 25/127 Le Service des Travaux de Première Urgence (31.12.18).
AJ 25/127 Instructions, actes officiels et documents (1918).
AJ 25/127 Office de Reconstitution Agricole, Lettre du 25.03.19.
AJ 25/127 Boret, V., Observations sur l'introduction en France du bétail provenant de l'étranger (23.05.19).
AJ 25/127 Bertrand, F., La main d'oeuvre dans les régions dévastées (1919).
AJ 25/128 Sociétés Tiers-Mandataire (06.06.19).

AN F2 2099–2103 Administration Financière des Communes: dommages de guerre, régions libérées 1914–1921

F2 2100 Etats généraux des régions dévastées (09.09.19).
F2 2100 Rapport du préfet de l'Aisne au comité consultatif de reconstruction (31.11.19).

F2 2102 Lettre du Préfet de l'Oise au Ministre de l'Intérieur (17.09.21).
F2 2103 Objets abandonnés dans la zone des opérations militaires, Somme (27.12.15).
F2 2103 Accambray, L., Mission de contrôle dans le département de l'Aisne (1919).

AN F2 2147 Dommages de Guerre

AN F10 2185 Agriculture: guerre de 1914–1918: mesures diverses

F10 2185 Lesueur, J., Machines agricoles et culture mécanique (02.16).

AN F12 7808 Ravitaillement du Nord de la France, 1917–18

AN F12 8025–8026 Questions du Temps de Guerre: problèmes agricoles

F12 8025 L'effort agricole, 13.12.16–20.03.17.
F12 8025 Programme de l'offensive agricole (12.16).
F12 8025 Note présentée au Comité d'Action Nationale (15.01.17).
F12 8025 La mise en culture des terres abandonnées (02.17).
F12 8025 Travaux agricoles (10.03.17).
F12 8026 Le Rouzic, M., Main d'oeuvre agricole (18.12.16).
F12 8026 Chauveau, M., Rapport pour faciliter le remembrement (15.05.17).

AN F12 8030 Reconstitution Agricole 1916–1920

F12 8030 Le Rôle de l'Office de Reconstitution Agricole (1917).
F12 8030 Warren, De. E., Note sur la remise en culture des terres dans les pays libérés et la coopération agricole (24.01.18).
F12 8030 Warren, De. E., Réorganisation des régions libérées (27.03.19).

AN F21 2904 Commission Consultative pour la Reconstitution des Régions Envahies

F21 2904 Hermant, J., Les conseils à donner aux sinistrés en vue des reconstructions (1917).
F21 2905 Rapport présenté par M. Léon Rosenthal (04.04.17).

AN F23 17 Documents Divers sur la Reconstitution des Régions Libérées 1915–1919

AN F23 213 Comité de Reconstitution des Régions Envahies 1915–1919

AN F23 213 Jacomet, D., Rapport sur les cimetières allemands créés en France pendant l'occupation ennemie.

AN 324 AP/47–64 Papiers: André Tardieu

324 AP/47 Leroux, M., Agriculture dans le département de la Somme (13.05.31).

324 AP/47 Historique de la Société des Agriculteurs de la Somme (16.05.31).
324 AP/60 Tardieu, A., A Blérancourt (08.07.30).
324 AP/60 Tardieu, A., Le discours de Laon (26.03.33).
324 AP/62 Reconstitution de la France dévastée (31.03.32).
324 AP/63 Tardieu, A., Ce que demandent les régions libérées (01.09.20).

SERVICE DES ARCHIVES ECONOMIQUES ET FINANCIERES, PARIS (AEF)

AEF 1A 384–386 Dommages de Guerre

1A 385 Services de l'Etat. Lettre au Ministre des Régions Libérées (03.20).
1A 385 Thomas, A., Rapport concernant les économies à réaliser (11.06.20).
1A 386 La question des subventions (03.10.20).
1A 386 Valeurs des avances en nature (11.20).

ARCHIVES DU MUSEE SOCIAL, PARIS (AMS)

AMS Compte-Rendu de l'Assemblée Générale (17.05.25).

ARCHIVES DEPARTEMENTALES

Archives Départementales des Ardennes, Charleville-Mezières (ADA)

ADA 12J 5 Collection Marlier. Guerre 1914–18, cartes.
ADA 12J 15 Roquère, M., Extraits du rapport sur la reconstruction (28.04.21).

Archives Départementales de la Marne, Châlons-sur-Marne (ADMa)

ADMa 140 M16 Lettre du Général Commandant (27.07.18).
ADMa 140 M16 Lettre du Ministre de l'Agriculture (30.07.18).
ADMa 140 M16 Lettre du Sous-Préfet de Reims (11.10.18).
ADMa 140 M16 Tatier, M., Letter (20.11.18).
ADMa 140 M17 Rapport (12.02.16).
ADMa 140 M17 Lettre du Préfet au Ministre de l'Agriculture (18.09.17).
ADMa 140 M17 Letter (18.11.17).
ADMa 140 M17 Général Commandant du Ve Armée, Letter (18.11.18).
ADMa 153 M21 Lettre du Maire de Dampierre (23.05.15).
ADMa 203 M198 Registre des délibérations du comité d'action agricole (03.03.18).
ADMa 203 M199 La mise en culture des terres abandonnées (07.02.17).
ADMa 203 M199 Rapport sur le recensement des terres abandonnées (24.11.16).
ADMa 203 M199 Rapport sur les résultats obtenus (25.12.17).
ADMa 203 M204 Commission de la main d'oeuvre agricole (12.03.19).
ADMa 203 M205 Armes et munitions (25.06.19).

Archives Départementales de Meurthe-et-Moselle, Nancy (ADMM)

ADMM W1312 Plans d'aménagement.

Archives Départementales de la Meuse, Bar-le-Duc (ADMe)

ADMe 976 Rp.2705 Note du préfet au sujet de la zone rouge (07.01.20).
ADMe 976 Rp.2705 Procès-verbaux de réutilisation de la zone rouge 1920–23.

ADMe 976 Rp.2705 Plans d'alignement.
ADMe 1008 Rp.1–20 La coopérative de reconstruction des églises du diocèse de Verdun.

Archives Départementales du Nord, Lille (ADN)

ADN 104J Comités de secours américains dans l'Aisne pendant la guerre 1914–18 et oeuvres américaines diverses.
ADN M 631(7) Enquête sur l'habitat rural. Rapport de l'Ingénieur en Chef du Génie Rural (26.12.36).
ADN 9R 500 Monsarrat, M., Etat de l'agriculture dans le département du Nord 1916.
ADN 9R 1098 Extension du camp de Bailleul, Letter (29.01.17).
ADN 10R 5569A Coopératives de reconstruction des églises des diocèses de Lille et de Cambrai.
ADN 10RA Plans généraux d'alignement et de nivellement.

Archives Départementales du Pas-de-Calais, Arras (ADPC)

ADPC 1J 200 Guyot, E., Enquête en Artois 1919.
ADPC 857 Briens, M., Lettre à M. Pichéry (04.17).

Archives Départementales de la Somme, Amiens (ADS)

ADS 332.252 O'Hanrahan, R.M., Letter (15.07.18).
ADS 332.252 Lettre du Préfet au Ministre des Régions Libérées (06.02.22).
ADS 336.256 Ministre des Régions Libérées, Lettre du 02.12.21.
ADS 336.256 Lettre de l'Inspecteur des Contributions Directes (01.06.22).

Anonymous reports and articles from newspapers and journals

The following titles have been abbreviated: *Annales de Géographie* (*AG*); *Annales de la Science Agronomique* (*ASA*); *Bulletin des Eglises Dévastées du Diocèse d'Arras* (*BEDA*); *La Construction Moderne* (*CM*); *La Défense Agricole* (*DA*); *Journal d'Agriculture Pratique* (*JAP*); *Journal des Départements Dévastés* (*JDD*); *Journal des Régions Dévastées* (*JRD*); *L'Architecture* (*LA*); *Le Peuple* (*LP*); *Le Monde Illustré* (*MI*); *The Statist* (*TS*). Entries are arranged alphabetically by title and year of publication.

Anon., 'L'exposition de l'architecture régionale dans les provinces envahies' *LA* (1917) p. 30.
Anon., 'Les types de constructions agricoles' *CM* (01.06.17) pp. 1–2.
Anon., 'Exposition du concours pour la reconstruction des habitations rurales dans les départements envahis' *LA* (1918) pp. 9–13.
Anon., 'Les églises dévastées' *BEDA* (01.05.19).
Anon., 'Aisne' *JRD* (25.05.19) p. 23.
Anon., 'Marne' *JRD* (15.06.19) p. 71.
Anon., 'Marne' *JRD* (27.07.19) p. 167.

Anon., 'Marne' *JRD* (10.08.19) p. 198.
Anon., 'Meurthe-et-Moselle' *JRD* (07.09.19) p. 267.
Anon., 'Meuse' *JRD* (06.07.19) p. 121.
Anon., 'Meuse' *JRD* (09.11.19) p. 18.
Anon., 'Oise' *JRD* (29.06.19) p. 107.
Anon., 'Les oubliés' *JRD* (06.07.19) p. 122.
Anon., 'Partie officielle: loi du 4 mars 1919' *JAP* 32 (1919) pp. 147–48.
Anon., 'Pas-de-Calais' *JRD* (24.08.19) p. 233.
Anon., 'Le péril jaune' *JRD* (02.11.19) p. 3.
Anon., 'Proposition de résolution concernant la délimitation de la partie dévastée du département de la Somme' *Annales de la Chambre des Députés (Documents)* 93 (1919) p. 2511.
Anon., 'La question des transplantés' *JRD* (18.05.19) p. 6.
Anon., 'La reconstitution des régions libérées' *ASA* (1919) p. 209.
Anon., 'Les sinistrés et les lenteurs' *JRD* (25.05.19) p. 26.
Anon., 'Sinistrés, méfions-nous des vampires!' *JRD* (19.10.19) p. 1.
Anon., 'Somme' *JRD* (15.06.19) p. 74.
Anon., 'Somme' *JRD* (29.06.19) p. 107.
Anon., 'Vers la renaissance des régions dévastées' *LA* (1919) pp. 401–04, 468, 501–03.
Anon., 'Vosges' *JRD* (03.08.19) p. 186.
Anon., 'Citations à l'ordre de l'armée' *Bulletin Départemental Meusien de la Reconstitution* 55 (1920) p. 671.
Anon., 'Le congrès des délégués communaux des régions sinistrées de l'Oise' *DA* (02.10.20).
Anon., 'Dans nos ruines, ils ne laisseront rien debout' *JRD* (21.03.20) p. 1.
Anon., *Département du Nord. Rapport du préfet sur la reconstitution. Session extraordinaire de novembre 1920* (Lille: Denel, 1920).
Anon., 'Le désobusage dans la zone anglaise' *JRD* (22.02.20) p. 1.
Anon., 'The devastated areas' *TS* (06.05.20) pp. 857–58.
Anon., 'Epernay' *TS* (03.06.20) pp. 1054–55.
Anon., 'Gentlemen colored!' *JRD* (01.02.20) p. 3.
Anon., 'L'initiative privée peut sauver les régions libérées' *JRD* (21.03.20) p. 2.
Anon., 'Pas-de-Calais: vers la renaissance' *LA* (1920) p. 28.
Anon., 'Réclamations des agriculteurs des régions libérées' *JAP* 33 (1920) pp. 88–9.
Anon., 'Reconstruction des agglomérations rurales: loi du 14 mars 1919' *JAP* 33 (1920) pp. 89–90.
Anon., 'Les régions libérées' *DA* (29.08.20).
Anon., 'The ruins of Arras' *TS* (17.06.20) p. 1138.
Anon., 'The wines of France' *TS* (27.05.20).
Anon., 'Albert' *LP* (25.01.21).
Anon., 'Après l'enquête de la CGT dans les régions dévastées' *LP* (05.02.21).
Anon., 'La CGT va exposer son plan de reconstruction' *LP* (20.03.21).
Anon., 'La commission des réparations visite nos ruines' *JRD* (17.04.21) p. 1.
Anon., 'La délégation ouvrière franco-allemande dans la zone rouge' *LP* (01.11.21).

Anon., 'La délégation syndicaliste a visité hier Arras et les mines de Lens' *LP* (23.01.21).
Anon., 'Une délégation ouvrière franco-allemande' *LP* (31.10.21).
Anon., 'La délégation ouvrière franco-allemande' *LP* (01.11.21).
Anon., 'Enlèvement des fils de fer barbelés' *JRD* (02.10.21) p. 3.
Anon., 'Une enquête de la CGT dans les régions dévastées' *LP* (11.01.21).
Anon., 'L'état déplorable de Tergnier et des cités construites à Chauny' *LP* (19.01.21).
Anon., 'La main-d'oeuvre allemande dans les régions dévastées' *LP* (08.02.21).
Anon., 'Monsieur Loucheur et les coopératives à Nancy' *JRD* (10.04.21) p. 1.
Anon., 'Le monument aux morts de Notre-Dame de Lorette' *CM* 37 (1921–2) p. 238.
Anon., 'Où en est la question de reconstruction par la main-d'oeuvre allemande?' *LP* (04.12.21).
Anon., 'La participation allemande' *LP* (13.01.21).
Anon., 'Les recours aux Allemands' *JRD* (06.11.21) p. 1.
Anon., 'Loucheur dit: Il faut que l'Allemagne paye! Pas de main-d'oeuvre allemande' *LP* (25.04.21).
Anon., 'Sociétés coopératives de reconstruction' *JRD* (03.07.21) p. 3.
Anon., 'Un succès coopérateur' *JRD* (13.11.21) p. 3.
Anon., 'La visite de Monsieur Loucheur aux Chemin-des-Dames' *LP* (08.08.21).
Anon., 'Après la guerre, l'ouragan' *LP* (10.03.22).
Anon., 'La Belgique qui reconstruit' *LP* (07.02.22).
Anon., 'Le Comité Américain pour les Régions Dévastées' *MI* 65 (1922) pp. 14–15.
Anon., 'Déclaration de Monsieur Reibel' *LP* (08.02.22).
Anon., 'L'ossuaire de Douaumont' *CM* (1922–3) pp. 361–62.
Anon., 'Le programme de Monsieur Reibel' *LP* (26.01.22).
Anon., 'La reconstitution dans la Somme' *JRD* (19.02.22) p. 1.
Anon., 'Les cités-jardins des chemins de fer du Nord' *CM* 39 (1923–4) pp. 13–16.
Anon., 'L'assemblée générale de l'Office du Bâtiment et des Travaux Publics' *Le Parlement et l'Opinion* (1924) pp. 507–23.
Anon., 'L'impasse' *JRD* (17.8.24) p. 1.
Anon., 'Meuse' *JDD* (27.07.24) p. 1.
Anon., 'La zone rouge' *JDD* (27.07.24) p. 1.
Anon., 'Lettre de Monsieur Dalbiez' LA 38 (1925) p. 9.
Anon., *L'agriculture dans le département de Meurthe-et-Moselle* (Nancy: Imprimerie Lorraine, 1927).
Anon., 'Les travaux' *Bulletin Mensuel de l'Union des Coopératives de Reconstruction des Arrondissements de Montdidier, Amiens, Doullens* (1927, 1932, 1936).
Anon., 'Les travaux faits depuis six ans' *Bulletin Mensuel de l'Union des Coopératives de Reconstruction des Arrondissements de Montdidier, Amiens, Doullens* (01.05.28) pp. 5–7.
Anon., 'Le boisement dans la zone rouge de la Meuse' *Revue des Eaux et Forêts* 68 (1930) pp. 789–92.

Anon., 'Les coopératives de reconstruction en France. Historique de leur rôle après la guerre de 1914–18' *Notes Documentaires et Etudes* 824 (1948) pp. 1–28.

Anon., *Atlas des nécropoles nationales* (Paris: La Documentation Française, 1994).

Published works

Abercrombie, P., 'Pinon' *Town Planning Review* 9 (1921) pp. 12–14.

Adam, G. ed., *L'agriculture dans le département des Ardennes* (Nancy: Rigot, 1928).

Adam, G. ed., *Les Ardennes: monographie agricole* (Paris: Ministère de l'Agriculture, 1937).

Agache, A., *Nos agglomérations rurales, comment les aménager* (Paris: Librairie de la Construction Moderne, 1917).

Agache, A., Auburtin, J.M. & Redont, E., *Comment reconstruire nos cités détruites: notions d'urbanisme s'appliquant aux villes, bourgs et villages* 2nd edn. (Paris: Armand Colin, 1916).

Aimond, C., *La guerre de 1914–1918 dans la Meuse* (Verdun & Bar-le-Duc, 1922)

Aldcroft, D.H., *The European economy 1914–1970* (London: Croom Helm, 1978).

Alexandre, A., *La vie agricole dans la Picardie orientale depuis la guerre* (Paris: Les Belles Lettres, 1928a).

Alexandre, A., 'L'économie agricole de la Picardie orientale depuis la guerre' *AG* 37 (1928b) pp. 61–73.

Alphand, G., *La France pendant la guerre 1914–1917* (Paris: Hachette, 1917).

Amat, J.P. , 'Montfaucon d'Argonne, commune forestière' *Horizons d'Argonne* 50 (1985) pp. 88–105.

Amat, J.P. , 'Guerre et milieux naturels: les forêts meurtries de l'Est de la France, 70 ans après Verdun' *L'Espace Géographique* 16 (1987) pp. 217–33.

Amat, J.P. , 'La forêt et la guerre, un exemple de sylvofaciès sur les champs de bataille de la Grande Guerre en Argonne' *Bulletin de l'Association de Géographes Français* 65 (1988a) pp. 191–201.

Amat, J.P. , 'Le souvenir monumental des Américains dans le paysage meusien' in J. Lanher, G. Canini & N. Cazin (eds) *Du Sergent York à Patton: les Américains en Meuse 1917–1919* (Société des Lettres, Sciences et Arts de Bar-le-Duc, 1988b) pp. 129–49.

American Battle Monuments Commission, *A guide to the American battlefields in Europe* (Washington: US Government Printing Office, 1927).

American Relief Committee, *Misery devastated, Somme, France* (Paris: Chaix, 1920).

Ardouin-Dumazet, 'Sur le remplacement des arbres détruits par la guerre' *Séances et Travaux de l'Académie d'Agriculture de France* (1915) pp. 572–79.

Ardouin-Dumazet, 'L'agriculture sur le champ de bataille de la Somme' *JAP* 29 (1916) pp. 305–07.

Arnould, P. *La guerre de 1914–18 et les forêts de l'Aisne, un bouleversement majeur* (Paris, 1992).

Aubigny, D'. M., 'La restauration des régions libérées' *Le Parlement et l'Opinion* (1921) pp. 1135–40.

Auburtin, J.M., *La reconstruction des agglomérations rurales dans les régions dévastées par la guerre* (Paris, 1916).

Auburtin, J.M., 'Quels matériaux employer dans la reconstruction des agglomérations rurales dévastées par la guerre?' *Annales d'Hygiène Publique et de Médecine Légale* 31 (1919a) pp. 193–213.

Auburtin, J.M., 'L'aménagement des villages' *La Nature* 47 (1919b) pp. 323–26.

Auburtin, J.M. & Blanchard, H., *La cité de demain dans les régions dévastées* (Paris: Armand Colin, 1915).

Augé-Laribé, M., *Le paysan français après la grande guerre* (Paris: Garnier, 1923).

Augé-Laribé, M., *L'agriculture pendant la guerre* (Paris: Presses Universitaires de France, 1925).

Augé-Laribé, M., *Situation de l'agriculture française* (Paris: Berger-Levrault, 1945).

Augé-Laribé, M. & Pinot, P., *Agriculture and food supply in France during the war* (New Haven: Yale University Press, 1927).

Auscher, E.S., 'La reconstruction des villes et villages' *Revue d'Hygiène* (1919) pp. 8–16.

Bach, M., 'Les forêts mitraillées en Lorraine' *Revue Forestière Française* 27 (1975) pp. 217–22.

Bachelet, M., 'L'activité des sociétés tiers-mandataire et le rôle des coopératives d'approvisionnement dans l'achat des engrais et des machines' in Fédération Nationale de la Mutualité et de la Coopération Agricole, *IXe Congrès National de la Mutualité et de la Coopération Agricole* (1921) pp. 93–102.

Bailly, P., *L'agriculture du département de Seine-et-Marne* (Melun: La République, 1937).

Barjot, D., 'Les entreprises du bâtiment et des travaux publics et de la reconstruction' in J. Favier (ed.) *Reconstructions et modernisation* (Paris: Archives de France, 1991) pp. 231–36.

Barral, P., *Les agrariens français de Méline à Pisani* (Paris: Armand Colin, 1968).

Bastide, C., 'La renaissance d'un département dévasté' *Revue des Sciences Politiques* (1923) pp. 589–94.

Baudoui, R., 'La reconstruction de Tergnier' in J. Favier (ed.) *Reconstructions et modernisation* (Paris: Archives de France, 1991) pp. 245–47.

Bechmann, M., 'Sur les moyens de venir en aide aux agriculteurs des régions libérées' *Séances et Travaux de l'Académie d'Agriculture de France* (1917) pp. 668–78.

Becker, A., *Les monuments aux morts: mémoire de la Grande Guerre* (Paris: Errance, 1988).

Becker, A., 'Le culte du souvenir après la Grande Guerre: les monuments aux morts' in J. Favier (ed.) *Reconstructions et modernisation* (Paris: Archives de France, 1991) pp. 25–30.

Becker, A., *La guerre et la foi. De la mort à la mémoire 1914–1930* (Paris: Armand Colin, 1994).

Becker, J.J., 'Les destructions de la guerre de 1914–1918: coût, ampleur, conséquences démographiques' in J. Favier (ed.) *Reconstructions et modernisation* (Paris: Archives de France, 1991) pp. 17–22.

Bédarida, M., '1918: une modernisation urbaine frileuse' in J. Favier (ed.) *Reconstructions et modernisation* (Paris: Archives de France, 1991) pp. 263–66.

Benns, F.L., *Europe since 1914* (London: Bell, 1930).

Berenguer, J., '*De l'Ardenne à l'Argonne: progrès et régressions dans le monde rural*' (Thèse pour le doctorat d'Etat, Université de Lyon III, 1984).

Bernard, P. & Dubief, H., *The decline of the Third Republic, 1914–1938* (Cambridge: Cambridge University Press, 1985).

Berthault, P., 'Pour les agriculteurs des régions envahies' *JAP* 31 (1918) pp. 153–56.

Blache, J. ed., *Géographie lorraine* (Paris: Berger-Levrault, 1938).

Blanchard, R., *La Flandre: étude géographique de la plaine flamande en France, Belgique et Hollande* (Dunkirk: Société Dunkerquoise, 1906).

Bloch, C., *Bibliographie méthodique de l'histoire économique et sociale de la France pendant la guerre* (Paris: Presses Universitaires de France, 1925).

Bluzet, A., *Reconstitution des moyens d'habitation dans les villages détruits: département de la Marne* (Châlons-sur-Marne, 1916).

Borg, A., *War memorials* (London: Leo Cooper, 1991).

Boulin, P., *L'organisation du travail dans la région envahie de la France pendant l'occupation* (Paris: Presses Universitaires de France, 1927).

Bousquet, M., 'La reconstruction des bâtiments ruraux des régions dévastées. Matériaux et procédés modernes' *La Nature* 47 (1919) pp. 23–28.

Boussard, I., 'L'agriculture au lendemain des guerres de 1914 et 1939' in J. Favier (ed.) *Reconstructions et modernisation* (Paris: Archives de France, 1991) pp. 187–93.

Bowden, M.J., 'Geographical changes in cities following distaster' in A.R.H. Baker & M. Billinge (eds) *Period and place. Research methods in historical geography* (Cambridge: Cambridge University Press, 1982) pp. 114–26.

Bowman, I., *The new world: problems in political geography* (New York: World Book Co., 1921).

Braibant, M., 'L'amélioration des abris provisoires' *JRD* (25.12.21) p. 3.

Braibant, M., *L'agriculture française: son tragique déclin, son avenir* (Paris: Armand Colin, 1936).

Braudel, F., & Labrousse, E., eds, *Histoire économique et sociale de la France tome IV*, vol. 2 (Paris: Presses Universitaires de France, 1980).

Brethe, J., *Les sociétés coopératives de reconstruction immobilière des régions dévastées* (Paris: Sirey, 1923).

Brion, S., 'Les transformations du village rural dans la zone dévastée de la Meuse 1914–1918' *Annales de l'Est* (1935) pp. 3–29.

Brisac, J., *Conseils sur les principales dispositions relatives à l'hygiène dont il convient de s'inspirer dans les projets de reconstruction des immeubles détruits par les événements de guerre* (Châlons-sur-Marne, 1922a).

Brisac, J., *Rapport du préfet sur le fonctionnement des services de la reconstitution de la Marne* (Châlons-sur-Marne, 1922b).

Brisac, J., *Rapport du préfet sur le fonctionnement des services de la reconstitution de la Marne* (Châlons-sur-Marne, 1923).

Brogan, D.W., *The development of modern France 1870–1939* (London: Hamish Hamilton, 1940).

Bros, M., *L'effort financier de l'état français dans l'oeuvre des réparations* (Meulan, 1924).

Brunet, P., *Structure agraire et économie rurale des plateaux tertiaires entre la Seine et l'Oise* (Caen: Caron, 1960).

Brunet, P. & Dionnet, M.C., 'Présentation d'un essai de carte des paysages ruraux de la France' *Bulletin de l'Association de Géographes Français* 305–306 (1962) pp. 98–103.

Brunet, R., *Atlas et géographie: Champagne, Pays de Meuse et Basse-Bourgogne* (Paris: Flammarion, 1981).

Brunhes, J. & Deffontaines, P., *Géographie humaine de la France* (Paris: Plon, 1926).

Brunhes, J. & Vallaux, C., *La géographie et l'histoire de la paix et de la guerre sur terre et sur mer* (Paris: Alcan, 1921).

Bury, J.P.T., *France: the insecure peace. From Versailles to the great depression* (London: MacDonald, 1972).

Busscher, De J.M., *L'architecture des dommages de guerre: aspects de la reconstruction des régions dévastées de la première guerre mondiale* (Paris: Ministère de l'Urbanisme et du Logement. Direction de l'Architecture. Secrétariat de la Recherche Architecturale, 1983).

Caplain, R., 'La reconstruction de l'église de Nomeny' *CM* 44 (1928–9) pp. 223–27.

Caraud, P., *L'oeuvre des sociétés coopératives de reconstruction dans les régions dévastées* (Coulommiers: Brodard, 1924).

Carpentier, G., *La reconstitution économique et immobilière dans la Somme dévastée* (Montdidier: Moderne du Santerre, 1928).

Cart de Lafontaine, H.P., 'The rebuilding of devastated France' *The Builder* 120 (1921a) pp. 195, 259, 402, 474, 804–06.

Cart de Lafontaine, H.P., 'The work of La Renaissance des Cités' *Town Planning Review* 9 (1921b) pp. 1–4.

Cart de Lafontaine, H.P., 'Town planning in France' *The Builder* 127 (1924) pp. 1021–22.

Catusse, R., *Service de reconstitution des régions libérées: rapport au conseil-général de la Meuse* (Bar-le-Duc: Comte-Jacquet, 1932).

Causel, C., *Service de reconstitution des régions atteintes par les événements de guerre* (Arras, 1922).

Cellerier, F., *Le remploi, dans les constructions, des vieux matériaux provenant des villes et villages détruits par la Guerre* (Paris: Ministère de la Guerre, 1917).

Cépède, M., *Agriculture et alimentation en France durant la IIe guerre mondiale* (Paris: Génin, 1961).

Chambre d'Agriculture de Meurthe-et-Moselle, *Enquête sur le remembrement* (Nancy: Imprimerie Lorraine, 1934).

Chantriot, E., *La Champagne: étude de géographie régionale* (Paris: Berger-Levrault, 1906).

Chappaz, G., *Le vignoble et le vin de Champagne* (Paris: Larmat, 1951).

Chauveau, C., *Le remembrement de la propriété rurale* (Paris: Baillière, 1918).

Chemin de Fer du Nord, *Souvenir de la Grande Guerre. Visite des régions dévastées du Nord de la France I. Albert, Arras, Lens* (Paris, 1919).

Chenevier, P., 'Le rappel des cultivateurs dans les campagnes dévastées' *La Reconstruction Lorraine* (15.12.17) pp. 15–21.

Chevalier, G., *Les bois d'oeuvre pendant la guerre* (Paris: Presses Universitaires de France, 1927).

Chevalier, L., *Les réparations des dommages résultant des faits de la guerre* (Tournai: Casterman, 1919).

Clause, G., 'La lutte contre le déclin 1870–1950' in M. Crubellier (ed.) *Histoire de la Champagne* (Toulouse: Privat, 1975) pp. 365–87.

Clout, H.D., *Agriculture in France on the eve of the railway age* (London: Croom Helm, 1980).

Clout, H.D., *The land of France 1815–1914* (London: Allen & Unwin, 1983).

Clout, H.D., 'The reconstruction of Reims 1919–30' *Planning Outlook* 32 (1989) pp. 23–34.

Clout, H.D., 'Rural reconstruction in Meuse after World War I' *Acta Geographica Lovaniensia* 33 (1992) pp. 599–607.

Clout, H.D., 'Rural reconstruction in Aisne after the Great War' *Rural History* 4 (1993a) pp. 165–85.

Clout, H.D., 'The revival of rural Lorraine after the Great War' *Geografiska Annaler* 75B (1993b) pp. 73–91.

Clout, H.D., 'Reconstructing the countryside of the eastern Somme after the Great War' *Erdkunde* 48 (1994a) pp. 136–49.

Clout, H.D., 'Rural revival in Marne 1914–1930' *Agricultural History Review* 42 (1994b) pp. 140–55.

Clout, H.D., 'Rural revival: the recovery of the Moselle after World War I' *Modern and Contemporary France* 2 (1994c) pp. 395–403.

Cochin, H., Bourgeois, N. & Poncheville, De A.M., *Le Nord dévasté* (Paris: Alcan, 1920).

Collinet, P. & Stahl, P., *Le ravitaillement de la France occupée* (Paris: Presses Universitaires de France, 1928).

Comité d'Action des Régions Dévastées, *Dans les régions dévastées: l'oeuvre de reconstitution et la solidarité française* (Paris, 1925).

Comité d'Action des Régions Dévastées, *L'encyclopédie des régions dévastées* (Paris, 1930).

Comité National de la Géographie, *Atlas de France* (Paris: CNRS, 1953).

Confédération Générale des Coopératives de Reconstruction des Régions Dévastées, *Les emprunts des coopératives de reconstruction* (Paris, 1923).

Confédération Générale du Travail, *Dans les régions dévastées: une politique de reconstruction. Rapport de la commission d'enquête du conseil économique du travail* (Villeneuve-Saint-Georges, 1921).

Conseil-Général de l'Aisne, *Rapport du préfet sur la reconstitution des régions libérées* (Laon: Courrier de l'Aisne, 1924).

Conseil-Général de l'Aisne, *Rapport du préfet sur la reconstitution des régions libérées* (Laon: Courrier de l'Aisne, 1929).

Conseil-Général de la Marne, *Rapport du préfet sur le fonctionnement des services de reconstitution* (Bar-le-Duc, 1926).

Conseil-Général de Meurthe-et-Moselle, *Reconstitution des régions libérées: Rapport de Monsieur le préfet* (Nancy: Berger-Levrault, 1919).

Conseil-Général de Meurthe-et-Moselle, *Reconstitution des régions libérées: rapport du préfet* (Nancy: Rigot, 1920).

Conseil-Général de la Meuse, *Rapport de M. Piette, préfet* (Bar-le-Duc, 1919).

Conseil-Général du Nord, *Rapport du préfet sur la reconstitution* (Lille: Danel, 1919).

Conseil-Général du Nord, *Rapport du préfet sur la reconstitution* (Lille: Danel, 1920).

Conseil-Général de l'Oise, *Rapport du Préfet de l'Oise sur la reconstitution des régions libérées, 1e session ordinaire du Conseil-Général* (Compiègne, 1925).

Conseil-Général du Pas-de-Calais, *Session Ordinaire* (Arras: 1919).

Conseil-Général du Pas-de-Calais, *Service de reconstitution des régions atteintes par les événements de guerre* (Arras, 1921).

Conseil-Général du Pas-de-Calais, *Sessions Ordinaires* (Arras, 1922–27).

Couedelo, R.A., 'Aménagement et urbanisme: l'insertion des pouvoirs publics 1919–1950' in J. Favier (ed.) *Reconstructions et modernisation* (Paris: Archives de France, 1991) pp. 211–20.

Couturaud, E., *Guide pratique pour la reconstruction, l'extension, l'aménagement et l'embellissement des villes et des communes rurales* (Paris, 1915).

Cuminal, J., *Rapport de la délégation nommée pour visiter les régions libérées* (Privas, 1918).

Cuvelette, M., *La destruction et la reconstitution des mines de Lens* (Paris, 1922).

Damade, A., *Les scandales des dommages de guerre et les parlémentaires* (Paris: Teillon, 1924).

Damuzeaux, E., 'Le remembrement dans les Ardennes' in *Congrès des Améliorations Agricoles: Les améliorations agricoles* (Paris: Fédération Nationale des Collectivités, 1931) pp. 9–12.

Damuzeaux, E., *Le remembrement de la propriété foncière dans les Ardennes en application de la loi du 4 mars 1919* (Sedan: Suzaine, 1933).

Dassonville, J., *Pour relever les ruines* (Paris: Perrin, 1919).

Dautresme, D., *Les conséquences de la guerre en Seine-et-Marne: étude historique, administrative et économique* (Melun: Legrand, 1919).

Debus, J.S., *La grande leçon: la rénovation du Nord de la France* (Lille: Mercure de Flandre, 1928).

Delaire, M., 'Restauration' *CM* 34 (1919–20) p. 89.

Demangeon, A., *La Picardie et les régions voisines: Artois, Cambrésis, Beauvaisis* (Paris: Armand Colin, 1905).

Demangeon, A., *Le déclin de l'Europe* (Paris: Payot, 1920).

Demangeon, A., *La France économique et humaine*, vol. I (Paris: Armand Colin, 1946).

Demangeon, A. & Matruchot, M., 'Les variations de la population de la France de 1881 à 1921' *AG* 35 (1926) pp. 499–510.

Dervaux, A., 'Comment reconstruire nos cités détruites' *La Réforme Sociale* 37 (1917) pp. 203–31.

Deschamps, G., 'Aux régions dévastées: avec la Croix-Rouge américaine' *Revue des Deux Mondes* 44 (1918) pp. 672–95.

Deschaseux, M., 'Eaux et forêts' in *Rapport du Préfet au Conseil-Général des Vosges* (Epinal, 1919) pp. 51–2.

Despagnet, E., 'Les habitations provisoires' *JRD* (26.10.19) p. 2.

Dessaint, J., 'Aux régions dévastées' *La Revue de Paris* 29 (1922) pp. 748–62.

Devaine, E., 'Les habitations' in Anon. *Exposition des oeuvres sociales du Nord* (Lille: Danel, 1922) pp. 122–24.

Diefendorf, J.M., ed., *Rebuilding Europe's Bombed Cities* (London: Macmillan, 1990).

Dietrich, G., 'L'économie agricole et vie rurale dans le canton nord de Lunéville' *Annales de l'Est* (1954) pp. 77–92.

Dike, A.M., *The American Committee for Devastated France* (New York: n.d).

Doumer, P., 'Signature ou révision' *JRD* (01.6.19) p. 33.

Dubreule, R. & Courtassol, J., *La France blessée et renaissante: bilan et inventaire* (Paris: Temps qui passe, 1950).

Ducasse, A., Meyer, J. & Perreux, G., *Vie et mort des Français 1914–1918* (Paris: Hachette, 1962).

Dufournet, P., 'Comment se sont construits les villages picards' *Techniques et Architecture* 11–12 (1943) pp. 313–23.

Dupuy, E., 'L'architecte dans les régions dévastées' *LA* (1919) pp. 609–15.

Dyer, G., *The missing of the Somme* (London: Hamish Hamilton, 1994).

Edmonds, J.E., ed., *History of the Great War based on official documents. Military operations: France and Belgium 1918*, vol. V (London: HMSO, 1947).

Elwood, P.H., The Argonne cemetery of the American Expeditionary Force at Romagne-sous-Montfaucon *Architectural Record* 47 (1920) pp. 507–10.

Emery, P., *Service de reconstitution des régions atteintes par les événements de guerre. Rapport au Conseil-Général du département de la Meuse* (Bar-le-Duc: Comte-Jacquet, 1922).

Emery, P., *Les régions libérées de la Somme après quatre ans de reconstitution* (Amiens: Progrès, 1923).

Emery, P., *Département de la Somme: la reconstitution des régions libérées. Rapport présenté au Conseil-Général* (Amiens: Progrès, 1924).

Emery, P., *La reconstitution des régions libérées. Rapport au Conseil-Général de la Somme* (Amiens: Progrès, 1925–8).

Ernest, G., 'Reconstitution des villes' *LA* (1919) pp. 90–91.
Estier, R., 'Les paysans et la guerre' in J.P. Houssel (ed.) *Histoire des paysans français du XVIIIe siècle à nos jours* (Roanne: Horvath, 1976) pp. 401–10.

Fagot, M., 'L'agriculture des Ardennes' *Comptes Rendus de Séances de l'Académie d'Agriculture de France* 4 (1918) p. 1087.
Fallon, L., 'La Meuse et les guerres: la grande guerre 1914–18' *Dossiers Documentaires Meusiens* 42 (1986) pp. 1–68.
Favier, J., ed., *Reconstructions et modernisation: la France après les ruines 1918, 1945* (Paris: Archives de France, 1991).
Fiel, P., *L'oeuvre de la coopérative de reconstruction des églises du diocèse de Nancy et de Toul* (Nancy: Vagner, 1927).
Fiel, P., *La reconstitution des régions dévastées en Lorraine* (Nancy: Pays Lorrain, 1935).
Flatrès, P., 'Les structures agraires du Nord de la France' in *Mélanges de géographie offerts à M. Omer Tulippe,* vol. I (Gembloux: Cuclot, 1967) pp. 309–21.
Flatrès, P., *Atlas et géographie du Nord et de la Picardie* (Paris: Flammarion, 1980).
Floremont, G., *L'économie agricole en Meurthe-et-Moselle entre les deux guerres* (Mémoire de Maîtrise, Université de Nancy II, 1983).
Fohlen, C., *La France de l'entre deux geurres 1917–39,* 2nd edn (Paris: Casterman, 1972).
Fondation Carnegie, *Pose de la première pierre des édifices communaux de Fargniers reconstruits avec le concours de la Dotation Carnegie 9 juillet 1922* (Paris, 1922).
Fontaine, A., *L'industrie française pendant la guerre* (Paris: Presses Universitaires de France, 1925).
Ford, G.B., *Out of the ruins* (New York: Century, 1919a).
Ford, G.B., 'The facts on the devastation and the present reconstruction efforts in France' *Engineering News Record* 82 (1919b) pp. 218–27.
Ford, G.B., 'Summary of war damage in France' *New York Times Current History: the European War* 18 (1919c) pp. 516–21.
Forget, J., 'La reconstitution forestière et la zone rouge dans la Meuse' *Bulletin de la Société des Lettres, Sciences et Arts de Bar-le-Duc* (1927) pp. 121–31.
Forget, J., 'La reconstitution forestière et la zone rouge dans la Meuse' *Revue des Eaux et Forêts* 66 (1928) pp. 336–39.
Fox, F., *GHQ: Montreuil-sur-Mer* (London: Allan, 1920).
Franklin, J.H., *In the track of the storm* (Philadelphia: American Baptist Publication Society, 1919).
Fromont, P., 'L'électrification des campagnes françaises' *AG* 34 (1925) pp. 385–97.
Fry, A.R., *A Quaker adventure* (London: Society of Friends, 1926).
Fry, A.R., *A Quaker adventure,* 2nd edn (London: Society of Friends, 1943).
Fussell, P., *The Great War and modern memory* (New York & London: Oxford University Press, 1975).

Gaines, R., *A village in Picardy* (New York: Dutton, 1918).

Gaines, R., *Ladies of Grécourt: the Smith College Relief Unit in the Somme* (New York: Dutton, 1920).

Garnotel, J., *L'ascension d'une grande agriculture: Champagne pouilleuse-Champagne crayeuse* (Paris: Economica, 1985).

Gavelle, E., *Les droits du passé et les exigences du présent dans la reconstruction de nos villes et villages* (Lille: Comité Flamand, 1920).

Gay, A., Le remembrement dans les régions dévastées *JAP* 37 (1922) pp. 250–53, 296–99.

Geipel, R., *Disaster and reconstruction: the Friuli (Italy) earthquakes of 1976* (London: Allen & Unwin, 1982).

Gérard, C., *Lorraine: l'architecture rurale française* (Paris: Berger-Levrault, 1981).

Gérard, C. & Peltre, J., *Les villages lorrains* (Nancy: Université de Nancy II, 1979).

Gibbons, H.A., *France and ourselves: interpretative studies 1917–1919* (New York: Century, 1920).

Gide, C., *Effects of the war upon French economic life* (Oxford: Clarendon Press, 1923).

Gide, C. & Oualid, W., *Le bilan de la guerre pour la France* (Paris: Presses Universitaires de France, 1931).

Gilbert, M., *First World War* (London: Weidenfeld & Nicolson, 1994).

Girault, A., 'Le remembrement de la propriété foncière dans les régions dévastées' *Economiste Français* 50 (1922) pp. 5–6, 99–101.

Goissaud, A., 'L'oeuvre de la Compagnie du Nord: la reconstitution dans les régions libérées' *CM* 42 (1925) pp. 39–47, 73–81, 120–24, 205–210, 287–91, 327–28.

Gonnet, G., 'Le remembrement augmente le rendement de nos terres cultivables' *JDD* (20.01.24) p. 1.

Gouge, R., 'Le problème de la reconstitution' *JRD* (08.02.20) p. 1.

Gouge, R., 'L'avenir des coopératives' *JRD* (27.02.21a) p. 1.

Gouge, R., 'Discours de M. René Gouge' *JRD* (12.06.21b) p. 1.

Gouguenheim, A., 'La situation dans les régions libérées' *Les Cahiers de Droits de l'Homme* (1921) pp. 181–86.

Gouttin, P., 'Les forêts mitraillées soixante ans après' *Revue Forestière Française* 31 (1979) pp. 318–22.

Grailles, B., *Mémoires de pierre: les monuments aux morts de la première guerre mondiale dans le Pas-de-Calais* (Arras: Archives Départementales du Pas-de-Calais, 1992).

Granveau, A., *Annuaire administratif, commercial et industriel de la Meuse* (Bar-le-Duc: Constant-Laguerre, 1922).

Gravier, G., 'La plaine lorraine' *AG* 19 (1910) pp. 440–55.

Greenwood, J.O., *Quaker encounters* (York: Ebor, 1975).

Grosdidier de Matons, M., 'La Woëvre' in J. Blache (ed.) *Géographie lorraine* (Paris: Berger-Levrault, 1938) pp. 260–65.

Groupement des Sociétés Coopératives Approuvées de Reconstruction des

Eglises Dévastées de France, *Emprunt pour la reconstruction des églises dévastées* (Paris, 1922).
Gruet, G., ed., *Monographie agricole du département de Meurthe-et-Moselle* (Nancy: Ministère de l'Agriculture, 1937).
Guérin, J., *Le réveil des pierres: histoire d'une coopérative 1919–1929* (Compiègne: Bourson, 1930).
Guicherd, J. & Maitrot, C., 'Les terres des régions dévastées' *JAP* 35 (1921) pp. 154–56, 332–35, 36 pp. 234–35, 314–15.
Guillon, J.M., 'Dans les régions dévastées par la guerre' *JAP* 28 (1915) pp. 630–32, 29 (1916) pp. 11–13,129–31.
Guillon, J.M., 'Mission anglaise de la Société des Amis' *JAP* 29 (1916) pp. 92–94.

Haas, J.E. Kates, R.W. & Bowden, M.J., *Reconstruction following disaster* (Cambridge Mass. & London: MIT Press, 1977).
Hanotaux, G. ed., *Circuits des champs de bataille de France: histoire et itinéraires de la grande guerre* (Paris: Edition Française Illustrée, 1920).
Hanotaux, G., 'L'Aisne dévastée 1918–21' *MI* 6 (1922) pp. 4–5.
Hanotaux, G., *En Belgique par les pays dévastés* (Paris: Plon, 1931).
Harbulot, J.P. , 'Villages meusiens' *Dossiers Documentaires Meusiens* 8 (1977) pp. 1–53.
Hartke, W., *Kulturgeographische Wandlungen in Nordostfrankreich seit dem Kriege* (Berlin: Berliner Geographische Arbeiten, 1932).
Harvey, T.E., *Behind the battlelines in France* (London: Society of Friends, 1915).
Heffernan, M., 'For ever England: the western front and the politics of remembrance in Britain' *Ecumene* 2 (1995) pp. 293–323.
Helot, J., 'Situation de la culture dans les régions dévastées' *Comptes Rendus des Séances de l'Académie d'Agriculture de France* 6 (1920a) pp. 544–47.
Helot, J., 'Situation de la culture dans les régions dévastées' *JAP* 33 (1920b) p. 491.
Hénard, M., 'La main d'oeuvre chinoise' *JRD* (26.10.19) p. 3.
Hénard, M., 'La politique de M Loucheur' *JRD* (02.10.21a) p. 1.
Hénard, M., Le coup de fouet *JRD* (20.11.21b) p. 1.
Herbette, M., *L'avenir de la France* (Paris: Alcan, 1918).
Héricault, G., *Les terres assassinées devant les dévastations 1914–1933* (Paris: Sirey, 1934).
Hersant, G., *Une politique de la construction après la guerre: travaux publics et bâtiment* (Paris: Payot, 1919).
Hilaire, Y.M., 'Le XXe siècle' in P. Bougard & A. Nolibos (eds) *Le Pas-de-Calais de la préhistoire à nos jours* (Saint-Jean d'Angély: Bourdessoules, 1988) pp. 340–60.
Hitier, H., 'Le village picard' *AG* 12 (1903) pp. 109–19.
Hitier, H., 'La situation agricole des régions récemment libérées du département de la Somme' *Comptes Rendus des Séances de l'Académie d'Agriculture de France* 3 (1917a) pp. 580–89.

Hitier, H., 'La situation des régions libérées du Santerre' *JAP* 30 (1917b) pp. 237–40.

Hitier, H., 'Situation de l'agriculture dans l'Aisne envahie' *Comptes Rendus des Séances de l'Académie d'Agriculture de France* 4 (1918) pp. 1076–87.

Hitier, H., 'Les régions dévastées par la guerre' *JAP* 34 (1920) pp. 80–82.

Hitier, H. & Pluchet, E., 'L'état des récoltes dans les régions libérées' *Comptes Rendus des Séances de l'Académie d'Agriculture de France* 6 (1920) pp. 34–44.

Hoc, P., 'Le remembrement de la propriété foncière' JAP 41 (1924) pp. 91–93.

Holliday, A.C., 'The rebuilding of Rheims' *Town Planning Review* 9 (1921) pp. 5–11.

Hottenger, G., *Morcellement et remembrement* (Paris: Baillière, 1914).

Houssel, J.P., *La montagne de Noyon* (Diplôme d'Etudes Supérieures, Université de Paris, 1960).

Huber, M., *La population de la France pendant la guerre* (Paris: Presses Universitaires de France, 1931).

Hubert, L., *La renaissance d'un département dévasté* (Paris: Boivin, 1923).

Huin, F., 'L'évolution des forêts ruinées d'Argonne' *Mémoires de la Société d'Agriculture, Commerce, Sciences et Arts du Département de la Marne* 77 (1962) pp. 159–66.

Hurst, S.C., *The silent cities. An illustrated guide to the war cemeteries and memorials to the 'missing' in France and Flanders: 1914–1918* (London: Methuen, 1929).

Hutchinson, G.S., *Pilgrimage* (London: Rich & Cowan, 1935).

Huysmans, E., *La réparation des dommages de guerre en Belgique* (Brussels: Van Oest, 1919).

Illaire, M., 'La loi du 17 avril 1919, charte des sinistrés' in J. Favier (ed.) *Reconstructions et modernisation* (Paris: Archives de France, 1991) pp. 105–11

Inghels, A., 'Le contrôle de l'hygiène dans les régions libérées et l'assainissement des champs de bataille' *Annales de la Chambre des Députés (Documents)* 93 (1919) pp. 2647–53.

Inghels, A., *Le panama des régions dévastées* (Paris: La Brochure Républicaine, 1924).

Javary, M., 'L'effort du réseau du Nord pendant et après la guerre' *Bulletin Mensuel de la Société Industrielle du Nord de la France* 215 (1921) pp. 17–129.

Johnson, D.W., *Topography and strategy in the war* (New York: Holt, 1917).

Johnson, D.W., 'A geographer at the front and at the peace conference' *Natural History* 19 (1919) pp. 511–21.

Johnson, D.W., *Battlefields of the world war: western and southern fronts. A study in military geography* (New York: Oxford University Press, 1921).

Jolivet, R. & Brousse, M., *Remembrements en Meuse* (Bar-le-Duc: Chambre d'Agriculture, 1959).

Jolyet, A., 'Restauration des forêts dévastées par les faits de guerre' *La Nature* 44 (1916) pp. 401–06.

Joyant, E., *Traité d'urbanisme,* 2 vols (Paris: Librairie de l'Enseignement Technique, 1923).

Juillard, E., *Atlas et géographie de l'Alsace et de la Lorraine* (Paris: Flammarion, 1977).

Klatzmann, J., *La localisation des cultures et des productions animales en France* (Paris: INSEE, 1955).

Kraus, H., *International relief in action 1914–1943* (Philadelphia: The Research Center, 1944).

Kuisel, R.F., *Capitalism and the state in modern France. Renovation and economic management in the twentieth century* (Cambridge: Cambridge University Press, 1981).

Labaste, A., 'Les relations par voie ferrée entre l'Est et le Nord de la France' *AG* 41 (1932) pp. 242–57.

Lançon, J. & Minon, R., *Les archives historique et patriotique du nord de l'Aisne pendant la guerre et l'après-guerre 1914–1921* (Paris, 1921).

Laurent, F., *L'agriculture de demain* (Paris, 1919).

Laurent, J., *L'Argonne et ses bordures* (Paris, 1948).

Lavollée, R., 'Comment on vit dans les villages libérés' *La Réforme Sociale* 79 (1920) pp. 16–35.

Le Mamer, Y., 'Le Pas-de-Calais aux XIXe et XXe siècles' *Bulletin de la Commission d'Histoire et d'Archéologie du Pas-de-Calais* 13 (1991) pp. 148–88.

Lebrun, A., 'Programme de la reconstitution agricole des régions libérées' *JAP* 31 (1918) pp. 492–94.

Lebrun, A., 'Comment a été reconstruit un village lorrain' *MI* (1922) pp. 3–4.

Lebrun, L. & Guille, L., *L'agriculture dans la Marne en 1926* (Troyes: Paton, 1926).

Lecq, H., 'La situation de l'agriculture en pays envahi, nord de la France' *Travaux et Notices publiés par l'Académie d'Agriculture de France* 1 (1918) pp. 285–315.

Léon, P., 'Les constructions rurales après la guerre' *Les Arts Français* 23 (1918) pp. 203–16.

Léon, P., 'The reconstruction of ancient edifices in the devastated regions of France' *The Builder* 124 (1923) p. 115.

Lequeux, A., 'La Thiérache' *Bulletin de la Société de Géographie de Lille* 6 (1936) pp. 203–20.

Leuillier, R., *Pas-de-Calais. La vie administrative, les oeuvres de solidarité, d'assistance, d'hygiène et d'enseignement et la vie économique du département pendant la guerre* (Boulogne-sur-Mer, 1918).

Leuillier, R., *Pas-de-Calais. Service de reconstitution des régions atteintes par les événements de guerre* (Arras, 1920).

Lidbetter, H. & Monk-Jones, N., *SSA14 Section sanitaire anglaise quatorze, 1915–1919* (Manchester: Benson, 1919).

Lill, H., 'Reconstruction des villages dévastés' *LA* (1916) pp. 175–78.

Lobeck, A.K., *Physiographic diagram of Europe* (New York: Geographical Press, 1944).

Loirat, A., *Le remembrement de la propriété foncière dans la Somme* (Amiens: Ministère de l'Agriculture, 1931).

Loupiac, P., *Pays libérés, ruines reconquises* (Albi: Corbière et Julien, 1918).

Lubersac, De G., *Les pariahs des régions dévastées* (Château-Thierry: Moderne, 1926).

MacDonald, W., *Reconstruction in France* (London: Macmillan, 1922).

Magny, C., *La reconstitution du département de la Meuse: la tenacité d'une courageuse population, l'effort de l'administration* (Bar-le-Duc: Comte-Jacquet, 1928).

Magre, A., *Département des Vosges: rapport sur la reconstitution des communes libérées au conseil-général* (Epinal, 1923).

Mahain, A. ed., *La Belgique restaurée: étude sociologique* (Brussels: Lamertin, 1926).

Mahuet, De A., *Les sociétés coopératives de reconstruction du département de Meurthe-et-Moselle* (Nancy: Berger-Levrault, 1927).

Maricourt, De A., *L'Oise dévastée* (Paris: Alcan, 1920).

Mauco, G., *Les étrangers en France: leur rôle dans l'activité économique* (Paris: Armand Colin, 1932).

Mauco, G., 'Les modes d'exploitation agricole en France' *AG* 46 (1937) pp. 485–93.

Mayeux, A., 'Monuments aux morts de l'état de Pennsylvanie à Varennes-en-Argonne, à Fismes et à Nantillois' *LA* 43 (1930) pp. 33–38.

Meissel, R., *La Picardie dans la Grande Guerre* (Amiens: Centre Régional de Documentation Pédagogique, 1986).

Mestrel, De A., 'Après la guerre dans les départements envahis' *JAP* 28 (1914–15) pp. 487–90.

Michael, L.G., Agricultural survey of Europe: France *United States Department of Agriculture, Technical Bulletin* 37 (1928) pp. 1–184.

Michel, E., *La réparation des dommages de guerre* (Paris: Berger-Levrault, 1923).

Michel, E., *Les dommages de guerre de la France et leur réparation* (Paris: Berger-Levrault, 1932).

Michelin Illustrated Guides to the Battlefields, *Verdun and the battles for its possession* (Clermont-Ferrand & London, 1919a).

Michelin Illustrated Guides to the Battlefields, *Battlefields of the Marne 1914* (Clermont-Ferrand & London, 1919b).

Michelin Illustrated Guides to the Battlefields, *The first battle of the Somme 1916–1917* (Clermont-Ferrand & London, 1919c).

Michelin Illustrated Guides to the Battlefields, *Arras, Lens, Douai and the Battles of Artois* (Clermont-Ferrand & London, 1920).

Middlebrook, M., *The first day on the Somme: 1 July 1916* (Harmondsworth: Penguin, 1984).

Middlebrook, M., *The Somme battlefields* (Harmondsworth: Penguin, 1994).

Millet, E., 'Traits permanents de la vie rurale' in Blache, J. (ed.) *Géographie lorraine* (Nancy: Berger-Levrault, 1938) pp. 140–63.

Minella-Bouchy, M., 'Remembrement, reconstruction et transformation du paysage rural dans le canton de Nomeny' *Annales de l'Est* (1956) pp. 39–54.

Ministère de l'Agriculture, *Statistique agricole de la France: résultats généraux de l'enquête décennale de 1892* (Paris: Imprimerie Nationale, 1897).

Ministère de l'Agriculture, *La petite propriété rurale en France: enquêtes monographiques 1908–1909* (Paris: Imprimerie Nationale, 1909).

Ministère de l'Agriculture, *Statistiques agricoles annuelles 1910–1913, 1919–1928* (Paris: Imprimerie Nationale, 1911–14, 1920–29).

Ministère de l'Agriculture, *L'effort agricole de la France pendant six mois de guerre, août 1914–janvier 1915* (Paris: Imprimerie Nationale, 1915).

Ministère de l'Agriculture, *Statistique de l'agriculture. Résultats généraux de l'enquête décennale de 1929* (Paris: Imprimerie Nationale, 1936).

Ministère de l'Intérieur, *Dénombrement de la population 1896, 1911, 1921, 1931* (Paris, Imprimerie Nationale, 1897, 1912, 1922, 1932).

Ministère des Régions Libérées, *Guide du cultivateur sinistré désireux de reprendre son exploitation* (Paris: Imprimerie Nationale, 1919a).

Ministère des Régions Libérées, *Notice sur les questions à examiner et sur la documentation à réunir en vue de l'établissement des projets d'aménagement, d'embellisssement et d'extension des agglomérations rurales* (Paris, 1919b).

Ministère des Régions Libérées, *L'oeuvre de la reconstitution: statistique au 1 octobre 1922* (Paris, 1923) unpaginated.

Ministère des Travaux Publics. Service des Régions Libérées, *La reconstitution de la France dévastée: statistique générale* (Paris, 1929) unpaginated.

Mireur, R., *Rapport du préfet au Conseil-Général des Vosges* (Epinal, 1924).

Monicault, De P., 'Sur les secours aux régions agricoles dévastées par la guerre' *Comptes Rendus des Séances de l'Académie d'Agriculture de France* 1 (1915) pp. 21–29.

Morain, A., *La situation économique du département au 1 août 1918: rapport présenté au Conseil-Général* (Amiens: Le Progrès, 1918).

Morain, A., *Département de la Somme: l'oeuvre de reconstitution de la région dévastée au 1 avril 1920* (Amiens: Le Progrès, 1920).

Morain, A., *Département de la Somme: la reconstitution de la région libérée au 1 avril 1921* (Amiens: Le Progrès, 1921).

Morain, A., *Département de la Somme: la reconstitution de la région libérée au 1 avril 1922* (Amiens: Le Progrès, 1922a).

Morain, A., *Département du Nord: le bilan de trois ans de reconstitution* (Lille: Danel, 1922b).

Morain, A., *Le remembrement de la propriété foncière dans la Somme* (Amiens: Le Progrès: 1922c).

Morain, A., *La reconstitution du Nord dévasté au 1 septembre 1923* (Lille: Martin-Mamy, 1923).

Moreau-Bérillon, C., *Au pays de la Champagne: le vignoble, le vin* (Reims: Michaud, 1924).

Moreau-Bérillon, C., *Le rôle de la coopération dans les régions dévastées* (Châlons, 1921).

Musset, R., 'La reconstitution agricole des régions dévastées du Nord et du Nord-Est de la France' *AG* 31 (1922) pp. 355–60.

Naudin, A., *Département du Nord: rapport du préfet sur la reconstitution* (Lille: Danel, 1919).

Naudin, A., *Département du Nord: un an de reconstitution* (Lille: Danel, 1920).

Naudin, A., *Département du Nord: deux ans de reconstitution* (Lille: Danel, 1921a).

Naudin, A., *Département du Nord: la reconstitution définitive, de la renaissance et du dévéloppement des oeuvres départementales d'hygiène sociale* (Lille: Danel, 1921b).

Naudin, A., *Département du Nord: trois ans de reconstitution* (Lille: Danel, 1922).

Nogaro, B. & Weil, L., *La main d'oeuvre étrangère et coloniale pendant la guerre* (Paris: Presses Universitaires de France, 1926).

Oeuvre des Secours aux Eglises Dévastées, *Le progrès de la reconstruction des églises* (Paris, 1923).

Ogburn, W.F. & Jaffé, W., *The economic development of post-war France* (New York: Columbia University Press, 1929).

Ogier, M., 'Touristes américains' *Bulletin Départemental Meusien de la Reconstitution* 8 (1919) pp. 118–19.

Ottavi, P., 'La situation' *Bulletin Mensuel de l'Union des Coopératives de Reconstruction des Arrondissements de Montdidier, Amiens, Doullens* (01.02.23) p. 1.

Ovise, L., *Etude sur le remembrement* (Laon: Chambre d'Agriculture, 1948).

Padieu, G., 'Une exploitation basée sur la culture mécanique dans les régions dévastées' *JAP* 43 (1925) pp. 156–59.

Parisot, D., *Le régime de l'indemnisation en matière de dommages causés aux biens par les faits de la guerre* (Paris: Presses Universitaires de France, 1923).

Parisot, J., *Enquête sur l'habitation rurale en France: Ministère de la Santé Publique,* 2 vols (Paris: Dannaud, 1939).

Patrix, L., 'Détermination, après enquête, des régions où le remembrement apparaît nécessaire' in *Congrès des Améliorations Rurales Les améliorations rurales* (Paris: Fédération Nationale des Collectivités, 1931) pp. 13–16

Peltre, J., 'De 16e au 18e siècle: une génération de nouveaux villages en Lorraine' *Revue Géographique de l'Est* 6 (1966) pp. 3–27.

Peltre, J., 'L'évolution des structures foncières en Lorraine' *Bulletin de la Société Géographique de Liège* 5 (1969) pp. 1–24.

Peltre, J., 'Insuffisante transformation des campagnes' in J.C. Bonnefont (ed.) *Histoire de la Lorraine de 1900 à nos jours* (Toulouse: Privat, 1979) pp. 210–37.

Petit, O., '*La naissance et le dévéloppement du syndicalisme et de la mutualité agricole dans le département de l'Aisne entre les deux guerres*' (Thèse pour le doctorat d'Etat, Université de Paris IV, 1986).

Peytral, P., *Rapport au Conseil-Général du Pas-de-Calais* (Arras: 1925).

Peytral, P., *Pas-de-Calais. Service de reconstitution des régions atteintes par les événements de guerre: rapport du préfet* (Arras: 1926).

Peytral, P., *La reconstitution des régions libérées du Pas-de-Calais: situation au 1 janvier 1927* (Hénin-Liétard: Plouvier, 1927).

Philippot, G., 'La récupération des munitions: désobusage et remise en état du sol' *MI* 5 (1921) p. 16.

Picard, E., *La reconstruction en Alsace* (Strasbourg: Alsace à l'Oeuvre, 1937).

Picard, R., 'La reconstruction des régions dévastées en France' *La Vie des Peuples* (1922) pp. 1009–29.

Pierson, C. & Désiré, J., 'Combats de 1914–18 en Picardie', planche N5 in *Atlas de Picardie* (Amiens: 1985).

Piette, M., *Conseil-Général de la Meuse: rapport de M. Piette, préfet* (Bar-le-Duc, 1919).

Pinchemel, P., *Structures sociales et dépopulation rurale dans les campagnes picardes de 1836 à 1936* (Paris: Armand Colin, 1957).

Pitrois, Y., *Les femmes de la grande guerre* (Geneva: Jeheber, 1916).

Polignac, De M., 'Renaissance de la Champagne' *MI* (25.09.20) p. 16.

Poquet, O., 'Le Porcien à l'heure allemande: le village de Rocquigny pendant la guerre 14–18' *Terres Ardennaises* 14 (1986) pp. 27–31.

Préaud, R. & Fiel, P., *Les coopératives de reconstruction du département de Meurthe-et-Moselle* (Nancy, 1922).

Préfecture de l'Oise, *Rapport du préfet sur la reconstitution des régions libérées. Première session ordinaire du Conseil-Général* (Beauvais, 1925).

Pye, E.M., *Relief work in the devastated department of the Marne* (London, Society of Friends, 1915).

Quénedey, C., *La reconstruction des maisons après la guerre. Les anciens types des pays dévastés* (Rouen: Cagniard, 1920).

Rabouille, E., 'La reconstitution naturelle des forêts dévastées du Nord' *Revue des Eaux et Forêts* 60 (1922) pp. 395–401.

Rabouille, E., 'Les forêts dévastées du Nord de la France' *Revue des Eaux et Forêts* 66 (1928) pp. 434–37.

Ratineau, J. & Gaillot, M., *L'agriculture dans l'Aisne* (Laon: Office Agricole Départemental de l'Aisne, 1928).

Raux, M., 'Le calcul de la perte de valeur d'avenir et la question des réparations forestières' *Revue des Eaux et Forêts* 59 (1921) pp. 1–10.

Reibel, C., 'La reconstitution des régions libérées' *CM* 39 (1923–4) pp. 565–69, 579–83.

Reibel, C., *La reconstitution des régions libérées* (Paris: Comité National d'Etudes Sociales et Politiques, 1924a).

Reibel, C., 'L'oeuvre magnifique de reconstitution accomplie dans les régions du Nord et de l'Est' *JDD* (23.03.14b) p. 3.

Reibel, C., 'La reconstitution des régions libérées' *JAP* (01.01.24c) p. 246.

Renaud, G., *Visite dans les régions dévastées par l'ennemi, octobre 1917. Rapport présenté au nom de la délégation du Conseil-Général des Vosges* (Epinal: Imprimerie Administrative, 1918).

Renaudin, C., 'La vie rurale dans le nord de la Champagne' *AG* 45 (1936) pp. 225–39.

Revault, L., 'Rapport fait au nom de la Commission des Régions Libérées chargée d'examiner le projet relatif à l'organisation des visites dans les régions libérées' *Annales de la Chambre des Députés* 95 (1920) p. 587.

Reynes, L., *Receuil officiel des sépultures militaires* (Paris: Alépée, 1929).

Rieucau, L., 'Le remembrement rural dans le département de la Somme' *Hommes et Terres du Nord* 1966(1) pp. 87–97.

Rigaud, O. & Bédarida, M., *Reims, reconstruction 1920–1930* (Reims: Ville de Reims, 1988).

Ringelmann, M., 'Sur les constructions temporaries à élever dans les régions envahies' *Séances et Travaux de l'Académie d'Agriculture de France* (1914) pp. 955–61.

Ringelmann, M., 'Le Génie Rural et la guerre de 1914–1916' *ASA* (1915) pp. 296–381.

Ringelmann, M., 'Reconstruction des bâtiments ruraux dans les régions envahies' *JAP* 31 (1918) pp. 129–31, 184–87.

Ringelmann, M., *Habitations rurales et bâtiments de ferme des régions libérées* (Paris: Librairie Agricole, 1920).

Roche, L., *L'agriculture dans la Meuse* (Bar-le-Duc, 1931).

Rodolphe-Rousseau, J., *Les coopératives de reconstruction dans les régions libérées* (Paris: Rousseau, 1920).

Rogers, L., 'The problems of reconstruction, international and national' *Documents of the American Association for International Conciliation* 1 (1920) pp. 1–164.

Rolin, C., 'Monseigneur Thouvenin: prêtre social et reconstructeur d'églises' *Mémoires de l'Académie de Stanislas* 38 (1950–3) pp. 155–74.

Rosenthal, L., *Villes et villages français après la guerre. Aménagement, restauration, embellissement, extension* (Payot: Paris, 1918).

Roussel, E., *Le département de l'Aisne après cinq ans de reconstitution: exposé présenté au Conseil-Général* (Nancy: Berger-Levrault, 1923).

Roussilhe, H., 'La photographie en avion appliquée à la reconstitution des régions dévastées' *La Nature* 48 (1920) pp. 197–201.

Sagnier, H., 'Dans les régions libérées: zone de l'armée britannique' *JAP* 30 (1917a) pp. 469–72.

Sagnier, H., 'La coopération dans les régions libérées' *JAP* 30 (1917b) pp. 322–25.

Sagnier, H., 'Dans les régions libérées, à Blérancourt' *JAP* 30 (1917c) pp. 427–28.

Sagnier, H., 'L'agriculture française pendant la guerre' *Travaux et Notices de l'Académie d'Agriculture de France* 1 (1918) pp. 493–520.

Saint, L., *La reconstitution de l'Aisne* (Nancy: Berger-Levrault, 1920).

Samson, F., *L'agriculture dans le département de la Meuse en 1931* (Troyes: Paton, 1931).

Sars, De M., *L'oeuvre des coopératives de reconstruction du département de l'Aisne* (Paris: Cofea, 1937).

Sauvy, A., *Histoire économique de la France entre les deux guerres,* vol. I (Paris: Fayard, 1965).
Schmerber, J.M., *La réorganisation foncière en France: le remembrement rural* (Cahors: Coueslant, 1949).
Schmitt, A., 'La population du département de la Meuse depuis le début du XIXe siècle; étude de géographie humaine' *Annales de l'Est* (1928–9) pp. 80–105.
Second, P., *Reconstitution des régions libérées: rapport du préfet, Meurthe-et-Moselle* (Nancy: Rigot, 1920).
Sellier, H. & Bruggeman, A., *Le problème du logement* (Paris: Presses Universitaires de France, 1927).
Sherman, D.J., 'Objects of memory: history and narrative in French war museums' *French Historical Studies* 19 (1995) pp. 49–74.
Simson, D.C.U., 'The Vimy memorial' *Canadian Geographical Journal* 26 (1943) pp. 41–43.
Slowe, P. & Woods, R., *Fields of death. Battle scenes of the First World War* (London: Robert Hale, 1988).
Smets, M., ed., *Resurgam. La reconstruction en Belgique après 1914* (Brussels: Crédit Communal, 1985).
Smets, M., 'Belgian reconstruction after World War I: a transition from civic art to urban planning' *Planning Perspectives* 2 (1987) pp. 1–26.
Smith, C.H. & Hill, C.R., *Rising above the ruins in France: an account of the progress made since the Armistice in the devastated regions in re-establishing industrial activities and the normal life of the people* (New York: Putnam, 1920).
Société Coopérative de Reconstruction des Eglises du Diocèse de Nancy, *Consécration de l'église d'Ancerviller* (Nancy, 1923).
Society of Friends, *Plan for the reconstruction of forty villages to the west of Verdun* (London, 1918).
Stapathi, M., 'Les travaux de reconstruction des régions libérées' *CM* 34 (1919) pp. 99–102.
Stephens, D.O., *With Quakers in France* (London: Daniel, 1921).
Swinton, E., *Twenty years after: the battlefields of 1914–18, then and now,* 3 vols (London: Newnes, 1936).
Syndicat des Sinistrés en Albert et sa Région, *Etude et plan de reconstitution et d'extension de la ville d'Albert* (Paris: Otis-Pifre, 1917).

Tardieu, A., *The truth about the treaty* (Indianapolis: Bobbs-Merrill, 1921).
Taylor, A.J.P., *The First World War: an illustrated history* (Harmondsworth: Penguin, 1966).
Théry, E., *Conférences sur les conditions économiques de la guerre* (Paris: Adrien Maréchal, 1918).
Thierry, H., 'L'assainissement du sol dans les régions ravagées pendant la guerre' in *Congrès interallié d'hygiène social pour les régions dévastées par la guerre,* vol. I (Paris: Levoux, 1919).
Thierry, M., *Dans la Picardie dévastée* (Paris: Boccard, 1918).
Thomassin, M., 'Situation agricole des régions libérées dans la zone de l'armée

anglaise' *Comptes Rendus des Séances de l'Académie d'Agriculture de France* 3 (1917) pp. 624–28.

Thumerelle, P.J., '*La population de la région Nord-Pas-de-Calais: étude géographique*' (Thèse pour le doctorat d'Etat, Université de Haute-Bretagne, 1979).

Tissier, M., *Au front de Champagne* (Châlons-sur-Marne, 1918).

Toulemon, A., *La réparation des dommages de guerre* (Paris: Plon, 1921).

Trenard, L., ed., *Histoire des Pays-Bas français* (Toulouse: Privat, 1972).

Tribondeau, J., *L'agriculture du Pas-de-Calais* (Arras: Ministère de l'Agriculture, 1927).

Tribondeau, J., *L'agriculture du Pas-de-Calais* (Arras: Ministère de l'Agriculture, 1937).

Troller, A., 'La reconstitution des chemins de fer du Nord' *La Nature* 47 (1919) pp. 248–53.

Troupeau-Housay, J., 'Une remise en état du sol dans les régions libérées' *JAP* 47 (1927) pp. 395–97.

Troyansky, D.G., 'Monumental politics: national history and local memory in French monuments aux morts in the department of the Aisne since 1870' *French Historical Studies* 15 (1987–8) pp. 121–41.

Vaillat, L., *La maison des pays de France: les provinces dévastées* (Paris: Niestlé, 1917).

Vaillat, L., 'La voie sacrée' *LA* (1919) pp. 780–82.

Vallaux, C., 'Péronne' *La Vie Urbaine* (1919) pp. 12–25.

Vandervynckt, E., *Le remembrement parmi les améliorations foncières rurales* (Lille, 1936).

Vezin, C. & Vandamme, P., *L'agriculture dans le département du Nord* (Lille, 1937).

Vidal de la Blache, J., *Etude sur la vallée lorraine de la Meuse* (Paris: Armand Colin, 1908).

Vigato, J.C., 'L'architecture du régionalisme: les origines du débat 1900–1950' *Dossiers et Documents de l'Institut Français d'Architecture* 4 (1983) pp. 33–38.

Vigato, J.C., *L'architecture régionaliste: France, 1890–1950* (Paris: Norma, 1994).

Villate, R., *Les conditions géographiques de la guerre. Etude de géographie militaire sur le front français de 1914 à 1918* (Paris: Payot, 1925).

Vincent, J., 'La reconstitution des régions dévastées' *Le Parlement et l'Opinion* (1919) pp. 2026–42.

Wallon, E. & Gobert, L,. *Rapport sur la visite faite dans la région du Nord (Somme, Pas-de-Calais et Nord) par une délégation de l'Union des Comités Centraux des Réfugiés des Départements Envahis* (Paris, 1919).

Weber, E., *The hollow years. France in the 1930s* (London: Sinclair-Stevenson, 1995).

Webster, D., 'The soldiers moved on; the war moved on; the bombs stayed' *Smithsonian Magazine* (1994) February pp. 26–37.

Whittick, A., *War memorials* (London: Country Life, 1946).
Willaert, M., *Historique de la Fédération des Coopératives pour Dommages de Guerre* (Brussels: Imprimerie Nationale, 1930).
Winter, J., *Sites of memory, sites of mourning: the Great War in European cultural history* (Cambridge: Cambridge University Press, 1995).

Zimmermann, M., 'La population de la France en 1921' *AG* 31 (1922) pp. 37–51.
Zimmermann, M., 'La population de la France d'après le recensement du 7 mai 1926' *AG* 36 (1927) pp. 328–35.

Index